What could be more important to our time than re-establishing the fundamentals for sustainable common wealth? This most timely book, written by one of the leading thinkers in the field, sets out a clear agenda that challenges all of us to act.
Dr Neil Ravenscroft, Professor of Land Economy, University of Brighton, and Director of Tablehurst Farm CSA

All around us we see evidence of the sort of life we create when we forget that all our wealth is common wealth. Let's celebrate a book which reminds us of that fact, and gives clear guidance on how to make it a reality in the modern world.
Molly Scott Cato, Reader in Green Economics, Cardiff School of Management

In the current climate of anxiety as to how we move on from the devastation of toxic capitalism (paradigm lost), Common Wealth *offers a human centred alternative (paradigm found) to this most pressing of questions.*
Patricia Rawlinson, lecturer, London School of Economics, author *From Fear to Fraternity: A Russian Tale of Crime, Economy and Modernity*, Pluto Press, 2010

This is a timely book, making the rare and important link between the crisis of our 'captive state' and the ways in which citizens and communities can mobilise to address it. More than a call to action, it offers practical and much needed pathways for actually taking action.
Rosemary Foggitt and Pat Conaty, *Common Futures*

While Common Wealth's *analysis is attractive, Martin Large offers a lucid, insightful and thought-provoking set of workable suggestions for putting them into practice. Many are already doing so. He should be listened to … and then acted upon.*
Professor Nigel Curry, Director of the Countryside and Community Research Institute, University of Gloucestershire

Only by sharing the value of our common resources more fairly, is humanity likely to be able to avoid the worldwide self-destruction towards which our present path of development is leading us.
In his masterly new book Martin Large explores the changes this implies for the structures of business, government and civil society and the relationships between them. He identifies land value taxation and a citizen's income as among the measures that will help to bring the changes about.
Please read it if you care about the future of our species.
James Robertson, a founder of the New Economics Foundation and author of *Transforming Economic Life*

From bitter searching of the heart
We rise to play a greater part
This is the faith by which we stand
Men shall know common wealth again

Leonard Cohen, from *Villanelle for our Time*

The earth shall become a common treasury to all, as it was first made and given to the
sons of men.

Gerard Winstanley, 1649

The law doth punish man or woman
That steals the goose from off the common
But lets the greater felon loose
That steals the common from the goose.

Anon

How can we put an end to unrestrained market fundamentalism and financial capitalism,
that are void of morals or moderation, in order to protect the finances and livelihoods of
our citizens? That is the issue we are now facing. In these times, we must return to the
idea of fraternity – as in the French slogan 'liberté, égalité, fraternité' – as a force for
moderating the danger inherent within freedom.

Yukio Hatoyama, Prime Minister, *A New Path for Japan*

The more that freedom informs civil society and the cultural sector, the more equality
informs the state sector with its rights and responsibilities, and the more that mutuality
or fraternity guide business and economic life – the more creative, just, democratic,
healthier, wealthier, the more sustainable, will be our society.

Martin Large, *Common Wealth*

There is no wealth but life. Life, including all its powers of love, of joy, and of admiration.
That country is richest which nourishes the greatest number of noble and happy
human beings; that man is richest who, having perfected the functions of his own life
to the utmost, has also the widest helpful influence, both personal, and by means of his
possessions, over the lives of others.

John Ruskin, *Unto this Last*

Common Wealth

For a free, equal, mutual
and sustainable society

MARTIN LARGE

HAWTHORN PRESS

Common Wealth © 2010 Martin Large

Martin Large is hereby identified as the author of this work in accordance with section 77 of
the Copyright, Designs and Patent Act, 1988. He asserts and gives notice of his moral right
under this Act.

First published by Hawthorn Press in 2010.
Hawthorn House, 1 Lansdown Lane,
Stroud, Gloucestershire,
GL5 1BJ, UK
Tel: (01453) 757040   Fax: (01453) 751138
Orders@booksource.net
Website: www.hawthornpress.com

A CIP catalogue record for this book is available from
The British Library

ISBN 978-1-903458-98-3

Cover image © Clifford Harper
Cover design and typesetting by Bookcraft Ltd, Stroud, Gloucestershire, UK

Printed by Cromwell Press Group in the UK

Printed on FSC approved paper

Every effort has been made to fulfil requirements with regard to reproducing copyright
material. If any omission has been made, please bring this to the publisher's attention so
that proper acknowledgement may be given in future editions.

Contents

List of boxes vi
List of figures vii
Acknowledgements viii
About the author ix
Foreword x

Part 1 Remaking Society 1
 Chapter 1 **What Social Future Do We Want?** 2
 Chapter 2 **Remaking Society** 15
 Chapter 3 **Tripolar Society: Government, Business and Civil Society** 31

**Part 2 From Capitalist to Civil Society: Clarifying Boundaries
    between Business, Government and Civil Society** 49
 Chapter 4 **The Emergence of Civil Society: Restoring Fences** 50
 Chapter 5 **Capturing the State** 66
 Chapter 6 **Capturing Culture** 89
 Chapter 7 **Capitalism Unleashed: The Seizure of Common Wealth** 118

Part 3 Redrawing Boundaries 142
 Chapter 8 **Transforming Capitalism: Stewarding Capital for
       Individual Enterprise and Common Good** 144
 Chapter 9 **Citizen's Income: Social Inclusion and
       Common Wealth for All** 172
 Chapter 10 **Land for People, Homes and Communities** 182
 Chapter 11 **Freeing Education** 214
 Chapter 12 **Common Wealth: Leading from the Social Future
       as it Emerges** 236

Appendix 1: Tools for Cross-Sectoral and Trisectoral Partnership Building 260
Appendix 2: Feedback and Next Steps 262
Appendix 3: Governing and Reclaiming the Commons 264
Notes 266
Resources 275
Glossary of terms 278
Index 281

List of boxes

1.1	Stroud co-op allotments	4
1.2	Letter to the *Guardian*, 19 September 2008	7
2.1	Baphumelele Educare Centre	19
2.2	Culture gets creative	21
2.3	Women of Britain say – 'Go'!	23
2.4	It's UP 2 Us!	25
3.1	Nuclear power consultation 'a sham': government versus civil society	32
3.2	The SPACE	42
3.3	Sweden: creating the 'folkhemhet', the people's home	46
5.1	Brown's PFI tube policy costs taxpayers £2 billion	72
5.2	Stroud Maternity Hospital matters	77
5.3	Tescopoly drives small newsagents out of business	79
6.1	Mission Musica and the power of culture	94
6.2	'We need a rebellion against a press that's damaging our national psyche'	100
6.3	Whose voice?	101
6.4	'Captured: a laddish, thuggish, snapshot of power'	105
6.5	What took the Food Standards Agency so long not to ban additives?	112
6.6	US copyright creep: from Thomas Jefferson to Mickey Mouse	115
6.7	Throwing Microsoft out of the Windows: freeing access to knowledge	116
7.1	Winners from privatisation	122
7.2	'The gap between rich and poor could lead to riots'	131
8.1	Can the arts support the arts?	152
8.2	Tolkien Trust received only £32,000 royalties from the £3 billion sales of the Lord of the Rings films	153
8.3	John Lewis's success	157
8.4	Quantitative easing, printing money and creating debt-free money	163
8.5	SCARF: Stroud Community Asset Reinvestment Fund	165
8.6	Norwegian Oil Fund shows way forward for Scotland's future	166
8.7	Scrooge Nouveau and the Spirit of Earth Day Past	170
10.1	Experiences with Land Value Tax in various countries	186
10.2	Britain's feudal land ownership system	187
10.3	The Development Land Tax Act 1976: how we nearly got it right	188
10.4	Harrisburg cuts crime and unemployment with LVT	190
10.5	Freedom to roam: access … what access?	192
10.6	Stonesfield Community Trust, Oxfordshire	198
10.7	Isle of Gigha Heritage Trust, Scottish Hebrides	199
10.8	The future is Fordhall	200
10.9	The benefits of mutual home ownership	204
10.10	The Cashes Green Hospital story	205
11.1	The 'Open Eye' campaign – for Open Early Years Learning	219
11.2	A practical manifesto for education on a human scale	230
11.3	Pluralist, free education systems	233
12.1	The Exchange	247
12.2	Dialogue: Mayor on a bench	250
12.3	Stroud Community Farm	253
12.4	Stroud Communiversity	255

List of figures

1.1	The three sectors: government, business and civil society	12
3.1	The three sectors and their constituents	37
3.2	Threefold image of an organisation	38
3.3	Summary: the key elements of the state, business and civil society/cultural sectors	47
4.1	The economic, political and cultural systems	52
4.2	Civil society	55
4.3	Capitalist society	57
4.4	Tripolar society	59
4.5	Commercialising, bureaucratising and ideologising forces	61
4.6	Diagram of leaves	63
5.1	Commercialising the state and culture	68
7.1	The enclosure and privatisation of common wealth	128
7.2	The power structure of neo-liberal dispossession	134
7.3	Summary: comparison of neo-liberal capitalist and tripolar society	141
8.1	The business transfer/takeover process	149
8.2	Money from nothing: how banks create capital from thin air	161
10.1	Land for People	191
10.2	Equity creation through a CLT	194
10.3	House and land	196
10.4	Cashes Green Hospital, Stroud	205
10.5	Springhill co-housing, Stroud	209
10.6	Redditch Co-operative Homes	210
12.1	Dialogue between government, business and civil society	248

Acknowledgements

This book draws on a variety of sources, which are more fully acknowledged in the Resources section on pp. 272–74. However, I would particularly like to acknowledge Nicanor Perlas's seminal book, *Shaping Globalization: Civil Society, Cultural Power and Threefolding* (2000). When we met, the question of writing on threefolding from a British perspective came up. A Right Livelihood Award winner in 2003, Nicanor is a candidate in the 2010 Philippines presidential election. He gives a profound theoretical and practical contribution to conceptualising a threefold society as an alternative to neo-liberal capitalist society.

Other acknowledgements include David Korten's books such as *When Corporations Ruled the World* (1999); Molly Scott Cato, *Green Economics* (2009); James Bruges, *The Big Earth Book* (2008); Christopher Schaefer's unpublished article, *Nine Propositions in Search of a Social Order*, in which he translated from German an English version of Christoph Strawe's aphorisms; George Monbiot's book *Captive State* (2000) and his website; Rudolf Steiner's *Threefold Social Order*; and Ros Tennyson's groundbreaking work in developing cross-sectoral partnerships with government, civil society and business, such as *Managing Partnerships* (1998). I am also indebted to Otto Scharmer's work on presencing, in his *Theory U: Leading from the Future as it Emerges*. Ken Sprague's cartoons, The Fishes, Mutilated World, and The Fruits of Labour, come from John Green (2002), *Ken Sprague, People's Artist*, with kind permission of the Ken Sprague fund. For design and production thanks to Christina Kesisoglou for her illustrations and layout, to Clifford Harper for the cover image, and to Lucy Guenot, Nick Morgan and John Button at Bookcraft.

My special gratitude goes to those who have read critically and given editorial feedback and encouragement on chapters, including my wife Judith Large, Andy Treacher, Philip Martyn, Molly Scott Cato, Max Comfort, Richard House, Rosemary Foggett, Michael Evans, Steven Hill, David Tuffield, my editor Christopher Feeney, and Tony Crofts. Thanks to Ros Tennyson of the Partnering Initiative for her editorial feedback on Appendix 1. Since key parts of *Common Wealth* are based on action research, I would like to acknowledge Greg Pilley for our work on developing community farm land trusts, such as at Fordhall Farm in 2005–7; Max Comfort for joint work on setting up Gloucestershire Land for People; Bob Paterson of the University of Salford's Community Finance Solutions; and Community Land Trust action research colleagues Pat Conaty, Rosemary Foggett, Steven Hill, Steve Bendle and David Rodgers. A Winston Churchill travelling fellowship to the USA enabled me to research CLTs and bring back what I had learned.

Lastly, I would like to acknowledge fellow directors and members of Stroud Common Wealth Ltd, a non-profit company set up in 1999 to help regenerate Stroud by developing social enterprise and community land trusteeship. Our motto is, 'Building economic, social and cultural wealth together.'

Martin Large, October 2009

About the author

Martin Large works as a facilitator in the field of individual, organisational, community and societal development; his clients have included civil society organisations, government agencies and businesses ranging from small to multinational. This involves creating the conditions for people to meet, engage and make the most of their resources; exploring the contexts and key issues they face; evaluating what works and doesn't work; and helping them to focus on emerging desired futures and how to achieve them.

He has worked as an educator, as an academic lecturing in management and organisational behaviour at what is now the University of Gloucestershire, and as a management consultant with Social Ecology Associates and Sustainable Futures. He has run a publishing company for 29 years, chairs Stroud Common Wealth, and has enabled the development of a variety of cultural projects, including a theatre, college, co-operatives, the Social Enterprise Centre and community land trusts.

Martin's motto is, 'It is better to light fires than to fill buckets.'

Foreword

It is extraordinarily difficult to understand quite how unwell our economy is, and why. Our instincts tell us to ignore it, to await the return of easy loans and rising house prices. Our brains, when we engage them, tell us something else.

The economy has been, for most of us in the West, 'everything'. We have judged others, and ourselves, by economic performance. We have developed a curious fear about money. However much we have, will we ever have enough? Bankers earning millions make us fearful of not being able to afford – well, something. Our obsession with money has blinded us to all the other things that make us feel good, happy and secure. It has also blinded us to the surging undercurrents of inequality, unfairness, distorted systems and structural weaknesses that make future crunches not only likely but inevitable. Stand by for the energy crunch, oil crunch, food crunch and water crunch. Stand by, too, to watch democracy buckle under the strain of these challenges.

It is time to pay attention. Most readers will be astonished to learn how land is distributed in the UK. It is now almost a thousand years after the Norman invasion when William parceled out much of the country to his nobility, or 'cronies' as one might call them now. The aristocracy, the church, the crown and the government all continue to own land on a vast scale. Spend a moment thinking about it and you may wonder how, with all our intelligence and concern for progress and democracy, the one thing – apart from air and water – which we might think of as ours in fellowship with our fellow citizens is owned by a very few. Land ownership in Britain is still almost mediaeval.

Do we not have the wit to think of a better and fairer way? Indeed, can we not dream up better ways of doing business, running cities, regenerating communities and energising food production?

A book like this, exploring the system which is – witness the credit crunch – so inadequate, is badly needed. There is no shortage of analysis of the way society works, but Martin brings us up to date and tackles difficult questions from the perspective of a man who has made new ideas work. He has pioneered new ways of sharing land and resources and knows what is possible. In fact, he has inspired me to re-think much of what I do. A Bristol city-centre development that I have been involved with will now be driven by the search for new ways of engaging the community and creating space for everyone, rather than for a few profiteers. We will work in transparent partnership with all concerned. This is Martin's way, and he has much to teach us.

Martin asks us to ponder the question of making the transition to a more free, equal, mutual and sustainable society. We are challenged to remember the history of land theft and land enclosure that has set the patterns of inequality that have remained largely unchanged in centuries. Then, by offering us examples of inspirational reform, of individuals challenging old ways of thinking, of new institutions and new ideas, Martin shows that there really are new ways of being. We certainly need them.

I am especially inspired by the story of Charlotte and Ben Hollins, who secured their father's tenanted organic farm with the help of thousands of investors in Fordhall Community Land Initiative, a community land trust. Martin was deeply engaged in the process and has shown what is possible. He explores practical theories of land trusteeship for permanently affordable homes, of freeing education and of land taxation. It is never dry; it is always hopeful. But unlike so many theorists, Martin makes it happen.

Alastair Sawday

PART 1

Remaking Society

The Fishes by Ken Sprague

Chapter 1

What Social Future Do We Want?

The market triumphalism of financial capitalism has gone. Yet City bankers' bonuses are creeping back, thanks to competing banks going bust and taxpayers propping up a shaky financial system, which nearly collapsed in October 2008. Whilst the belief that 'unfettered markets know best' has been shattered, with nearly one million young people aged 16–25 unemployed, people are asking, 'What is our new vision of society? If not the market, what are our guiding values?' A young friend asked, 'Is life just about economics? What values can I live by?' Michael Sandell, the 2009 BBC Reith lecturer, suggests that we face the challenge of the re-moralisation of society saying, 'Most political questions are at their core moral or spiritual ... they are about our vision for the common good.' So *Common Wealth* takes up Professor Sandell's invitation to explore how the values of freedom, equality, mutuality and sustainability can help transform society: an economy that works well for all, a vibrant cultural life that enables every human being realise their potential, a political life rooted in equality, human rights and social justice, and the sustainable care for the environment.

Westminster parliamentary democracy also faces a crisis of legitimacy. With the massive public bailouts, have the too-big-to-fail banks captured the state? Who rules? There is public outrage at the MPs' expenses scandal, at cash for legislation, at a part time parliament failing to protect our civil liberties and do its job of holding government to account. Faced by the credit, food, climate, energy, water and poverty crunches, it is clear our way of life may be unsustainable. Our social future is being mortgaged up to the hilt to prop up the financial system; government prints money to support the banks, yet four million people are waiting for social housing. There has been little debate about the choices we face, say between free university tuition versus bankers' bonuses. There is also denial and conflicting information about Britain's real financial situation.

The British government has spent £95.5 billion propping up the Royal Bank of Scotland, which it believes is too big to fail. Taxpayers, however, have no clear idea just how risky RBS really is, as the accounts which hide toxic assets are so obscure. Lloyds/HBOS is also too big to fail. The government has insured these imploded banks with taxpayers' money against future losses. The banks are also supposed to both build up their capital and keep lending to homeowners and businesses – two conflicting tasks. Alistair Darling's grim April 2009 budget made it clear just how mortgaged Britain's future is, with the projected national deficit for 2009–10 increasing from an estimate of £38 billion in 2008 to £175 billion. Projected borrowing for the four years from 2009 is £606 billion, national debt will be 79 per cent of GDP, the highest ever in peacetime, the economy will have its worst year since 1945 and the debt will cost £35–47 billion per annum to service. This means people losing their jobs, government spending cuts, a falling pound, personal and company bankruptcies. And Britain, compared with other countries, is in deep economic trouble, with a unique combination of a bust housing boom, a consumer credit bubble, an economy based on financial services and an overspending government with the motto of 'debt, debt, debt'.[1] And in a pre-election year, both government and opposition are concealing the hard choices and hoping for a return to business as usual, rather than making a thorough evaluation of why things went wrong.

However, this crisis offers an opportunity to remake society – a wake-up call that invites the questions, 'What social future do we want?' and 'How can we create a sustainable society for people and planet?'

Some people want a 'business as usual' social future. They want to kick-start the economy with tax cuts, printing money and bailing out the banks to get the economy booming again. Others want a Green New Deal, creating a low-carbon economy and doing more with less. The deep-green transition movement looks to a whole redesign of the way we live and work so as to cope with the challenge of peak oil through an energy descent. The British government wants a surveillance society to deal with rising terrorism, the anti-social individualism triggered by thirty years of 'selfish capitalism,' strikes from factory closures and social unrest from unemployment. However, the Nobel laureate Amartya Sen considers that real democracy is central to sustainable development if it is to work for all. And many people want to get on with building the social future where they are, whether this means developing more sustainable businesses, caring for the environment, renewing democracy or community development.

Mutilated World by Ken Sprague

For those who want to get engaged practically, a first step is to analyse the causes of what is happening; secondly, decide what social future they want; and thirdly, to develop positive solutions that work. Examples of positive, practical solutions are anyway already emerging, whether it is an innovative social enterprise, conversation cafés, environmental improvement or renewed interest in allotments and the transition towns' movement. This book, whilst drawing on such solutions, offers perspective on 'work on the social future in progress'. Reflecting on some of the learning from the social future as this emerges can help clarify the context of our changing world, raise relevant questions and find some workable solutions that point the way ahead.

Box 1.1   Stroud co-op allotments

Allotments are now so popular that many towns have as many people on the waiting list as they have allotments. People value growing good food along with the benefits of gardening, health and conviviality. The seven members of the informally organised Stroud co-op allotments make the most of their land by sharing work on a total of 4.5 allotments, which are formally held by individual members. Children join in. 'On Friday we work from 10 a.m. to 1 p.m. with a coffee break around a fire to boil water for hot drinks in the winter. We have built a curved bench by our hut. We plan our crop list and rotation every year, so that we are harvesting something every week of the year. In autumn we preserve a lot of our produce to cover the following year's "hungry gap".'

Source: Nick Weir

It is good to engage practically with developing positive solutions; however, it is also vital to understand how we got here. One major cause of the various energy, credit, climate, poverty, food and democratic crunches we face is that much of our commons, our common wealth of shared resources such as land, water, culture, radio bandwidth, publicly owned utilities, and many public services such as water, have been enclosed, privatised and then sold back to us. James Robertson gives one helpful definition of the commons as 'common or shared resources'. These 'are resources whose value is due to Nature and to the activities and demands of society as a whole, and not to the efforts or skill of individual people or organisations.'[2] The story of the enclosure of common land in Britain is familiar; however, the enclosure of other commons has intensified over the last thirty years. This is an age of enclosure, of privatization, where our commons – whether the gifts of nature such as land, water, air, seeds, the human genome, or the commons resulting from human creativity – such as capital, the financial system, public assets, culture, health, education – have been made into commodities for sale on the market. Everything is now for sale. Just as the banks plundered our financial commons in a market-fundamentalist free-for-all, so some Westminster MPs took as much in the way of expenses as they could within their rules from our taxes. At the same time, a compliant parliament forgot it was their job to secure the common good. Parliament failed to preserve our common wealth, the family silver of, for example, our public utilities, from privatising Conservative and New Labour governments. MPs failed to scrutinise the corporate capture of government for private gain and so much else. [3]

So this book is about reclaiming our common wealth in order to help bring about a more free, equitable, mutual and sustainable society. Developing small-scale, positive solutions is a good start, but this needs resourcing, for example with affordable access to land for community-supported food growing. So I argue that it is vital to recognise that things like land and capital are commons: rights, not commodities. At worst, utter desolation and at best market failure results from treating, say, land as a commodity, as we see from the lack of affordable homes and one in nine households being in negative equity.

However, traditionally, much common wealth was stewarded by community-based organisations such as churches, charities and commons associations outside both the public sector of the government and the private business market sector. As 'the voluntary and community organisation sector' is now reinventing itself as 'civil society', new forms of communalising or mutualising assets such as community land trusts are emerging. (Community land trusteeship will be explored in Chapter 10, 'Land for People'.)

Common Wealth goes on to argue that, after thirty years of successive governments unleashing a neo-liberal capitalist society, the 'crunch' now gives space to think through the shape of our emerging society. For example, the current captive, corporate state can be replaced by a government that works for the common good; the economy can be freed from neo-liberal capitalism by developing an associative, fair trade economy; and public services such as education and health can be liberated from both state dominance and from commercialisation. So government, business and civil society can rebuild common wealth, based on such guiding principles as freedom, equality, mutuality and sustainability. I argue that the wellbeing, wealth and resilience of society will be greater, the more we recognise the distinct, unique contributions of government, business and civil society, which embrace cultural, voluntary and community organisations. So, the more the principle of freedom informs civil society and culture, the more equality informs the state sector of human rights and the more that mutuality guides business and economic life, the more creative, just, democratic, healthy, the more resilient, will be our society.

I hope that the renewed understanding of the commons and of the emerging tripolar society of civil society, business and government will lead to limiting markets to the economic system and removing the recently imposed markets from the public, statutory sector and from the cultural and community sector. This would mean stopping the marketisation of the NHS and of education, for example. Professor Michael Sandell, in his 2009 Reith Lectures, also invites people to rethink the moral limits to markets, as the free market triumphalism of the last thirty years has now been replaced by market scepticism. There is much hope, he says, for cultural, moral and civil renewal, in working for the public good.

I also aim to offer people interested in co-creating their desired social future some practical solutions and tools for change. These tools include useful social maps for analysis, strategic planning tools and practical partnership-building resources for making the transition to a more sustainable, creative and just society, a transition from capitalist to civil society. Such partnerships can focus on a variety of themes such as improving energy use, transport, housing, health or education. Anyone who wants to get engaged – business leaders, political leaders, government officials, civil society/community activists and facilitators – will find the tools and maps useful.

But what led to this analysis of common wealth and the need for a new understanding of the need for civil, not capitalist society? Firstly, I wrote to the *Guardian* about the credit crunch. When the Stroud Conservative parliamentary candidate then told me on the street that 'Your *Guardian* letter was wrong – it's not a meltdown of the financial system, it's only a correction', I retorted, 'Wake up! We face a major crisis!'

Some media space has since been given to discussing the 'new politics', economic analysis and how companies have been avoiding tax. But too little space has been given to more fundamental social analysis and the emerging practical solutions – hence this book.

The second reason for writing *Common Wealth* is that the corporate media and government give little space for the inspiring, practical solutions that can help rebuild our democracy, economy and way of life. The emerging alternatives are below the radar of both government and the media. This is not surprising. The corporate financial, business, media and political elites that control the current failing system both created it and still profit from it. Like Stroud's Conservative parliamentary candidate, they are in denial, hoping things can be patched up for business as usual. But they are not reflecting and doing things differently. They are still looking in the rear-view mirror for guidance. But as Einstein once said, 'We cannot solve our problems with the same thinking we used when we created them.'

For example, soon after the HBOS and Bradford and Bingley banks went bust in September 2008, partly from short selling, the FSA banned the short selling of shares. This is where speculators borrow shares they do not own in order to buy them later at a cheaper price. The ban was lifted by the FSA on Friday 16 January 2009. Chancellor Alistair Darling, who thought the ban should stay in force, was given an hour's notice of the end of the ban. Barclays Bank then lost 25 per cent of its share value in frenzied trading. The defensive Lord Turner, the new FSA chair, said that abusive short selling was not playing a major role in the Barclays' share meltdown. However, the hedge fund Lansdown Partners, who also bet on Northern Rock's crash, made a profit of £12 million from short selling Barclays.[4] Lansdown also help fund the Tory Party. One wonders how much political and financial elites actually care for the common wealth and wellbeing of ordinary people.

Thirdly, it is not just the financial meltdown that has triggered *Common Wealth*. We face destructive forces, locally, nationally and globally. Christmas 2008 saw the brutal assault on Gaza by the Israeli Army, professing to target Hamas soldiers whilst killing and injuring children and civilians. The Israeli Army, government and mainstream media vilified some young Israeli soldiers who told their Gaza stories factually, for example how they were ordered to shoot anyone on sight. The destructive forces of war, nationalism and terrorism are easy to unleash but hard to stop. We saw this in the 1990s with the Yugoslav civil war and the ensuing break-up into nationalist states:- what my wife, Judith Large, called *The War Next*

Box 1.2   *Letter to the* Guardian, *19 September 2008*

Dear Editor,

Capitalism is imploding with the credit crunch, just as communism fell with the Berlin Wall in 1989, with both systems morally bankrupt. Successive British governments have sold off public assets and utilities at knock-down prices, leaving us defenseless against massive energy price increases. Politicians have engineered a disastrous housing boom and bust, with parliament allowing Blair/Brown and Bush their murderous $3 trillion Iraq war.

And now corporate socialism is being extended by Prime Minister Brown at vast taxpayer expense to the predatory city bankers whose only value is that 'greed is good', even whilst the same bankers are destroying HBOS through speculative short selling. This is a defining historic moment with the collapse of light-touch, laissez-faire turbo capitalism.

So how can we the people reassert democratic power over our elitist parliamentary shamocracy? Reclaim a people's banking sector that serves society? And will your newspaper give space to inspiring and practical solutions that will help re-vision our democracy, economy and way of life?'

Martin Large

Door.[5] The British government continues to wage wars, including the Iraq War, which has cost up to a million Iraqi lives, 3 million refugees and the deaths of 179 British soldiers. British soldiers are still fighting in Afghanistan with to date over 200 deaths and 1000 injured. Given the destructive forces we face, which can so easily be mobilised by rabble-rousing politicians and the corporate media who want to divert attention away from domestic problems, this book is about taking constructive action to build a human-friendly society with a more resilient democracy, economy and culture. Better to light candles than curse the darkness, as the old saying goes.

The need for this constructive approach was vividly brought home to me when I was working as a facilitator in post-civil-war Croatia in 1997 with the Osijek-based Zentar za Mir or Centre for Peace. I was working near the devastated town of Vukovar, where Serb militias had massacred several hundred Croatians at the hospital in the recent civil war. I vividly remember driving past the ruined high school and church of my translator, Tanya, and my feelings of shock at her stories. Vukovar was a ghost town with several miles of shot-up buildings along the road, evoking the worst pictures of bombed-out cities from the end of the Second World War.

I was working with thirty-five members of newly forming 'peace teams' that would provide human rights support, legal advice and community development in the civil-war-torn areas bordering on Bosnia and Serbia. We were staying at an old, castle-like hotel overlooking the Danube, which was partly blocked by a wrecked ship. There was the occasional sound of gunfire at night. Participants of all ages came from former Yugoslav backgrounds – a patchwork of vibrant, positive people who had tough, harrowing stories to tell. When they were prioritising strategic tasks, I suggested, 'Don't try to do too much, too soon; after all, Rome wasn't built in a day.' Tanya muttered to me bitterly, 'Yes, but it was destroyed in a day, like Vukovar. It is much easier to destroy than to create.'

So when apologists for the current financial meltdown glibly talk about the inevitability of capitalist cycles of creative destruction, I remember Tanya's words, 'It is much easier to destroy than to create!' Think of the costs of this neo-liberal capitalist destruction. Who loses and who benefits?

However, constructive action to help build a more sustainable society, like the work of the Zentar za Mir peace teams, has significant positive results. As a result of my first Croatian visit, I returned to work for the peace teams on a new arts centre, Roma community development, a Bosnian human rights centre and a youth centre for Vucovar. One young member of the original peace teams had even been elected to the new Croat parliament in Zagreb as a social democrat.

The fourth reason for writing *Common Wealth* is to show how a rebalancing of business, government and civil society is happening. There is a growing global and local civil-society-led movement working practically for a more sustainable planet, a movement of movements that works to counter the destructive forces of war, the climate and credit crunches and much more. This work goes largely unreported, though President Obama, as a former community organiser, knows about the huge potential of 'we, the people' to remake the world, in partnership with government and business.

So, the purpose of this book is to nurture the seeds of change. It will show how individuals, companies, communities and government can develop a more resilient society in our workplaces and communities. The social future is already visible.

Seed questions

We face the credit, climate, peak oil and food crunches, just to mention a few pressing issues. How do we collaborate to resolve such complex challenges? *Common Wealth* analyses how we got to here and suggests what we can do about it.

My strategic planning work with people in companies, government and communities was one key trigger for writing this book. Whether it was the Post Office or the Croatian peace teams, people kept coming up with strikingly similar key questions about their desired social future. Colleagues around the planet noticed the same questions coming up.

This is how questions can come up, for example in strategic planning workshops. As the first step, participants describe all the changes in the wider world over the last few years that strike them as novel or significant. They then describe, firstly, what the world will be like in five years' time if all the trends they identify continue *without anyone doing anything*, and, secondly, they describe the future in seven years if *people work hard to make a difference*. The contrast between the desirable and the probable futures of the world are so striking that people get fired up to then make a plan for the future of an issue, their community, company or organisation. This dialogue creates the space for people to analyse and wake up to what is happening in the wider world as well as in their organisational or community contexts and to explore what they really want.

When then asked to discuss the desired future scenarios and to formulate the significant points arising, the following seed questions frequently come up:

- How can we build a more efficient, collaborative, sustainable, resilient economy that meets people's needs and respects the planet's carrying capacity?
- How are we building a more peaceful, democratic, just and equitable society?
- How are we enabling all human beings to reach their full spiritual, creative, social and physical potential?
- How are we creating a more beautiful world and environment? How are we caring for the earth and all its living beings?

Help with tackling the above seed questions that people are asking can only start here, using a few transformational action points. Readers of course will know what is most pressing in their community, company or organisation, and will decide their own entry points.

Who will find this book useful?

This book is for anyone wanting to make a difference in their community, company or organisation in enabling the transition to a more creative, just and sustainable society. It offers strategic planning tools and processes for transformation. Business leaders will find the book useful not just for their own company success, but also for mapping how to collaborate more effectively for mutual benefit with government and civil society over pressing questions. Successful businesses have an enlightened self-interest in supporting a more sustainable society. Civil society activists and cultural and community leaders will see how their initiatives and advocacy can complement the work of government and companies. Politicians and civil servants will be able to re-imagine their role as the heart of society rather than as bureaucratic controllers. This book is for those who want to build practical social futures wherever they are, and who find this more motivating than getting depressed just talking about problems and what 'they' should do.

Entry points for transformational change

Take housing as one practical entry point. The causes of the lack of affordable housing in Britain can be identified as housing market failure, a dysfunctional financial system, successive governments that deliberately created the conditions for a house-price bubble in order to engineer 'economic growth' and the treating of land as a market commodity rather than a socially shared 'commons' like the air. This analysis, outlined in more depth in Chapter 10, Land for People, leads to tried and tested workable solutions such as a land value tax and developing community land trusts for urban neighbourhoods, towns and villages for permanently afford- able access to homes, workspace, land for food growing and community facilities. The transformative action of treating land as a right, as a common wealth for us all, redraws the boundaries so that land is no longer a commodity as understood by neo-liberal economics. Other entry points will include treating capital as common wealth, liberating work through the citizen's income and freeing education from capture by the state.

This book will also describe the 'big picture' of the social, economic and political landscape as a strategic change map to help business, civil society and political leaders chart their organisations' courses in a turbulent world. The reason for offering this social map is that we are in a social, environmental, political and economic crisis caused by a runaway capitalist system, fully unleashed since the end of communism in 1989. It could be that just as the morally bankrupt commu- nist system collapsed in 1989, the current system of neo-liberal capitalism is now collapsing step by step with a self-destroying, debtonating financial system. The state cannot take on any more banking failures, let alone the toxic unsecured debts of trillions of dollars in the shadow banking system. Just as the 1929 Wall Street Crash and ensuing Depression showed how a ruling political and economic system dominated by the 'masters of the universe' in Wall Street and the City of London destroyed itself, we are now facing a systemic breakdown over a few years. But no one really knows the timetable.

I argue that society has come to be dominated by the corporate business and financial sector, with a captive state that secures citizen compliance and chan- nels increasing amounts of our taxes to the corporations for delivering ever more costly and less effective services. For example, consider how successive British governments have handed over low-priced publicly owned energy utilities to corporations, allowing them to charge above-inflation price increases for energy and then get away with windfall profits. Or consider how much public money has been used to support the banks with shares and loans, and how much risk the taxpayers have taken on by insuring the toxic debts of banks.

However, the argument goes further, advocating that it is now time to separate the corporate business sector from the state and balance both with a dynamic, emerging new societal partner variously called 'civil society', 'the community' or the 'cultural sector'. News broadcasts covering disasters now commonly announce that 'Government, civil society and business are working together to bring relief.' I will argue that the civil society or community sector is emerging as a leading body of a 'third societal sector' to challenge and counterbalance the dominance of the business and government sectors. Civil society led in the 1989 toppling of the Berlin Wall, the 1999 'Battle of Seattle', the 2003 global opposition to the Iraq War and the 1 April 2009 G20 'Financial Fool's Day'. Civil society organisations at Seattle challenged the cosy collusion between the business and government sectors as represented by the World Trade Organization, which was then bidding for world economic dictatorship. Civil society organisations or CSOs are advocating democracy, social justice and holistic sustainable development. Environmental CSOs and consumers are pressing the supermarkets to start a green conversion, to set environmental standards far higher than governments set for themselves. For example, to become carbon neutral, to stop sending waste to landfill and to stop selling paper, wood or fish that does not come from sustainable sources.

Business, government and civil society: partners for sustainable development

Society can be likened to a three-legged stool whose legs are government, business and civil society. If each sector focuses on its strengths and engages appropriately in dialogue and partnerships with the other two sectors then there can be social renewal and effective practical action.

Conversely, when business, the state and civil society overstep their appropriate boundaries, society suffers. For example, the state is held captive by business when the large supermarkets bully governments to set industry-friendly standards, get planning permission to build in green belts and drive small shops out of business so that we get 'ghost town Britain'. When the state allows the commoditisation and selling of the commons, such as land, water, air and natural resources, then people no longer have affordable access. When business commercialises the cultural space of civil society, we see health and education treated as profit-making businesses. When the public sector runs businesses or civil society organisations there is the danger of red tape, waste and bureaucracy.

Clarifying boundaries

Each sector will be able to contribute more effectively to the common good by clarifying boundaries between business, the public sector and civil society. There is currently much confusion; for example the government treats health as if it were only a business, with patients as consumers. The clarification of society's threefold boundaries leads to a separation of powers and of governance. This separation in

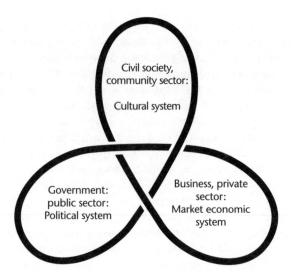

Figure 1.1   The three sectors: government, business and civil society

society as a whole could become as useful a piece of social architecture as James Madison's separation of statutory powers between the legislature, executive government and judiciary in the US Constitution of 1787.

Fortunately, people have a practical sense of the differences between the state, business and civil society in everyday life. People have a gut feeling that citizenship is not a commodity that should be 'bought', that the content of education should not be politically decided and that religion is a private, not a state affair, for example.

The separation of powers between state, business and civil society results in a new guiding principle:

> The well-being, wealth and resilience of society will be greater, the more the separation of the three societal sectors is recognised. So, the more that freedom informs civil society and the cultural sector, the more equality informs the state sector with its rights and responsibilities, and the more that mutuality guides business and economic life – the more creative, just, democratic, healthier, the more resilient, our society.[6]

It is all very well to argue for such high principles as a society based on freedom, equality, mutuality and sustainability, but what are the *practical* benefits of this threefold analysis of society? I will argue that the recognition of the appropriate boundaries and positive contributions of state, civil society and business will result in such practical outcomes as:

- identifying ways the three sectors can work together for holistic sustainable development, so that we can live much better on much less and tackle hitherto intractable challenges;

- reclaiming the dignity of labour through the citizen's basic income, so that people can be freed for real work and social contribution;
- recapturing capital for social benefit and respecting individual enterprise;
- reclaiming land and capital as common wealth, so that they are no longer commodities traded on the market but are held in trust for common benefits – including permanently affordable homes, farms and capital for enterprise;
- freeing human potential, for example by the state again becoming a partner rather than a provider of public services such as the arts, health and education.

One danger is to cover too much. This is not a book that is 95 per cent critique with 5 per cent solutions at the end. I will focus on analysis, on identifying principles for social renewal and suggesting a few practical, transformational entry points for action.

You may not really understand a system until you try to change it. For example, I have learned a huge amount about Britain's farmland ownership system through carrying out a community farmland trust action research project that has resulted in setting up a number of successful farmland trusts.[7] One striking thing I learned was that around 70 per cent of British land is owned by only 157,000 landowners, and that 10 per cent of Britain is still owned by descendents of the Plantagenets who benefited from William the Conqueror's 1066 land-grab!

I hope this book will help you with maps and some guiding theory for the journey. Theory without practice or experience is useless, and practice without theory can be dangerous, because you don't understand the underlying principles, only the recipes. You have the know-how, but not necessarily the 'know-why'.

What will be covered?

Part 1   Remaking society
1. What social future do we want?
2. Remaking society
3. Tripolar society: government, business and civil society

Part 2   From capitalist to civil society
4. The emergence of civil society
5. Capturing the state
6. Capturing culture
7. Capitalism unleashed: the seizure of common wealth

Part 3   Redrawing boundaries
8. Transforming capitalism
9. The citizen's income
10. Land for people, homes and communities
11. Freeing education
12. Common wealth: leading from the social future as it emerges

How to best use this book

The book is structured so that it can be dipped into, as well as read straight through. Diagrams and pictures tell one story. Boxes offer solutions, stories and examples. Part 1 describes the new social landscape of the three societal powers, as an alternative to the bipolar state- and business-dominated society now collapsing. Some readers will want to focus on the practical applications of threefold analysis such as transforming capitalism, land and labour in Part 3. People concerned with strategic community, business or governmental planning will be interested in the partnership-building and planning tools and participative design tools for organisation redesign in Chapter 12 and Appendix 1. Part 2, on the move from capitalist to civil society, offers a political, economic and cultural analysis of how we got here. It offers an analysis of neo-liberalism, which threatens to destroy the planet, business and the community as well as undermine individual wellbeing through affluenza. It culminates in a summary table comparing tripolar society with neo-liberal society. There are follow-up resources in the Appendices, as well as a glossary and index.

The first question to address is, 'How is it that more and more people want to make a difference?'

Chapter 2

Remaking Society

*Stroud community
planning motto*

Just as the power of old social structures fades, more and more people want to make a difference – to their communities, workplaces and the planet. The global breakdown of old social, economic and cultural forms is creating the conditions for individual initiative and agency. This marks a historic shift in human development from dependency on traditional social structures where '*they* should do something', to emerging social movements where people take action to make a difference. The 'more people want to make a difference' virus is spreading globally with travel, the Internet, business and the rise of global civil society. For example, I heard a West Papuan elder give an inspiring talk about the indigenous independence movement's struggle with Indonesia and the mining corporations, with two young filmmakers who had risked their lives to make an undercover film there. President Obama is another example. He worked as a community organiser for three years on Chicago's South Side, and then went into law and politics.

The aim of this chapter is to describe this seismic shift from a more collective consciousness formed by gender, class, work or ethnicity to an individual consciousness emancipated from traditional roles. Without wanting to recap twentieth-century history, the taking of refuge in outdated collective identities, such as nationalism or religious fundamentalism, can be seen as an expression of a fear of freedom in a bewildering world of rapid change. The current historic shift from collective consciousness to more self-aware, responsible individuals points a way forward. This shift is one foundation stone for a more creative, equitable, just, sustainable society. It is vital for business, government and civil society leaders to understand this change, as people simply do not know 'their place' any more. We won't behave or defer as authority would like us to.

This consciousness shift means that effective business managers have given up the outdated Theory X assumptions about workers, which stemmed from the old hierarchical command and control organisational structures. Employees were expected to leave their brains at the door, to do as they were told and not to think for themselves. Tight control systems were based on the assumption that staff were basically selfish and lazy and would avoid work if they could, or at least try to get away with doing as little as possible, were motivated by money and status and did not like responsibility. Now, successful businesses recognise that workers want wider involvement, are keen to develop themselves and want more responsibility and are motivated when they see the company making a positive difference to society. Moreover, high-performing businesses now encourage staff participation, flexible work structures, learning, responsibility, autonomy and discretion.

The shift is also happening in the statutory sector. Traditional representative government expects citizens to vote every five years and then to comply with policy made by their betters. Nowadays, old-style authoritarian politicians who get to the top either have to force things through at huge cost, enlisting autocratic 'czars' to galvanise action, or engage with citizens using a wide variety of partici- pative democratic processes, joint analysis of problems and the development of workable solutions. Otherwise people resist, saying, 'Not invented here'. The age of deference is gone. Many people see government support for the building of the third runway at Heathrow as going against policy commitments to reducing carbon and to an integrated, fairer, affordable transport policy for all. As many as 4,000 protestors are pursuing the creative strategy of buying small plots of a one- acre field wanted by BAA for its runway. This will force the government to pursue costly and time-consuming compulsory purchase orders with all 4,000 owners if the runway is to be built.

This chapter will cover how this shift arose and what it means for individuals and for the remaking of society. The topics it addresses include:

- blessed unrest: a global movement of movements
- waking up to our individual potential
- cultural creatives multiply
- the shift from collective to the individual: the basic societal law
- the process of getting engaged and civil disobedience
- vision building.

Blessed unrest: a global movement of movements

Paul Hawken was so struck by the worldwide emergence of civil society movements below the radar of the corporate media, business and government, that he wrote a book called *Blessed Unrest*. He is a successful American businessman and activist, a respected authority on sustainable business and co-author of a groundbreaking book with Amory and Hunter Lovins called *Natural Capitalism*. He helps business do much more with fewer resources through good design.

He describes the 'making a difference' virus as like catching 'a blessed unrest', borrowing the expression from choreographer Martha Graham. Like artists, people feel a life-force, a sense of flow, openness, awareness to what is happening and a kind of divine dissatisfaction. This blessed unrest 'keeps us marching' and makes people feel more alive.[1]

He describes in his book how blessed unrest, the wanting to make a difference virus, has led to a movement of millions of people worldwide working to remake the world, writing that:

> The movement has three basic roots: the environmental and social justice movements, and indigenous cultures' resistance to globalization – all of which are intertwining. It arises spontaneously from different economic sectors, cultures, regions, and cohorts, resulting in a global, classless, diverse, and embedded movement, spreading worldwide without exception. In a world grown too complex for constrictive ideologies, the very word movement may be too small, for it is the largest coming together of citizens in history.

The rise of this 'global movement of movements' was largely ignored by the media, business and government for many years, though now academics are researching the global civil society movements. By giving voice, witnessing, advocating values, creating alternatives, demonstrating for or against government or business policies and informing society about key issues, civil society movements are changing business and bringing down governments all over the world. We often see only the tip of the iceberg. For example, the everyday work of thousands of African women's groups for environmental and social justice was ignored in the celebrity-dominated news stories when Wangari Maathai of the Kenyan Green Belt Movement was awarded the Nobel Peace Prize.

The global emergence of civil society and new social movements is complex to analyse. There seems to be no common ideology, even though underlying values indicate a significant cultural shift. These values include social justice, the need for equity for all people living on the planet, non-violence, empathy, sustainability and respect for culture. Hawken considers that, 'The promise of this unnamed movement is to offer solutions to what appear to be insoluble dilemmas: poverty, global climate change, terrorism, ecological degradation, polarization of income, loss of culture. It is not burdened with a syndrome of trying to save the world; it is trying to remake the world.'[2]

So, how do you get started – or keep going? What issues get you going and spark blessed unrest in your community or workplace?

The answer depends where you are in your life, what challenges life brings and what question really concerns you enough to get engaged. The spark may come through travel, neighbourhood issues, work or friends. But once you are engaged, one thing leads to another, as life becomes more interesting. A first step can be to wake up to your individual potential, the acorn in you that bursts to become an oak tree.

Waking up to our individual potential

When Nelson Mandela was inaugurated as the President of South Africa in 1994, he challenged the people in the audience to wake up to their individual potential, so that they could also more freely contribute. He quoted Marianne Williamson's words:

> Our deepest fear is not that we are inadequate. Our deepest fear is that we are powerful beyond measure. It is our light, not our darkness, that most frightens us. We ask ourselves, who am I to be brilliant, gorgeous, talented and fabulous? Actually, who are you not to be? You are a child of God. Your playing small doesn't serve the world. There is nothing enlightened about shrinking so that other people won't feel insecure around you. We were born to make manifest the glory of God within us. It's not just in some of us; it's in everyone. And as we let our own light shine, we unconsciously give other people permission to do the same. As we are liberated from our fear, our presence automatically liberates others.

Born and brought up to rule in a kingly family, Mandela left his people, got a good education, became a lawyer and joined the ANC. He became a leader and then was imprisoned by the white apartheid regime on Robben Island. With ANC colleagues there, he made every attempt to educate and develop himself to the full. After nearly thirty years, he emerged as the leader of the new South Africa, able to forgive, have compassion, help reconciliation and provide wise statesmanship for an orderly transition from white apartheid rule.

Mandela invites people to wake up, as all over the world, people are passing the threshold from the collective to the individual. They are emancipating themselves from tradition, from old roles, from their families and nations, from class, from their gender – and emerging as self-aware, developing individuals who are freer than ever before in history to choose. It may not be easy, as some may fear freedom, or not get the help they need to overcome personal blockages. Some may get stuck in therapy or competitive individualism, finding it hard to realise the relatedness of 'Because you are, I am' to contributing to wider society in whatever ways work for them.

But in spite of all the blockages, people are nevertheless waking up to their individual potential, even in the midst of hyper-materialist modernism. For example, I met a Korean woman who had been a successful journalist, a beauty queen and a TV newsreader. She was taking an MA in Human Resource Management in Britain after profound spiritual experiences that had healed her of the anorexia and bulimia which were 'the destructive effects of media celebrity'. She described how her first husband had been violent to her and her exploitation by the patriarchal, dog-eat-dog media company she had worked for. She was now writing a book, completing her thesis, looking forward to marriage and children – and living her own life from within, rather than from others' constricting expectations.

Or take Charlotte Hollins, the young tenant farmer who in 2005 refused to allow the family organic farm to be sold from under them for development. She, her younger brother Ben and their friend Sophie Hopkins mobilised people successfully in a community buy-out of Fordhall Farm in Shropshire. They won a 2006 Schumacher Award for human-scale development, social innovation, sustainability and replicability – along with the other 8,300 shareholders in Fordhall Community Land Initiative who saved the farm.[3] Or the Chinese human rights and democracy dissident Hu Jia and his wife Zeng, who suffered Chinese government surveillance for exposing human rights abuses ahead of the 2008 Olympic Games.[4]

Without Heather Brooke and her journalist colleagues we would not have known about the secret world of Westminster MPs' expenses. She is an investigative journalist who used the Freedom of Information Act for years to try to get Westminster MPs' expenses, which were secret until leaked in 2009, published. Her first Freedom of Information request was met by baffled silence. Speaker Martin blocked her request for the names and salaries of MPs' staff. Richard Thomas, the 'independent' information commissioner, delayed her request for information on MPs' second homes for a year, then refused to support the publishing of their expenses' receipts. She successfully appealed at a tribunal and won the High Court case in May 2008, which required MPs' expenses to be published in the public interest, to ensure accountability and transparency. The courts were astonished to discover that Andrew Walker of the Commons fees office believed that 'transparency will damage democracy' and that 'there is checking where

---

Box 2.1   Baphumelele Educare Centre

In 1989, Rosalia Mashale, 'Rosie' to those around her, a trained primary school teacher, moved from the Eastern Cape to Khayelitsha in the Western Cape Province.

Rosie was disturbed to see young children going through the rubbish dump in search for food while their parents were away during the day, either at work or in search of work.

She responded by taking children into her home, and together with a group of women from the community, began looking after these unsupervised children. After the first week, thirty-six children had joined their charge.The name given to this project was Baphumelele, a Xhosa word meaning 'progress'.

From these humble beginnings the Baphumelele Educare Centre was founded, which today is an established community crèche caring for roughly 230 children aged three months to six years.

While the Educare Centre had developed a reputation for looking after children, Rosie also felt a calling to reach out to orphaned children in the community. To that end, the Baphumelele Children's Home was created as a place of safety for abandoned, abused, neglected or orphaned children, most of whom are either infected with or affected by HIV/Aids.

Continued overleaf

Through the hard work, determination and help of the community and overseas friends, Baphumelele has developed into a thriving community project over the years. In addition to the Children's Home and Educare Centre, today Baphumelele encompasses other community outreach initiatives such as: Baphumelele Woodwork Shop, Rosie's Kitchen, Baphumelele Second-Hand Shop, and the HIV Respite Care Centre. Susan Perrow tells the story of how she met Rosie:

'I first met Rosie in 1996 and our friendship was instant. I stayed overnight sometimes in her little house in Khayelitsha and despite her poor living conditions she always insisted in treating me like a queen, putting me in her bed and sleeping on a mattress on the floor next to me. However this royal treatment never came before the needs of her work.

One day she had offered to drive me through the slums and deliver me safely back to my friend's house on the other side of Cape Town. On the way she stopped to pick up the weekly bread for her soup kitchen, the leftovers from the week's food at a posh boys school. On this particular day there were many more boxes of bread than usual, and I helped Rosie pile them into the back of her car and the boot. There were two boxes out of about twenty that couldn't fit in, so I offered to hold one on my knee in the front seat. Rosie's reply was to point out a bus stop at the end of the street – if I caught the bus then she could fold down the seat and fit both boxes in. So I walked to the bus stop and eventually a bus came by that took me in the right direction, and all the bread made it back to the soup kitchen.

Source: www.baphumelele.org.za and Susan Perrow, author, Healing Stories

there are receipts. When there are no receipts there is no checking … If it's below £250 then the assumption is that it's going to be reasonable.' The 'John Lewis list' for the allowable purchase of white goods was uncovered. In the end, the Commons said MPs' expenses would be published in October 2008. In January 2009 MPs tried to pass a law exempting them from the Freedom of Information Act. Then publication was promised in July 2009, but the expenses were leaked to the *Daily Telegraph* in May 2009. Brooke wrote that MPs had 'plenty of opportunities to do the right thing by parliament and by the people. At every juncture they behaved in the worst possible way. They refused legitimate requests, they wasted public money going to the high court, they delayed publication, they tried to exempt themselves from their own law, they succeeded in passing a law to keep secret their addresses from their constituents so as to hide the house-flipping scandal.'[5]

These are just a few stories of people who get engaged, and readers will know many other such wake-up stories. It is fascinating to listen to people's life stories, what they are engaged in, how they got involved – and what their vision for society is. This awakening is especially obvious with young people, who want to travel, understand cultural differences, see the world, offer service in their gap years and find a worthwhile job if they can.

But whether young people at an idealistic age actually get the positive understanding, education, mentoring and support they need to wake up to their full potential is another question. For example, some disaffected and well-travelled young British Muslim men were skilfully manipulated by older jihadists into carrying out the 7 July 2005 London suicide bombings with tragic results and fifty-three deaths.

Box 2.2   Culture gets creative

Interview with Paul Ray and Sarah van Gelder, *Yes* **magazine, Winter 2001**

Sarah: Where did all these Cultural Creatives come from? You say that prior to World War II there were few, if any, Cultural Creatives. Instead, almost all Americans belonged to one of two other subcultures. Could you describe what those two were?

Paul: The two subcultures are what we call the Traditionals and the Moderns. The Modern culture is the dominant, parent culture of this civilization, and it goes back 500 years to the Renaissance. Then around 1750 to 1800, we started getting a major backlash against the materialistic, urban, industrial, bureaucratic, culture of Modernism from the people who were losing – the Traditionalists. These people were reacting against the tendencies of the Modern world to undercut the legitimacy of churches, the Bible, the patriarchal family, and so on.

Sarah: So beginning after World War II, this third subculture emerges?

Paul: First of all, we're talking today about a quarter of the adults in the United States, 50 million adults, and probably 80 to 90 million adults in Western Europe. These people take the ideas of ecology very seriously, and they support slowing business growth in order to save the planet. They also take very seriously women's issues and issues of personal growth and relationships. We found that the typical Cultural Creative cares intensely about the issues raised by post-World War II social movements. These movements include those focused on civil rights, the environment, women's rights, peace, jobs and social justice, gay and lesbian rights, alternative health care, spirituality, personal growth, and now, of course, stopping corporate globalization. All of those concerns are now converging into a strong concern for the whole planet.

Cultural creatives multiply

The awakening of human potential is one of the most significant changes of our time. We live in a highly creative age. It is like Lorenzo de Medici's Renaissance Florence, except that now every person can be creative in their own right. Culturally creative people want to build the social, economic and cultural future, seek transformational and personal change and address the social, spiritual and ecological challenges of our time as opportunities for positive change. 'Be the change you want to see in the world', said Gandhi.

However, the freedom to choose lifeways, partners, work and values, whilst acceptable to culturally creative people, can also be threatening to traditionalists and modernists. Such freedom is out of their comfort zone – it can cause insecurity and fear. The traditionalists, threatened by change, can retreat into various forms of fundamentalism, polarising the world into good and bad, us and them. Some want to return to the past, reviving old religious forms. The modernists adopt the latest fashions, enjoy technological and economic progress, want to get to the top and have it all. Having is more important than being or becoming. They defend the current 'business as usual' model of society and scientific materialism, believing that a combination of new technology and more of the same will help us all muddle through the credit crunch and peak oil.

Paul Ray and Sherry Anderson first researched the emergence of cultural creatives in the 1990s and concluded that there is a profound shift taking place as their numbers increase worldwide.[6]

The shift from the collective to the individual

So there is a historic transformation from the individual serving a collective-driven society to a society serving individual growth. This shift leads to individuals choosing to contribute what they can and clarifying their values to live by. This transition from the collective to individualisation was foreshadowed in the Scientific Revolution, and by post-Reformation non-conformist movements such as the Quakers and the Romantic movement. However, thinkers such as Freud, Weber, Jung and Rudolf Steiner noticed individualisation as a change with wide historic significance in the late nineteenth century.

In 1898, Rudolf Steiner observed this unfolding change in human consciousness from the collective to the individual. He described this historic shift as follows:

> At the beginning of culture, humanity strives to create social arrangements in which the interests of the individual are sacrificed for the interests of the whole. Later developments lead to a gradual freeing of the individual from the interest of the community, and to an unfolding of individual needs and capacities.[7]

At the time Steiner made this observation, most people had to sacrifice themselves without question for the collective. Average life expectancy in Europe was around thirty-one years; men and women worked long hours to raise children,

Box 2.3 *Women of Britain say – 'Go!'*

Source: Parliamentary Recruiting Committee, 1915

men were expected to die if conscripted for their country, women were expected to have children and many died in childbirth. Today, at least in wiser social democratic countries, the conditions for individual freedom are in place. These include the right of conscientious objection, civil liberties, free education, healthcare, a minimum wage, decent housing, social security and contraception. A whole range of personal development paths has developed, such as coaching, counselling and psychotherapy. These can help individuals transform blockages to personal health, wellbeing and fulfilment and explore how to best cope with personal freedom in an age of the existential insecurity that inevitably comes with individualisation.

Here are four other significant changes in human consciousness that emerge with increasing individualisation.

Firstly, when people wake up to their individual potential, they can then also choose to see the world that we humans have created for what it is. This can be a shock. It is hard to ignore the electronic-media-driven, high consumption lifestyle fired by turbo capitalism and how this is destroying both the planet and humans. Yet this social world is our humanly created world. Yes, we are part of the naturally created world of the earth, seas, trees and animals. However, we also create the world of conversations, technology, shops, farms, companies, government and entertainment. If we don't like what we find, we can choose to say 'no'. Then we can join with others to co-create what we do want. However, it is clear that many people choose not to see the world as socially created, regarding it as 'nothing to do with them'. And others may continue to pursue selfish individualism, without developing ethical individualism.

Secondly, the modern social world we have created both mirrors and shapes our human consciousness interactively. Scarcely fifteen years ago, there was relatively little use of broadband or mobiles. Now walk down any street, and many people are texting, or looking at their mobiles, or engaged in phone conversations, as if no one else in the street was there. This mirroring and shaping is part of a huge social learning process we are all involved in – like it or not. The extent to which technology or humans are in control is another question.

Thirdly, our unprecedented power to transform nature and to create the social world we live in invites us to take more responsibility for building healthy neighbourhoods, families, businesses, organisations and society. 'They', whoever they are, won't or can't do it any more. As we said in Stroud during our Community Planning Conference, 'It's UP 2 US'.

We have moved from a rural, through an urban/industrial and now to a post-industrial society. On the way, we have largely lost the old sustaining connection with the cycle of the seasons and with nature. Traditional social structures – such as hierarchical, command and control bureaucratic organisations – don't really work any more. Tradition, shared values, religion and social instincts once guided community life and shaped the social fabric. But now, the capacity to use technology to exploit the earth invites also the responsibility for co-creating the social world and caring for the earth. Paradoxically, the testing and use of weapons of mass destruction – or the destruction of the living earth by our wasteful economy – can also invite a new age of social responsibility. We do not value what we have until we have nearly lost it …

Fourthly, the new social phenomenon of 'reflexivity' is an outcome of the above three social shifts in our relationship with the world. How we see the world has significant consequences. At the same time people are becoming more reflective about themselves, their lives and work. Individuals have the power to shape social life, according to their perceptions – whether these are accurate or not.

For example 'confidence' keeps the financial markets going up or down, and 'reflexivity' has dramatic effects on the global financial markets – with self-fulfilling prophecies that can lead to market meltdown. The hedge-fund speculator George Soros has made a fortune – at least $2.9 billion in 2007 – from his successful practice of reflexivity. Rather than see financial markets as efficient and rational, Soros sees people's knowledge as imperfect. People have a stubborn attachment to wrongheaded ideas, so that bankers' expectations and feelings can influence economic basics like share prices. For him, reflexivity is a two-way interaction between people's perceptions and the real situation. People decide to buy or sell

Box 2.4   *It's UP 2 Us!*

The early 1990s saw the small Cotswold market town of Stroud in decline, triggered by the district council moving its offices out of the centre, and new out-of-town supermarkets putting many small shops out of business. Civil society, with business and local government support, led regeneration through designing and facilitating a far-reaching community planning process which involved over 1,000 people in 1994–5. Significant parts of their vision have since been realised, for example the repopulation of the town centre through 'living over the shops' and the conversion of the iconic Hill Paul Mill for flats, rather than being knocked down.

on their perception and interpretation of the situation. However, their decisions also influence or manipulate the situation, and changes in the economic situation also change their perceptions. So for many years bankers such as Alan Greenspan believed that insured sub-prime debt was secure and profitable, even though it was pumping up the biggest credit bubble in history.[8] This economic neo-liberal, former head of the US Federal Reserve Bank, actually believed naïvely that banks acted rationally and responsibly. He lamely told US Congressman Henry Waxman that, 'Those of us who have looked to the self-interest of lending institutions to protect shareholders' equity (including myself) are in a state of shocked disbelief.'[9] No wonder speculators like Soros, with a more accurate perception of reality, have been so successful with market fundamentalists like Greenspan in charge.

How we see 'the world' is important, as this influences how we act. If you see yourself as a responsible and reflective co-creator who can make a modest difference, this is very different from seeing yourself as powerless in a world created by 'them'.

Getting engaged: 'I felt I was sleepwalking before'

It just takes one action to get engaged. Anita Roddick, the Body Shop founder, suggested we 'take it personally'. She said that to challenge corporate globalisation where the World Trade Organization is the unelected world government, we need a revolution in kindness. 'We are surrounded by inequalities, but we must react with sympathy, and then act with imagination, hope and courage, because things can change.' She said that, 'The future of the world depends on us all taking it personally.'[10]

So you can cut down on personal resource consumption, reuse plastic bags, save energy or pick up litter whilst on a morning walk. You can demonstrate by returning all the unnecessary packaging to a supermarket – dumping it back at the check-out. You can support fair trade products where possible and invest ethically.

Change becomes self-reinforcing as more and more people get involved. There has been a Stroud High Street weekly vigil against the renewal of Trident, as Gordon Brown, who professes to be inspired by Mahatma Gandhi, wanted to spend £30 billion of our money on Trident. There was a monthly Quaker meeting for worship at the gates of the USAF Air Base at RAF Fairford in Gloucestershire, to give witness for peace and against the weapons of mass nuclear destruction once stored there.

Thus we meet the challenges that life brings and pay attention to what can be done within our spheres of influence. Actions can be openings for greater understanding, learning and more engagement. For example, Gandhi used to spin cotton into thread himself and encouraged others to do so, in order to both empower people and also undermine the British cotton industry exports through local self-reliance. Change happens by example. Think of the French priest, Abbé Pierre, who founded the Emmaus communities to help homeless people make a living through recycling, house clearance and selling refurbished goods so as to combat social exclusion and recover dignity. Consider Princess Diana, who went well beyond her privileged background with its military trappings and campaigned against landmines. Or the group of school children in Market Drayton, Shropshire, who raised a few pounds to help save their local Fordhall Farm for the community.

Many try to make a difference, in spite of feeling that their actions are like a drop in the bucket in the bigger scheme of things. Think of the story of the boy on a seashore strewn with hundreds of storm-stranded starfish, who was throwing them back into the sea. When asked what difference his action made, he answered, whilst throwing another starfish into the sea, 'It makes a lot of difference to this one!'

Rebecca Hosking has been called 'the bag lady of Modbury' in Devon. She led the successful campaign for a first plastic-bag-free town in Britain. Louise Carpenter writes of her BBC film that:

> Through Message in the Waves, Hosking revealed some horrible truths: how plastic rubbish on a mammoth scale – anything from lighters and asthma inhalers to bags, toys, bottles, toothbrushes and pens – is being blown into the sea, where it then chokes or poisons the wildlife. Hosking had held a dying

albatross in her arms and fished a plastic bag out of the mouth of a choking 50-year-old turtle. The horror of it all meant she returned to England a changed woman, with a desperate need to feel rooted in a community: 'I felt I was sleepwalking before', she says. 'I suppose I was like everybody else. It was my job to be ethically minded but I wasn't really. I bought things and didn't think about the bills, I drove a lot, I was doing all the things that everybody does on a normal day and doesn't think about.'[11]

Citizen engagement is even now official government policy, as the flagship policy of Hazel Blears when Secretary of State for Communities and Local Government (2007–9). She once went so far as to say it's a 'sin' to waste people's time in engaging them on issues and then disregarding what they have to say. Her political rhetoric, however, did not match the reality of what she and her ministerial team did. Basically her version of citizen engagement boiled down to aspirations for keeping people informed. One of her junior housing ministers, Ian Wright MP, asked me, 'What is the secret of community engagement?' when we met him on 27 February 2008 at Westminster to lobby for community land trusts. Mentally wondering why he and his ministerial colleagues were not 'engaging with' the six members of Plane Stupid who had demonstrated on the Palace of Westminster rooftop against building the third Heathrow runway that very morning, I replied that:

> The more people see a direct connection between their efforts and the community benefits they value, such as more affordable homes, safer neighbourhoods, better community facilities, more jobs and a better environment, the more they will be likely to engage – especially if they see a direct connection between their efforts and the results. And if their time is not wasted.

This assumes that most people, when given the opportunity, will cooperate for mutual and the public good, can take responsibility and can organise – especially if facilitative leaders work to develop democratic skills and capacity for civic and community development through practical work on issues that affect them.

Our meeting was interrupted by his having to vote, and he did not acknowledge my follow-up letter.[12]

Civil disobedience

So looked at positively, the world situation is a wake-up call. We can choose action or, like the Easter Islander cutting down the last tree, 'obey orders' unthinkingly. (The collapse of Easter Island into cannibalism and poverty was partly caused by cutting down trees for the expensive death rituals and monuments for the ruling elite.) We can do 'business as usual' without thought for the mess we are leaving for our grandchildren. The distinguished American historian and civil rights activist Howard Zinn once wrote:

> Civil disobedience is not our problem. Our problem is civil obedience. Our problem is that numbers of people all over the world have obeyed the dictates

of the leaders of their government and have gone to war, and millions have been killed because of this obedience.

Our problem is that people are obedient all over the world in the face of poverty and starvation and stupidity, and war, and cruelty.

Our problem is that people are obedient while the jails are full of petty thieves, and all the while the grand thieves are running the country. That's our problem.[13]

Maybe you think that Zinn is exaggerating about the grand thieves running the country. In January 2007, Prime Minister Blair refused to attend the first parliamentary debate on Iraq since 2004 to answer for his actions. His refusal is set against the war-related deaths of several hundred thousand Iraqis, the deaths of over 179 British soldiers and the estimated $3 trillion cost of this war. He also stopped the Serious Fraud Office inquiry into the alleged £1 billion bribery of Saudi Arabian officials by British Aerospace, declaring it was against the 'public interest'. Blair's hypocritical decision broke his government-supported OECD anti-bribery convention, which states that the prosecution of foreign bribery, 'shall not be influenced by considerations of national economic interests or the potential effect upon relations with another state'.

Principled civil disobedience can meet with understanding from juries. The six climate change activists who scaled the chimney of the Kingsnorth coal-fired power station in Kent in October 2007 were charged with criminal damage estimated at £30,000. They were protesting against the building of a new coal-fired station that would not capture carbon. They argued that their action had prevented damage to more valuable property, so by closing the station for a day, they had each prevented 3,300 tonnes of carbon entering the atmosphere. Supported by a cast of expert witnesses, they were acquitted by the jury. The bravery of the Kingsnorth Six showed that direct action raised public support, changed people's minds, caused a cabinet reshuffle and shifted government policy.[14]

From vision-building to action

But individual change and action, whilst important, can only go so far. As Goethe once famously said, one alone can do little, but when several join together with a common purpose, much can be achieved. We can join together with others to take action on an issue in the community, or work on changing a business practice of our employer, or influence government. We can co-create a desired future of what we want to achieve, define our objectives, agree our guiding values, make plans, decide who will do what and implement our plans.

Vision-building and action for a more peaceful, just, human-centred and sustainable life needs facilitation to be most effective. This helps us learn and build capacity as we develop the economy, political processes and cultural forms we want on the local level. The global movement for freedom, democracy and social justice – once known as the anti-globalisation movement – is leading the way with the World Social Forums. These complement practical grassroots regeneration work by providing global space for networking, vision-building for 'another world', organising, learning and dialogue.

But to create 'another world' we need shared vision so we can create desirable futures. It helps to ask, 'What do we want, and how do we get there?' The question, 'is my work leading to a desirable future?' is important for individuals to ask from time to time. It is also vital for companies, communities and civil society organisations to work on vision, purpose and guiding values as stars to steer by. It is essential to develop a future image of what we want to do about the complex issues we face.

Behavioural science research found that as long as people talked about problems, their energy sank. But when they started planning what they wanted for the future and achievable solutions, people's energy immediately rose.[15]

Consider how all over the world in the early 1990s, communities – encouraged by the UN Rio Summit and Local Agenda 21 – started to envision what they wanted for a sustainable community, with lasting results. The Dutch psychiatrist Bernard Lievegoed once told me how when he was living in Amsterdam during the Second World War, he used to gather with others in 'rooftop' meetings. People had to crawl across dangerous roofs to get to the meeting place despite the curfews. Each person would share their dream of how they wanted Holland to be after the war – and what they wanted to do about it. Such meetings happened all over Holland, even in prisons. After the war was over, the relationships established enabled participants to help each other achieve their visions. For example, Dr Lievegoed gave a talk on youth education at a rooftop meeting. The future head of the Dutch employers' association was there and later invited Lievegoed to set up the NPI Institute for Organisational Development.[16] Similarly, in Britain, the 1939–45 war saw a ferment of new thinking that led to the establishment of the NHS. 'Without vision, the people perish', as the old saying goes.

Small actions can have big effects. Heather Brooke's investigation of MPs' expenses led to the exposure of the House of Commons to public scrutiny and the call for thoroughgoing democratic reform. A faxed question from Greenpeace to a food manufacturer in 1999 resulted in the removal of GM ingredients from their baby food. In a chaotic situation, for example the current financial market meltdown, small groups of people can take thoughtful action with significant outcomes. From chaos theory, we know that when a butterfly beats its wings in the Gulf of Siam, it could result in a hurricane in the Gulf of Mexico. People all over the world want to take more responsibility and make a difference. We can build on productive work in progress to create more positive futures.

But it is important to see what we can and what we cannot change, to recognise where we have concerns, but no influence, and where we just have influence. And it is very easy to forget if you are comfortably off. The daily reality of poverty, conflict, injustice, environmental degradation and poor social conditions for two-thirds of humanity goes largely unreported. Even so, we know in our hearts what is really going on. The social artist Joseph Beuys wrote on one of his blackboard drawings which was displayed at the Tate Modern in spring 2005:

He who ... can live carefree and sleep peacefully despite knowing that two-thirds of humanity are hungry or dying of starvation while a large proportion of the well-fed third must take slimming cures in order to stay alive, he should ask himself what kind of a man he is and whether, moreover, he is a man at all.

Alice Walker once said, 'If one person is poor, how can others say they are rich?'

Finally, when I work as a facilitator with people in companies, government and communities to build practical vision and to make strategic plans for their future, the key social questions of our time come up to set the context for change. The following common questions often emerge:

- How can we build a more efficient, collaborative, fair, sustainable economy that meets people's needs and respects the planet's carrying capacity and the needs of future generations?
- How are we building a more peaceful, participative, democratic, just and equitable society?
- How are we enabling all human beings reach their full spiritual, creative, social and physical potential?
- How are we caring for the earth?

Summary

To summarise, more and more people want to make a difference and contribute to creating a better world. People are waking up to their individual potential. Individuals no longer blindly sacrifice themselves for the collective, but want to develop themselves and clarify their values. As traditional social forms break down, as technology offers the choice of destroying or sustaining the planet, we can 'take it personally'. There is a renewed sense of taking responsibility for society and the planet. How we see the social world – reflexivity – is very important, because perceptions can become self-fulfilling prophecies. Reflection and reality-checking is important. Joining with others, we have the opportunity to co-create and realise the desired future for our community or organisation. It's now up to us, not them.

The old political and economic structures are falling apart. People are emancipating themselves from these structures, which are bursting at the seams like old suits. However, in order to exercise citizenship, to work as a responsible consumer or producer and live as a free thinking individual it is useful to now ask 'What map of emerging society can help? What power do we have and what kind of power will be most effective? How can we best use the emerging map of the three social powers of business, the state and civil society for public good?'

Chapter 3

Tripolar Society: Government, Business and Civil Society

This chapter asks and seeks to answer the question, 'What map can help guide action for a more sustainable society and planet?' Now that political ideologies such as neo-liberal capitalism, socialism and communism have passed their sell-by dates, what new image of society is emerging?

The two societal powers of business and government dominated the social landscape up to the 1980s, paying only lip-service to the idea of 'community'. According to the economic neo-liberal Mrs Thatcher, there was no such thing as society, only self-seeking individuals. 'The market' dominated the political and cultural spaces of society. But when civil society movements brought down Eastern European communist governments, culminating with the November 1989 toppling of the Berlin Wall, the emerging third societal power of civil society was hard to ignore.

Despite Francis Fukuyama heralding the fall of communism as the victory of capitalism and the 'end of history', global civil society developed as a countervailing power to the neo-liberal capitalism that was then fully unleashed as Bush Senior's 'new world order' and the 1991 Washington neo-liberal consensus. Global civil society raised concerns about the destruction of the environment, rising inequality, the destruction of indigenous cultures, social exclusion and the capture by corporate globalisation of nation states and cultures. Global civil society led the 1999 Battle of Seattle against the corporation-dominated World Trade Organization, bringing its destructive agenda out into the open. Then the 2003 worldwide anti-Iraq War demonstrations successfully delegitimised Bush and Blair's war. Greenpeace projected an image of 'Bliar' on to the Thameside wall of the Houses of Parliament, and Brian Haw's demonstration in Parliament Square continues to speak truth to government power. And civil society is not just about being against the government or the big corporations – it is also about developing solutions and partnerships to tackle some of the big issues we face. And when 2 million people celebrated President Obama's inauguration on 20 January 2009 in Washington, this was a positive expression of hope by civil society, with 'we the people' welcoming a new government led by someone with deep roots in community organising.

So the new tripolar world is made up of three societal powers – those of business, the government and civil society. The cosy marriage between big business and government has been disrupted by the emergence of civil society, which has changed societal dynamics for ever through triangulation. So when the government espouses carbon reduction to tackle global warming, but in practice is soft on the construction of new coal-fired power stations by electricity companies delighted to be let off the expense of low-carbon technology, civil society can act decisively. Civil society organisations such as Greenpeace, advocating for alternatives such as the Green New Deal, demonstrate to get the message across and change values.

The British voluntary and community sector, along with the NGOs, is reinventing itself as civil society, following global usage. Sometimes civil society is loosely referred to as 'the third sector', though this includes a mix of charities, non-profits as well as social enterprise, which can be seen as part of the economy. Civil society and the community sector is challenged to assert itself more strongly, as the British government wants to control such instances of people power. The government's default position is that of bureaucratic, top-down control and of marginalising, co-opting and paying lip-service to civil society organisations. People see a stream of government-led, time-wasting consultations that recommend what the government wanted to do in the first place, like the new nuclear power programme. Interestingly, Labour and Conservatives are in conflict about how to best relate to civil society. Oliver Letwin MP, for example, claims that a new Conservative government, now rebranding itself as the 'party of society', will enable full civil society development such as Community Land Trusts for affordable homes.

Box 3.1   Nuclear power consultation 'a sham': government versus civil society

A government-backed consultation on new nuclear power stations came under fire from a market research watchdog, which said it breached the industry code of conduct because insufficient steps were taken to ensure members of the public were not led into giving the required response. It is the second time the process has run into difficulties, following a High Court ruling in 2006 which found the government's decision-making process had been unlawful as it had failed to engage in the fullest possible consultation.

Environmental campaigners Greenpeace said the ruling by the Market Research Standards Board revealed the consultation to be 'a sham and an insult to the people who took part' and left the government's plans for new nuclear power stations 'in disarray'.[1]

However, when faced by civil society taking the lead – for example with the Transition Towns movement or the Community Land Trust movement – government finds it hard to respond with anything other than 'warm words', sometimes obstructing whilst professing to help. So, whilst housing ministers said they wanted to remove block-ages to Community Land Trust development for affordable homes, they also for long opposed Housing Bill amendments to put the definition of Community Land Trusts into law. The Transition Towns movement, with over a hundred member towns and cities across Britain, has been raising questions about the implications of peak oil for our economy and way of life. Yet government 'does not believe that global oil produc-tion will peak between now and 2020' and so will make no contingency plans.[2]

This chapter explores the emerging tripolar image of society. I will suggest that society is not a monolithic structure, but is formed from the dynamic interplay between the autonomous but interconnected economic, political and cultural systems. A simple image is that of society as a three-legged stool with business, the state and civil society as the legs, each standing in the economic, political and cultural systems respectively. The topics addressed include:

- the costs of confusion between business, government and civil society
- from the neo-liberal to tripolar societal maps
- recognising business, government and civil society in action
- trisectoral partnerships for sustainable development
- tripolar society, organisations and the human being
- reinventing business, government and civil society
- cultural, political and economic power
- from bipolar to tripolar social power dynamics.

The costs of confusion between business, government and civil society

What we currently have is confusion, not clarity, between the contribution of busi-ness, government and civil society. The results of this confusion are very costly. For example, in September 2008, the US Treasury Secretary Hank Paulson, former CEO of Goldman Sachs bank, refused to bail out a leading competitor, Lehman Brothers. His decision was a crucial trigger in making the financial meltdown much worse. Did he let Lehman go bankrupt because this would be would be in Goldman Sachs' interest? Or did he let Lehman go down because it was in the interest of the US government and people? Whose interest was Paulson serving when he wanted the dictatorial power to spend the $700 billion from Congress on toxic debt, with his decisions exempt from legal redress? Was Paulson acting in the public interest for the government, or in the bankers' private interest?

There is currently little clarity about what the healthy boundaries between busi-ness, government and civil society should be. When Rupert Murdoch invited David Cameron, George Osborne and Lord Peter Mandelson to attend his daughter Elisabeth Murdoch's birthday party on his yacht in Corfu in summer 2008, it looked like a case of business buying politicians for present and future favours. A grounded respect for healthy boundaries would have kept the politicians away from the party.

The government seems to want to make hospitals into businesses, rather than run hospitals in a businesslike way. Some British politicians want a privatised health market run by profit making business, not a public health service. Hamish Meldrum, the BMA chairman, said at the 2008 BMA annual conference that 'the market is now a peculiarly English disease. The BMA wants to see an NHS untarnished by a market economy, true to its beginnings, giving the public a fair, caring, equitable and cost-effective health service – not a service run like a shoddy supermarket war … Let's stop pretending that healing the sick is like trading a commodity.'[3] Government has even hollowed its own core statutory functions out by privatising chunks of the prison service, data services, security and the Army. The new British census contract has apparently been given to the US defence firm Northrop.

Another example of confusion is the question of whether the Post Office is a business or a public service. New Labour sees post offices as profit-making businesses. So it has closed 4,500 post offices, undermined profitability by withdrawing contracts, and plans to close 2,500 of the remaining 14,000. It's a hot issue. In 2006, 4 million people signed petitions against closures planned by Alistair Darling, then Secretary of State at the Department of Trade and Industry.

We are all poorer for the government seeing the Post Office as a profit-making business rather than as a social service and social business. Postal monopolies have been progressively lifted by government so that private companies can compete, thus taking away PO profits that were formerly used to cross-subsidise other socially beneficial, but 'loss making' postal services. At this point, the government then starts paying a subsidy from taxes to the PO. This subsidy is not enough, so smaller local post offices have to close, only for local authorities and communities to then reopen them, as with Stroud's Uplands post office, which gets a grant from the Town Council. The government seems to have forgotten its International Postal Union obligations, which require that the inland postal rate is the same anywhere in Britain, even to expensive-to-deliver-to destinations like the Outer Hebrides. Finally, at the time of writing, having perhaps fatally undermined the viability of Royal Mail, Lord Mandelson, Secretary of State for Business, Innovation and Skills, has tried to sell off a large share to the TNT Corporation with support from his Conservative opposite number Kenneth Clarke MP. This is in the teeth of popular, Post Office, trade union and backbench parliamentary opposition in the form of John Cruddas MP, who proposes to reinvent the Post Office as a People's Bank. There is no doubt, however, that Royal Mail needs to find a viable new business or social business model.

From the neo-liberal to tripolar society

So, to prevent such confusion, this chapter argues for clear boundaries between the business, government and civil society sectors. I will argue that the health, wealth and justice of a society is greater, the more it works with the principles of freedom in the creative cultural life of individuals in civil society, equality in human rights of citizens in the political system and mutuality in economic life between producers, distributors and consumers.

The boundaries of social maps are important, as they shape perceptions. The politicians, who believe that 'business is good, public services are bad', will privatise everything they can, even in the face of evidence that goes against their policies. In Britain, public utilities were sold off in the 1980s and 1990s by government at two-thirds of their market value, thus also sacrificing significant ongoing income streams that would have been of public benefit.

As Keynes once observed, many so-called practical men are the unwitting slaves of the theories of long-dead economists, in this case those of the neo-liberal economics pioneer Friedrich Hayek. So the neo-liberal societal map guides the World Bank and the IMF, for example, when they impose draconian structural adjustment programmes on poor countries. The IMF forces cuts in education and the privatisation of public services such as water supply, so that 'the invisible hand of the market' can flourish. The precaution is usually taken of increasing spending on security to quell the anti-IMF riots. This is how neo-liberal economists such as Milton Friedman interpreted the ideas of Adam Smith, which resulted in the 1992 'Washington consensus'. Successive British governments, through privatising our public assets and parts of our health service, have pioneered the implementation of these ideas. These neo-liberal values are so embedded that many believe that 'there is no alternative'.[4] Such values, of course, are now challenged by the credit crunch, the banking crisis and the worst recession since the 1930s.

However, the emergent tripolar society described here is very different from the neo-liberal model of society, where the corporate market economy dominates both the state and civil society.

Recognising business, government and civil society in action

The 'three-legged stool' map of the three social powers or sectors of society first dawned on me when I was facilitating an Agenda 21 housing conference. This multi-stakeholder conference was analysing the options for increasing sustainable housing in Gloucestershire. As soon as it started, it was like having people from at least three different planets in the room.

The conference was held because in the mid-1990s the government announced that Gloucestershire had to make plans for at least 50,000 new homes to be built by 2010 as projected housing demand was rising. This was a very hot topic. NIMBYs[5] did not want new houses in their back yards, perceiving these as afford-able homes for problem families; employers wanted affordable homes for staff; house builders and land owners wanted planning permission – and big windfall profits – to build executive homes in the green belt. Local government had to make plans by squaring the circle between all these interests.

There were many stakeholder groups at the conference. But it was clear from the start, even by the clothes being worn, that the business people thought and behaved very differently from public sector officials and elected representatives on the one hand and people from a variety of community-based organisations, non-profits, cultural and civil society organisations (CSOs) on the other. CSO participants were strong on values, community engagement, social inclusion and what made for a diverse, sustainable community, environmentally, socially and culturally. They had vivid stories about the needs of a range of marginalised groups, had demon-strated initiative in getting pilot housing projects going, were good at advocacy and brought clearly articulated values to the process. They participated actively, were keen to get things moving and saw their input of time as worth while if it both achieved more homes for their particular locality and also brought about value change. They were good at using cultural power. Some were impatient with the perceived sluggishness of the public sector, which was concerned about fairness, equity, detail, setting precedents and following correct procedures. They seemed happier to block plans rather than work with community groups and business on pressing housing problems.

It was striking how public sector officials and elected politicians from several levels of local government kept dipping in and out of the process. They met to exchange information in huddles from time to time. Their concern was fairness for all, standard provision, representation, getting the overall housing, structure and area plans correct, ensuring that there was good information about real overall housing needs and not making planning precedents. They seemed to always have time and money for another meeting, much to the annoyance of business and civil society people, who had more pressing work. The public sector people had the legitimate and coercive power of granting planning permission for homes and funding. They were concerned about the sustainability and stability of community and civil society groups, about how representative they were. They were impatient with seemingly endless discussions of values, such as the low-impact rural settlements desired by *The Land Is Ours*[6] and the social exclusion of travellers and young people.

The business people, such as employers, farmers, house builders and developers, were highly focused, clear about their objectives and collectively knew every bit of land in the county with actual or potential planning permission, no matter how far in the future this might be. They wanted to get profitable up-market homes built, but houses built for low-income people were low on the agenda. They had economic and resource power. When different housing options were discussed, they could quickly calculate budgets and projected profits. They shared an entrepreneurial flair with the civil society organisations and were keen to explore how the planning system could help unlock land value. Planning permission from government could deliver land uplift value, in some cases from £5,000 per agricultural acre to up to £1 million an acre. The stakes were high for them.

No wonder it was like having people from three different planets in the room. All three sectors were there for different reasons, but needed to cooperate to secure their respective interests and objectives. They knew that the alternative to partnership between the three sectors was conflict, attrition or stalemate. With hindsight, given the conflicts and the fact that housing is a complex, 'wicked issue', recognising in advance the need for a three-way partnership for sustainable housing could have helped break the logjam.

My experience at the housing conference was similar to that of Ros Tennyson, who observed the three sectors in action and now works all over the world to develop the capacity for three-way partnerships. She saw the importance of recognising and including the three sectors when developing a cross-sector partnership in the early 1990s in Krakow, in post-communist Poland.[7] She works for the Prince of Wales's International Business Leaders' Forum, developing partnerships around the world for sustainable development. She uses the triangular dynamics of the three sectors productively to build partnerships. Each sector is invited to identify its strengths and weaknesses and share their perceptions of the other two sectors' strengths and weaknesses. They then agree to play to their strengths and make positive contributions in a trisectoral partnership. These approaches are used around the world to tackle burning social problems and build partnerships for sustainable development where appropriate.[8] Ros Tennyson's representation of the three sectors is shown in Figure 3.1.

Trisectoral partnerships for sustainable development

A practical way of using the tripolar societal map is to help guide action on key questions using trisectoral partnerships. The three sectors bring very different working principles, skills, knowledge and qualities. For example, there is the need to combat global warming and social inequality. Business, the state and civil society can do something to reduce carbon use in their own sectors. However, there is the danger that state-enforced action such as a massive nuclear power programme may make things much worse. On the other hand, effective trisectoral partnerships – with each sector playing to their unique strengths – can achieve more through open-ended, effective and transparent collaboration than by forcing through a predetermined plan to favour corporate interests.

Figure 3.1   The three sectors and their constituents
Source: Ros Tennyson and Luke Wilde, The Guiding Hand: Brokering Partnerships for Sustainable Development, *Prince of Wales Business Leaders Forum and the United Nations Staff College, 2000, Figure 1, p. 8*

Real dialogue can help business explore a variety of sustainable energy options. Civil society can help individuals engage with the issues involved in global warming, help make sense of what is happening and what it means, enable value change for sustainability and take action through inspirational projects in the community. Examples of this include the Centre for Alternative Technology at Machynlleth, Wales, and the Centre for Sustainable Energy in Bristol. The state can engage with business and civil society with strategic planning frameworks about what is needed, for example for waste management or energy-efficient house-design rules or sustainable transport frameworks. It can pass both enabling legislation and regulation, as well as resourcing civil society initiatives and education, and encouraging business to work within the new sustainable planning frameworks. Business itself can reconfigure how it works, for example through doing much more with far fewer resources through 'natural capitalism', engaging with consumers about saving resources, implementing fair trade, and supporting civil society with research funds, grants for education and pilot demonstration projects. Such dialogue, learning and action can all be made much more effective through open three-way partnerships at global, regional, national and local levels as appropriate.

Tripolar society, organisations and human beings

So business, the government and civil society can be seen as forming together the three-legged stool of society. They have 'dotcom', 'dotgov' and 'dotorg' email addresses respectively. But society also reflects the human being. Just as humans are basically threefold, having a physical body, an inner life of experience or soul and an identity which enables us to say 'I' to ourselves as the centre of our experience, so also organisations can be seen as having a threefold structure. You can recognise the 'essence', 'spirit' or 'identity' of an organisation as expressed by its purpose, mission, guiding values and story; the 'soul' of the organisation is expressed in

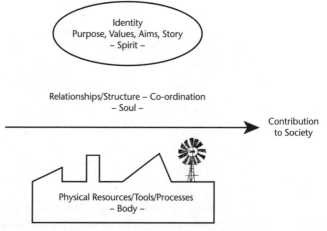

Figure 3.2   Threefold image of an organisation
Source: Martin Large, Social Ecology, *1981, p. 62*

the patterns and quality of relationships forming the structure; the 'body' can be seen in the life processes, energy, activities, the buildings, the equipment and the physical resources of an organisation.

Threefolding comes from our personal experience. As human beings we think, we feel and we have the will to take action. At the same time, these human faculties of thinking, feeling and willing are alive in our relationships. In conversation with others, we exchange ideas, feel likes and dislikes and notice our intentions for action. In groups of people, thinking is shared through the content of what is said; the will of the group members is expressed through the procedure and the purpose; feeling is expressed through the interaction of participation and communication, speaking and listening.

An important further consideration is the human body itself. Studying the human body – one of the most complex organic systems – can help clarify more about the dynamics of society. For example, an interesting fact is that body tissues are largely self-regulating in determining what oxygen and nutrients are needed. Although there are many ways of analysing the various organic systems forming the body, one 'big picture' of how the body works is of 'head, heart and hands'. The human body has a threefold structure formed from the dynamic yet semi-autonomous, self-organising interaction of the head (the nervous and senses system), heart (circulatory and breathing system) and limbs (metabolic system).

A healthy society, like the human body, is not dominated by any one system, but formed from the dynamic interplay of the economic, cultural and political systems. So studying the human body can help clarify how a self-organising tripolar structure can work, though the analogy should not be taken too far. One key observation from the human body is that there is no overall centralisation. Health results from the differentiation and partnership working of the three organic systems. Whenever one system starts to dominate, the body suffers ill health.

By observing the human body, therefore, you can recognise three functionally distinct but interacting physiological systems working semi-autonomously. Firstly, there is the nerves and senses system, which gathers sensory information about the world for the mind to then process into concepts. Whilst the nervous system functions and is active throughout the whole body, it is also focused in the head and the brain. If the nervous system centred in the head really exercised the absolute command and central control of the other two systems – as is sometimes imagined – then the neck would need to be very thick to carry all the command nerves!

Secondly, there is the circulatory or rhythmic system. This is formed from breathing and the circulation of oxygen through the blood. It carries nutrients to the nervous system from the metabolic system and carries waste products away, through breathing (as with carbon dioxide) and through excretion. The heart is not just a pump that drives blood through the veins and arteries, as physiologists such as Harvey once theorised, but also a sensing, balancing and rhythm-bringing organ. Unlike the conscious brain, the heart never sleeps or stops. To be a pump according to the old simplistic, mechanistic conceptions, the heart would have to be massive.

The heart responds directly to the metabolic system. For example it responds to the increased activity of muscles by beating more rapidly, as anyone will notice when walking uphill. Physiologically, it does so by responding to the increase in venous return – the increased amount of blood coming back through the veins to the heart. Muscular activity vigorously massages the veins through the fact of having one-way valves, pushing the blood back to the heart. This all happens without the mediation of the brain or nerves. Fear and frightening thoughts can also increase your pulse, and have direct effects on the metabolism, such as speeding up the gut, going pale, or getting a dry mouth. The heart is very responsive to the body, and whilst it's true that it works as a pump to get blood into the arteries and capillaries, it is more of a mystery how the blood then returns to the heart, as pressure gets low in the capillaries and veins. So a combination of muscular pushing and suction gets the blood back, from the feet, for example, up to the heart. One fascinating fact is that tissues auto-regulate themselves – each tissue controls its own blood flow according to its need for oxygen.[9] The heart gives rhythm to the blood circulation, and has its own independent nervous system inter-connected with the amygdala or 'feeling brain' in the cerebral cortex, with the brain appearing to respond to messages from the heart. So the heart is a kind of listening organ, rather than a pump, and as the heart listens to the body the heartbeat varies. The heartbeat of healthy people goes up or down according to demand, whereas the heart can beat only regularly in ill people, as if the heart had lost contact with its organic listening function.

Thirdly, there is the metabolic-limb system of all the organs and activities connected with digestion and the metabolism. Coordination is achieved by means of a 'gut' or abdominal brain, a kind of network of nerves spread through the solar plexus. This semi-autonomous gut brain controls the digestive system and unconscious metabolic processes.

The interconnections between the three systems are subtle, complex and operate at many levels throughout the body. For example, within the brain there is a cerebral cortex, a limbic and a reptilian brain, or 'thinking', 'feeling' and 'willing' brains. The head itself has the skull protecting and enclosing the brain, the nose connecting with the rhythmic breathing and circulatory system and the jaw, a small limb connecting with the metabolic-limb system. There is also the rhythmic system in the gut, with the rhythmic movement of peristalsis, waves of nerve fibres, moving the digesting food along.

Several key conclusions can be drawn from observing the human organism:

1.   There is no organic centralisation. No one organic system dominates in a healthy body. The human body is sustained by three functionally independent, yet interacting systems. There is no organic command and control system in overall charge.

2.   Each organic system has a special, unique relationship with the world. The head connects with the world by means of the senses; breathing links the circulatory system and our lungs to the air; and the metabolic system relates to the world through taking in and digesting substances and through the movement of the limbs.

3.   Each system works semi-autonomously, controlling its own functions, whilst keeping the other two systems informed and supported.
4.   Each system performs unique functions, whilst serving the human body in a specialist way.
5.   Each system works in partnership, interconnecting with the other two systems.
6.   Bodily health is maintained by positive and negative, homeostatic feedback that keeps each system from overstepping its natural functioning and boundaries. Under- and over-active systems produce ill health – so an over-active stomach can cause a headache, for example.

Such insights can be used to deepen our understanding of the partnership working of tripolar society, with three autonomous, but interacting systems or legs. One 'leg' is the economy with the market as the home territory of business. The economy serves human needs by producing, distributing and consuming goods, services and commodities. Whether as producers, distributors or consumers, we all participate in the economic system. We mutually satisfy our needs. Goods acquire value through people's needs, when trading products for money. We can observe, think through and calculate what is needed, and associate with others to produce and distribute or to meet our needs and establish a price.

Associative working is inherent in healthy economic development, for example through the Toyota lean production system,[10] where suppliers share risks and benefits of collaboration, waste reduction, quality improvement and R&D up and down the supply chain, which is pulled along by consumer demand. Another example is through fair trade, where producers, suppliers and consumers upstream and downstream in the supply chain can calculate and agree the prices and level of profit needed at each transaction along the chain.

The second leg is the political system or polity, the home territory of the state, government or public sector, which is concerned with civil, cultural and economic rights, legal regulation, security and political life. We are engaged as citizens, and elect representatives to pass laws, agree civil rights and entitlements, for example to health or education, to develop policy, choose an executive government and a judiciary, as well as ensuring law and order and security. This sphere is concerned with equality, where legal regulation ensures we all have the same rights and are treated alike before the law. The public sector makes sure that business works within the legal frameworks of environmental, health, privacy, intellectual copyright and labour laws, for example. It ensures that some businesses and individuals are not more equal than others. The essence of political life is the regulation of relationships between people according to a sense of fairness, a sense for what is right. This activity is a bit like the human heart and circulatory system, which tirelessly senses the health of the whole and brings rhythm to the human body. Without such regulation by the public sector, for example, powerful businesses could impose low wages and dump waste on the environment. The public sector makes sure that resources get to all parts of society equitably. All are equitably entitled. The public sector can identify what the needs are with those affected, make plans and engage with business and civil society to enable these needs to be met.

Lastly, the economic and political systems are nurtured and renewed by the creative cultural system, by people contributing their work, capacities and talents. Civil society and creative organisations, which serve the realisation of individual potential, are on home ground in the cultural system, with their stress on values, empowerment, advocacy of policies to the public sector and innovation with exemplar projects. The freer people are to develop their talents, make the most of their abilities, get the health care they need, develop their sense of meaning, values and purpose in life, the more they can contribute positively to a vibrant cultural life, a living economy and a resilient polity. And the converse applies. Think of the lifelong cost to society of people who have not had a whole education and a nurturing upbringing that helps them make the most of their potential. For example many of the 80,000 or so people in the British prison system at an annual cost of £40,000 per offender will re-offend, partly because a significant number are barely literate, mentally unstable and have not had the training to get jobs. They just get punished, rather than rehabilitated.

The creative cultural system thrives on freedom, on initiative, experimentation and exploration. Whether it is in the fields of education, science, technology, art,

Box 3.2   The SPACE, Stroud Performing Arts Centre

health, spirituality, religion or in personal growth, the more freedom there is, the more vibrant will be people's creative human contributions.

This practical principle has been long known in the economic regeneration field. For example, Stroud was economically run-down in the 1990s with over seventy empty properties in the centre. Various cultural initiatives were started, such as Stroud Performing Arts Centre (SPACE), to raise the creative spirit, rather than focus only on jobs and business development. Together with other initiatives such as Stroud Artspace, which provides affordable studios for artists, Stroud Festival and regenerating the local food culture through the farmers' market, it worked. As the town became known for innovation and artistic creativity, this attracted more entrepreneurs and artists.

There are plenty of other examples. Take St Ives in Cornwall, a town which was regenerated partly by the building of the Tate St Ives, for which local artists prepared the way. The Swedish government, seeing the huge export revenues generated by its excellent sound recording industry, and seeing that ordinary schools gave little space and time for students to develop creatively, are now encouraging creative centres in 250 municipalities, for young people aged from six to their mid-twenties to access the creative arts. The direct benefits to individual children are important for their lives. But in the long term, the Swedish government is asking, 'Who knows what creative industries will arise as an indirect result of these cultural centres? Another Abba? Another unforeseen outcome such as Sweden's world-class music recording studios?'

So initiative, creativity, meaning, new values, health, energy and will are liberated by free cultural space, and can have massive positive effects far into the future. But cultural life can be constrained, even killed, by the focus on narrow economic payoffs. For example a university recently told lecturers that they had to generate two patents a year to keep their jobs. I was once told by former colleagues, 'We are no longer a liberal university, but a business.' In England, there is a deterrent effect on sparky teachers entering the profession with the rise of assessment-driven state control of the content and delivery of education. For example, a civil servant told a teacher colleague that, 'We cannot trust teachers, that is why we specify to you what should be taught, when and how, for example the literacy hour.' In contrast, innovative businesses know full well the power of free cultural space. For example, Racal-Redac, a Gloucestershire company, encouraged its young engineers to experiment and have long inventive coffee breaks, and to then spin off their inventions, such as the cell phone, into new companies like Vodafone.

Where can you see examples of this tripolar society at work? Firstly, tripolar society is already embedded in how we live, though we don't realise it. People have a practical grasp of the healthy separation of the three powers of society. This guiding insight at a certain time in history came to be embedded in traditional constitutional and social structures. So Thomas Jefferson, no doubt remembering the theocratic tyranny of the Salem witch trials, formulated a boundary principle between polity and culture: 'There shall be a wall between religion and politics'. That is why the US has no official state religion, and there is no religious teaching in state schools to this day.

The US Constitution is based on a clear tripolar separation of legislative, executive and judicial powers. Even though this was undermined in the Bush years by the revolving door between business and government, the separation of powers has been reaffirmed by Obama. In Britain following the 1939–45 war, the free-market economy that had led to the Depression was rolled back and the Attlee government shaped a mixed economy. The government also brought in a state-maintained but semi-autonomous education sector, and an autonomous National Health Service. There was a significant separation of the three societal sectors in Britain between 1945 and 1979, seen for example in the public broadcasting system, where it was clearly but tacitly understood that the more freedom the BBC had, the better the service. The one-sided, disastrously laissez-faire, classical liberal economy that caused the Depression was rolled back for a generation, only to be brought back in a different form in the 1980s. People often refer to the 1950s and 60s as a golden era, pointing to the cultural revolution of the 1960s, rising real incomes, more equitable wealth redistribution and increasing public common wealth. The key elements were in place for a tripolar society that emerged as a pragmatic solution following the 1939–45 war.

So tripolar society emerges from practice, from seeing what works and does not work. As a Churchill Fellow on a travelling scholarship, I remember visiting Mayor Peter Clavelle at Burlington, Vermont, in the fall of 2003. He described his personal map of how the city worked and how this guided development. He told me:

> As the city government, we create a social/political, economic and cultural plan with civil society and the private business sector. We make an annual budget, which is passed – often argued line by line overnight – in the Town Hall Meeting by local citizens. And, for example, if there is a housing need we set up an independent, non-profit civil society provider, the Burlington Community Land Trust, to deliver our social housing programme in partnership with the city. So for example we channel a housing sales tax to the CLT, and our city pension fund invests in it. What happens if there is a new need? Well, for example a while back a small group wanted to set up a women's refuge, I said, 'Fine. Come back in a month with more supporters and present your plans to the Councillors at the next town meeting. If they support your proposal, we will work with you to help develop the plan, get you start up funding, and help you become viable as a civil society organisation providing this service.'

As a thought experiment, just consider the social challenge if there were a hundred or so survivors of a shipwreck or plane crash who landed on a desert island. How could the group best organise itself to survive until eventual rescue? People would have to organise ways of gathering food, fishing, growing food, then storing and distributing food in return for bartering or even a form of exchange, thus developing a simple economy. In addition, the whole community would need to find ways of recognising everyone's rights, ways of making decisions affecting everyone, mandating people to carry out tasks for the community, a means of dispute resolution and sanctions to preserve security, with each person's vote or voice counting when taking decisions. Finally, depending on their talents, individuals would create a cultural life – storytelling, celebrations, common meals, a food culture and education if there were children – and share hobbies if there was interest. Different people with different capacities could come to the fore in the three areas.

Another way of understanding the tripolar view of society in everyday life is that of the 'you, we and I' perspective. When working in the economy, you are meeting the needs of other people, asking, 'How can I serve *you*?' When making laws, policies and working for the public good, there is a sense of '*we*'. When nurturing your own growth, learning, health and sense for meaning, you are more '*I*'-centred. Understanding foreground and background can also help. Whilst working in, say, a local government job, this is supported by taxes from the economy and you use skills acquired at college. Teachers' and doctors' work is resourced from the surplus revenues from the economy, whilst also being held in a legal framework. When you work in business, you use your skills and knowledge from school, and the employment relationship is governed by a contract.

Summary

To conclude, society can be understood as having a dynamic tripolar structure. Society emerges from the dynamic working together of business, the state and civil society, which have their home territory in the economy, political system and culture respectively, a kind of three-legged stool. The health, wealth, resilience and justice of a society is greater, the more individuals work with the principles of freedom in creative cultural and civil life, citizens respect the equality of human rights in political life and consumers and producers are guided by mutuality in economic life – and the more sustainability guides our care for the earth.

This threefold model of society contrasts with the market-driven Thatcher, Blair and Brown neo-liberal model of society, where big finance and business has captured the state and dominates culture and civil society. The threefold analysis of society also contrasts with one-sided models of society such as the Iranian Shia theocracy, which under Khomeini dominated both business and the state as a throw-back to the caliphate of former times, or the state bureaucratic model, where the state dominates both civil society and business.

In the next chapter, I will argue that the current confusion in the boundaries between business, government and civil society is undermining social health, well-being, justice, sustainability and wealth. I will also argue that at the same time, people have a gut-level sense for these boundaries, and have a practical understanding of the qualitatively different dynamics of the cultural, political and economic spaces of society. And that there is concern when these boundaries are not recognised and respected.

Box 3.3   Sweden: creating the 'folkhemhet', the people's home

The Swedish story is relevant here, because it shows how people can realise their vision of society. Nineteenth-century Sweden was a poor country, and saw tragic famines and the emigration to the USA of up to a million people. Towards the end of the nineteenth century, as modern business arose, so did the social democratic movement, with a strong emphasis on co-operation for mutual benefit, on education, health, on co-operative housing and social equality. When the Social Democrats came to power in the early twentieth century, they brought in universal education and the development of a society focusing, not on empire, as with Britain, but on the welfare of the people. This was called creating the 'folkhemhet', the people's home. In the 1920s and 1930s, Swedish social democrats drew strongly on British thinkers like Keynes, Leonard Hobhouse and J. A. Hobson, finding ideas that helped Sweden chart a course between Depression-creating, laissez-faire liberal economics on the one hand and, on the other, the Soviet communist command state. Today, when you visit Sweden, it is striking how many aspects of life, such as transport, the environment, education, work and culture, are designed carefully with real people, children and families in mind. Business and the state are there to serve the people. As a result, 'poor' people in Sweden are significantly healthier than rich people in Britain, there is a right to warmth, and there is free university education as this is considered the best kind of social investment in Sweden's future, rather than a 'private commodity' to be paid for on the Blairite neo-liberal model. Of course, some could argue that with Sweden the scope for individual initiative, for cultural freedom and for civil society/community development has been crowded out by the state, and the boundaries could be redrawn to redress the balance. Perhaps the fact that Swedes drew selectively on the ideas of leading British thinkers explains partly why the success of egalitarian Sweden was used to berate both Thatcher and New Labour, according to the historian Tristram Hunt. People can also see common ground between the Swedish model and the better aspects of Britain between 1945 and 1979. Now the Swedes are engaged in creating an action plan to wean themselves from oil dependency by 2020. A new national mission to create a green 'folkhemhet' could be gathering strength.

However, there is a widespread concern that through a lack of under-standing of Sweden's social democratic achievements, and the cultural movements that inspired them, the common wealth of the 'folkhemhet' is being thrown away by the current neo-liberal-influenced 'moderate' government.

	State	Business	Civil society
System	Political	Economic	Cultural
Governance – basis for relationships	Laws, rules	Market, mutuality, exchange, transactions	Values-based
Main power source	Coercive, legal power, mandated by representative democracy	Resource and reward power	Normative, information, soft power
Control agents	Citizens/voters, executive government, legislators, judges	Owners, directors, managers, unions, staff, consumers	Cultural and community organisations, professional bodies, members and representatives of CSOs
Goals	Social order, social justice, equity, human security; human rights and entitlements	Meeting human needs Creating wealth Sustainability	Realising and maintaining human potential and wellbeing; realising and respecting values, common good
Evaluation, success criteria for assessment	Legality, social cohesion, human security, inclusion, social equity and justice	Satisfying human needs profitably, ethically and in environmentally sustainable ways	Extent human potential is realised through education, health, arts, science and spirituality
Leading legal and organisational forms	Bureaucratic, governmental/ statutory structures authorities and agencies	For-profit PLCs, private companies, partnerships, etc.; shared-profit mutuals, co-ops, community interest companies, social enterprise	Charities, foundations, community benefit trusteeship bodies and co-ops, non-profit organisations/ companies, NGOs
Guiding principle	Equality	Mutuality/association	Freedom
Funding and resourcing	Taxes and public loans; creating new money through the Bank of England	Income from profitable/surplus sale of goods, services and carrying out contracts	Gifts of money, time and resources; business grants; government grants and contracts; grants from trusts and Lottery Fund; income from profitable social businesses
Extreme, one-sided forms	Bureaucracy: over-centralised bureaucratic states	Plutocracy or corpocracy	Theocracy

Figure 3.3   Summary: the key elements of the state, business and civil society/cultural sectors

PART 2

From Capitalist to Civil Society
Clarifying Boundaries between Business, Government and Civil Society

Good fences make good neighbours.

Robert Frost, 'Mending Wall'

Part 2 uses the tripolar societal map to clarify the boundaries between business, government and civil society. It will analyse how boundaries are crossed unhealthily, for example when business captures government, or government captures civil society. People have an intuitive grasp of the three spaces of society and the need for a separation of powers. When the boundaries are respected, each societal power recognises the integrity of the other two. This intuitive grasp can lead to self-limitation, where for example the state disestablishes the church, thus withdrawing from religion (or vice versa), or the government withdraws from running business through privatising state enterprises.

What are the benefits of the tripolar separation of powers? People with a grasp of the boundaries between the three societal powers can better analyse the strategic context of their business, government agency or civil society organisation. Such insights can help inform organisational strategic planning, sectoral strategic planning, and when to engage in cross-sectoral partnerships for mutual benefit or common good. People also gain tools for analysing unhealthy boundary-crossing, such as when corporate business is invited by the British government to set up profit-making polyclinics in supermarkets, to undercut local GP practices and the role of the NHS as a public service.

If you want to dip into Part 2, use the summaries as stepping-stones. Then come the transformative entry points in Part 3 on Capturing Capitalism: Solving the Social Question with the Citizen's Income, Land for People and Freeing Education.

Part 2 has chapters on:

- the emergence of civil society: clarifying boundaries
- capturing the state
- capturing culture
- capitalism unleashed: seizing our common wealth.

Chapter 4

The Emergence of Civil Society:
Restoring Fences

Meanwhile, some very necessary fences are under attack; in the rush to privatisation, the barriers that once existed between many public and private spaces – keeping advertisements out of schools, for instance, profit-making interests out of health care, or news outlets from acting purely as promotional vehicles for their owners' other holdings – have nearly all been levelled. Every protected public space has been cracked open, only to be re-enclosed by the market.

Naomi Klein, *Fences and Windows*[1]

The purpose of this chapter is to clarify the importance of boundaries between the economy, polity and culture. The emergence of civil society will be described, to help gain further insight into the leading principles and dynamics of the three sectors of society. The analysis is useful because it shows how the corporate capture of the state happens, meaning that citizens pay more in taxes to subsidise private profits, as in the corporate welfare of the US government-industrial-military complex, the part-privatised British rail system and now the banking sector. Healthy fences between the three sectors and unhealthy boundary-crossing will be analysed. The themes of this chapter are:

- an overview of tripolar society
- clarifying the different meanings of 'civil society'
- from capitalist to civil society
- how do we get there?
- why boundaries matter
- negative boundary-crossing
- intuitive practical grasp of boundaries
- theocracy, bureaucracy and plutocracy: the three extremes.

An overview of tripolar society

The economic system

Economic wellbeing is secured through the profitable production, distribution and consumption of goods and services by mutual exchange and associative working in the market. The guiding principle is *mutuality* or cooperation. 'Business', whether profit-making, not for private profit distribution or a social enterprise such as a co-operative, is the leading institution of this sector.

The political system

Governance and citizenship in the polity secures equity, justice and security through law, human rights, agreements, entitlements and regulation. The guiding principle is *equality*. Government, including elected legislatures and local councils, the executive and the judiciary, is the leading institution of this sector.

The cultural system

Individual growth, wellbeing and meaning are secured through health, the arts, sciences, ethics, spirituality, sport, education and culture. The guiding principle is *freedom*. A leading institution is civil society, though by its very essence the cultural system will have a variety of organisations that give voices to its many diverse branches and movements.

Figure 4.1 offers another way of picturing the three societal powers.

People have an everyday understanding of how business and the state shape their lives. Civil society or the community/third sector is an emerging concept, a sector that is now becoming distinct from business and state. The web of local voluntary and community associations is being reframed as civil society. But civil society is made up of a wide variety of organisations, ranging from the local to the global. This includes NGOs, voluntary and community-based organisations, church groups, charities, social movements, philanthropic organisations, campaign groups – a whole variety of active associations which are working in the cultural space. Civil society is the creative space of society, where issues are discussed, learning happens, identity is developed and values clarified. Civil society organisations (CSOs) are funded by gifts from individuals, government or charitable grants, membership fees and people giving their time. Global CSOs such as Amnesty, Greenpeace or Oxfam now have large resources from gifts, fund-raising and grants. Some CSOs, because a lot of their funding is from government, are less independent, being known as GONGOs or government NGOs. Business-dominated NGOs are known as BUNGOs.

Whereas government uses coercive and legal power and business uses resource and economic power, civil society uses cultural, normative, expert or soft power to achieve its aims. The cultural sphere cultivates values, ideas, worldviews, meaning, symbols, art, spirituality, science, ethics and knowledge. This is where people realise their potential and nurture their values, sense of meaning, purpose, identity, qualities and capacities. This is where learning, value shifts and creative renewal happen in the cultural space of civil society. This helps every individual to become

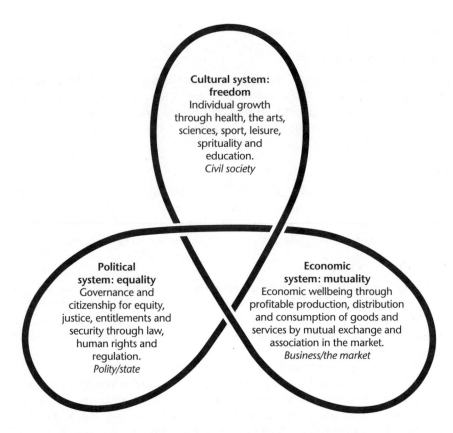

Figure 4.1   The economic, political and cultural systems

at least potentially a positive contributor. The Filipino thinker, civil society leader and 2003 Right Livelihood award winner Nicanor Perlas writes:

> Culture is, in fact, that social space where identity and meaning are generated. The two are inseparable. Identity and meaning give human beings their cognitive, affective and ethical orientation. In short, culture is the wellspring that determines and sustains human behaviour. Loss of meaning results in a cluster of aberrant and destructive behaviours. Discovery of meaning brings greater creativity, compassion, and productivity. It is clear that the institution, in this case civil society, which controls meaning and identity and, therefore, behaviour, will have tremendous clout in the direction and affairs of national and world society.[2]

Politicians respect cultural power. Soon after Prime Minister Gordon Brown exhorted British people to eat up all their food as a way of saving money, he attended the G8 world food shortages summit at Hokkaido in July 2008, which cost £238 million. The media in this case, as a cultural, normative power, high-lighted the huge irony of the eight-course, nineteen-dish dinner cooked there by twenty-five chefs to indicate the G8 leaders' commitment to belt-tightening.

There are many examples of the successful exercise of cultural power by civil society organisations.

The energy and petrochemical company Shell was shocked in the 1990s by civil society organisations such as Greenpeace and Friends of the Earth, which highlighted the potential ecological problems posed by the obsolete Brent Spar oil platform being dumped in the North Sea. At the same time, Shell faced massive civil society challenges over their cosy relationship with the Nigerian government, the execution of the Ogoni leader, Ken Saro Wiwa, and Shell's envi-ronmentally destructive oil extraction practices in the Niger Delta, where the Ogoni live.

At the personal level, the loss of meaning can be disastrous, leading to suicide or poor health. Though normally suicide rates amongst soldiers go down during war, from 2001–7 Thomas Insel, head of the US National Institute of Mental Health, reported that for Iraq and Afghanistan veterans, suicides and psychological mortality were trumping combat deaths. James Carroll writes:

> The war in Iraq, in particular, is an exercise in the obliteration of meaning. The war's essence is its lack of essence. The war's catch 22 is that its stated goal is social order, while the American presence itself creates disorder. Our troops know this. They arrive in the war zone with every intention of protecting an innocent population from the enemy, only to discover that they are the enemy and the population are indistinguishable. 'Insurgents' often turn out to be, not ideologues much less 'terrorists', but only cousins of those already killed … Suspicion is ubiquitous. No one trusts Americans. Such conditions make the war controversial in the US, but in Iraq they make the soldiers' situation intolerable. These particular problems exist within a larger context of collapsing sources of meaning. The myths on which the military ethos depend have been broken.[3]

Carroll argues that there is a historic value shift from soldiers fighting for their nation, to working for the value of global citizenship. He considers it naïve to think any more that the myth of using violence to end violence can be sustained. Soldiers get their sense of meaning from loyalty to comrades and their unit. But on return home, veterans are on their own, abandoned on discharge.

So, CSOs can use cultural power positively, advocating for new policies, opposing destructive practices, building capacity and demonstrating sustainable alternatives, as with the rapidly developing local food movements.

Clarifying the different meanings of 'civil society'

'Civil society' can have four distinct, but related meanings. This is why the term can be confusing. Just as business can take many forms, ranging from sole traders, part-nerships, small and medium-sized companies to large corporations, so government has many levels, going from the parish to the UN. Mapping the civil society sector can also be complex.

Firstly, there is 'civil society' as the whole web of informal and formal associations in community life, which build social capital and wellbeing. For example, many Norwegian towns have a 'kvell' association that cares for community wellbeing, run by individuals who freely engage to organise festivals, create community gardens, voice concerns and raise development opportunities with the local government.

Secondly, Nicanor Perlas uses 'civil society' to mean those values-based organisations, such as NGOs, environmental, women's and youth groups, which are working for comprehensive sustainable development, peace or social justice, from the local to global levels.

Thirdly, 'civil society' can be used as an overall description of cultural organisations, such as the media, religious or spiritual groups, charitable trusts and foundations, non-profit health organisations, educational organisations, professional associations, voluntary bodies and community organisations. (To complicate things further, there is a question about the extent to which the 'third sector' overlaps with civil society in Britain. The complex mix of charities, social enterprises and non-profits confusingly includes both social businesses working primarily in the economy such as co-ops, as well as advocacy organisations and traditional charities with trading arms. The US has clearer laws on non-profits.)

Fourthly, 'Civil Society' can be used for describing society as a whole in a visionary sense, when civil values have been embedded in all spaces of society, replacing capitalist values. David Korten describes how he sees Civil Society in this last, visionary sense being realised.

From capitalist to civil society

Figure 4.2 shows how David Korten contrasts Civil Society with Capitalist Society. He considers that the 'defining political struggle of the 21st century is not so much between political ideologies as between life values and financial values – between a civil society and a capitalist society'.[4]

In Figure 4.2, Civil Society is formed from a foundation of holistic spiritual values that are embedded in its whole culture. Society is continually renewed by the work and contribution of people and a dynamic, creative community life. In this Civil Society, people make sure that politics and economics serve society and the planet, rather than dominate. They transform the polity with openness, equality, active citizen participation and representation. People, who associate as consumers, producers or distributors in self-organising markets that result in productive lifeways and a sustainable relationship with the planet, run the economy. According to Korten:

> The Civil Society is radically self organising and predominantly cooperative in the manner of all healthy living systems, and seeks to maximise the opportunity for each individual to fully and freely develop their creative potential in service to the whole of life. Thus a Civil Society differs in every dimension from the capitalist economy in which we currently live.[5]

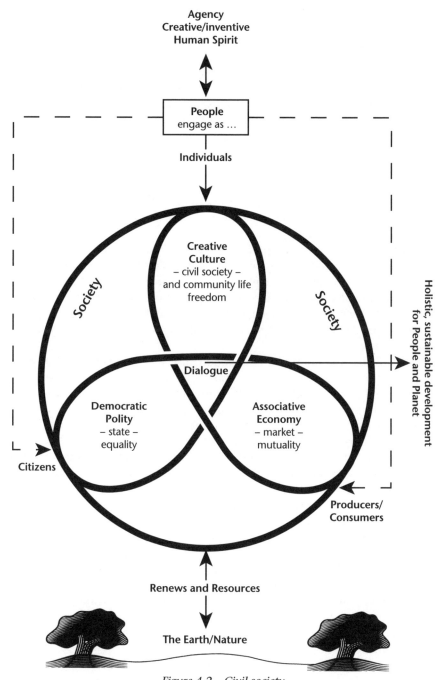

Figure 4.2   Civil society
Source: Adapted from David Korten, Creating a Post-Corporate World, twentieth
annual E. F. Schumacher Lectures, October 2001, Great Barrington, MA, USA, p. 4

Korten describes the Capitalist Society that is now collapsing:

> In the capitalist economy, money is the defining value and the primary medi-
> ator of the relationship among persons and institutions. The whole of public
> life is dominated by global financial markets that value life only for its liquida-
> tion price. Using money as an instrument of control, the capitalist economy
> co-opts the life energies of each individual and directs them to the task of
> replicating money as the defining purpose of capitalist society.
>
> The control of productive resources is consolidated in global mega-corpo-
> rations answerable only to the managers of huge investment funds who in
> turn are answerable only for the financial returns produced on their portfolios.
> The wages of working people are suppressed to increase the returns of those
> who already command vast financial holdings. Economic affairs are centrally
> planned by the heads of corporations that command internal economies larger
> than those of most states.
>
> Through their ownership of mass media, influence over school curricula,
> commercialisation of the arts, and mass advertising, global mega-corporations
> dominate the processes of cultural regeneration – creating a global mono-
> culture grounded in values of materialism and consumerism that strengthen
> corporate legitimacy and alienate each individual from their inner spiritual
> life, so that corporate logos become the individual's primary source of identity
> and meaning.
>
> Similarly, the dominant corporations use their massive financial power
> and control of the mass media, corporate think tanks, public relations firms,
> and pseudo citizen front groups to control the institutions of polity – buying
> politicians and dominating public discourse to create a grossly distorted one
> dollar one vote democracy. All but a tiny elite is deprived of a meaningful
> political voice and are alienated from the political process.
>
> Spiritually impoverished and pressed into a struggle for survival, those
> deprived of both political voice and an adequate means of livelihood become
> increasingly indebted to a system that demands they devote ever more of their
> life energies to its imperatives. Ideals of equity are out of the window and indi-
> vidual freedom becomes largely illusory.
>
> Destructive of both life and spirit, the capitalist economy must be
> considered a social pathology. Even its apparent capacity to create vast
> wealth is largely illusory, as while it produces ever more glitzy gadgets and
> diversions, it is destroying the life support systems of the planet and the
> social fabric of society – and thereby impoverishes the whole of humanity.
> Its institutions function as cancers that have forgotten they are part of a
> larger whole and seek their own unlimited growth without regard to the
> consequences.

So this description of Capitalist Society is a stark analysis of where we are now.
Korten's future Civil Society is where we could be if we work hard at cultural,
social and economic transformation. Korten's summary of Capitalist Society is

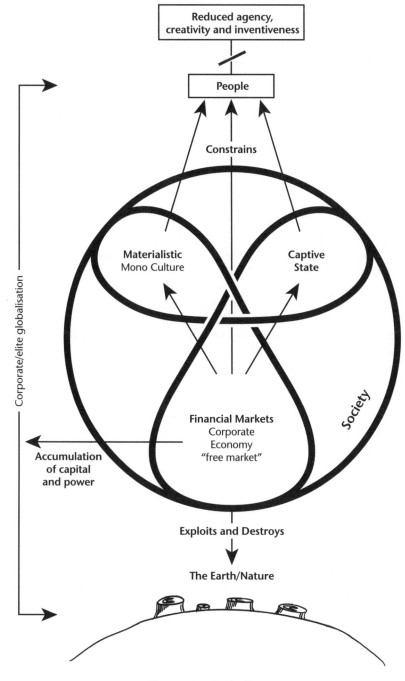

Figure 4.3   Capitalist society
Source: Adapted from David Korten, Creating a Post-Corporate World, *twentieth annual E. F. Schumacher Lectures, October 2001, Great Barrington, MA, USA, p. 4*

also a good analysis of the capture of the state and culture by corporations, of negative boundary-crossing, which will be explored in more detail in Chapters 5, 6 and 7.

However, how can a Civil Society be brought about?

How to get there

Nicanor Perlas describes how to bring about Civil Society in the visionary sense, grounding his analysis in a clear theoretical framework and developmental steps. The first step is when civil society, comprising a powerful range of civic, community and cultural organisations, emerged and challenged the Eastern European communist regimes in the 1980s, when Western peace movements challenged the nuclear arms race, and when at Seattle in 1999 an alliance of civil society organisations successfully challenged the WTO with its corporate globalisation agenda. So here is civil society both in the first associative sense and also the second sense of mobilising for sustainable development and peace. We saw an unprecedented mobilisation of 1.5 to 2 million people in London in February 2003 against the Iraq War, and 10 million worldwide. This was a powerful expression of 'we, the people'.

The third use of 'civil society', for cultural organisations as a whole sector, happens when these become aware of the potential for mobilisation, advocacy and experiment to achieve their aims more fully by challenging the other two sectors. So health organisations, for example, instead of just treating the symptoms of illness, actively tackle the systemic causes of illness through campaigning for public health, better housing, more equitable income levels, safer roads, for smoking bans and for healthy food.

Such mobilisation inevitably brings civil society and cultural organisations both into opposition and then into partnership with government and business. Thomas Insel, the head of the US National Institute of Mental Health, for example, was unpopular with the Bush government for linking the Iraq War with rising veteran suicides. As cultural life becomes more engaged and assertive, so new values, knowledge and research change political and economic life. The smoking ban in pubs, for example, is an example of the institutionalisation, or embedding, of health values. There is a movement for rolling back the influence of corporations on families by banning advertising to children. The mainstreaming of such values such as respecting the right to childhood or sustainability by civil society organisations alone, of course, takes years of work. However, as President Obama, with experience of community organising on the one hand and of politics on the other, writes, 'Sometimes we need both cultural transformation and government action – a change in values and a change in policy to promote the kind of society we want.'[6] So he argues that more money for schools won't make much of a difference by itself unless parents encourage their children to work hard.

In this way, over time, civil society organisations act as the wellsprings in the visionary sense for developing a future Civil Society, that will come to replace Capitalist Society. Civil Society will be brought about as cultural and then political and economic life are transformed by values such as sustainability and social justice.

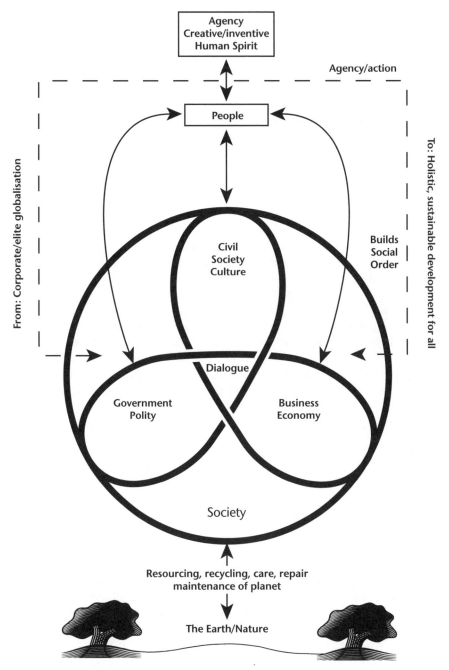

Figure 4.4   Tripolar society
Source: adapted from Nicanor Perlas, Shaping Globalisation: Civil Society,
Cultural Power, and Threefolding, *Quezon City, Philippines, Center for Alternative
Development Initiatives, 2000, p. 25*

Nicanor Perlas describes the steps for bringing about Civil Society in his visionary sense. His theoretical framework, outlined in Figure 4.4, understands society as tripolar, with government, business and civil society at home in the polity, the economy and culture respectively. Civil society becomes empowered and self-aware in critical opposition to business and government, and so ready to engage for sustainable development through transforming corporate globalisation.

Tripolar society is energised by a dynamic, productive relationship between the earth, individual human beings and the creative spirit. So firstly, people in this tripolar society can renew their relationship with the earth and the whole of nature on the basis of respect, care and sustainability.

Secondly, millions of people around the world are engaged in creative cultural transformation, through personal growth, a healthy food culture, education, value changes, art, science and spirituality. Drawing on the creative human spirit, they are engaged in transforming capitalist society around the world. Some develop socially and environmentally responsible businesses. Others in government work to bring about sustainable change in government, and also with civil society and business. Many get active in civil society organisations, developing alternatives. Culturally creative people working in business, civil society and government from strategic partnerships, guided by values such as sustainability or social justice. As the values of culturally creative people come to be embedded in political, civil society and business organisations, the power of capitalist society and corporate globalisation fades.

In order to further clarify the boundaries of the three systems, and how corporations have captured culture and the state, here is another perspective on boundaries.

Why boundaries matter

Clear boundaries in personal and public life are important. If you confide in a friend, you want personal secrets to be respected. You declare a conflict of interest if you might benefit, say, from a company board decision if you are a director. Big accountancy firms are supposed to have 'Chinese walls' between their consultancy, accountancy and audit departments. Arthur Andersons, the former accountancy firm, famously failed to hold Enron to account through their public auditing function of an ongoing, massive corporate fraud. In the City of London audit firms ignored the trillions of unsecured debt their banking and financial clients were piling up until the August 2007 debtonation. Part of the toxic speculation in derivatives was caused by the repeal in the US of the Glass-Stegall Act, which had put a wall between retail banks and merchant banks. These walls had already been removed in Britain in 1986 by Thatcher's 'Big Bang', which allowed the City casino banks free rein.

Setting boundaries between personal life and paid work is a big issue for many people. The rise of laptops, email and mobile phones has resulted in some people having to work without boundaries between their work and personal lives, 24/7. Fuzzy boundaries can mean that you don't have a life – you are all over the place. Clear personal boundaries are important because they support your life-work

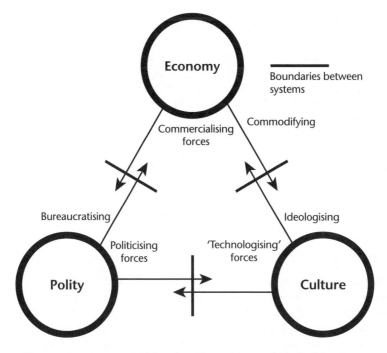

Figure 4.5   Commercialising, bureaucratising and ideologising forces
Source: Martin Large, Social Ecology, *1981, p. 66*

balance, privacy, work and relationships. You know where you are. This is also true when there are clear boundaries between the business, state and cultural sectors.

Here are some examples illustrating both the importance of respecting boundaries and the confusion when boundaries are violated, taken from everyday life.

- You have been invited to a friend's party, only to discover it is in fact a book sale in their home. Commercialism ruins the friendship.
- As a parent, you have to counter pester power from your children and their peers, as advertisers invade the free cultural space of your family and children.
- It is clear that the state has been captured or commercialised by business in significant ways, for favourable legislation, regulation and tax breaks, such as tax-free aviation fuel for airlines when at the same time petrol for your own car is highly taxed.
- You are astonished that, in spite of the free-market rhetoric, profits are guaranteed to companies by the state for thirty years under the Private Finance Initiative.
- The former chief government scientist, Sir David King, announced on the one hand that global warming was causing more loss of life than terrorism and is a serious challenge. Yet on the other, he advocated more nuclear power. The question arises, 'Is this a soundly researched argument from independent science or his personal opinion?' And to what extent can a 'government' scientist be an independent scientist?

Furthermore, the private business model can dominate the state and culture. So cultural organisations like schools and hospitals are run as businesses, whilst the state has been captured by business. The market has enclosed both the state and culture. Universities now have CEOs rather than Vice-Chancellors.

But clarifying and resetting boundaries will liberate business, culture and state to focus on their unique contributions to society, rather than continue to cause confusion by overstepping the boundaries.

The examples above are of negative boundary-crossing, where confusion is caused by overstepping the boundaries and by removing fences. The aim of the following chapters is to show how a clear understanding of the boundaries between the economic, political and cultural systems or spaces can prevent confusion. Clarifying boundaries can not only prevent confusion, but also help the economy, the polity and culture focus on what they do best. Fortunately, most people have a gut-level grasp of social boundaries.

An intuitive, gut-level grasp of social boundaries

The intuitive grasp of healthy and unhealthy social boundaries is in our culture. For example our political system is based on a clear separation of powers. As citizens, we elect our representatives to the local council, national or European parliaments. They pass laws, agree priorities for the annual budget which reflects our entitlements to public services such as security, education and health, they scrutinise the work of the executive and debate burning issues that may lead to new laws and policies. The executive government is the second leg of the state. And the third leg is the independent judiciary. Each political leg is clear about its independence and functional autonomy, yet all three work for the common good in their different ways. The triangulation between the three political powers creates a healthy dynamic of checks and balances.

When this clear separation and dynamic balance of political powers is not respected and goes out of balance, there is conflict and citizens and civil society express concern. People feel it is not 'right'. So when Lord Goldsmith, the Attorney General or government lawyer, gave the advice that Prime Minister Blair wanted – that the 2003 Iraq War was legal under his interpretation of international law – there was widespread condemnation from the public, by international lawyers such as Philippe Sands and from some MPs. Elizabeth Wilmshurst, a senior lawyer at the Foreign Office, resigned in March 2003 because of the illegality of the Iraq War. Lord Bingham, the retiring Lord Chief Justice, in November 2008 called the Iraq War illegal, commenting that Britain had acted as a 'world vigilante'.

The separation of constitutional powers has been a hard struggle over the centuries and is still developing. For example parliament has now asserted its right to declare war, rather than the Prime Minister as 'king in parliament'. Judges have used the Human Rights Act as the basis for restricting the government's terrorist detention laws and preventing the erosion of civil liberties.

But it is not just in social life that we have an intuitive sense for form, order and structure, but also in science. This sense for form once struck me very forcibly when as a publisher I had to ask the printer to reprint a book because a critical

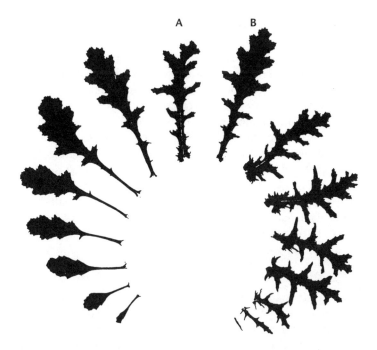

*Figure 4.6   What about this groundsel leaf sequence? People 'know' intuitively that
leaves A and B have been swapped, and are not in the 'right' sequence.*
Source: Margaret Colquhoun and Axel Ewald, New Eyes for Plants: A Workbook for
Observing and Drawing Plants, *Stroud, Hawthorn Press, 1996*

'mistake' had to be reinstated. The author had originally asked the reader to spot
the deliberate mistake in a sequence of dandelion leaves. There were two leaves
in the leaf sequence that the author had swapped, so the reader could then work
out the correct sequence by their 'feel for form'. But the printer, unable to resist *his*
strong feeling for form and also not reading the instructions to the reader in the
text, physically swapped the two leaves back into the correct sequence!

Intuitive social thinking senses the way that society works in social or anti-social
ways. We have a sound hunch that high house prices have a devastating effect on
young families and that inequality is damaging. We have a 'feel' for the conditions for the healthy development of the economy, political system or culture.
We have a hunch that whenever former Prime Minister Blair met press tycoon
Rupert Murdoch there would be an ongoing trade of favourable news coverage
for concessions on cross-media ownership sooner or later. The sense for healthy
social boundaries was activated when Bernie Ecclestone, director of Formula One,
gave £1 million to New Labour ; the suspicion was that favours would sometime
be forthcoming in return.

This sense for boundaries, and where they are drawn, changes over time. For
example, as formal religion declines, many people feel there is no longer a place in
Britain for a state church. So they feel it is high time to disestablish the Church of

England with its twenty-six bishops sitting in the House of Lords, to separate it from the state and political system. It can then stand on its own two feet in the cultural system, as a self-supporting church with a religious purpose. The separation of church and state has been part of the US constitution since the first amendment of 1791, the founding fathers clearly seeing the potential mayhem that could be caused if Congress was dominated by religious factions, as had happened in some of the short-lived Puritan theocracies of New England. Thomas Jefferson wrote that, 'building a wall of separation between church and state' was the 'expression of the supreme will of the nation in behalf of the rights of conscience'. And as Alastair Campbell, Blair's Press Secretary, once correctly said, 'We don't do God.'

Traditionally, just like the threefold separation of political powers in the state, the societal threefolding between the economy, polity and culture was implicit rather than explicit. Such de facto practical threefolding was widespread in Britain before 1979 – for example with the state guaranteeing citizens free health care, through resourcing an arm's-length, semi-independent, public-service NHS.

Theocracy, bureaucracy and plutocracy: the three extremes

The tripolar societal map can also help clarify the nature of theocracy, bureaucracy and plutocracy. There are societies where one of the three systems dominates the two others. Firstly, theocracy. In Iran under Ayatollah Khomeini, there was theocracy, rule by religion or ideology. The state, culture and the economy were dominated by the autocratic/theocratic rule of the Shia Islamic ayatollahs. Today, Iranian democrats oppose what they call 'the mullah state'. Restoring the caliphate is a theocratic dream of Usama bin Laden. The ideological domination of the USSR and China by their Communist Parties can be seen as a kind of ideological theocracy, where moral tyranny was exercised. The party line had to be obeyed, and this dominated the state and the economy. The reason why poets were so dangerous in the USSR was that they exercised independent cultural power, thus challenging the ideological dominance of the party. The Chinese communist crackdown on the Falun Gong movement was prompted by their fear of a cultural challenge. Similarly, the Chinese communist leadership demonises the Buddhist spiritual leader, the Dalai Lama. The more bankrupt the ruling ideology, the more the leaders are afraid of cultural challenges.

Secondly, bureaucracy develops where society is dominated by the state, with stifling over-governance and crippling red tape. The 'war against terrorism' in Britain has been used shamelessly to increase the power of the bureaucratic state, with the systematic erosion of civil liberties, the pressing for forty-two-day detention without charge, proposals for identity cards and the relentless rise of surveillance. Bureaucracies are averse to taking risks, want conformity and are dominated by the need for control.

Finally, with neo-liberalism comes the rise in the West of plutocracy, the rule of the rich, and the domination by financial institutions and transnational corporations. Rich elites come to control most of the wealth through the corporate control of finance, business and the state. Culture, such as the media, is used to bolster plutocratic power through information control over people.

Summary

Tripolar society is made up of business, civil society and government, working in the economic, cultural and political sectors respectively. Charting the rise of civil society clarifies the different, and still contested, meanings of 'civil society'. These include civil society as associational, community-based organisations; secondly, as an engaged core of active cultural-based CSOs concerned with advocating for peace and sustainable development; and thirdly, emerging as a global societal power at Seattle in 1999 as 'we the global people'. CSOs are now engaging more and more cultural organisations as an increasingly self-aware civil society sector emerges. Finally, there is a more visionary understanding of civil society, where creative cultural values are embedded in the transition from Capitalist to Civil Society. This is achieved through creative individuals working to transform society and embed new values, like care for the planet.

Clarifying boundaries between the three societal powers can help people, who already have an intuitive, practical grasp of boundaries, spot negative boundary-crossing such as the captive state. Finally the three extremes of theocracy, bureaucracy and plutocracy were described as one-sided, unchecked developments of the three societal powers.

The tripolar framework of boundaries will now be used in the next chapter to analyse the captive, corporate state, where we have the best democracy that money can buy.

Chapter 5

Capturing the State

I see in the near future a crisis approaching that unnerves me and causes me to tremble for the safety of my country ... corporations have been enthroned and an era of corruption in high places will follow.
Abraham Lincoln, letter to Col. Williams F. Ekins, 21 November 1864

In Goldman Sachs and the City we trust.
Epitaph, Labour and Conservative governments, 1979–2010

This chapter analyses how corporations and the big banks have captured the state. The question is, 'To what extent have corporations been enthroned in high places?' This is important because it helps understand how failed bankers such as Fred Goodwin get a massive pension from RBS with the agreement of Finance Minister Lord Myners, whilst the unemployed get a mere £64 a week Jobseeker's Allowance.

To summarise, clear boundaries between the state, civil society and business make for strong government, thriving business and a vibrant community. Strong government is needed to make policy, legislate, regulate, resource and enable public service provision. The political system sets the rules within which business works, whether it is environmental, labour, planning or competition law. The government is like the referee of a football game, there to ensure the rules of the game are respected. If the government itself becomes a player in the game, it can lose the ability to be a fair, independent referee. It is a conflict of interests. And if business captures the government, then profit and self-interest rules, which is what we see now. For example, Silvio Berlusconi went from dominating Italy's media, to setting up a political party and becoming a Prime Minister able to pass laws that exempt him from the law. These are such fundamental conflicts of interest between business and state that Italy cannot be called a democracy.

To analyse how the corporations have captured the state, this chapter will examine:

- the captive state: why does plutocracy matter?
- privatising public assets
- PFI: getting guaranteed profits and cheap public assets
- buying the planning system
- ending High Street competition
- the rise of corporate power and privilege
- revolving doors and fat cats
- the arms industry and government
- the captive state and restoring boundaries.

The captive state

Statesmen, civil society and business leaders of integrity see the vital importance of a clear separation of business and state, of economy from politics and from culture. Abraham Lincoln prophetically wrote of the future crisis in America that would result from the 'enthronement of corporations' and the 'corruption in high places' that would follow.[1] This process was reversed by the anti-trust legislation of Theodore Roosevelt which rolled back the power of the robber barons, and then the regulation of Roosevelt's New Deal. President Eisenhower in his farewell address in 1961 again warned of the overweening power and threat to democracy of what he called the 'military-industrial complex'. This is the overlap in people, profits and common interests between arms companies and the US military which has such a big influence on government policy, and which since the early 1950s has used fear with misinformation to extract ever-larger taxes from the American people to pay for the war machine and deliver arms company profits.

We now see how the credit crunch is being used by the financial sector to socialise its losses. The revolving doors of bankers and industrialists with government ministers and civil servants make it highly confusing to know the boundaries between their public and private financial interests, and whether there are in fact boundaries at all.

Business leaders need a clear, well-enforced legal and regulatory framework to work within. They see the benefits from security, from laws protecting property rights, from good health and safety legislation, from paying taxes for providing a good transport, educational, environmental and health infrastructure, from economic stability, from clear rules about fair and unfair competition. They dislike captive or partial government, which gives preferential treatment to favoured companies: they see the need for a level regulatory playing field.

When some industrial sectors get large government handouts – such as the arms industry with a £500 million to £1 billion subsidy every year, the car industry in 2009 with up to £2 billion in handouts and the banking sector receiving up to £1.3 trillion – other industrial sectors and taxpayers ask, 'Why?'[2] Companies which are good environmental citizens and employers dislike the 'race to the bottom' with

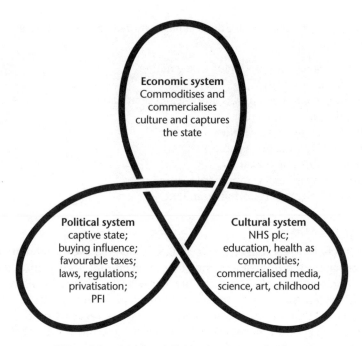

Economic system
Commoditises and
commercialises
culture and captures
the state

Political system
captive state;
buying influence;
favourable taxes;
laws, regulations;
privatisation;
PFI

Cultural system
NHS plc;
education, health as
commodities;
commercialised media,
science, art, childhood

Figure 5.1   Commercialising the state and culture

other companies as different states compete for company relocation by lowering minimum wages and health standards.

Take Rupert Murdoch, of News Corporation, which owns HarperCollins, *The Times*, the *Sun*, *News of the World* and Sky TV. Newscorp, or rather its UK arm, Newscorp Investments, roundly criticises such wrongdoing as 'social security scroungers', bankers' bonuses or MPs' expenses through its media outlets while at the same time itself freeloading on Britain. At least until 1999 one might be forgiven for thinking that it was not paying its fair dues as a corporate citizen. *The Economist* wrote that News Corporation made £1.4 billion in pre-tax profits in the twelve years until 1999, but by means of legal tax avoidance paid no net British corporation tax.[3] In 1998, for example, News Corporation's £309 million UK profits would have resulted in £92 million in tax, but this was offset against rebates.

George Monbiot argues cogently that big business has captured the British state in his book *Captive State: The Corporate Takeover of Britain*.[4] However, I would argue that the picture is more complex. Many businesses do respect the boundaries between the economy and the state, while some famously do not. For example, it is argued that the US government was influenced to invade Iraq by the ex-Halliburton oilman Vice President Dick Cheney and the US oil companies. It was a war for oil. This would be a good example of Abraham Lincoln's 'corruption in high places'. But on the other hand, according to the late Anthony Sampson, a distinguished journalist, the CEOs of both Shell and BP 'had the keys of Number 10'.

They argued with Prime Minister Blair against invasion as it would cause instability and threaten oil supplies.

To recap, business works in the economic system through the production, distribution and consumption of products through mutual exchange. The natural territory of business is the economy, providing needed goods and services profitably. Business wields economic power, but governments, working in their natural territory of the political system, have political power, comprising the power to coerce, legislate, regulate, legitimate, provide law and order. The state or the polity deals with how people relate to other human beings through the equality of their human rights as citizens. The state makes sure there are laws, regulations, security, safety nets, social order and that citizens are treated equitably according to their rights and entitlements. Government is not a business and vice versa. Where big business dominates the state, corporations will rule the world in their economic interest and the corporate state will limit human rights and social justice for profit. This is corporate plutocracy. But equally, where the state dominates business, economic life is bureaucratised and enterprise crippled. However, where each sector respects the appropriate boundaries, all three sectors can flourish and play to their strengths.

There are many examples of where big business oversteps the boundaries. Business does so *because it can*, because of weak regulation by the state, the lack of clarity about boundaries and because especially stock market quoted companies are dominated by the overwhelming drive for increased profits. Examples of commercialising the state will include privatisation to get cut-price public assets, securing favourable contracts from the state through Private Finance Initiatives, influencing the planning system for gain, the ending of retail market competition that we see now on every High Street in Ghost Town Britain, corporations getting the same rights as citizens, the way that the captive state is strengthened by revolving job doors and finally how we get the best democracy money can buy.

I will argue that there has been a corporate takeover of Britain, with New Labour selling itself as the 'natural party of business', creating 'the most business friendly environment in the world'.[5] Tony Blair claimed in 1997 that, 'Britain will have the most lightly regulated labour market of any leading economy in the world.' This means that Britain is run by a corpocracy, supported by governments that have 'no objection to people being filthy rich', to quote Lord Mandelson, First Secretary of State and Business Secretary.

Take Bob Diamond, the CEO of Barclays Capital who 'earned' £22 million in 2006. He shamelessly pressed Mervyn King of the Bank of England for the same bank bailouts as the Fed was providing in the US. Larry Elliott likens this to the police being forced to give a getaway car to bank thieves. He and Dan Atkinson conclude that:

> The response to the market meltdown helps illustrate ... the principles that govern the modern world. One is that despite the lip service paid to democracy, Western societies are effectively run by moneyed oligarchies, who have as little time for their wage slaves as did the ruling elite of ancient Athens. In

February 2008, Gordon Brown and his ministers opposed a private members bill designed to give greater rights in the workplace to agency workers, part-timers who face some of the lowest wages and toughest working conditions of any group.[6]

Two weeks earlier, Chancellor Darling had announced the end of his proposals to tax the 120,000 or so wealthy non-domiciled residents who use London as a tax haven.

So, just how have corporations taken over?

Privatising public assets

Britain was the first test bed in the world after Pinochet's Chile for piloting key neo-liberal policies such as privatising state-owned companies, privatising public services such as health and selling off publicly owned assets. Contrary to popular perceptions of the ultra-capitalist USA, it is common there for cities to own their own water and power companies as public services. New York's Twin Towers, which were destroyed on 9/11, were not actually so much a symbol of US capitalism, but of city enterprise. The NY Port Authority owned the World Trade Center land with profits from rents going into public services. The US federal government and the US taxpayer fund the water supply system in the mountain and western states gener-ously, to the huge benefit of farmers and desert cities such as Las Vegas, which get cheap, federal-taxpayer-subsidised water. Whilst rightwing Americans may deplore the 'socialised medicine' or universal health care of Canada and European social democracies, they ignore the US socialised water system and the arms companies' corporate welfare system.[7]

A key neo-liberal policy to be piloted by Margaret Thatcher in the 1980s was the privatisation of state-owned companies and the selling of public assets. Former Conservative Prime Minister Harold Macmillan opposed this policy as 'selling off the family silver'. Starting with British Telecom, British Gas, the water and electricity boards, the public asset sales continue. Chancellor Gordon Brown announced his plan to sell off public assets worth £46 billion in his 2007 budget. He sold the Inland Revenue Tax Office Buildings in 2001 to 'tax avoiding' Mapeley, an offshore property company, on a leaseback deal. The company's profits cannot be taxed.

Privatisation was marketed by the Thatcher government through selling undervalued shares to the public. They were bought off as the new share-owning democracy, with the carrot of making windfall gains. She appealed to greed and self-interest, as she believed 'there was no such thing as society'.

Her populist argument was that state-run businesses were by definition inef-ficient, limiting enterprise by red tape and needing public subsidies. She further argued that political control was bad for business and restrictive borrowing rules should be changed. In the face of an explosion of electronic technology, new consumer demands and market changes, the state-run corporations were unre-sponsive and lacked enterprise. People wanted choice – it was no longer good enough for British Telecom to only provide one type of black telephone. The state monopoly of a sector through nationalised companies was bad for the consumer and for business. With greater competition, the discipline of the free market, the ability to raise share capital and accountability to shareholders rather than government, competent private sector management would privatise state corporations. These would then become more efficient, competitive and profitable and give better service to customers. It was argued that government's main strength was government, not running businesses.

These arguments made some practical sense but with caveats. Bureaucracy and enterprise do not mix easily. Government could privatise, step back and provide an effective regulatory framework that in theory protected the public interest, the consumer, labour and the environment. When and if done well, privatisation could help redraw the boundaries between state and business.

But several critical, costly strategic mistakes were made. As a result, privatisation was often a huge windfall gift to business, a reckless cut-price selling of the family silver. The extent of this massive windfall gift from British politicians to business has still not been calculated.

The first mistake was to sell off the capital and fixed assets (such as land, natural resources such as water rights, oil, property, patents, tools, equipment, capital goods) of each publicly owned business, instead of leasing them on a full repairing lease for long-term income and capital gain for the public.

A similar mistake was made in the sixteenth century by Henry VIII, who sold off land for short-term profit and at knock-down prices. Much of the 20 per cent of British land that his father Henry VII had patiently acquired to fund the running costs of the monarchy and the state was squandered. Later monarchs had therefore to go cap in hand to parliament for more tax income – which came with strings attached. In sharp contrast to privatising Conservative and New Labour governments, successive Dukes of Westminster only normally lease rather than sell land and property. As a result of long term stewardship, this estate has prospered greatly since 1066.

Leasing the national electricity distribution grid, on a full repairing lease, would have yielded far more income in the long term than selling it. The argument is that a capital 'commons' has been built up through long-term public investment, as in the construction of our transport system and utilities. Because such capital is a socially created 'commons' it is very hard to value, as it is not a commodity like a chair. By definition a 'commons', a shared resource, is a right to be leased, to be socially and democratically controlled, rather than a commodity to be bought and sold on the market.

However, the British Treasury knows that the commons *can* be leased, as Chancellor Gordon Brown leased the right to mobile telecoms companies to use the electro-magnetic spectrum for £22 billion. Just consider the rising annual national income that citizens and the state could have gained from leasing the capital and fixed assets of the former nationalised industries, rather than selling off the family silver.

Conservative Prime Minister John Major was so keen to privatise British Rail that he deliberately designed the privatisation to be well-nigh impossible and expensive to reverse. So the rail system was sold off to over 100 companies. The rolling stock was sold off to a leasing company, which has profited greatly at public expense, by overcharging. The rail-leasing firm Porterbrook was sold in 1996 to Charterhouse Capital Partners, turning an investment of £73.6 million into £825 million on selling the firm in August 1996 to Stagecoach. Parliament criticised the sale, saying the Treasury lost £900 million from the sale of the rail-leasing companies. Then Abbey bought Porterbrook in 2000 for £1.4 billion. Serious rail accidents occurred as a result of safety being compromised by cutting costs on maintenance and subcontracting by the privatised Railtrack. The publicly owned Network Rail had to then take over from a failing Railtrack.

Instead of saving taxpayers' money, subsidies to the rail industry are now higher than ever, and rail fares have gone up at a much higher rate than inflation. In 2006, 'The total amount paid in fares by rail passengers has doubled since privatization to more than £5 billion a year. But the total subsidy has risen even faster, reaching £6.3 billion last year, four times what British Rail received in a typical year.'[8] There is still no coherent, integrated, connected, affordable public British transport system. In Sweden, where government strategic transport planning is thorough, integrated, user-friendly, environmentally sensitive and connected, the state leasing to private rail companies has been successful compared with Britain.

The second mistake of privatisation was poor regulation in the consumer and public interest. Thirdly, the government failed to plan the whole transport system effectively for maximum public benefit. One exception was former London Mayor Ken Livingstone, whose Transport for London carried out effective public transport planning, service commissioning and congestion charging. He had to fight with the Labour government, which initially opposed congestion charging.

Box 5.1: Brown's PFI tube policy costs taxpayers £2 billion

In late 2007, Metronet went into receivership with a £2 billion loss, and gave up its £17 billion, thirty-year contract back to Transport for London. Prime Minister Blair and Chancellor Brown had forced the Metronet PFI deal through against Livingstone's wishes between 2001 and 2003, spending £450 million on legal, contract and consulting fees in the process. In addition to funding the £2 billion loss, TfL had to make infrastructure payments to Metronet of £3 billion between 2003 and 2007. 'It is the shocking naiveté with which the Treasury allowed the taxpayer to be taken to the cleaners which is a disgrace: there was no substantive transfer of risk to the private sector.'[10] Norman Baker, the Liberal Democrat transport spokesman, said that the Metronet fiasco was 'an appalling waste of public money … Taxpayers are forking out for this multimillion deal to a failed company to save Gordon Brown's blushes. Just like Northern Rock, the private sector takes the profit when they can, and the public sector bails them out when matters go pear-shaped.'[11]

Chancellor Brown forced through tube privatisation and the Metronet PFI. This, in Livingstone's view, cost more than keeping the Underground in public hands and compromised safety through cutting corners.[9]

Lastly, the fourth strategic mistake was that the government did not understand that selling ownership means less control or no control. So Thames Water has been sold several times to asset-stripping investors, first German and now Australian, which are loath to put money into maintenance and capital investment, even though water consumers are paying higher rates, supposedly for such investment. Consequently, Thames Water is profitable for the owners, who are sweating the asset for all they can get, though with an ancient, leaky water-supply system. On the other hand, Wales Water has been mutualised, rather than renationalised by the state, after privatisation got derailed. All water consumers are now owners of the mutual, and can exercise direct control as both consumers and members who help elect Dr Cymru's board, who work on an expenses-only basis. Not-for-private-profit Glas Cymru is committed to reinvest profits to keep bills low.

The government, however, is more comfortable with the privatisation of public assets to corporations than with the localisation, communalisation or mutualisa-tion of such assets for permanent public benefit. The communalisation of assets in local open membership, democratically accountable bodies is a real, human-scale alternative to the nationalisation and privatisation of assets. But 'business and privatisation is good, community is bad' is the government mantra.

For example, when Standish Hospital near Stroud, Gloucestershire, was no longer needed as a NHS hospital in 2006, the government invited bids for the site to be continued for some form of health care provision, as it had originally been given for this purpose. So a local partnership of civil society organisations, health businesses and charities made a civil society-led bid in 2005. This would have put the beautiful 32-acre site into a community land trust for leasing to a partnership of specialist health providers, such as hospital after-care and specialist surgery. John Hutton MP, then Labour Health Minister, said before the 2005 election that the community 'Save Standish' bid was the NHS's 'preferred bid' over those of private bidders. After the election, the new Minister, Lord Warner, then froze out the Standish community bid and invited new bidders. As a result of ministerial delay, the hospital is still empty and much degraded. Now, as of summer 2009, the local PCT (health authority) has had a rescue plan accepted by the NHS, which is strikingly similar to the 'Save Standish' bid. However, local people think that communalising this asset would have delivered a wider range of health, business, social and environmental benefits more promptly without the buildings falling into disrepair, with local democratic control via open community land trust member-ship. Local trusteeship would better ensure that Standish Hospital was kept for public benefit.

It is not clear that the lessons of effective, public-interest privatisation have been learned. For example, privatisation is being pushed abroad by the Department for International Development, which paid out £118 million in consultancy fees to the five big accountancy firms in 1997–2002 for privatisation contracts. John Hilary, director of policy at War on Want, commented that 'There is a solid body of evidence which shows that privatisation of public services increases poverty in developing countries.'[12] And the same can be argued for Britain, with increasing fuel, transport and water poverty.

PFI: getting guaranteed profits and cheap public assets

The Private Finance Initiative was invented to help the government build and run the schools, hospitals and transport system that it otherwise said it could not afford. Gordon Brown believed that if the state borrowed too much money, then the financial markets got nervous. This is now ironic, given the bank bailouts. However, by an ingenious sleight of hand that fools no one, it is all right for private companies to borrow for government-backed PFI schemes. So companies raise the capital, build hospitals, schools and roads, and then run them for the next thirty years. The government pays for the lease and service charges. Politicians claim this gets much new investment into public services, and, as they believe that business is more efficient than the state, that services will thus be cheaper and better.

However, this has been a licence to print money for PFI companies, at public expense. Take road schemes. According to George Monbiot, the Skye Bridge PFI contract allowed companies to fleece the taxpayer. The Skye Bridge should have cost £23 million, according to the original estimates, but under PFI has cost the public £93 million! This was the first PFI scheme in Britain, and after nine years from its opening in 1995, the companies that built the bridge had charged a total of £33 million in tolls. The government had originally given the PFI companies £13 million in sweeteners for approach roads, £3 million for consultants and £4 million for risks such as construction delays. The European Investment Bank lent £13 million, breaking the bank's rules, which were to lend only when there were no funds from other sources. The government closed the alternative ferry service on the day of the bridge's opening, so as to eliminate competition. With further government subsidies for lowering tolls of £7.6 million and buying back the bridge contract from the PFI companies at £27 million, Monbiot estimates the total cost to the taxpayer at £93.6 million and not the original £23 million or an independent estimate of £15 million. But it is impossible to hold government and business to account because the contract is secret, and both Conservative and Labour governments hid behind 'commercial confidentiality'. Monbiot writes of PFI that 'the lesson of the Skye Bridge is obvious. If we are not allowed to see what is being done in our name, there's a pretty good chance we are being ripped off.'[13] Typically, local Labour politicians such as Brian Wilson MP advocated abolishing bridge tolls before the 1997 election, but went back on their promises afterwards. As protestor John Campbell said, 'what hurts the most is the sense of betrayal. These ministers were campaigners before they got into power. Now they are just suits.'[14]

Take schools and PFI. Building Schools for the Future is a £45 billion programme aiming to rebuild every secondary school and half of all primaries in England by 2020. Instead of LEAs building their own new schools – as happened with Hampshire County Council, which became a school design exemplar – the Treasury has forced LEAs into PFI. There is a built-in conflict between what local authorities and schools want (flexible contracts to provide up-to-date schools), what contractors want (to make money) and what the Treasury wants (a guarantee of what it will cost). PFI for schools is complex, hard to manage and results in cost overruns, glitches and design problems. Furthermore, given the choice, the new academies have all opted out of PFI, sensibly preferring to keep control over the building of their schools and to hold on to ownership. One academy head, unhampered by a government-enforced PFI, said, 'Why would we want to not be in total control of our buildings?'[15]

Take hospitals. The Walsgrave Hospital in Coventry was to have been renewed at the cost of £30 million and so was not profitable enough for a PFI. It was rebuilt for £330 million. Altcourse Prison in Liverpool was built by a consortium, which broke even after two and a half years and now enjoys twenty-two years of profit. The PFI companies that built Norfolk and Norwich University Hospital gained millions from refinancing the scheme with cheaper loans. According to Monbiot: 'Many of these projects offer far worse services than their publicly funded equivalents. Beds are crammed together ... operating theatres are flooded with sewage; children try to study in permanent building sites; underpaid prison guards sign off sick and look for work elsewhere. The experiment keeps failing but the government keeps repeating it.'[16]

PFI has contributed to the paradox whereby the UK has the highest health spending ever, yet at the same time there are cuts in front-line services. Before the 1997 General Election, Alistair Darling MP, then shadow Treasury Secretary, already predicted that PFI's 'apparent savings now could be countered by the formidable commitment on revenue expenditure in years to come'.[17] As the figures are 'commercially confidential' it is hard to assess government claims that PFI schemes represent value for money and are cheaper than schemes that are public sector financed and run. Even though New Labour when in opposition opposed PFI on moral as well as on secrecy grounds, when in power they went ahead regardless. Jack Straw MP in 1996 said that it was 'morally unacceptable' to have PFI gaols, that this 'was one area where a free market does not exist', then as the new Home Secretary signed PFI contracts for new gaols already in the pipeline. The merchant banker Adrian Montague, one-time head of the Treasury PFI task force, said, 'The prison sector is becoming a commodity product. It is almost on a production line.'[18]

George Monbiot concludes his analysis of PFI thus:

Among the many costs of the Private Finance Initiative is the transfer of control and ownership of the nation's critical infrastructure to private business, whose interests are often wholly distinct from those of the electorate. Complicated and confidential, it has been able to penetrate areas of public life whose overt privatisation would be politically impossible. It has enabled companies to harness the great untapped resources they coveted, sustaining their share prices by turning public capital into private cash. *The purpose of the Private Finance Initiative is to deliver the assets of the state to the corporations.*[19] [author's italics]

However, the careful privatisation of state-run corporations *can*, under the right conditions, redraw the boundaries between state and business appropriately and to mutual benefit. One key condition is that the capital assets should be leased so as to preserve public ownership into the future and provide a public income stream. For example, many local authorities retain ownership of facilities such as leisure centres and lease them out to businesses that run them. Capital is a commons to be democratically controlled in the public interest, yet leased on conditions to business. This balances business enterprise on the one hand, and public interest on the other.

However, PFI is a massive negative overstepping of the boundaries between business and the state, between the economy and the polity. Rather than offering transparent, accountable commissioning of public services such as hospital-, road- and school-building, PFI is costly, unaccountable, untransparent and forces the state to tax us more so as to guarantee long-term corporate profits. So we have the paradox of more money being spent on health than ever, whilst civil society has to fight service cutting and hospital closures to pay for expensive PFI contracts, as in Stroud, where a successful campaign in 2007 eventually forced the local health authority to keep the maternity unit open.

Democracy is also under attack from the buying of our planning system by developers and corporations, who are seeking to realise huge capital gains from favourable planning permission and real estate development. Again, the boundaries are being shifted by compliant government in favour of the developers.

Buying the planning system

Planning land use is a key local, regional and national government strategic task. Deciding how we use our scarce land is at the heart of democracy and the state. Yet in 2004 national government abolished local structure plans and gave the task to Whitehall officials, who also got veto rights over local community plans. The May 2007 White Paper announced by Department of Communities and Local Government Minister Ruth Kelly further limited the scope for local councils and protestors to object to 'national' projects such as motorways, pipelines, airports, power stations and new out-of-town supermarkets. A national commission in 'the national interest' would decide these.

Coincidentally, the government's energy review also announced the need for a whole new generation of nuclear power stations These were no doubt to be forced through by the national planning commission against local opposition. According to Simon Jenkins, this 'Tesco clause betrays big business's grip over Labour'.[20] In spite of Gordon Brown's lip service to empowering communities and enabling rather than centralising government his government clearly wants to dismantle local democratic planning.

The control of the planning system is anyway weighted in favour of developers, who can keep appealing against local councils' decisions. They can reapply for planning permission after two years. Even though councils may want to oppose a development, they may not have the money to pay legal bills, and are worried about paying costs if they lose. Local people who object to a development have to fund their case themselves, and if the council approves of a scheme, only developers, not local people, can object, unlike other democratic European countries.

Box 5.2   Stroud Maternity Hospital matters

Put the knife down, you can't take a piece of our town
The family silver isn't safe in your hands
Because after all this time you still refuse to understand
That value isn't only something you can measure out in pounds
And once you kill a thing, it's gone; that's why we're asking you to put
the knife down

John Dougherty

Stroud Maternity Hospital is a midwife-led unit praised by its clients and for which a great deal of affection is felt in the town. So when the health trust running it decided to shut it down in the interests of cost-saving, it might have guessed in advance that this would not be a popular decision.

A team made up of midwives and recent parents quickly coordinated a campaign which included: a march of thousands through the town centre; a media offensive which made effective use of local celebrities, getting both local and national attention; a series of meetings with the trust managers; and the hiring of an analyst who was able to highlight serious but basic flaws in the calculations used by the trust to make its case.

In the face of this sustained criticism and effective counter-argument, the trust eventually backed down and the unit remains open.

Photos by Cyril Laffort

Granting planning permission is a highly sensitive political activity, as it can raise the value of land from a few thousand pounds an acre to over a £1 million an acre. The resulting capital gain on the increase of land value is not taxed. But usually, the local council makes a Section 106 'planning gain' agreement with the developer – who may have to do a variety of things such as fund new roads, pay cash, contribute to a new school and allocate land for affordable homes – all in return for gaining lucrative planning permission.

Again, the planning system is heavily weighted against communities trying to control their future development and capture land value for enduring public benefit. For example, High Bickington in Devon carried out a village appraisal and then agreed a twenty-year plan for the future, which included community facilities, a new school, community woodlands, more workspace to reduce car journeys to work for local business and building permanently affordable homes so as to expand the village from around 600 to a thousand people, thus also helping the school, pub and shops survive. High Bickington Community Property Trust was set up, with £5 million of potential assets in the form of permanently affordable houses, which would have eventually yielded an income stream for community services. Devon County Council had offered land from a county farm, outside the village planning envelope, to the village. The Parish, District and County Councils and planners were behind the scheme, which was lauded by Alun Michael MP, the then Minister for Rural Affairs.

But the government planners, the Government Office South West, called in the High Bickington plan on Christmas Eve 2004, and their inquiry ruled against the plans. Department of Communities and Local Government Minster Ruth Kelly upheld her inspector's decision, in spite of her token support for community land trusts. This is an example of government blocking community-led initiatives. After nine years' dogged effort, High Bickington Community Property Trust finally got planning permission for a more limited housing scheme in 2009. This could set a workable model for every neighbourhood, town and village in Britain to follow for community-owned, affordable homes, workspace and facilities. One question asked was whether High Bickington was blocked for so long because it captured value for the community rather than for developers? Or was it blocked by senior civil servants and Ruth Kelly because it was civil society led with local government support, rather than national government controlled?

Ending High Street competition: Ghost Town Britain

Successive governments have allowed the big supermarkets to almost eliminate competition from corner shops and drastically reduce consumer diversity and choice. For example, in 2006 the government allowed Waterstone's to take over Ottakar's, effectively leaving WH Smith as the only other 'bookshop' on the High Street. By allowing the big supermarkets to open up smaller 'corner shops', many locally owned and run shops have gone out of business. As supermarket chains grow, small shops decline. With the decline of small shops comes the decline of the local economy, because money spent in such shops tends to circulate longer in the local economy, rather than being extracted by the large chains. So we have Ghost Town Britain and cloned High Street shops. Furthermore, the supermarkets have special tax advantages, such as tax-free parking, and pay proportionately lower rates than small shops. The taxpayer also has to pay for the transport infrastructure that the supermarkets need.

Box 5.3   Tescopoly drives small newsagents out of business

In April 2009 Lord Mandelson's Business, Enterprise and Regulatory Reform unit in the Department of Trade and Industry deregulated newspaper distribution. Supermarkets will benefit hugely, but not small newsagents. Free speech and cultural freedom will suffer. Historically, the newspaper distribution firm guaranteed '... in return for exclusive delivery rights, to supply whatever stock a shop requests, however small the order might be. This allowed small newsagents to survive and protected publishers from censorship by powerful retailers. (In the United States, supermarkets often dictate the contents of the magazines they sell.) Tesco has been trying to break the distribution agreement since 2000; now Mandelson has delivered.'

Source: George Monbiot, 'This £2bn Mandelson Fiefdom Is an Open Door to Corporate Predators', Guardian, 4 May 2009

Even though studies show that supermarkets charge overall more for their products, comparing the prices with local markets and independent retailers, the Office of Fair Trading takes no remedial action. The supermarkets also have huge land banks and are keen to build more out-of-town supermarkets when and if the moratorium on such building schemes is lifted. The big four supermarkets control nearly 80 per cent of the British retail food market. Their control of food retailing also means that farmers are getting very little more for the food they produce than ten years ago, that is until the recent 2008 food-price increase. Furthermore, a web of personal connections and revolving doors maintains supermarket influence on the government. For example, David, now Lord, Sainsbury has given over £5 million to the Labour Party, was the Science Minister (in spite of his GM company connections) and was the former CEO of Sainsbury's. Archie Norman, once CEO of Asda Wal-Mart, was once also a Conservative MP and shadow spokesman for the environment.

Clearly, the ability of the government to maintain a healthy competitive environment for food retailing has been blocked by corporate influence, to the detriment of consumers, small businesses and producers. The supermarkets have bought influence, whether by political party donations or by gifts like Tesco's donation for the Millennium Dome learning area of £12 million. The return for such 'gifts' is favourable planning, tax and competition rulings. It may have been totally coincidental that soon after Tesco's millennium gift, a car-park tax proposal that would have cost the supermarket £40 million a year was dropped.

The boundaries need shifting back so that government can exercise effective planning in the public and community interest, charge the supermarkets their true infrastructure support costs and break up the retail monopolies for consumer and producer benefit.

The capture of government by the supermarkets means the end of many of Britain's small shopkeepers.

The rise of global corporate power and privilege

The historical development of the state and corporations shows how the state has been increasingly influenced by big, publicly quoted corporations. The legal form of the corporation was one of the significant social inventions of the nineteenth century. Whereas the state has been dominant since the Middle Ages, now it is the corporations. Corporations are legally accountable to shareholders, not the public or stakeholders, for maximising profit. They have grown so powerful that they have managed to acquire many of the rights previously reserved for people, and at the same time have shed their responsibilities.

Corporations originated in the need of charities such as schools, churches and hospitals for viable continuity. Incorporation helped them avoid things like death duties, which had to be paid when the founders died. These bodies were licensed by the crown, and at first excluded profit-making business. The crown then started to grant charters to trade associations, which then became the great merchant companies such as the Dutch East India Company in 1602 and the British East India Company in 1600. These got powers to act like states in the exploitation of colonies. For example, the British East India Company exported tea from China to Europe and paid for this in illegal opium, which Britain forced on China through the 1838–42 Opium War, enforcing unequal trade treaties at the same time.

The activities of commercial corporations were strictly controlled after the bursting of the South Sea Bubble in 1720. But after the Bubble Act was repealed in 1825, incorporations were again legally permitted. They slowly acquired the rights hitherto only belonging to individuals, plus one key right, that of limited liability. Hitherto, individuals investing in companies had unlimited liability, but from 1856 there was limited liability. By the end of the nineteenth century, the corporation became a separate legal 'person', empowered to carry out business in its own name, buy assets, hire workers, pay taxes. As a result governments could no longer terminate a corporation if it exceeded its chartered powers, because now corporations were persons, protected by law in the same way as free persons.

President Roosevelt implemented the New Deal in 1932, designed to restore economic wellbeing though regulatory reforms, including regulation of the out-of-control banks. The 1933 Glass-Steagall Act separated retail banking from investment banking. Government regulation, trade unions, consumer power and the welfare state rebalanced the power of the corporations. For example, in the USA power companies could not operate beyond their state, and there were strict borrowing rules for banks, as so many had gone bankrupt in the USA in the early 1930s from excess speculation. But in the late 1970s Keynesian economic management by the state came under fire from neo-liberals. They wanted economic 'freedom' for banks, corporations and individuals. This led to deregulation, privatisation, social spending cuts and rolling back the state in favour of corporations.

With better air transport, telecommunications and information technology, corporations could emancipate themselves from their home national states and go global. They could source cheap labour and materials globally and start to dictate to governments, threatening to move on to cheaper offshore locations.

Corporations developed new ways of avoiding social obligations, such as shifting to offshore subsidiaries, using tax havens, exempting themselves from, say, injury claims made by workers in the South. For example in 1999, the British Court of Appeal stopped 3,000 South Africans with asbestosis suing Cape plc, in spite of the fact that Cape is a British company. In Britain, though companies enjoy police protection, can sue for libel and use the law as legal persons, when it comes to health and safety or corporate manslaughter – where people are killed by avoidable accidents at work – they are largely exempt.

The dominance of global corporations over nation states was formalised in 1993 with the formation of the World Trade Organization. Big corporations increasingly govern society through what is called 'corporate or elite globalisation'. According to William Niskanen of the Cato Institute, 'Corporations have become sufficiently powerful to pose a threat to governments.'[21] Corporate leaders are the new high priests and kings, with unprecedented power. David Korten, author of *When Corporations Ruled the World*, writes that, 'The publicly traded, limited liability corporation is an institutional form that allows for the virtually unlimited concentration of economic power for the exclusive financial benefit of its shareholders without public accountability for the consequences of its use.'[22]

So the corporations deliver needed products and create unparalleled wealth. But according to Korten, they have outgrown their clothes and dominate government. So the boundaries between corporations and government need redrawing, globally, nationally and locally. Corporations have an important job to do, but without regulation they can become 'Frankenstein monsters'. US Chief Justice Louis Brandeis considered that these corporate monsters could overpower their creators and no longer serve the needs of society.

In July 2008, when working on the first draft of this chapter, I wrote that:

> It could be that unless civil society and government balance the power of the corporations, there could be a world economic, environmental, political and social crash. Just as the legitimacy of Eastern European communist regimes unexpectedly imploded under challenges from civil society movements and economic decline in 1989, so the runaway growth of corporate globalisation could also burst like the South Sea Bubble. The corporate global bubble is financially unstable, environmentally unsustainable and based on massive social inequality. There are limits to how far global corporations can freeload on society through captive governments and a muzzled civil society. It is not whether the global corporate bubble will burst, but when.

Since then, the credit crunch and financial meltdown have seen bail-outs of the failing banks, governments propping up economies and widespread job losses as the most grotesque credit bubble in history burst. The question is, will the power of the corporations and banks be rebalanced by redrawing the boundaries between state and the market, as happened after the South Sea Bubble, with Roosevelt's New Deal and with the post-1945 British welfare state and mixed economy?

Revolving doors and fat cats

Corporations can influence government policy and regulatory frameworks through corporate leaders becoming ministers, advisers, members of policy working parties and working on secondment. Whilst the expertise that individual business leaders can bring to government may be useful, there can be conflicts of interest. When 'fat cats' are co-opted by government to advise on a burning question, there may be the exclusion of a diverse range of people, each with information, experience and a piece of the puzzle. Whose voices are heard? How transparent and accountable are these processes? There are choices. For example, the process of appointing elite business leaders and experts to conduct inquiries or to advise is different, say, from participative inquiries, from citizens' juries or assemblies composed of a cross-section of people.

Revolving doors and co-opting leaders with conflicts of interest severely weaken government's ability to act in the overall public interest. George Monbiot's list of fat cats,[23] with their previous gluttony and subsequent creamery, is a striking way of getting the point across. Lord Marshall of Kingsbridge was the chair of British Airways, which campaigned against aviation fuel tax, yet he was put in charge of Chancellor Gordon Brown's energy tax review to investigate how fuel taxes on corporations could reduce global warming. Ewen Cameron, former chair of the government's now disbanded Countryside Agency, which introduced the right to roam, tackled rural social exclusion, and kept footpaths open, personally opposed the right to roam as the Country Landowners' Association president. He owns 3,000 acres of Somerset and was reported by the Ramblers Association for twice blocking a footpath across his estate. Take Robert Osborne, who headed the Special Projects unit at Tarmac, a major builder of PFI hospitals, commissioned by the Department of Health. His subsequent creamery was being Chief Executive of the Department of Health's Private Finance Unit. He then returned to Tarmac in 1998 to lead its PFI division. Tony Edwards was Director of the TI Group, owner of Matrix Churchill, which sold machine tools for arms-making to Saddam Hussein – subsidised by British taxpayers. But he was also head of the government's Defence Export Sales Organisation, advising on the granting of arms export licences. Professor Peter Schroeder, as Director of Research and Development at Nestlé, then became director of the government's Institute of Food Research. Professor Sir John Cadogan, former research director of BP, became Director-General of the Research Councils, which are tasked with pure research, not supposedly immediately applicable to corporate work. Or Michael Mallinson, president of the British Property Federation, which lobbies government for property developers. His creamery was being Deputy Chairman of English Partnerships, which sold and developed government land.

John Reid, former home secretary, consults with private security firm G4S. Stephen Byers, former trade and industry secretary, advised Consolidated Contractors, an oil and construction multinational. Anji Hunter, a Blair aide, became BP's director of communications. Jonathan Powell, another Blair aide now works for Morgan Stanley. Peter Wilby writes that:

In office, they and others may honestly claim they are acting in the public interest. But, to a remarkable extent, politicians now identify the public interest with the corporate interest. Taking on powerful corporations is a thankless task at the best of times; to do so when a corner of your mind must know the implications for your future career prospects requires exceptional courage and determination.[24]

The US was no different. Did Hank Paulson, when US Treasury Secretary, allow Lehman Brothers to go bankrupt because he was acting in the US interest, or in the interest of his former bank, Goldman Sachs? Vice President Dick Cheney was a Halliburton oilman, and Halliburton gained massive contracts in Iraq. President Obama has now brought in stringent new rules to try to curtail the revolving doors and fat cats of the Bush era.

In a democracy, citizens elect a government, which is supposed to run the country in the public interest. However, if the fat cats and corporate leaders using the revolving doors between state and business exert undue influence on policy and regulation, then we have a façade democracy. The boundaries between business and government are not respected.

The arms industry and government

The arms industry has a particularly strong hold on government, in order to secure taxpayers' money and favourable regulation. Massive subsidies are given to the arms industry, almost £1 billion a year for the UK defence industry. By 2003, £1,015,166,892 had been guaranteed by the British government's Export Credit Guarantee Department. The government promotes arms sales, with taxes that would otherwise go for education or health. The Serious Fraud Office was forced by Prime Minister Blair to stop investigating the BAE Saudi arms deal in 2007 for reasons of 'national security'. Robert Wardle of the SFO was pressured three times by the Prime Minister to drop his investigation into alleged bribery by BAE, though investigation continues with BAE Systems contracts in Tanzania, Chile, Qatar, Romania, South Africa and the Czech Republic. So even though the British government has signed up to the OECD anti-corruption convention, it refused to continue investigating the Saudi arms deal and directed the SFO to discontinue the investigation, thus compromising the independence of prosecutors. Furthermore, it was revealed in December 2004 that the British government in a hitherto secret deal would pay BAE insurance of £1 billion if the Saudi regime collapsed. The ECGD insures arms exports, which are too risky for private insurers, and under the Thatcher and Major governments accumulated £10 billion in bad debts from exporting arms to unstable countries like Saddam's Iraq.

Both Prime Minister Blair in a July 2005 visit to Riyadh and then Defence Secretary John Reid pushed for the sale of seventy-two Eurofighter Typhoon jets at £5.4 billion, plus extras which made a total of £10 billion. The British taxpayer will subsidise this deal with export insurance. Both the Saudis and BAE had asked for the SFO bribery investigation to be called off. It is plain that the real power lies with the Saudi royal family. BAE and the British government act as arms salesmen for a deal which is not in ordinary people's interests. And other British industrialists may well say that it is not fair that the arms industry gets so much preferential help, and ask, 'Why can't the arms industry stand on its own feet?'[25]

Governments justify subsidising the arms industry because of the need to retain a home 'defence industrial base'. Exporting arms makes British companies more viable, and so able to keep supplying the Ministry of Defence. But this is outdated: BAE is trying to become more American, by taking over medium-sized US arms companies, so it can get US contracts; furthermore, French companies such as Thales are acquiring UK companies. Effectively, there is no British defence industrial base any longer, because its place has been taken by the global arms corporations – which the British government is subsidising.

The best democracy money can buy[26]

So just how have British politicians, elected by citizens to serve the public interest, allowed big business to capture the state? Typical of Britain's captive state is the fact that one of Gordon Brown's first acts as Prime Minister in June 2007 was to appoint Digby Jones, former head of the CBI, to be a minister in the Department of Trade and Industry to lead the task of reducing the burden of red tape on industry. Whose interests, one asks, was Digby Jones serving? And his successors include Lord Carter, the former CEO of the Brunswick Group, a big PR firm working for BA, Unilever, Barclays, Rolls Royce and BT. Lord Davies, Minister for Trade and Investment was a former non-executive director of Tesco and chair of Standard Chartered Bank. No wonder there is light-touch regulation of the banks, with this kind of entry point for banks and corporations into a captive government.

Gone are the days of old-style bribery, nicely caught by the US bumper sticker that read, 'Get into politics – buy a congressman!' In the good old days of the Major Conservative government, Mohamed al Fayed, owner of Harrods, gave large amounts of cash in brown envelopes to MPs such as Neil Hamilton to ask helpful questions in parliament, as revealed by the 'cash for questions' scandal.

And it's not just the scandal of ex-Prime Minister Tony Blair's 'cash for peerages' practices, where rich donors or lenders to the Labour Party were allegedly promised or were given peerages in return for cash or loans. Or the revelation that peers requested cash to change legislation and ask questions in the Lords. We are talking about a boundary shift in favour of business, as politicians meekly gave up state power to what has been called 'market democracy', welcomed business rewriting the rules of public procurement and rolled back the state's powers to intervene in the market for public benefit and protection.

Adam Curtis's 2007 BBC television documentary *The Trap* shows how Bill Clinton and Tony Blair allowed 'the market' to take over the responsibility of running society. The concept of 'market democracy' arose from the thinking of economists such as Professor James Buchanan. He set out to discredit politicians and civil servants as hypocrites. They professed to represent the public interest, but in fact serve their own interest. There was no such thing as public service, only civil servants' self-interest. The popular comedy series *Yes, Minister* was based on this theory of the conflicts in self-interest between ministers and civil servants. The public interest is whatever the politicians say it is, according to public choice theory. Buchanan said the idea of the public good is just 'not meaningful'. Why? It is logically impossible for politicians to express the will of the people, because social life is a game with competitive individuals seeking their rational self-interest. Everyone is out for number one, and the only system that can express people's preferences is the market. Humans are calculating information processors, and voting is a weak form of information processing that can at best only indirectly express preferences. So the economy is superior to democracy, buying is a better way of expressing preferences and markets are the only accurate voting machines. The CEO of Citibank/ Citicorp, Walter Wriston, wrote a best-selling book in 1992 called *The Twilight of Sovereignty*, where he argued for markets to take over from government in running society. (This now seems highly ironic and arrogant, as in November 2008 the US government bailed out Citicorp's freeloading successor, Citigroup, with a $306 billion guarantee and $20 billion capital injection, after massive sub-prime losses. Citigroup was valued at $20.5 billion, down from $250 billion in 2007.)

Freedom was reframed as the ability of the individual to get what they wanted. The image of the human being was a simplified economic model, a rational calculating machine. This narrow view of humans originated in Cold War games theory, pioneered by the mathematician John Nash, who saw the human being as a financial analyst, as a computer that constantly strategised for self-interest. Behaviour change happened when people were incentivised, not because they were guided by values. So get them to pay for black plastic bags for rubbish, rather than setting up helpful recycling systems that people will anyway want to use freely because they value sustainability. Humans are genetically programed as bio-computers, merely machines for passing on genes. Buchanan and Nash saw society as a market-place of competitive humans, which complemented the neo-liberal free marketeers' image of the 'invisible hand of the market', where altruism gets in the way of efficiency and greed is the motor.

So when Bill Clinton was voted in as President of the USA on a platform of using state power to create jobs, improve welfare and housing and bring in a new health care system, he was met in January 1993 by Alan Greenspan, of the US Federal Reserve, and Robert Rubin of Goldman Sachs. They told him his programme could not be funded with such a big government borrowing deficit, that he could not borrow more money without a collapse of confidence. However, they suggested that the way to build a better society was to give power to the market. People and business would flourish when market restrictions were lifted. So Clinton cut public spending, reduced welfare programmes, dismantled the welfare state piecemeal and abandoned public health reforms. In 1996, Clinton spoke of giving up the power of big government to change the world, announcing the end of the imposition on people by government of what they thought people needed, declaring that government didn't have all the answers and that the state had to live within its means. He agreed to further deregulation of the financial markets, which helped lead to the sub-prime crisis. Clinton ended the vision of liberal politics that Franklin Roosevelt had brought in with the New Deal, where the state intervened to protect people against the market, by providing a supportive safety net and regulating business.

Clinton repealed Roosevelt's Glass-Steagall Act in 1999, thus allowing ordinary banks to enter the casino economy of speculative investment banking.

John Major (who after the 1997 General Election became the chair of the armaments and private equity company Carlyle, which had benefited massively from the first Gulf War) also followed Margaret Thatcher down the market democracy path. He announced a 'revolution' in how public services like health were delivered. He introduced, to mimic self-interest, the internal market into the NHS and performance targets, exhorted by such 'liberation management' gurus such as Tom Peters, who extolled, without any research evidence, how such targets would liberate people from bureaucracy.

New Labour followed on from Major and Clinton. In 1997 Tony Blair in a victory speech said Labour were, 'The new radicals. A Labour Party modernised that must undertake this historic mission: to liberate Britain from all the old social class divisions, old structures, old prejudices, old ways of working and of doing things that will not do in this world of change.' What he really meant was 'let the market rule'. So the power to set interest rates was given to the Bank of England, the task of light-touch regulation was given to the FSA and Chancellor Gordon Brown at the Treasury implemented a wide-ranging programme of performance targets, incentives and efficiency measures. To show his sense of humour, Brown's Treasury even announced the target of reducing world conflict by 6 per cent, a dog turd reduction target and a community vibrancy index.

So New Labour professed to improve public services through a rational system of efficiency targets and more funding, but in practice this led to more control, more expensive regulation and audit. NHS managers massaged the waiting-list figures by doing the easy operations first. The police reduced the crime figures by reclassifying crimes as 'suspicious occurrences', or wily school heads made sure teachers 'taught to get students through the league table tests'. No one knows whether to believe the numbers. The school league tables were introduced to incentivise schools to compete so that standards would rise and to identify failing schools. Even though most parents wanted their local school or hospital to be a good one, the government introduced a market system where already good schools became better. Mobile parents accelerated this process by moving into the right school-catchment areas. Meanwhile, the government introduced business-led, central-government-controlled and generously state-funded academies to provide 'competition'.

One result of New Labour's market friendly policies has been the death of social mobility, as education policies led to increasing segregation based on wealth. So rich children were more likely to live and die rich than poor children. Blair's aim in 1997 to liberate Britain has resulted in a more rigid, unequal and stratified society appearing than at any time since 1945, brought about by a massive boundary shift between the state and the market, a society that provided welfare for the wealthy, guaranteeing profits for PFI companies and, according to David Craig in *Plundering the Public Sector*, paying over £70 billion for management consultants. He wrote:

> To treat the possible waste of £70 billion of taxpayers' money, the desecration of our public services, the plundering of our cash starved NHS as anything but

a national emergency is to fail to understand what is happening in this country
... despite all the faults of the British public services, there is such a thing as a
'public service work ethic' and that this is quite different from the private sector
profit motive. We must understand that health, education, defence, policing,
prisons and social services are too important in a modern democratic society
to be handed over to organisations that only have a goal of profit maximisa-
tion regardless of human costs. Of course the public sector can and should
learn better management techniques from private sector companies. But they
should learn from, and not be taken over by, the private sector.[27]

But just how did Britain get the best democracy that money can buy? According
to investigative journalist Greg Palast, one way was through cash for access to the
New Labour government for then selling Britain. According to the *Observer* of 5
July 1998, lobbyists revealed that:

- in return for favourable tabloid news, the government offered News International
  valuable changes to the union recognition and competition bills;
- after Tesco gave £12 million towards the Millennium Dome, Tesco got the
  proposed supermarket car-park tax lifted, saving £40 million a year, though
  there might not have been a direct connection;
- Enron was able to reverse a government block on building new gas-fired power
  stations;
- PowerGen got approval for merger plans previously rejected by the Tory government, approval worth billions.

According to Palast, cash for access was systemic: 'New Labour had opened up
secret routes of special access to allow selected corporate chiefs to bargain, alter
or veto the government's key decisions.' Trade and Industry Minister Margaret
Beckett, who opposed the takeover by PowerGen of East Midlands Electricity
and who opposed new gas plants, was removed from office on 27 July 1998 by
Blair. Her replacement, Peter Mandelson, signed off the PowerGen takeover on 22
September and removed the moratorium on new gas plants.[28]

However, it is not just New Labour that has been captured, it is also the
Conservatives. The Tories are being funded by wealthy offshore businessmen like
Lord Ashcroft, a banking and telecoms security millionaire worth £800 million;
Julian Schild, chair of Huntleigh Technology which supplies the NHS with beds;
Michael Hintze, a hedge fund owner; and Lord Harris, the carpet millionaire. Big
City firms like PriceWaterhouseCoopers and the Boston Consulting Group are
advising on policy.[29] What payoff they want for their investment is not known. But
the bumper sticker should now read, 'Get into politics, buy a political party!'

Summary: from captive state to re-establishing boundaries

To summarise, business needs to lobby government on improving legislation and
regulation. When this is done openly, when the boundaries are clear, when there
is fairness and a level playing field for all, this can work. As long as businesses
were small, medium-sized or based in home-nation states, reasonably healthy

state–business boundaries could be maintained if lobbying was done transparently. The US New Deal framework created by Roosevelt, which lasted until the 1980s, and the Keynesian mixed economy and welfare state in the UK, built clear boundaries that contained the corporations. However, the analysis of privatisation, the selling of public assets at knock-down prices, PFI, the fat cat/revolving door syndrome between business and government, the favourable legislation for corporate privileges, tax avoidance, the buying of planning permission, the military-industrial complex, the ending of High Street retail competition and cash for access all indicate a historic shift in the boundaries to a captive state and corpocracy. Compliant government has failed to uphold public interest, allowing business to influence policy, regulation, planning and tax, acquire knock-down assets and get thirty-year PFI profits.

The story gets worse, however, as since the 1980s large corporations have made a global bid for power. They have bypassed national governments by creating institutions, for example the World Trade Organization in 1993, which aim to develop a globalised single market using carrots and sticks. When the governments of nation states signed up to the WTO, they signed away much of their sovereignty over taxes, labour, and environmental, social and health protection. The WTO treaty went through the Westminster parliament with hardly a mention, with very few MPs reading the small print. Whilst Eurosceptic MPs were opposing giving up sovereignty to Brussels, they were at the same time ignoring the more serious signing away of British economic sovereignty to the WTO.

Few people knew about the WTO treaty because, firstly, governments chose not to debate the issues with the public; secondly, parliament failed to exercise thorough scrutiny; and, thirdly, because of the information control exercised by a small number of global media corporations, which wield huge influence over public opinion.

Chapter 6 will now analyse the corporate capture of the media and culture, exploring the question of how the few control the many.

Chapter 6

Capturing Culture

But the reasons for our decline are never made clear because the corporate ownership of the country has absolute control of the populist pulpit – 'the media' – as well as the schoolroom.

Gore Vidal[1]

A popular government without popular information or the means of acquiring it is but a prologue to a farce or a tragedy; or perhaps both. Knowledge will forever govern ignorance; and a people who mean to be their own governors must arm themselves with the power which knowledge gives.

James Madison[2]

The corporate control of the media and culture is a major blockage to creating a sustainable, democratic and just society. Offshore global media corporations aim to undermine the relative independence of Britain's public broadcasting system. The reason? On the one hand, governments, through the manufacture of opinion and consent, can control citizens, and on the other, corporations can control consumers through cradle-to-grave advertising. David Hume wrote that the first principle for governments who wanted to stay in power was to ensure the control of the many by the few through shaping opinion.

The aim of this chapter is to unmask the ways that commercial and political interests capture cultural organisations, such as the media, for profit and power. These are crucial issues: how the mainstream media ignored the growing financial bubble; how life-threatening issues such as global warming have been sidelined until recently; how favourable scientific research is bought; how the arts are compromised; how advertisers manipulate children; and how the mass media news is shaped by corporate and political elites for their own ends. This is a major boundary question, and relates directly to one of this book's major arguments, that there should be clear boundaries between culture – including the media, health, education, science and the arts – the state and business.

Two recent examples illustrate the power and importance of an independent culture and media. Firstly, journalist Heather Brooke persevered in her investigation of MPs' secretive expenses and self-made rules despite years of blocked Freedom of Information requests. Her tenacious reporting resulted in the exposure of MPs' expenses in May 2009, via the *Telegraph* leak. The expenses scandal has triggered resignations, a parliamentary crisis and public demands for reform. Secondly, the *Guardian's* investigative reporting of massive corporate and banking tax avoidance in early 2009 shamed the government and the Inland Revenue into taking action.

The following themes will set the scene:

- co-opting cultural power
- what blocks the freeing of cultural space?
- cultural power and social movements[3]
- denial that 'the few' condition the opinion of 'the many'.

The chapter will then focus on some key areas of the corporate and state capture of culture. As a result, readers will be able to analyse their own examples of negative boundary-crossing as they arise. The following examples of capture will be analysed:

- the corporate control of the media
- privatising healthcare: NHS plc
- the commercialisation of childhood
- buying science
- the enclosure of the intellectual and genetic commons.

Co-opting cultural power

Co-opting cultural power is vital for corporations' profits. They want people to identify with brands, to shape their buying habits, identify with logos and to find meaning in consumerism. One television advertisement shows a toddler strapped into the back of a new car, a voice intoning 'And his first word was Ford.' And indeed, one survey found that most of the words and images recognised by British toddlers were brand names and logos.

What this shows is that culture – the ways we see, understand and make meaning in the world – really matters. Today, the real battle is for cultural power. The winners will have the best songs, music and stories that give meaning and sense to our lives. Think of the moving power of John Lennon's song 'Imagine'. If the state has coercive, legally backed power and business has resource and reward power, then cultural power offers the support of truth, evidence, of norms, of meaning and identity. The state needs legitimation, not just from elections or bishops blessing battleships, but from supportive media representation, from helpful stories and being seen to base its actions on accepted values.

On the other hand, with cultural power, artists, scientists, religious and spiritual teachers, individuals, parents, educators and doctors can speak their truth to political power. When Martin Luther King announced 'I have a dream', the civil rights vision and agenda was renewed for generations. The pen is more powerful than the sword, and there is nothing more powerful than an idea whose time has come. 'Even though I know that I might die tomorrow, I'd still plant a tree today', said King. And now Obama is President of the USA.

So Britain's shamocratic parliament, stung by Brian Haw's permanent anti-Iraq War witness in Parliament Square, declared a 1-kilometre protest exclusion zone around the Houses of Parliament. On 23 May 2006, the police forcibly stole many of Haw's protest signs. Perhaps what parliament really objected to was Haw's hard-hitting poster highlighting the fact that MPs had spent an astonishing 700 hours debating foxhunting and only seven hours on whether to invade Iraq. Haw's example of cultural power was celebrated by Mark Wallinger's installation *State Britain*, located exactly on parliament's protest exclusion line going through Tate Britain. The unmasking of Westminster parliamentary democracy as a sham was also illustrated by Maya Evans, the courageous woman who was arrested by the police whilst standing by the Cenotaph reading out the names of the ninety-seven British soldiers killed in Iraq up to October 2005. Maya Evans was prosecuted – receiving a twelve-month conditional discharge and being ordered to pay £100 costs – under Section 132 of the Serious Organized Crime and Police Act, which prohibits 'unauthorized demonstrations' near parliament. Government was afraid because she exposed their hypocrisy; her truth undermined their shamocratic power. A friend brought up in East Germany commented that 'This kind of repression is all too familiar from my childhood!'

Cultural power can trump both the power of the state and that of the market. Consider the opposition of the Blair and Brown governments to a *real* open inquiry into the process and decisions leading up to the 2003 Iraq War. They do not want the real story of how British parliamentary democracy works and doesn't work to come out. Such an inquiry would threaten their power and unmask the massive democratic deficit behind the cosy Big Ben 'mother of parliaments' public image. Such an inquiry might expose the parliamentary monarchy, where a majority of just one MP can guarantee the executive government the power of 'the king in parliament'.

So because the truth really matters, both government and corporations employ skilled spin doctors to spin 'good' stories like spiders. These are the favourable stories that they want people to hear, not necessarily the story of what really happened. Occasionally, the cynicism of spin doctors comes out. Jo Moore, the spin doctor advising Steven Byers, Secretary of State for Trade and Industry, sent a memo on 11 September 2001 saying that this was 'now a very good day to get out anything we want to bury'.

Culture is like the water we swim in, and, like fish, we normally don't notice this taken-for-granted world of perception, language and meaning. Culture is crucial as it offers the space for creating identity and meaning, for clarifying the values, ideals, principles and norms we live by. Our culture-given identity informs our thinking, feeling and willing – our values. Culture is the wellspring that helps shape human behaviour. Losing meaning puts us in a vacuum. Finding meaning is liberating, energising and sustaining. It follows that if you control the sources of meaning, you can control society, which is one reason why the US Founding Fathers didn't want a state religion. So human beings are meaning makers. We want to feel that our lives are meaningful.

The free exercise of cultural power can have impressive results. For example, the WTO's secret Multilateral Agreement on Investment, which would have enabled companies to sue states for losses, and even potential losses, from the application of national environmental, social and labour laws to their products, was defeated by a global swarm of opposing CSOs in 1998. They exposed what political and corporate leaders were secretly signing up to 'in our name'. This is the Dracula principle of cultural power – as soon as a secret deal is exposed to the fresh air, it withers. British MPs' secret expenses system collapsed in May 2009 when claims such as those for Douglas Hogg's moat, David Cameron's wisteria pruning and Elliot Morley's £16,000 claim for interest payments on a mortgage that had already been paid off surfaced.

Renaming GM food as 'Frankenstein food' is an example of the ability of cultural power to reframe issues and thus create big value shifts. The consumer boycott of GM food in Europe resulted in supermarket bans on 'Frankenstein foods'. People are now remaking old clothes into beautiful bespoke garments, rather than buying new – a shift from consumerism to making, from fashion to trashion.

Cultural power is exercised in the political system through voting, lobbying, discussion, debating, advocacy and demonstrating. Cultural power confers or withholds legitimacy, which goes along with positive meaning, an ethical approach and getting a good press. In the economy, cultural power is expressed through buying or not buying a product and in investment choices.

There are many outcomes of corporate cultural dominance. One lethal outcome is what psychologist Oliver James calls 'affluenza'. Physically unfit, competitive, isolated individuals under the influence of 'wild capitalism' are depressed, unhappy and unable to find meaning in the consumer malls and corporate life and work ways. People with the affluenza virus keep comparing themselves negatively with others. They place a high value on money, possessions, fame and image when they already have enough income to meet their basic needs. According to James, needy, unhappy people make greedy consumers and competitive workaholics. Affluenza is most virulent in Britain and the US, wherever Selfish Capitalism has been thoroughly implemented. British children are obvious casualties of affluenza. They came bottom of the 2006 UNESCO happiness and wellbeing survey.

A second outcome of the corporate dominance of culture is that scientific research about the seriousness of global warming has been systematically trashed by oil companies such as Exxon Mobil and in misleading documentaries like Channel 4's *The Great Global Warming Swindle*. Consequently, up to 60 per cent of British people are still sceptical. Just imagine if the corporate media had given the same coverage to global warming or child poverty as to MPs' expenses!

A further outcome is that even though there is more research than ever about what makes for healthy lifestyles, this is not getting through to people. The research is blocked by the vested interests in government, the health professions and in the food corporations. For example, even though there is an epidemic of obesity, it is hard – even with good eyesight – to read the 8-point small print on processed food packaging and to spot the presence of corn sugar, which is hard to digest and just accumulates as fat in the body.

I mean by culture all the activities that enable people to develop their potential, to maintain their health, wellbeing, and sense of meaning. *The argument is that the freer and more independent from political and/or corporate control they are, the more vibrant our schools, arts, sports, science and health will be.* The more political and commercial control there is, the more the media are likely to become mere propaganda or advertising outlets. The more concentrated the media ownership, the less diversity of culture and the fewer voices. The more the process and content of children's education is state-determined, the less creative the teachers, students, parents, schools and communities will be. The more health professionals are constrained by industrialised, incentivised, target-driven medical systems, the less real health they can deliver. The freer scientists, artists, teachers, health workers and journalists are to compete with themselves, or together with others, for excellence, the more good work they will do. The more you trust creative cultural workers to do productive work, the more they will deliver. Of course, there are always negative examples where these guidelines do not hold, but on the whole people do good work when given the chance and the conditions are right.

For example, Jesse Owens won several gold athletics medals at the 1936 Berlin Olympics under Hitler's Aryan nose. When asked if he was competing against the Germans, he said, 'No, I was competing against Jesse Owens!' So whether you are a health worker, artist, teacher or journalist, the nature of your creative cultural work normally means that you will try to do your best and, if anything, over-work or over-prepare so as to exceed expectations and better serve the client. Creative cultural work is about the giving of yourself, serving others, making a difference and walking an extra mile. Even though you get paid for the results of your work, the pay may not truly compensate for the creative effort involved. This is of course one reason why the dedicated, giving work of cultural workers such as nurses can unfortunately be so much taken for granted and exploited. Some employers even cynically say that because people like their work, and make a creative contribution, this can be seen as a compensation for less pay. Such attitudes kill the goose that lays such golden eggs.

Community leaders know that culture really matters when trying to regenerate a run-down area or city. They know that economic, social and political regeneration follows from cultural renewal. They agree intuitively with the artist Joseph Beuys that culture is really capital, intelligence or the creative human spirit. That is why activities like community arts projects, festivals, arts centres, innovative schools, sparky libraries, literacy programmes, sports facilities, arts for children, local food celebrations, a vibrant university, a dynamic research centre, affordable workspace for artists and musical events can inspire cultural, social and economic regeneration. A creative, exciting school, for example, will inspire students to make the most of their talents, widen horizons, attract lively families, spark the development of small businesses, start regenerating local neighbourhoods and raise the community spirit.

The leading, creative role of culture is as old as democracy. In fifth-century-bce Athens, political leaders like Pericles knew that the provision of theatres, arts and

---

Box 6.1   *Mission Musica and the power of culture*

José Antonio Abreu, aged sixty-eight, is an economist and inspired musician who started giving music lessons to some poor children thirty years ago. He says the purpose is to help 'the fight of a poor and abandoned child against everything that opposes his full realisation as a human being'. Mission Musica spread throughout Venezuela, across the barrios of Caracas and other cities, attracting thousands of children with parents who say music as a way out of poverty. With current arts funding of £15 million it reaches 285,000 children, and with more funding will reach 1 million poor children.

When Mission Musica's leading orchestra, the Simón Bolívar Youth Orchestra, performed at a Prom concert at the Royal Albert Hall, on 19 August 2007, it got rapturous reviews. Gustavo Dudamel, a graduate of the programme, is now conductor of the Los Angeles Philharmonic.[4] Mission Musica is now being piloted in Scotland.

---

a beautiful environment was vital for individual health, meaning, wellbeing and growth. A positive creative cultural context led to active citizenship and productive work. St Ives, Cornwall, had a big creative boost in the 1990s when local artists successfully helped found the Tate St Ives, now a world-class gallery and arts magnet that has in turn led to the transformation of the Leach Pottery and more recently the restoration of the Porthmeor fishermen's lofts. In Stroud, which was in the mid-1990s a run-down former mill town, a range of cultural activities and facilities was developed such as another art college, festivals, Artspace, open studios and a performing arts centre with many courses for children. This helped stir up a creative vortex, which in turn drew in more creative arts, business and culturally active people, leading to a virtuous circle of innovation, civil society vibrancy and business development. Ruskin Mill College has pioneered the therapeutic education of maladjusted teenagers aged sixteen to nineteen, inspired by John Ruskin's motto, 'There is no wealth but life.' The Nailsworth and Stroud Valleys campus builds on the arts and crafts movement and the local textile heritage – powerfully resonating with the spirit and heritage of the locality.

What blocks the freeing of cultural space?

So, given the inherent, dynamic power of culture, what blocks the freeing of cultural space? Why have we not asserted free cultural power more than we have? These are big questions, but here are some answers.

1.   In spite of this being the most creative time in history, paradoxically, the dynamic power of the cultural system to generate a succession of social movements in the twentieth and twenty-first centuries has gone largely unrecognised. This is partly due to the corporate and state mass media not making the connections. It

was below their radar. For example the strength of the European peace and human rights movements of the 1980s, which opposed both US cruise missiles being based at USAF bases like Greenham and Russian SS20 missiles, helped Gorbachov stop the nuclear arms stand-off. He recognised the value changes brought about by emerging civil society in East and West.

2.   The dominant materialist ideologies, such as Marxism, consumerism and neo-economic liberalism play down the dynamic role of the individual creative human spirit and of original culture. These ideologies hold that culture reflects only economics and politics, rather than being an innovative power in its own right.

3.   Cultural activities and institutions such as education and health have come to be dominated by government and or business, 'because they can'. Traditional boundaries between education and the state, for example, have been eroded in Britain, with relatively little opposition, except in Wales and Scotland. Many people are so used to this that they cannot imagine free, self-standing, viable cultural activities, such as the 1930s Peckham Health Experiment in south London. This was based on a social, holistic approach to community health. The Blackthorn Trust at Barming, Maidstone, in Kent, is a dynamic contemporary example of a transformative general health practice.[5]

4.   Because government and business elites know full well the power of culture, they are all the more conscious of the need to control, co-opt and channel culture for their own ends rather than allow cultural freedom. So science can be bought; the Arts Councils will favour official and commercially fashionable art; there is a sanitised 'national curriculum' in schools that favours ICT rather than art; health services are strictly limited by the profitable orthodoxies; governments allow companies to capture life through patenting life; intellectual property is redefined for corporate gain; drug companies influence drug prescription by rigging research, bribing doctors and seducing consumers; childhood is commercialised; and schools are opened up to business.

5.   The concentration of media in fewer and fewer corporate hands and increasing cross-media ownership of the different media channels of television, radio, books, magazines, films and the electronic media results in limiting diversity.

6.   The value, time and energy given to creative cultural and civic life has eroded, as opposed, say, to television and the electronic media. A 2009 survey found that most seven-year-olds spent around six hours a day using computer games, the Internet and television. As a comparison, consider that indigenous Australian peoples once spent around twelve hours a week on subsistence – what we might call economic – activities. The rest of their time was spent on social life and on spiritual/cultural practices. Or consider the ancient ethical value of giving a tenth or tithe of your time to the community.

7.   The ignoring of civil society and social movements by the corporate media. Paul Hawken describes how the global rise of millions of active people and CSOs happened below the radar of corporate media and the government. When there was reporting, it tended to be negative coverage of more newsworthy violent highlights rather than what was really happening. For example, when a rainbow of

CSOs came to Seattle in November 1999 to challenge the WTO, the corporate media reported on political leaders like Prime Minister Blair, who said: 'People who indulge in the protests are completely misguided. World trade is good for people's jobs and people's living standards. These protests are a complete outrage.'

8.   The corporate media largely ignored the serious, well-argued, thoroughly researched and documented concerns about social justice, human rights, jobs and the environment put forward by CSOs at Seattle. The reason many people may still say they don't know what the 'anti- globalisers' actually want is the lack of coverage by the corporate media of what the real alternatives are. The 2007–9 global financial meltdown saw the media invite a narrow range of neo-liberal and mainstream academics, journalists and think-tank policy wonks to comment. Those outside 'the mainstream', with different perspectives, were seldom invited.

Many politicians and corporate leaders do not want people to wake up to the impact of cultural power, preferring to publicise state and corporate power. So Stalin dismissed the pope by asking, 'How many battalions does the pope command?' Margaret Thatcher claimed that Gorbachov called off the arms race at the end of the 1980s because the West had won, rather than acknowledging how the peace and human rights movements had influenced Gorbachov. Guns, law enforcement or cash can seem more powerful than soft cultural forms of power, such as Shelley claiming that, 'Poets are the unacknowledged legislators of the world.'

9.   Until recently, culture in the form of traditional religion and morality was strong enough to stand up to the state and the market. People understood that the religious, moral sphere was healthily independent from the state and the market. Similarly, education, medicine, the arts and science were free, beyond the reach of the market. This cultural independence has been weakened over the last thirty years of relentless marketisation and increased state control.

10. Finally, like the water fish swim in, so culture – the way we see things, all the things we take for granted – can easily be overlooked. But with reflexivity and deepening self-awareness, people are more and more culturally aware, as well as politically and economically aware. People exercising their cultural power in a series of life-changing social movements are expressing this practically.

Cultural power and the waves of social movements[6]

Successive waves of social movements have exerted significant cultural power for change over the last century. The waves are getting both stronger and more frequent as more people want to make a difference. A rainbow of social movements participated in the 1999 Battle of Seattle, where a coalition of CSOs, trades unions, environmentalists, human rights workers, churches and others came from all over the world. The 2003 anti-Iraq War demonstrations were a massive global civil society mobilisation.

Historically, there has been a series of unfolding, interconnected social movements. Here are a few:

- *The women's suffrage movement*, which worked towards everyone, not just women, getting the vote.

- *Successive women's movements,* including the 1920s home economics movement, the 1960s women's liberation movement, the equal opportunities movement and now the diversity movement.
- *The anti-war, peace and non violent change movements,* including Gandhi's peaceful resistance to the British Empire in India, CND, the anti-Vietnam and Iraq War protests, the gaining of the right to conscientious objection to military service and peace taxes.
- *The personal growth movement,* expressed through humanistic and transpersonal psychology and resulting in many ways of realising personal potential through psychotherapy, adult education, the arts, sciences, bodywork, holistic health, holistic sports and non-denominational spirituality. This personal development movement – when it links personal to social change – has been a foundation for a global, powerful current for renewing society. Nicanor Perlas told me that a researcher had found that all his forty or so fellow winners of the Right Livelihood Awards were inspired by significant spiritual practices.
- *The environmental movement* developed from the 1960s, reaching prominence in the 1980s. It is now a massive global movement of CSOs and millions of people concerned about green issues of environmental, cultural and economic sustainability. Its power grows with the rising challenges of global warming, peak oil and the need to take care of the planet. In Britain membership of environmental organisations dwarfs membership of the declining political parties.
- *The civil rights movements,* starting with the 1944 San Francisco Universal Declaration of Human Rights and embracing Martin Luther King in the 1960s and the South African Anti-Apartheid movement. With the signing into British law of the European Convention on Human Rights, British judges can now exercise countervailing power to check the government and undermine legislation that goes against the HRA. An example of this is the ruling in July 2008 that the torture and killing of the Iraqi hotel worker Baha Mousa by British soldiers was an abuse of his human rights. His family was awarded £2.6 million compensation. The Ministry of Defence has now to exercise a thoroughgoing duty of care under the HRA for soldiers, as families have brought cases against them for poor aircraft maintenance resulting in deaths, or for contributing to the death of a soldier serving in Iraq from heatstroke.
- *The global movement for democracy,* the 'movement of movements' led by CSOs from around the world using conferences like the World Social Forums. This first started in Porto Allegre in Brazil in 2000 for networking, learning and organising.

But there is a paradox here. Even though civil society movements originate in the cultural life space, which movement speaks for the freedom of the cultural system itself? How can diverse cultural leaders such as scientists, artists, religious leaders, spiritual teachers, educators, health professionals and community activists come together on common ground and assert the development conditions for cultural freedom? Perhaps this will emerge more and more, as CSOs carve out more free cultural space, and cultural organisations see that their aims can better be achieved through a healthy separation from the economic and political sectors.

Denial that the few condition the opinion of the many

This is an uncomfortable subject. It is hard to admit that 'the facts' we think we know, and our opinions, may have been shaped by sophisticated influencing powers beyond our critical, conscious control. How many of us really know what happened on 9/11, in spite of it being so heavily reported? A New York friend said that at first he disbelieved his children when they said that several elite Saudi students at their high school had been flown out of the US on the day after the attack on the Twin Towers. It later came out that in spite of all planes being grounded, special planes had flown Bin Laden family members and elite Saudis out of the US. It took a while to learn that some of the favourable conditions for the terrorist attacks on 9/11 were caused by privatisation and corporate cost-cutting on security, combined with federal government and military incompetence. The airlines had cut costs on security checks and Boston's Logan Airport had poor security systems, with security staff paid minimum wages. The air traffic control system, which was privatised and downsized under Reagan, was unable to track the hijacked planes.

It takes a determined search to check the facts and angle of a news story. It's fine to Google the background information on the Internet, but how do we know this is accurate? Anyone dealing with the press, and taking pains to supply accurate press releases, knows how many of the 'facts' then published are inaccurate, or people misquoted.

This brings us back to the importance of reflexivity – we create the world as we see it. We also reflect on what has happened and what we see. This is why cultural activities such as health, education, the news media, the arts, sciences and religion need to be independent, free of political and economic control. Otherwise they become propaganda or advertising. For example new 'wonder' drugs are often carefully marketed through apparently independent patient groups, which actually get secret drug company funding. The tragic story of a sufferer whose condition would be cured by the new drug is then spun in the media, to bring pressure on the NHS to fund the new wonder cure.

Corporate control of the media: how government allows media concentration

Information is power. Karl Marx would have written *Das Information* not *Das Kapital* if he were living today. Freedom of the press is fine, as long as you own a press, as the old saying goes. When in the early nineteenth century there were many free printing presses in Britain, press freedom worked well. Press freedom is now problematic when there are only six or so global media conglomerates. The purpose of this section is to argue that in spite of a growing wealth of minority news, culture and information sources from the web, indie media, small presses, specialist periodicals, radio and television channels, the mainstream media are firmly under either plutocratic, corporate or government control. Consequently, there is a lack of real information, different perspectives and analysis. Which financial journalists systematically warned readers about the risks of saving in Iceland banks well in advance of their collapse? Why did it take so long for the real Enron fraud story to come out? The Queen could have asked financial journalists as well as economists why they didn't spot the credit crunch coming. So why did the corporate media largely not see what was coming?

Firstly, even though a free and independent media has long been seen as essential for healthy economic, political and cultural life, much of our media is compromised by hidden interests, one-sided agendas, exclusion and even propaganda. This is important to recognise, as unless media are free, how can people gain the information they need to be well-informed citizens, productive workers and creative spirits?

James Madison, one of the founding fathers of US democracy, once wrote that, 'A popular government without popular information or the means of acquiring it is but a prologue to a farce or a tragedy; or perhaps both. Knowledge will forever govern ignorance; and a people who mean to be their own governors must arm themselves with the power which knowledge gives.'[7] Yet we saw how the Thatcher and Blair governments relaxed the regulation of the media, so that newspaper ownership was concentrated in ever fewer corporate hands. Media empires now embrace books, magazines, the Internet, radio and television. This matters, as media control enables owners to exercise unchecked cultural and normative power – to influence how we think about and see the world, to set the agenda. 'Reflexivity' means that how we see the world has consequences, as individuals have the power to shape social life according to their perceptions. But reflexivity also means that a few media owners can exercise disproportionate cultural power, and well they know it. So Murdoch's HarperCollins, for example, turned down Chris Patten's book on Hong Kong because it was critical of China. The Chinese government could have threatened Murdoch's Star TV interests. The same power is evident when, as an independent publisher for Steve Biddulph, usually a HarperCollins author, I was pleasantly surprised to get reviews so easily in the *Sun*, *The Times* and the *Sunday Times*. It wasn't a coincidence, as normally any book review is very hard to get.

Politicians know they have to get the media owners on their side to get noticed, elected and to keep power. Hence their reluctance to regulate, to limit the number of newspapers one company can own and to prevent rising levels of cross-media ownership and the concentration of media power. Blair went to court Murdoch in Australia in 1994 in the first year of his leadership of the Labour Party in a key strategic act. According to Lance Price, a media adviser to Tony Blair from 1998 to 2001:

> It's true that Rupert Murdoch doesn't leave a paper trail that could ever prove his influence over policy, but the trail of politicians beating their way to him and his papers tells a different story ... I was told by somebody who would know, that we wouldn't change policy on Europe without talking to him first. The continued support of the *News International* titles was supposed to be

---

Box 6.2   *'We need a rebellion against a press that's damaging our national psyche'*

Polly Toynbee wrote that it was a shame that a Blair speech on the British press left out the root of the problem, the ownership structure that he did nothing to break. 'Had he been brave, he could have restored media ownership rules to pre-Thatcher days. She let Murdoch burn the rulebook to acquire over 40% of national newspaper ownership. She arranged a unique get out clause in EU media law to allow him to launch Sky. Now as he stalks the *Wall Street Journal,* shudders run down American spines at the possibility of the owner of the *New York Post* and the corrosive *Fox News* seizing this business bastion … An eloquent protest against his *Wall Street Journal* bid came from the FT's economics writer, Martin Wolf, "How many even of his admirers would argue that Mr Murdoch for all his successes has created one serious, authoritative and truly independent newspaper?"

'… The newspaper agenda, slavishly followed by the BBC, reflects a profoundly dystopic image of society where nothing works, everything gets worse, public officials are inept, public services fail, tax is wasted, lethal dangers proliferate and everyone conspires to lie about it.'

Source: Polly Toynbee, Guardian, *16 June 2007*

---

self-evident proof of the value of this special relationship … The *Sun* and *The Times,* in particular, received innumerable 'scoops' and favours. In return, New Labour got very favourable coverage from newspapers that are bought and read by classic swing voters – on the face of it, too good a deal to pass up. Rupert Murdoch loves power and loves the feeling that he has the ear of other powerful men.[8]

Price argues that Rupert Murdoch was effectively a member of Blair's cabinet, and that only an employed spin doctor would deny that the media tycoon had a say in major Downing Street decisions.

'Mass producers of distortion'

Nick Davies, an award-winning investigative journalist, thinks that newspapers have become a conduit for propaganda and second-hand news. He writes that 'The mass media generally are no longer a reliable source of information.' A Cardiff University survey he commissioned looking at 2,000 UK news stories from *The Times, Telegraph, Guardian* and *Independent,* found that only 12 per cent of the 'facts' from the stories were from stories wholly researched by the reporters; with 8 per cent of the stories, they were not sure; the other 80 per cent were wholly, mainly or partially constructed from second-hand material

---

Box 6.3   Whose voice?

This is the triumphalist advertisement from News International celebrating the takeover of the *Wall Street Journal*:

'Free people
Free markets
Free thinking
That's what we believe in.
Confronting the issues, pushing the debate, breaking the story,
creating the new format, producing the next blockbuster.
That's what we do.
We make the stuff that excites, entertains, informs, enriches and
infuriates billions of imaginations. We create choice where none
existed. And by doing so, we find a voice for people the world
over …
a global media business made up of 53,000 passionate individuals
with revenues of US $30 billion reaching an audience of nearly one
billion people, every day'[10]

Rupert Murdoch's global $60 billion News International Corporation's
UK subsidiary Newscorp Investments owns *The Times*, the *Sunday Times*,
the *TES*, the *TLS*, the *Sun*, *News of the World*, Sky TV, Fox TV, Harper
Collins, MySpace, Twentieth Century Fox Films, Star TV, the *Australian*
and the *Wall Street Journal* (with the Dow Jones Index). One of the global
conglomerate's aims is to undermine public service broadcasting, such as
the BBC, so as to further increase power and profits. Politicians who seek
to curb his power will not get a good press, as seen in their opposition
to potentially tough new EU regulation. Tighter EU public interest media
regulation is one of the historic reasons the Murdoch press has been so
hostile to the EU.

---

produced by news agencies and PR sources. So only in 12 per cent of the stories
were the 'facts' thoroughly checked. Most journalists are therefore churnalists.
Newspapers, whose 'primary task has been to filter out falsehood, have become
so vulnerable to manipulation that [they are] now involved in the production of
falsehood, distortion and propaganda.'[9]

Noam Chomsky's analysis of the corporate media is presented in his book
Manufacturing Consent. He argues that the media corporations influence Western
electorates by news control and setting a partial news agenda, far more subtly than
clunky Soviet-style censorship. The term 'manufacturing consent' comes from the
journalist Walter Lippman, who said that government in the modern 'democratic'

age needed to step up control of the media in the face of an ever more educated electorate. Chomsky summarises his analysis thus:

> The 'societal' purpose of the media is to inculcate and defend the economic, social and political agenda of privileged groups that dominate domestic society and the state. The media serve this purpose in many ways: through selection of topics, distribution of concerns, framing of issues, filtering of information, emphasis and tone, and by keeping debate within the bounds of acceptable premises.[11]

So media power comes from what is said, what is not said and what gets on to the news agenda. The current status quo is uncritically accepted, and uncomfortable questions about society and the economy are ignored. For example, on the one hand Chancellor Gordon Brown was saying in his Labour leadership campaign that he was a Gandhian and how much he admired Gandhi. Yet he was also campaigning for a replacement for the Trident nuclear system that could cost anything from £30 billion to £70 billion, even though Britain's annual military budget at the time was around £33 billion. But mainstream journalists who may have wanted to confront Brown on such hypocrisy would lose access to government sources of information and become unpopular with their editors, who get 'called in' to Number 10. Brown's 14 May 2009 decision to purchase the costly, wasteful Eurofighter – at a time when front-line soldiers fighting in Afghanistan are poorly equipped and when there are public spending cuts – was largely ignored by the media, concentrating as they were at the time on the MPs' expenses scandal.

Greg Palast maintains that unlike other democratic countries, where there is a real free press, British journalists have to kiss the government whip that lashes them. So they self-censor the stories they write, otherwise they are frozen out. On 17 March 1999, on the orders of the police, an Old Bailey judge ordered Martin Bright of the *Observer* and Roger Alton and Alan Rusbridger, the editors of the *Observer* and the *Guardian* respectively, to hand over their notes on David Shayler, the former MI5 employee, on pain of imprisonment and unlimited fines. They refused. Even though the European Convention on Human Rights says the freedom of the press shall not be restricted, the judge considered that the freedom of the press in this case was subject to 'restrictions and penalties in the interests of national security'. In other words the law stops the government controlling the press, unless the government decides to control it. 'Rarely does government have to brandish the implements of coercion because British news people are bred to a strong sense of the boundaries of public discourse. In this class-poisoned society, elite reporters and editors are lured by the thrill of joining the inner circle of cognoscenti with ministers and titled military men. The cost of admission is gentlemanly circumspection.'[12]

A sophisticated use of the media to manage public perceptions has been employed to secure consent in recent wars. These are the media weapons of mass deception. When on 2 August 1990 Saddam Hussein invaded Kuwait, he had been a loyal US ally for ten years. So the US government used a PR firm, Hill &

Knowlton, to conduct a massive PR campaign to persuade the US public to support the war to reconquer Kuwait. On 10 October 1990 they set up what looked like a congressional hearing on human rights violations where 'witnesses' could give information without taking an oath. Fifteen-year-old Nayirah stole the show. She, it was later revealed, was the daughter of the Kuwaiti ambassador to the US, and had been carefully coached to say what she claimed to have seen with her own eyes in a Kuwait city hospital: 'I volunteered at the al Addan hospital. When I was there, I saw the Iraqi soldiers come into the hospital with guns, and go into the room where ... babies were in incubators. They took the babies out of the incubators, took the incubators, and left the babies on the cold floor to die.' This had happened to hundreds of babies. The story had a massive impact on public opinion and was used by President Bush. However, it took till after the war for the hoax to be uncovered by human rights investigators.[13] This is an example of framing an issue to secure consent to a war.

Rupert Murdoch's newspapers helped sell the 2003 Iraq War. His worldwide network of 140 newspapers, with 40 million copies sold every week, all editorially supported the war. His US *New York Post* named France and Germany as the 'axis of weasel', its front page a doctored colour photograph with weasel heads superimposed on the German and French UN ambassadors. His French newspaper carried a story calling President Chirac a worm, with a large worm bearing Chirac's head. And which newspaper, one may ask, carries headlines on News International's tax record?

Government pressure on BBC freedom

In Britain, it is not only the concentration of media ownership in a handful of corporations that has eroded independent reporting. The New Labour government has been undermining the independence of the BBC, using intense pressure for positive war coverage. BBC news anyway keeps within the Westminster political spectrum. The 2003–4 Hutton inquiry revealed the huge level of pressure put on the BBC by Prime Minister Blair and Alastair Campbell to influence favourable coverage in the lead-up to the Iraq War. Campbell's criticism of BBC coverage started in November 2001, with tough treatment of the stories being covered and statements made by reporters in a letter to Richard Sambrook, director of BBC News. In March 2003 Campbell wrote to the BBC saying that 'the PM has also expressed real concern about some of the reports' and threatening public controversy about them.

The sloppy reporting of the 'sexed-up' September 2002 Iraq dossier by Andrew Gilligan on the *Today* programme on 29 May 2003 gave Campbell the opportunity to attack the BBC about accuracy. Many people had noticed, despite what Campbell said, that in the run-up to the war, BBC news was noticeably *less* critical of the government than, say, ITN or Sky News. In the US, there had already been a great deal of sceptical news reporting about US and British government claims for Saddam having WMD. So Gilligan's 'sexed-up' charge may have been generally correct, though specifically inaccurate. And, crucially, if it was a mistake to broadcast Gilligan's report, then one cost of a free press is that it occasionally makes reporting mistakes.[14]

So, following the argument of this book, that the BBC should be much more independent of government control if it is to offer free and independent reporting as a public service, some key questions to ask include:

- What is the correct position of a government when it disagrees with news reporting? Bullying and pressure behind the scenes or open debate and respecting boundaries?
- How can real BBC editorial independence be strengthened?
- How can the BBC become free of government control of content?
- How can BBC governance include both representation from and participation by licence payers and other stakeholders such as staff, in voting for BBC Governors so as to balance government nominees with civil society and consumer members?

With the BBC Britain has had for over eighty years a public broadcasting service that is respected for news accuracy, cultural innovation and critical commentary. It has been sufficiently free from government to offer occasional hard-hitting investigative reporting and protected enough from commercialism to offer quality programming. It has been a working model for the world. However, the BBC could be even more the envy of the world if it was disestablished from the state as a free, independently constituted public service funded by licence payers with a real voice in governance. After all, licence payers do pay for the service.

The Hutton report was critical of the BBC's handling of the Dr Kelly and Gilligan affair. The BBC chair, Gavin Davies, and the Director General, Greg Dyke, felt they had to resign. They could have challenged the government to a public debate about the independence of the BBC and stayed on with support from civil society, listeners, viewers and BBC staff. In the end, they gave in. The opportunity for a historic reframing moment to further establish the independence of the BBC was missed.

But by fighting Alastair Campbell with his macho methods, Dyke and Davies lost the initiative. The *Guardian* quotes a senior BBC reporter: 'These men seem to have got into a huddle, saying we're going to fight this in a macho, arrogant, and narcissistic way. They have behaved like fighting cocks, spurred on to compete with Alastair Campbell ... They didn't sit down as rigorous people should, and go through the Gilligan report with a fine tooth comb.'[15] So crucially when the British public needed the BBC to critically scrutinise and report accurately on Blair's war, visionary leadership was lacking.

Onora O'Neill, in her 2002 BBC Reith Lectures, pointed out the inherent contradiction of the media corporations, who champion transparency, accuracy and accountability, being themselves unaccountable. She considered that freedom of the press was all very well when there was a plurality of printing presses in the early nineteenth century. But, she asks, what of press freedom when there are global media conglomerates broadcasting across frontiers, using electronic media, where states have limited regulatory powers? How can free speech be protected against state power and corporate media power? Like Chomsky, she is concerned that powerful media companies can dominate communications and the public mind,

> ### Box 6.4   *'Captured: a laddish, thuggish, snapshot of power'*
>
> Julian Glover summarised the *Alastair Campbell Diaries* as: 'How me and Tony stuffed the media and changed the world.' The book 'captures strikingly the laddish, hungry, boastful side of New Labour, a thuggish competition to acquire and use power. The details are realistic and for the most part depressing ... He loves power and the men who hold it ... He revels in brutality: he wants to "kill Gilligan" and suggests in a note passed across the Cabinet table that Blair shoots Short [i.e. Clare Short, Secretary of State for International Development] in the same way as Saddam shot his health minister. He offers to "get a gun". Blair's joking reply: "Yes." And he hates the media. His contempt for political journalists is absolute: even in 1997 he records, "I was sick of dealing with wankers."
>
> The obsession blinds him at times – he regards news that the dodgy dossier on Iraq weapons was copied off the Internet as just "another spin story". He missed completely the harm it did to his boss and trust in politics ... Meanwhile, Britain went to war.'
>
> *Source: Julian Glover,* Guardian, *10 July 2007*
>
> No wonder ex-Chief Justice Bingham used the term 'world vigilante' to describe the Blair government's handling of the Iraq War.

limiting the opportunities for individual debate and thus constraining individual free speech.[16]

So media freedom needs rethinking in a time of media market failure to deliver a plurality of voices. Corporate media ownership needs limiting, cross-media ownership needs breaking up, editors and journalists need to state their interests. The media conglomerates also need to pay their fair share of taxes. For example, News International is able to largely avoid taxes in the UK by clever accounting, switching profits and costs around the world. We have the hypocrisy of papers like the *Telegraph* chasing MPs on expenses, tax dodgers or social security scroungers whilst themselves being located offshore.

But what practical ways are there to develop a free press in Britain? One way is to follow the lead of the *Guardian*, which is owned for public benefit by the Scott Trust. Profits from the Guardian Media Groups are reinvested in improving news services such as the Guardian Unlimited website, now a global cultural resource. Another is to follow William Gladstone, who saw taxing culture such as books and newspapers as a tax on knowledge. So government could decide whether a media organ is primarily commercial/private interest or primarily public interest and choose to tax the commercial media, and not tax the public interest, independent media, just as books are not taxed as Gladstone opposed taxes on knowledge. The tax and membership revenues could then be used to fund an independent, public-interest Press Service supporting a range of newspapers, Internet services and magazines.

The BBC itself can be strengthened by further detaching itself from the government through independent editorial, informed by stronger public interest guidelines, and also with, say, one-third of the governors elected by licence payers to represent listeners and viewers. Of course the Internet already offers many opportunities for independent publishing, for example the Open Democracy website, which is funded by member contributions.

NHS plc. Privatising the NHS: from health as a right to health as a commodity

Governments have privatised the NHS by stealth since 1979. Health is now not so much a right but becoming more a commodity to be bought, as in pre-1948 days. Dentistry is one example, with affordable, accessible NHS dentistry all but disappearing. The original NHS was a remarkable success, based on the values of universality, comprehensiveness and equality. It gave value for money, because it was integrated, well planned and had a workforce committed to a public service ethos of care. The philosophy of promoting public health from prevention to cure and of free health as a right was basic. The elimination of market mechanisms meant that the NHS was very economical to run, with lean administration and management

However, the NHS came under pressure in the late 1970s, with chronic under-funding and relentless attacks from the 'new right', which wanted to roll back the boundaries of the NHS and open up new markets for the private health businesses. In 1980 the NHS spent £555 per head on health at a time when the EU average was £837 and the US £1,553. But private health companies wanted to get into publicly funded health care. This opportunity was provided by the Conservative government in 1991 with the introduction of the internal market as a simplistic, but expensive, magic cure-all bullet. New Labour, after criticising the internal market in opposition, then reintroduced it in government. According to Professor Allyson Pollock:

> The NHS, after serving as a model for comprehensive and universal health care, was now to become a laboratory for market mechanisms – mechanisms that would in turn be exported across the other welfare states of Europe … Belief in the superior efficiency of the private sector became the new shibboleth. The costs – in terms of a progressive loss of comprehensiveness, universality and equity, as well as in terms of money – were brushed aside. The Labour Party, which had created the NHS, became dedicated to its destruction.[17]

Labour opposed both PFI hospitals and privatisation through the internal health market when in opposition. Harriet Harman, a social security minister, said in 1997 that PFI was a 'Trojan horse for privatisation'. But Alan Milburn, Health Minister from 1999 to 2003 and later a private health care business consultant, initiated what he called the largest hospital-building programme in the world using PFI. This resulted in cuts in clinical budgets, the reduction of hospital beds and greatly increased costs. Under PFI, the government makes an agreement with a consortium of banks, health service operators and builders, which raises the money for building and running a hospital for thirty years with guaranteed profits.

PFI hospitals are much more expensive than NHS and government-built hospitals, as the private sector cannot borrow money as cheaply as government. Secondly, the PFI scheme must generate profits for private investors. Thirdly, it costs a lot to service the bureaucracies needed to run the PFI contract. The new Dartford and Gravesend PFI Hospital cost £94 million to build, but this escalated to £115 million when extra fees and financing costs were added. At Gravesend, the cost of servicing capital rose from 6 per cent of revenue budget to 32 per cent. This was offset by sales of public assets, Treasury support, cuts in beds, salaries, staff and levels of service. PFI is the cuckoo in the NHS nest.

New Labour, instead of reaffirming the founding NHS values of comprehensiveness, universality and equality, implemented a series of piecemeal market solutions. These were designed as destabilising entry points for private companies to gain a profitable foothold. The NHS became fragmented, in danger of losing its public health and overall planning focus. There were revolving doors between Labour policy makers and the private health sector. For example in May 2004 Blair's senior health policy adviser, Simon Stevens, left to become European president of United Health Group, an American HMO, and his place was taken by Julian Le Grand, a private health marketeer, management consultant and academic.

Up and down Britain, local communities had to demonstrate to protect essential health services such as Accident and Emergency or Maternity from the cuts needed to fund the government's privatisation programme. Ever more amounts of money were being spent on health, yet because of the huge extra amounts of money being spent on health privatisation, paradoxically there were service cuts.

One important reason for NHS privatisation was the fact that the government wanted British health companies to capitalise on emerging world markets for health care as state health provision was rolled back. Under the General Agreement on Trade in Services (GATS) within the World Trade Organization, the market for public services was being opened up worldwide. Few ordinary people knew about such secret negotiations, which were driven by investors who wanted low risk government-guaranteed profits from running public services. In 1995, when the GATS agreement was signed, only 27 per cent of GATS members opened their countries' health services to market competition. However, if some services were already supplied on a commercial basis, or in competition with other service providers, the right to exempt public services did not apply. With the privatisation of optics, dentistry, long-term care of the elderly, PFI and commissioning treatment from private hospitals, Blair and Brown opened up Britain for GATS privatisation for turning health into a commodity. They called it 'modernisation' and 'reform'.

New Labour gave enthusiastic backing to the list of public services put forward by the EU for privatisation, a list that included energy, sewerage, telecommunications, the post and financial services.[18] So the British government has been secretly rewriting the rules of public ownership in favour of the private sector. Government ministers like Lord Mandelson then hypocritically blame the EU when they 'have to' close post offices. By translating the WTO/GATS rules into British law, we no longer have sovereignty over health, education and social welfare. These are being redefined as economic services subject to international competition policy, rather than not-for-private-profit, cultural, public services that were protected from the market.

This is what Tony Blair really meant when he talked repeatedly about modernising public services. He meant rolling back the boundaries of the state, with the state's role being limited to funding a variety of fragmented, privately delivered health services, known collectively as NHS plc. This why in Stroud, we had to demonstrate vigorously to save our maternity unit, because the money was needed to fund PFI projects. And according to Allyson Pollock, the hospital operating budget cuts to fund extra PFI costs are the real reason NHS hospital cleaning and catering budgets have been cut, with the possible consequence of rising levels of lethal infections from super-bugs.

But just how has New Labour managed to privatise so much of the NHS without the public understanding what is happening, and without much opposition from the Labour Party and health care staff? Allyson Pollock asks, 'How was it able to convince so many people that it was still committed to comprehensive, universal and equal-access healthcare, when its policies were clearly running in the opposite direction?'[19]

New Labour used its PR skills to influence the national media, and activated the private health care industry, pro-health market think tanks, lawyers, academics and management consultants to pursue its privatisation agenda. These people stood to gain. For example the New Health Network had backing from Superdrug, the private health company Westminster Health Care and from consultants KPMG. The chair was Claire Perry, former CEO of Bromley Health Authority, who had driven through the intensely opposed PFI for Bromley Hospital.[20]

New Labour used the following ways to undermine public confidence in the NHS and introduce privatisation.

- Firstly, criticise and denigrate existing NHS services. After years of under-funding and twenty years of piecemeal privatisation and political centralisation, government spinners labelled the NHS negatively as a '1940s NHS', as a Stalinist, bureaucratic state monolith. Misinformation was fed to uncritical journalists, some of whom were co-opted on to pro-market interest groups. Hard evidence was not presented to back up the anti-NHS spin. Complex questions were reduced to slogans. The fact that the NHS was being shrunk was denied.
- Secondly, the claimed superior benefits of private health services in other countries such as the USA were well publicised. The research evidence and the downside were ignored, such as the fact that the USA demonstrated just what happens when health is left to the free market. There are at least 47 million Americans who are not able to get affordable health insurance and many are driven to bankruptcy by health costs.
- Thirdly, New Labour aggravated public concerns using the 'moral panic' scare technique about the NHS by highlighting problems. The *Daily Mail* does such outrage really well. The league table and star ratings systems were purportedly introduced so that patients could choose the hospital where they would have treatment. In reality, most people wanted their local hospital to be a good one, and the ratings themselves were statistically invalid.

- Fourthly, internal critics were muzzled. If they did raise concerns, they were punished, excluded and censured. So critics of PFI were threatened, as were critics of hospital closure. People critical of the private business health model were not selected for leadership jobs or for funding.
- Fifthly, scientific research evidence was discredited and undermined when it suited New Labour by a rapid rebuttal unit, which was set up in the Department of Health press office. In 1999, the editor of the *British Medical Journal* published an editorial entitled 'Perfidious Financial Idiocy' to accompany a series of four PFI articles. A week later, Prime Minister Blair made a hostile speech about PFI critics when he laid the cornerstone of the new Greenwich PFI Hospital. The Department of Health press office thereafter issued press releases rubbishing any article critical of PFIs, but without any hard evidence to back the spin. As a result of the four *BMJ* articles, Colin Reeves, director of finance at the NHS Executive, wrote a rebuttal letter, but failed to write a publishable article when invited by the *BMJ*.[21]
- Finally, government health critics are systematically discredited and intimidated as a way of silencing the source of scientific evidence. Allyson Pollock describes how, as a special adviser to the first House of Commons Health Select Committee inquiry into PFI, she was taken aside by the head of the Department of Health's PFI Unit, Peter Coates, 'to ask me whether it was wise or in my career interests to brief MPs against senior NHS officials'.[22] The eventual report – hiding behind parliamentary privilege – endorsed PFI and accused PFI critics of a 'lack of sound analysis' and 'antagonistic extreme views' without any evidence to back its views.

To conclude, NHS plc has replaced the original vision of the NHS as provider of the right to free health. New Labour are pushing back the boundaries of a health service in the form of an independently delivered NHS guaranteed by the state in favour of a piecemeal private health care market which is progressively captured by profit-making health companies. The founders of the NHS saw clearly that health was a right, not a commodity, and that the NHS had to be free within funding limits to give the best health care. So under successive governments, health has ceased to be a semi-autonomous public service and has become commercialised. And the government, via the WTO and GATS, aims to make sure that publicly funded and delivered health services become marketised in Britain and globally through the force of international law.

The commercialisation of childhood: turning children into commodities

The commercialisation of childhood is a major cause of toxic childhood. The government, through lax laws and poor regulation, and business, through relentless advertising, have worked together to commercialise childhood. But in most societies, childhood and family life is a protected cultural life space. Sweden bans television advertising to children of twelve and under in a family-friendly culture. In sharp contrast to Sweden, where children's right to a free childhood is respected, in Britain, marketeers have turned children into commodities.

This has been a disaster for children, with rising levels of obesity, learning diffi-culties, inequality, poverty and relatively poor physical and mental health. In 2006, Britain's children came bottom of the UNESCO advanced industrial coun-tries wellbeing survey.

On the one hand, the government brings in good programmes like Sure Start to help young children and parents, yet on the other allows junk food adver-tising, rising levels of social inequality and a shortage of decent, affordable homes. The poorest people in Sweden have better health outcomes, such as less infant mortality, than the richest in Britain. One factor is that childhood in Sweden is still slow, whereas in Britain it is on 'fast forward', unless families take extra care in protecting their children from relentless commercialism.[23]

How has the cultural space for childhood been commercialised?

The British children's market is worth at least £30 billion a year and influences how children learn and play and what they eat. Advertising shapes children's self-image and how they see the world, and exerts an influence as well on values, health and attitudes. The average child may see between 10,000 and 20,000 televi-sion advertisements a year, with films containing many product placements and ubiquitous endorsements by television characters like the Tweenies. The Internet is used by marketeers to sell junk food through social networking, competitions, chat rooms to arouse pester power and brand loyalties. It is not possible to get away from the advertisements in public spaces, on clothing, bags, shops or public transport. Marketeers use the 'cool factor' to get children to spread the word virally, exploiting children's vulnerabilities and the fact that under-sevens find it hard to assess persuasive intent. [24]

All this has damaging results: for example, low levels of wellbeing, anxiety, stress, poor relationships, dissatisfaction and mental health problems. Children grow up too soon, but development suffers, with for example language difficulties or an imagination limited by commercial toys rather than being liberated by free play. Junk food advertising on television costs £480 million annually, yet the UK has the highest level of child obesity in Europe with 35 per cent of boys and 45 per cent of girls being overweight or obese. Parents are asked to collect £250,000 worth of Tesco vouchers for a computer priced at £1,000, and children were offered a basketball costing £71 if they ate 170 chocolate bars. Companies that want to brand children for life target schools and families.

So, just who is bringing up children – parents, family, the community and teachers? Or a highly paid marketing profession of psychologists, marketeers and branding experts who spend billions to target our children for profit and unleash pester power on parents in the process? Why are the marketeers toler-ated? The reason that marketeers target children is 'because they can', and because the corporate media have captured the government on this issue. Tessa Jowell, when Minister for Culture, once said that commercials couldn't be banned, because how otherwise could children's television programmes be paid for?

One solution is to ban advertising directed at children under twelve so as to reclaim free cultural space. Research shows that marketeers will get around any partial regulations controlling advertising to children. Furthermore, even tight regulation does not work, except perhaps as gesture politics. So the simplest way to stop companies profiting from exploiting children would be a ban on *all* forms of advertising directed at children below twelve. This ban would improve children's wellbeing and stop advertisers manipulating families through pester power. It would show that children's health comes before company profits.

Childhood can be decommercialised through re-establishing the boundary around childhood as a free, protected cultural space. There should be a wall between children and commercialism. There needs to be ban on all forms of advertising directed at children as a way of reclaiming childhood for children and of respecting the right to a childhood.[25] It would be one of the most significant, and most welcome, child welfare measures the government could take.

Buying science

Buying favourable scientific research is a violation of boundaries where commercial interests corrupt independent scientific enquiry. It is vital to know who funded a particular piece of scientific research, and whether or not the results favoured the funder's interests. There are cross-cutting ties and revolving doors between government, business and universities that may be untransparent. This system was portrayed vividly in John Le Carré's novel, now a film, *The Constant Gardener*. Sometimes, the contradictions are farcical, such as British American Tobacco sponsoring the University of Nottingham Chair of Corporate Social Responsibility. Readers will recall examples of their own about industry-influenced science and where government bodies have failed to stand up for independence. Here are two examples, one concerned with the effects of food additives on children, and the other about how Dr Pusztai's research into GM potatoes was ditched.

The links between hyperactivity in children and food additives have been known about for over thirty years by parents, health professionals and educators. Parents and teachers have long seen dramatic changes in children's behaviour when they stopped having food and soft drinks containing such additives as sodium benzoate or tartrazine. Yet the Food Standards Agency has moved only reluctantly to look at the issue. When it received the Isle of Wight study by the University of Southampton, which showed that significant improvements in children's behaviour resulted from removing colourings and additives such as sodium benzoate from diets, the FSA did not act, except to delay by asking for more research. Even in the face of the September 2007 research results, the FSA still did not ban the additives.

So why is the FSA so slow to protect children's health and wellbeing? Has it been 'bought'? The global additives market is worth £12.4 billion a year and rising. And why is the government, so apparently keen on improving children's health, so slow to act on additives? And why did it take so long to fund and carry out the research? Could it be that research that suits corporate interests gets funded and challenging research does not get done?[26] Whose interests is the FSA representing – those of

---

**Box 6.5   What took the Food Standards Agency
so long not to ban additives?**

Links between Hyperactive Children and Food Additives

A study by researchers at the University of Southampton has shown
evidence of increased levels of hyperactivity in young children consuming
mixtures of some artificial food colours and the preservative sodium
benzoate.

The possibility of food colours and preservatives affecting children's
behaviour has long been an unresolved question for parents. This significant new research by a team from the University of Southampton's
Schools of Psychology and Medicine provides a clear demonstration that
changes in behaviour can be detected in three-year-old and eight-year-
old children

Professor of Psychology, Jim Stevenson, who led the research, comments:
"We now have clear evidence that mixtures of certain food colours and
benzoate preservative can adversely influence the behaviour of children. There is some previous evidence that some children with behavioural disorders could benefit from the removal of certain food colours
from their diet. We have now shown that for a large group of children
in the general population, consumption of certain mixtures of artificial
food colours and benzoate preservative can influence their hyperactive
behaviour."'[27]

---

ordinary people who fund it as a supposedly independent government body or
those of the food industry, government officials who have been influenced by
commercial interests and researchers wanting future corporate funding?

Corporations buy science and favourable regulation through both funding
research, directly or indirectly, and through funding political parties. The big
drug firms, such as Pfizer, GlaxoSmithKline, Astra Zeneca, Novartis and Aventis,
reach the heart of government in order to get favourable patents on drugs, even
though these have often been developed with public money in the first place.
For example in 1998, the US National Institutes of Health spent $1 billion on
drug and vaccine development, and only received $27 million in royalties, even
though HIV drugs they had invented were sold at high prices by big pharma
companies.[28] Former US Secretary of Defense Donald Rumsfeld was on the board
of a corporation that produced the damaging food additive aspartame, found in
NutraSweet.[29]

In Britain, consider Lord Sainsbury, who had a conflict of interest between his
GM company investments and his job as Blair's Science Minister. Whilst the public
were opposed to GM 'Frankenstein foods', scientists were trying to research GM
foods.

When Dr Árpád Pusztai of the Rowett Institute in Scotland was taken off his GM potato research after thirty-three months, the case illustrated many of the conflicts between independent science, government-influenced science and the corporate GM interests. He writes that his research was

> on the potential human/animal health aspects of genetically modified, GM food. It is based on the results of our nutritional, toxicological and immuno-logical studies with rats fed on diets containing two different samples of GM potatoes expressing the gene of the snowdrop bulb ... *What makes this study exceptional is that it was one of the very few studies, which had not been industrially funded but publicly financed by a major grant from the Scottish Office Agriculture, Environment and Fisheries Department (SOAEFD).* [author's italics] A part of these findings had also been published in a peer-reviewed scientific journal. Although our pioneering experimental work was interrupted and stopped after 33 months, the results were serious enough to sound a general warning to the public (who after all financed our project) about the possible health dangers of GM food. This I did in August 1998 in a short (150 sec.) TV interview given with the full consent of the Director of the Institute (Rowett Research Institute, Bucksburn, Aberdeen, Scotland, UK) because our concern became particularly acute with the realisation that whereas the GM potatoes we tested and found to have adverse effects on the metabolism, organ development and the immune system of young, rapidly growing rats had not been approved for human/animal consumption by the regulatory authorities, the British public had been eating GM soya, maize and tomatoes for nearly two years with their full approval even though these had not been as rigorously tested as our GM potatoes.

> As our GM potato nutritional trials were one of the very few independent works carried out to date, it is thought to be instructive to describe the back-ground to the project, the results and conclusions reached and the potential consequences of our studies in some detail, particularly as these can then be used in a more general context about the need for safety testing of GM food-stuffs ...

> In conclusion: our extensive nutritional, developmental and immune studies with GM potatoes expressing the GNA gene have shown that genetic engineering has not only substantially altered their composition but that it has also affected their nutritional value and wholesomeness. Although our study was abruptly terminated and it remains to be established whether its potential implications for human health could be substantiated, the often-heard view that there is no evidence, which indicates the possibility of potential harmful effects of GM food, can no longer be maintained. There is an urgent need for an at least five year but preferably a ten-year moratorium for the inclusion of GM foodstuffs in the human/animal food/feedchain and also the start of a corresponding and intensive research programme to investigate the potential health hazards and the associated risks of GM food for both human and animal

consumers. This will have to be done as per the motto of the Edinburgh OECD Conference: openly, transparently and inclusively with independent verification because without this the GM technology that promised so much for the 21st Century might not be accepted by the public and will disappear.[30]

Pusztai's independent GM research results had a devastating effect on government and corporate GM interests. This was an example of cultural, expert power. Eventually Whitehall admitted that the 'aged and frail' scientist, seventy-two years old in 2002, had been martyred[31] by a campaign to discredit him as the scientist who questioned the safety of genetically modified foods. Robert Evans of the *Guardian* writes, 'Dr Puzhtai [sic] was told to retire from his research institute after he described on a television programme how rats had become stunted, and their immune systems had been depressed, when they were fed genetically altered potatoes. Ministers sought to undermine his results, and scientists from opposing camps fought over the validity of the work. A group from the Royal Society, Britain's most distinguished scientific body, investigated his experiments and claimed that the tests were "flawed in many aspects of design, execution and analysis".' Who the members of the Royal Society group that criticised Dr Pusztai's work were, who funded their work and what their interests were was not mentioned in the article. But this incident clearly illustrates the power of publicly funded, independent or free science, and why governments and corporations want to control science for their own ends.

The enclosure of the intellectual and genetic commons

Corporations are enclosing the cultural, intellectual and genetic commons, and charging us for it. Take Canadian farmers Percy Schmeiser and his wife, who were seed savers. They saved canola seed for many years to replant the following season. But Monsanto, noticing there were GM canola plants growing on the roadside near their farm, brought a lawsuit against them for infringing their canola copyright. Even though the farmers argued that they had only used their traditional saved canola, Monsanto took them to the Canadian Supreme Court and won, thanks to the finer points of various WTO and NAFTA treaties that the Canadian government had signed. There has since been an out of court settlement, and Schmeiser won a Right Livelihood award for the defence of the genetic commons.

Even though seeds are a unique part of our common heritage, with farmers saving seeds for the following year, agribusinesses like Monsanto want to patent seeds. So to buy Monsanto seeds, farmers must agree not to save seeds or use any pesticides or fertilisers other than Monsanto's. Farmers must allow the Monsanto 'police' to inspect their fields and records at any time. Monsanto has brought over 400 lawsuits against farmers for misusing seeds. The cost of seeds has risen sharply, and whereas in 1997 in the USA transgenic soybeans had a 2 per cent market share, in 2002 it was 74 per cent. Cotton went up from 4 per cent to 70 per cent.[32]

Defending the cultural commons

A key question that the defenders of the genetic and creative commons ask is, 'Do we want a culture that is authentic and diverse? Or a commercial monoculture in which "content providers" sell proprietary products to consumers?'[33] So what are the creative commons? The commons are the creations of nature and society that we inherit jointly and freely, and hold in trust for future generations. The creative commons are a kind of knowledge bank and seedbed, holding humanity's vast store of science, art, customs, languages and law. The creative commons is the seedbed of human creativity. According to Lewis Hyde, author of *The Gift*, the carrying capacity of the cultural commons is endless, unless fenced in by copyright and patents. The law allows authors and inventors exclusive rights over their creative work for a limited time. This enables the author to benefit during their life, but then also society benefits in the long run. Copyright thus balances private wealth and initiative with the public interest or common wealth. The law allows a market in creative property, but puts a boundary on that market. Fair use rights allow rights to quote from works in copyright without asking permission. We have the rights to use purchased works as we wish privately, though there are public lending rights.

The creative commons matter because they are being enclosed and stolen from us. But the corporate onslaught over the last thirty years has led to major copyright creep. The positive trade-off between private copyright and public benefits has shifted to corporate benefit. Film studios, publishers and record labels asserted new intellectual property rights, and in 1998 got the US Congress to pass the Sonny Bono Copyright Term Extension Act, which makes copyrights nearly perpetual. Now Google, aiming to organise the world's information, is copying books in and out of copyright to sell downloads, not necessarily with the permission of the author or the publisher.

Corporations own fictional characters, so the Disney Corporation not only owns Mickey Mouse, but also Winnie the Pooh and even fairy stories such as 'Snow White' taken from the public cultural domain. A driver for copyright extension was that Disney could not survive if its Mickey Mouse copyright ended. One result is the increasing commercial enclosure of childhood, with their stories and games coming mainly from corporations. Children spend from thirty to forty hours a week with commercial television, DVDs, electronic games and propriety toys, not to mention their exposure to brands and junk food.

Box 6.6   US copyright creep: from Thomas Jefferson to Mickey Mouse

1790   First copyright term is fourteen years plus a fourteen-year renewal.
1976   Copyright extended to author's life plus fifty years (seventy years if owned by a corporation).
1998   Sonny Bono Act extends copyright by another twenty years.
2003   Supreme Court says Sonny Bono Act doesn't violate the constitution's intent of limited duration.[34]
2008–9 Google lays claim to the electronic rights to copy and disseminate out of copyright books.

The financial attraction of patents has shifted scientific research from areas of common need to areas of greatest private profit. This goes against the values of many scientists, who want their work to be freely available. Benjamin Franklin never wanted a patent for his most popular invention, the Franklin stove. 'As we enjoy great advantages from the inventions of others, we should be glad to serve others by any invention of ours.' This spirit of giving and sharing prevailed for 200 years, as research was shared through publication and conferences. The scientific knowledge commons flourished. Then in the USA the 1980 Bayh-Dole Act let universities get patents on tax-funded research and then license these patents to corporations. University science was for put up sale as corporate money flowed into university laboratories. The new UK Economic and Social Research Council grant application guidelines now stress the economic pay off of unversity research.

One result has been secrecy and distrust, with a reluctance on the part of research scientists to discuss research lest someone else beat them to the patent office. The common wealth of science is increasingly eroded and enclosed. Scientists are expected to come up with profitable patents, as opposed to pure research. The

---

Box 6.7   *Throwing Microsoft out of the Windows: freeing access to knowledge*

When IBM asked Bill Gates to come up with an operating system for their new PC, he bought DOS or 'Dirty Operating System' from someone he knew in Seattle for reportedly $60,000. His genius, apart from knowing where to find the original inventors, lay in then licensing, not selling, DOS to IBM. The rest is history, as we have to pay around £100 a time or so for Microsoft proprietary software such as Microsoft Word.

So, in the spirit of the creative commons, inventors around the world have collaborated to create, develop and continually improve the Linux operating system as an open-source, free alternative to the Microsoft near-monopoly. Linux is in many ways better than the Windows operating system and its derivatives. There are no 'Microsoft moments' on Linux, which, like senior moments, are short system losses.

Many people just cannot afford Windows. The president of Brazil's National Institute for Information technology (ITI), Sergio Amadeu de Silveira, argues that access to cheap computing is essential; otherwise there will be digital information exclusion. In a country where there are 46 million people living below the poverty line, Amadeu is against proprietary software such as Windows, mainly because of the excessive licensing costs. Free software, he believes, will 'democratise access to knowledge'. He has built a network of free computing centres and will get all federal government to use open-source software, replacing the Windows operating system.[35]

funders may not allow scientists to talk. For example, when a research study at the University of California in San Francisco found that a thyroid drug was no better than three cheaper alternatives, the sponsoring manufacturer hushed up the results. In Europe, scientific publishers wanted to charge for downloading scientific papers, even though the research had been paid for by public finds.

Summary: Capturing culture

To summarise, this chapter has analysed the ways that corporations, and government, have captured culture. The arts, scientific research, the genetic and intellectual commons, health, childhood and the media have been enclosed and co-opted by large corporations. As Gore Vidal writes, 'the corporate ownership of the country has absolute control of the populist pulpit – "the media" – as well as the school-room'.[36] The corporate domination of culture, with rising levels of affluenza, is so well developed in Britain that there are double the levels of mental ill-health than in Northern European social democratic countries.

The selfish capitalist domination of culture has masked the theft of our society's common wealth. The next chapter analyses how this dispossession happened, and how we were bought.

Chapter 7

Capitalism Unleashed:
The Seizure of Common Wealth[1]

Faced by the failure of credit they have proposed only the lending of more money. Stripped of the lure of profit by which to induce our people to follow their false leadership they have resorted to exhortations, pleading tearfully for restored confidence. They know only the rules of a generation of self-seekers.

Franklin Roosevelt, inaugural address, March 1933

The corporate capture of the state and of culture has masked the theft of our common wealth. Savings, wages, pensions, public services, the financial system, jobs, the environment, commons such as air, water, land, capital and genetic inheritance are being stolen from society, from 'us the people', by the financial and corporate elites, with the help of the captive state and a bought parliament, under the cover of a compliant media. The financial journalists Larry Elliott and Dan Atkinson see the financial elite gambling away our future wealth and putting us on the path to debt serfdom.

The situation is serious. Will Hutton, chair of the Work Foundation, called in January 2008 for the government to control the financial industry as it is destabilising not just the economy but all our lives with its pursuit of naked profits: 'Never in human affairs have so few been allowed to make so much money for so little wider benefit. Across the globe, societies and governments have been hoodwinked by a collection of self-confident chancers in the guise of investment bankers, hedge and private equity fund partners and bankers who, in the cause of their monumental self-enrichment, have taken the world to the brink of a major recession. It has been economic history's most one-sided bargain.'[2] But by blaming individual bankers, it is easy to ignore the captive corporate state which encouraged 'making money' from the seizure of common wealth.

This chapter analyses how this seizure is happening. Since the first step to reclaiming common wealth is to recognise the methods used to steal the commons, the next chapter suggests how to transform capitalism, for the benefit of people, society and the planet.

The financial market collapse in 2007 has triggered a rethink of the costs of the dominance of neo-liberal economics since 1979. The financial elites of the City and Wall Street have been exposed as the credit crunch takes hold and failing financial institutions run to government for support. The British government has nationalised the Royal Bank of Scotland (RBS), taken a large shareholding in several banks at a cost of £37 billion in October 2008 and is spending billions in taxpayers' money on risky loan guarantees and shoring up the financial system. Taking on RBS means that the government has added £1.6 trillion of unsecured banking debt to Britain's national debt of around £900 billion. We have little real idea of just how far our futures have been mortgaged, and whether the bailout will 'work', whatever 'work' means. Governments seem united in wanting to return to the boom years of business as usual, rather than use the crisis as an opportunity to develop a sustainable, equitable economy that works for all. There is a widespread feeling across Europe, expressed in demonstrations, strikes and public debate that governments were complicit in allowing the financial sector to rob society. They then proceeded to help the banks rather than ordinary people.

In Britain, expressing dissent at government economic policy can be dangerous. For example the largely peaceful demonstrations at the April 2009 London G20 summit were in part brutally put down by members of the Metropolitan Police's infamous Territorial Support Group. Some police illegally removed their identifying numbers and there was a fatal, unprovoked attack on a bystander, Ian Tomlinson, which the Met then tried clumsily to cover up.

The US government nationalised Fanny Mae and Freddy Mac with their $5 trillion mortgage loan books in summer 2008. These are huge mortgage lenders accounting for around half American home loans. President Obama supports bailouts for the banking system and New Deal-type public works schemes for job creation. John Kenneth Galbraith's book on how laissez-faire economic liberalism destroyed itself in 1929, *The Crash*, has become useful reading. Could it be that we are seeing again how neo-liberal capitalism is destroying itself; and taking down ordinary people, industry and the economy with it? Can remedial action be taken in time? Or will the remedial action taken by Prime Minister Gordon Brown, who helped cause the credit crunch in the first place, merely delay financial collapse?

The financial meltdown is a huge challenge, but what are the causes? One key cause is the corporate enclosure of our common wealth, the enclosing of our capital and financial commons. Enclosure of the commons underpins many other challenges that face us such as global warming, fuel poverty, the patenting of seeds, the privatisation of public utilities, the loss of public spaces and the public bailout of failing banks. Market fundamentalism, selfish capitalism, Blatcherism or neo-economic liberalism – call it what you like, this is the ideology that has greased the corporate theft of our common wealth.

This analysis leads to ways of reclaiming the common wealth, as is happening with community land trusts, mutualising assets, securing the capital commons and with the development of the shared creative commons such as the Linux operating system, for example.

This chapter will cover:

* the credit crunch: privatising profits and nationalising losses
* neo-economic liberalism
* commoditising the polity and culture
* the upward transfer of wealth to the plutocratic elite: accumulation by dispossession:
  1. privatisation and commoditisation: from commons to market
  2. financialisation
  3. managing and manipulating crises through the debt trap and economic shock therapy
  4. forced state redistribution
* the crisis we are in
* a summary comparison of neo-liberal capitalist and tripolar societies.

The credit crunch: privatising profits and nationalising losses

Controlling the runaway financial corporate sector requires the rolling back of the boundaries between the public and business sectors and reclaiming the financial capital commons. But, firstly, how has the financial sector been able to privatise its profits, whilst offloading its risks and losses on to society for so long?

The collapse of the Northern Rock bank in summer 2007 was brought home by pictures of thousands of panicking people queuing to withdraw their savings. The origins of the bank collapse started with the demutualisation of Northern Rock. The once prudent, member-owned building society became a shareholder-owned bank in a deregulated free market. Chancellor Gordon Brown in 1997 set up 'light-touch regulation' by the Treasury, the Bank of England and the Financial Services Authority (FSA). This allowed Northern Rock to lend mortgages at 125 per cent of house value, at five times borrowers' incomes and to borrow risky short-term capital using complex offshore methods to fund mortgage lending, rather than using the usual method of loaning out building society members' deposits.

When house prices stalled in 2007 and Northern Rock's risky business model unravelled, it was bailed out by the British taxpayer, with loans of £24 billion from the Treasury. The danger was that if other banks collapsed, savers would then lose their deposits and mortgagees would lose their homes.

Northern Rock is a telling example of the victory, the instability and the crisis of neo-economic liberal capitalism. Victory, because if financial services had not been deregulated, Northern Rock would have still been a cautious, mutually owned building society. Crisis, because neo-liberalism, far from being able to stand on its own free-market two feet, relies heavily on taxpayer handouts and is highly unstable. It is a unique way of privatising profits and nationalising losses.

So who are the neo-economic liberals in charge of banks such as Northern Rock? Take the free marketeer and biologist Matthew Ridley PhD. He was the chair of 'Northern Wreck' and led it to ignominious collapse in 2007 with the disgraced CEO Adam Applegarth by pushing an aggressive business model to the limit and trusting that credit would always be there.[3] Ridley comes from a wealthy Northumberland landowning family. A relative, Nicholas Ridley, was one of Thatcher's ministers and a leading privatiser. Matthew Ridley took up the chair of Northern Rock in 2004, a post once held by his father.

Ridley, as a columnist for the *Telegraph*, wrote of farm subsidies in 1994 that, 'The little-known ninth law of thermodynamics states that the more money a group receives from the taxpayer, the more it demands and the more it complains.' He opposed government intervention and as an academic evolutionary biologist offered an apparently scientific rationale for deregulating business. He argued, as a social Darwinist, that people, guided by natural selection, act in their own interests. However, selfishness can result in us *appearing* to be altruistic, cooperative and generous – thus gaining others' trust. This is a better strategy than lying or cheating. Government should therefore stop interfering with business and people's private lives, so that human selfish instincts can flourish. This social Darwinist argument advocates the invisible hand of the market, based on realising a self-interest that somehow delivers public benefit. Capitalism is people doing nasty things to each other from self-interest, with somehow beneficial results.

Dr Ridley, as well as at one time denying climate change and wanting to stop recycling, also advocated the scrapping of planning laws, criticised taxes, subsidies and government regulation in his *Telegraph* columns and books. He once famously wrote that bureaucracy 'is a self-seeking flea on the backs of the more productive people of this world. Governments do not run countries, they parasitize them.' So when Ridley tested out his neo-liberal business model as chair of Northern Rock, he had to rely on the state to clear up his mess, otherwise panic could have undermined the banking system. George Monbiot concluded his analysis of Ridley by writing that economic neo-liberalism 'Destroys people's savings, wrecks their lives and trashes their environment. It is the belief system of the free rider, who is perpetually subsidised by responsible citizens.'⁴

But where did these neo-liberal free riders come from and how did we allow them to seize our wealth?

The implementation of the neo-liberal social model by successive British governments since 1979 underpins diverse phenomena such as the commercialisation of childhood, climate change, the lack of affordable homes, rising social inequality, declining public infrastructure, the privatisation of public assets and the high level of British consumer debt (over £1.3 trillion), which means that personal debt now exceeds our GNP. The neo-liberal social model provides the ideological justification for the market to enclose our commons such as culture, public services, public assets, labour, land, childhood and even the financial system itself. The walls protecting these commons were torn down. So we now pay more for using what was once ours. What once were common assets became market commodities.

Take the once publicly owned water utilities, which were sold for £3.5 billion in 1989. The British government privatised Thames Water in 1989. The German RWE Group bought it in 2000 for £4.8 billion. RWE raised loans of £1.4 billion, which are being repaid by Thames customers as part of their water rates, already high because of the profits allowed for by the British government, and the need to reinvest in renewing old water pipes. RWE sold Thames Water to the Australian Macquarie Bank in 2006 for £8 billion, making a windfall profit of 500 million Euros for RWE. Enron bought Wessex Water. Even though then opposition leader Tony Blair said that 'millions of people feel disgusted and outraged at this excess and greed', New Labour did nothing to reverse privatisation.[5]

This sell-off by the British government of a public asset has robbed taxpayers of the capital asset they helped create. It results in water consumers paying more for the extra profits demanded by private corporate owners, leads to asset stripping of the water company for profits and to skimping on maintenance. But global investors such as Macquarie value British water companies for delivering good profits. And you may ask, just how good is the Macquarie Bank, which prides itself on being 'a factory for millionaires', at running and maintaining a water utility in the public interest?

Neo-liberalism and its origins

The world took a decisive, revolutionary turn towards neo-liberalism in 1978–80. In China, Deng Shao Ping proclaimed that 'to get rich is glorious'. He initiated the path to a dynamic capitalist economy, policed by a privileged Communist Party and producing record growth rates. At the same time, Paul Volcker at the Federal Reserve Bank, with the newly elected President Ronald Reagan, began to fight inflation with high interest rates and high unemployment. This undermined the strength of labour unions, deregulating industry, liberating finance nationally and globally. Margaret Thatcher was elected British Prime Minister in 1979, on an anti-union ticket, proclaiming, 'There is no such thing as society – only individuals and families.' Her friend General Pinochet was already leading the way in Chile, implementing at gunpoint the neo-liberal agenda of the Chicago Boys, Chilean students of the free-market economist Milton Friedman.

Box 7.1   *Winners from privatisation*

The big winners from privatisation were those that sold share issues for quick profits, City firms who earned big fees for organising privatisation share issues, and management, who got higher pay. Research shows that UK privatisations generated an average immediate price increase of 40%.

Source: Andrew Glyn, Capitalism Unleashed, *Oxford, 2007, p. 40*

So British taxpayers lost 40 per cent of the asset value of their nationalised industries on privatisation and governments got very poor value for money. Clearly, successive British governments and the political elites have not acted in the public interest. They have acted more like fire sale auctioneers.

These leaders took the obscure neo-liberal ideas of Friedrich von Hayek and Milton Friedman, and applied them to transforming their respective societies with free-market principles. They were trying to turn the clock back to the 1920s, to the days of laissez-faire economic liberalism, which had failed with the 1929 Crash and Depression. This time, though 'things would be different'.

Neo-liberalism is a theory of political economy that advocates freeing individual enterprise within a framework of tough private property rights, free markets and free trade. The minimal state's task is to maintain the legal and financial frameworks for business. It secures private property rights though the army, police, law and order and the courts and guarantees free markets through force if necessary. If no markets already exist, such as in commons like land, water, air, education, culture, science, health care, pensions, social security or the environment, then new markets must be created by the state at public expense. The state should then withdraw so business can benefit. The state must not intervene in markets because it lacks the information that prices give, and because in a democracy the market will inevitably be distorted for politicians to get elected. The interests of the wealthy elite and corporations in this self-serving ideology, however, are apparently ignored. By appealing to the self-interest of enterprising small business people and advertising shares in utilities like Gas as bargains, Thatcher cleverly masked these plutocratic interests in Britain.

In practice, neo-liberalism meant deregulation, privatisation and the state withdrawing from providing essential public services itself and privatising public services like health, education, public media and welfare.

The term 'neo-liberalism' comes from the laissez-faire, classical liberal economics that was discredited by the collapse of capitalism in the 1929 Wall Street Crash and the subsequent Depression in the 1930s. Strictly speaking, it should be called neo-economic liberalism, as liberalism is a distinct political philosophy that advocates personal liberties and cultural freedom. Roosevelt's New Deal, Keynesian economics, social democracy, the mixed economy and the welfare state replaced laissez-faire liberal economics from the 1930s to the 1970s.

When Friedrich von Hayek, Milton Friedman and their colleagues founded the Mont Pelerin Society in 1947 to promote neo-liberalism, they professed that they were concerned about the threats to individual human freedom and dignity and the freedom of voluntary groups by the suppression of freedom of thought and expression by what they saw as the totalitarian powers of the welfare state, social democracy and the mixed economy. They were concerned about the rise of moral relativism and the rise of theories that undermined the rule of law.

So far, so typical of libertarian concerns about maintaining individual and cultural freedom. However, the founding statement of the Mont Pelerin Society goes on *to marry cultural freedom on the one hand, with free enterprise in the economy on the other*, by announcing, 'It holds further that they [i.e. moral relativism, suppression of freedom of thought, the desirability of the rule of law, etc.] have been fostered by a decline of belief in private property and the competitive market; for without the diffused power and initiative associated with these institutions it is difficult to imagine a society in which freedom may be effectively preserved.'[6]

By conflating cultural freedom with free economic enterprise, neo-liberals neatly hijacked the principle of 'freedom' for capitalism. Freedom as the informing principle for cultural life is healthy. Free enterprise is also economically healthy when entrepreneurs start new businesses, work productively and take initiatives to improve workplaces. But in reality, mutually beneficial collaboration is the leading principle of the economy, not the dog-eats-dog, win/lose competition espoused by the free marketeers. The economy relies on the division of labour, joint ventures, partnership and associative working, on collaboration. Too much free enterprise and competition results in waste, duplication, over-supply and bankruptcies. In fact modern business relies on a high degree of marketing, planning, just-in-time production and co-ordination along a whole supply chain of producers, distributors and consumers. Companies such as Toyota which are best at lean production and service are the most successful.

Karl Polanyi criticised the founding ideas of the Mont Pelerin Society by pointing out that there were two contradictory ideas of good and bad freedoms. The bad freedoms included the freedom to exploit people, to make excessive personal gains, to prevent useful inventions being implemented and to profit from disasters secretly brought about for private gain. But arising with the market economy there also developed separately good freedoms like the freedom of speech, association, research, job choice and conscience. He looked forward to the passing of the market economy as the beginning of an era of unprecedented freedom. But he saw that the achievement of such a desired future was blocked by the neo-liberal utopianism of Hayek where:

> Planning and control are being attacked as a denial of freedom. Free enterprise and private ownership are declared the essentials of freedom. No society built on other foundations is said to deserve to be called free. The freedom that regulating creates is denounced as unfreedom; the justice, liberty and welfare it offers are decried as a camouflage of slavery.[7]

According to Polanyi, the ideal of cultural freedom soon degenerates into advocating unleashed business enterprise, or in other words, 'the fullness of freedom for those whose income, leisure and security need no enhancing, and a mere pittance of liberty for the people, who may in vain attempt to make use of their democratic rights to gain shelter from the power of the owners of property.' He then argues that because there is no society unless it is maintained by force and power, the main way the neo-liberal utopian vision can be implemented is by force, autocracy and violence, even fascism, as the good freedoms are lost and the bad ones dominate.

So Polanyi's prescient analysis helps us understand why Pinochet was the first to implement neo-liberal 'reforms' in Chile from 1973 using force; why Thatcher had to smash the miners, using all the powers of the state, before undertaking the extensive privatisation of public assets; and why, when President Bush announced that the US is obliged 'to help the spread of freedom', what he really means is the unconstrained spread of corporate monopoly power and McDonalds. It also helps explain how members of the British elite like Dr Matthew Ridley are such strong advocates of neo-liberalism, as it serves their economic interests. Consider how arms races and now wars on terror have been deliberately engineered to get public consent for high arms spending and corporate profits. According to Naomi Klein, 'the shock doctrine' of neo-liberal economics was imposed on country after country in the name of the free market, for the ultimate benefit of predatory corporations such as Cheney's Halliburton.

It is clear from this argument why the wealthy global elite have funded the neo-liberal movement so generously through compliant think tanks, business schools, free-market research institutes, university departments of neo-liberal economics, prizes such as the Bank of Sweden-funded Nobel prize for economics, the corporate media, the World Economic Forum at Davos and business lobby groups. Such organisations have repaid their sponsors' investment handsomely by providing the ideas, policies, advocacy and language that have disguised their real purpose. This purpose is that of restoring elite corporate power and plutocratic wealth in the guise of 'modernisation' or 'reform'. Such well-funded advocacy has influenced a massive shift of wealth and power back to the elite, with ever-widening inequality. For example, in 1979, 1 per cent of people in Britain owned 6 per cent of national wealth, rising ten years later to 9 per cent under Thatcher, now 13 per cent under New Labour and growing. The poor half of the population had 7 per cent of national wealth in 1996, and now the figure has fallen to below 5 per cent.[8] The gap is getting wider.

The corporate media have also helped promote the neo-liberal project by marginalising alternative ideas, so that people come to believe uncritically the 'common sense' that 'there is no alternative' to neo-liberal capitalism. It becomes perceived as 'radical' for the anti-economic globalisers such as the French farmer, McDonalds manurer and presidential candidate José Bové to advocate that 'another world is possible'. A handful of multimillionaires and corporate media empires have come to have a massive influence on culture, on politics and on economic thinking as captured governments allowed the concentration of media ownership in order to get a 'good press' and manufacture consent. A news agenda can be set that serves their interests, whilst ignoring or ridiculing the ideas that are threats. How many times, for example, have you read in the popular newspapers of 'benefit cheats' yet similar coverage is seldom given to the tax avoidance activities of the media conglomerates or of wealthy tax exiles such as Philip Green of British Home Stores who avoided paying tax on £1 billion by transferring this sum to his wife? The corporate media have a big incentive to persuade us that we are better off under Thatcher and Sons Ltd, rather than offer sustained critical analysis and alternatives.

For example, the uncritical reporting of 'economic growth' was a leading story in the media, in spite of the negative effects of such growth undermining people's wellbeing and damaging the environment. This is not reported. One real story is that even though Britain's GDP has risen by 50 per cent in twenty-five years, the Index of Sustainable Economic Welfare (ISEW) indicates a slow reduction of our quality of life, using indicators such as mental health. According to Oliver

James, US and British 'selfish capitalism' has led to affluenza, with record levels of depression.

It just so happens that the conditions that neo-liberals say are needed to free people from the 'serfdom' of the state, such as low taxes, lowering wages through weakening the unions, privatising health and reducing public services, are exactly, according to George Monbiot, 'the conditions required to make the wealthy elite even richer, while leaving everyone else to sink or swim. In practice the philosophy developed at Mont Pelerin is little more than an elaborate disguise for a wealth grab.'[9]

Commercialising and commoditising the polity and culture

To summarise, whilst liberal principles of freedom, of competition for excellence, of realising individual potential, are at home in the cultural space of the arts, media, health, education, science and spirituality, they are toxic when applied to the economy as an organising principle. Competing for excellence in science and the arts is a spur for development, invention and creativity. As the artist Joseph Beuys once said, 'Capital is spirit'[10], as real wealth comes from new ideas, inventions, imaginations and innovative ways of doing things. The essence of cultural life is a kind of marketplace, where people are striving for excellence – often against themselves, sometimes against or with each other.

Cultural freedom of course needs underpinning rights that guarantee free expression, for example, as well as resourcing, so that schools or health services can serve individual human needs as rights with entitlements. This secures the required resources to ensure that rights are realised in practice. Childhood as a cultural space needs protecting from harmful influences, both political and commercial – children have a right to childhood. Even in sport, which apparently encourages win/lose competition, the really successful athletes are in fact competing against themselves for excellence.

What has happened is that liberal principles have been mistranslated from culture and imposed on economic life by the neo-liberals. This ideology has made neo-liberal capitalism toxic and anti-social. This mistranslation both undermines free cultural activities on the one side and the economy, which thrives on collaboration, on the other. Because the initial prime movers in the early capitalist economy were pioneering entrepreneurs and merchant adventurers, neo-liberals made the mistake of basing their theory on the development needs of this early model of 'free enterprise', rather than on the sophisticated collaboration and teamwork needed to make the modern economy and division of labour work.

The upward transfer of wealth to the plutocracy: accumulation by dispossession

Britain has the contradiction of economic growth in a wealthy country on the one hand, and on the other, the fact that many modest income families need two incomes to get by. Many people feel constantly behind. This is a sharp contrast to the 1960s, when one income sufficed. Young families in their twenties and thirties now spend a much larger proportion of their net incomes on mortgage interest or rent, as the cost of homes has tripled in Britain since 1997. We can see the process of the upward transfer of wealth in Britain more clearly when we make comparisons with other countries. From the 1980s onwards, Northern European visitors remarked increasingly on the Third World look of parts of Britain outside the elite rich areas, and British visitors abroad saw the widening public/private wealth gap.

Compare Britain with Sweden, where the strength of social democracy has been able to contain neo-liberalisation within boundaries and to retain common wealth. Average incomes are higher in Sweden, inflation lower; national competitiveness is better, as is the business climate. The quality of life is higher, for example children experience far higher levels of wellbeing than in Britain. Sweden comes third in life expectancy; Britain is an astonishing twenty-ninth in the rankings. The poverty rate is 6.3 per cent in Sweden, and 15.7 per cent in Britain. The richest 10 per cent earn 6.2 times that of the bottom 10 per cent, as opposed to Britain, where it is 13.6 times. Illiteracy is lower and social mobility higher. Everyone has the right to warmth in Sweden; there is no fuel poverty as in Britain, where one in six people suffer. It is a family-friendly country, where university education is free – and where there is a pluralist education system. The right to education has been redefined as an entitlement, with students able to take their education 'grant' to apply for education in other Scandinavian countries and even in Britain. Whilst there is high direct taxation, the Swedes benefit in return from excellent transport, housing, education, environmental policies, health care and social welfare. One downside is a higher unemployment level, though it depends on how the comparative figures are collected. There is a smaller entrepreneurial small business sector and more cultural conformity. One striking feature is that the life expectancy of the poor in Sweden is better than that of the rich in Britain. Clearly, Sweden, unlike Britain, has retained and improved its common wealth, and, above all, those on modest incomes have benefited.[11]

One reason that Sweden is so publicly wealthy in comparison to Britain is that wealth has been captured there permanently for public benefit. Swedish people have not been progressively dispossessed of their common wealth, as has been happening in Britain since 1979.

How does accumulation by dispossession work?

Reviewing the achievements of neo-liberalism, David Harvey concluded that the control of inflation was the only real success. Growth was, however, poor. World aggregate growth rates fell from 3.5 per cent in the 1960s to 1 per cent since the 1980s. Countries such as Russia, which submitted to the neo-liberal shock doctrine in the 1990s, suffered catastrophic economic decline. Most global indicators of health, life expectancy and infant mortality show losses, not gains in wellbeing since the 1960s. Improvements in China and India largely contributed until recently to the reduction of the proportion of the world's people living in poverty. However, according to Harvey, apart from the highly visible growth of financial services and IT in the global financial centres like the City of London, which have become elite islands of wealth, the real neo-liberal success has been the elite's accumulation of wealth by dispossession. This is characterised by four key vacuuming processes.

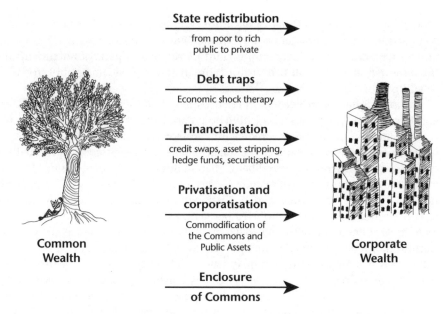

State redistribution
from poor to rich
public to private

Debt traps
Economic shock therapy

Financialisation
credit swaps, asset stripping,
hedge funds, securitisation

Privatisation and
corporatisation
Commodification of
the Commons and
Public Assets

Enclosure
of Commons

Common
Wealth

Corporate
Wealth

Figure 7.1   The enclosure and privatisation of common wealth

1   Privatisation and commoditisation: from commons to market

A key neo-liberal aim is to commoditise, privatise and corporatise the commons. These commons are public assets, rights if you like, that the community shares or holds in trust, with use rights clearly regulated. For example, in rural communities, farms neighbouring the fells as commons often have grazing rights for a customary number of sheep on the fell, rights regulated by tradition. Such practices are survivals of the over 5 million acres of common land enclosed in Britain in the eighteenth and nineteenth centuries.

Such enclosures are still going on today, with Monsanto, for example, privatising and commoditising our genetic commons in the form of seeds and genetic material. Seed savers find their government has signed away their traditional rights to saving seed, allowing Monsanto to sue them for breach of patent, as farmer Percy Schmeiser found in Canada (see Chapter 6).

By commoditising the genetic commons, taking the commons of water or land into private ownership, corporations can then create a new market and make profits from having dispossessed people's common rights. This has happened and is still happening with the privatisation and commoditisation of:

- public utilities such as transport, water, telecommunications, post, electricity and gas;
- social housing, education, health care, pensions, social welfare;
- cultural organisations such as prisons, universities and research institutes;
- warfare and security: some of the work of the army and police, core functions of the state, are being subcontracted to security companies, as in Iraq, and in Britain

the rise of the surveillance industry is also dependent on subcontracting;
- common intellectual property rights, such as the Indian Neem tree, seeds and genetic material have been privatised under the WTO's TRIPS agreement;
- labour is being commoditised through the loss of rights;
- nature is being commoditised through the rolling back of regulatory frameworks and the exploitation of the environmental commons of land, air and water;
- culture is being commoditised by drug companies and the tourist industry's exploitation of indigenous cultures;
- rights over commons such as pensions, education, welfare and health care are subject to creeping privatisation.

These processes all involve the transfer of public assets and commons away from free or affordable, equitable public access, to the ownership of corporations and the wealthy elite. We have to then pay them user fees for what was once ours.

2   Financialisation

The main aim of the financial sector should be to serve business with capital, savers with a return on investment and to provide loans and financial mechanisms for trade and industry. The state regulates and guarantees the financial system as the lender of last resort. A healthy financial system is maintained as a socially created commons for public benefit. Between 1945 and 1979 governments regulated the financial sector, for example through exchange and capital controls, so as to maintain a mixed economy, a welfare state and full employment.

The 1980s deregulation enabled the financial system to redistribute wealth through speculation, bankers' bonuses, hedge fund betting, asset stripping through mergers or takeovers, private equity takeovers that looted pension funds, betting on currency fluctuations as on Black Wednesday in 1992 and corporate fraud as at Enron and World Com. One of the triggers for all this was the City of London 'Big Bang' in 1986, which allowed High Street retail banks to start speculating in the casino economy as investment merchant bankers, just as in the Roaring Twenties before the 1929 crash. The 1999 repeal of Roosevelt's 1933 Glass-Steagall Act allowed Wall Street to follow the City.

'Financialisation' gathered strength after 1980. According to David Harvey, the value of daily financial transactions in international financial markets was $2.3 billion in 1983, and rose to $130 billion by 2001. The speculation gap is calculated by the difference between the estimated $800 billion needed to support international trade and productive investment in 2001 and the $40 trillion annual turnover.

The collapse of Enron was symptomatic of the ways the public interest audit system was manipulated for so long to cover up corporate fraud, and of how this collapse ditched the company's employees' pension rights. After Enron, auditors and credit rating agencies failed to notice the toxic assets financial institutions such as RBS were hiding in their accounts, preferring to get their fees.

The collapse of the US and UK sub-prime mortgage market in 2007 also dispossessed people of their savings and their homes, yet also benefited the waiting predators. Mortgage lenders such as Northern Rock knew they were making risky loans to modest-income families, desperate for homes. This risk was disguised by the arcane practice of 'securitising' the risk, getting 'Triple A' credit ratings and selling it on to banks as a high-earning investment. Credit ratings agencies such as Standard & Poor's were corrupted by giving Triple A ratings to incomprehensible mortgage-backed securities, and earned fees from the banks for doing so. In the early 1990s, Goldman Sachs pioneered 'securitisation' when they 'packaged up' the mortgage payments from an Arizona trailer park, putting the site's income into a new company, which then issued Goldman-backed securities. There are now over $8 trillion of such toxic or worthless securities.

Compare this to the boring banks in France, where home prices are still relatively low and where banks exercise prudence by making careful checks on new mortgage borrowers.

But many bankers didn't really understand the banking casino created by financialisation. For example, currency gambling involves billions being traded around the world every day. The risks are high, so they are spread through hedge funds, derivatives, which repackage securities such as mortgages, shares and debt, and private equity groups with collateral debt obligations – a whole range of financial fiddles, and it's hard concretely to really understand how they 'work'.

Hedge funds are part of the unregulated 'shadow economy' that arose. They helped destroy the economies of several Asian nations in 1997. Ben Bernanke, now boss of the US Federal Reserve, once said he didn't know how hedge funds worked, but he trusted 'sophisticated financial institutions that did' (!) The top twenty-five hedge fund managers each earned around £250 million a year. In Britain in 2005, 250 hedge fund managers, who added no real value, each got around £40 million. No wonder the banking casino has been called an asylum run by its inmates.[12]

John Maynard Keynes wrote in his seminal work *The General Theory of Employment, Interest and Money* of 1936 that:

> Speculators may do no harm on a steady stream of enterprise. But the position is serious when enterprise becomes a bubble on the whirlpool of speculation. When the capital development of a country becomes the by-product of a casino, the job is likely to be ill done.

However, banks such as Merrill made sure that, even though they made huge sub-prime losses, the disgraced chief executive gained financially through stock options. These are ways of linking the common interests of owners and managers of capital by paying the latter in stock options. This led to stock market gains that brought wealth to the managers, at the expense of workers, customers and ordinary stockholders. Stan O'Neal, CEO of Merrill Lynch, the Wall Street investment bank, lost $8 to $12 billion on betting billions on American mortgage-backed securities, making the biggest loss in ninety-three years. He received a $159 million payoff.[13] The real motto of financialisation, then, is that 'greed is good'. Apparently, paying excessive stock options to failing CEOs is OK, as it does not upset 'the market'.

Box 7.2   'The gap between rich and poor could lead to riots'

The *Guardian* reported on 28 August 2007 that 'City bonuses hit a record high with £14bn payout', against a background of record debt, rising bankruptcies, home repossessions and the Northern Rock meltdown. Bonuses paid to private equity directors of GLG Partners Noam Gotesman and Pierre Lagrange were £200 million and £250 million respectively. Sir Ronald Cohen, of private equity group Apax, 'warned recently that the gap between rich and poor could lead to riots'. On 29 August 2007 it was reported that the 1,389 directors of FTSE 100 companies received pay packages of over £1 billion, with Lord Browne of BP getting £10,623,764 and Bob Diamond of Barclays £23 million.

On 29 January 2009, President Obama called for bankers to act responsibly, saying that it was unacceptable for bankers to get the estimated $18 billion bonuses they awarded themselves in 2008, when taxpayers were bailing them out: 'It is shameful, and part of what we are going to need is for the folks on Wall Street who are asking for help to show some restraint and show some discipline and show some sense of responsibility.'

It seems that some top bankers don't know how to cut their personal spending. The Citigroup bank cancelled a new corporate jet after Obama questioned the wisdom of the purchase given that the bank had taken $45 billion (£31.6 billion) of public money in autumn 2008.[15] John Thain, former Merrill Lynch CEO, apologised for spending £860,000 on antique furniture, carpeting and curtains for his executive offices, promising to repay the money. He had requested a $10 million bonus. He refused to take responsibility for Merrill's quarterly losses of $15 billion after being fired by new owners Bank of America. He said it was necessary to pay $4 billion in bonuses to keep Merrill's key staff. In early 2007 Thain bought an $87,784 rug, a George IV chair costing $18,468, a commode worth $35,115 and a waste-paper basket priced at $1,405.[16]

So far, there has not been much evidence of the famous neo-liberal principle of the trickle-down effect. Otherwise the cleaners at Goldman Sachs would get paid £20 an hour.

New Labour has continued the bankers' bonus culture. They hired Sir Philip Hampton as the chair of RBS, which is 70 per cent owned by the state. In effect a civil servant, he will get a £1.5 million bonus with this part-time job, if he hits secret targets. He is also part-time chair of Sainsbury's, at £395,000 p.a.

David Harvey summarises the dispossession of the common wealth wrought by financialisation:

> Deregulation allowed the financial system to become one of the main centres of redistributive activity through speculation, predation, fraud, and thievery. Stock promotions, Ponzi schemes, structured asset destruction through inflation, asset stripping through mergers and acquisitions, the promotion of levels of debt incumbency that reduced whole populations, even in the advanced capitalist countries, to debt peonage, to say nothing of corporate fraud, dispossession of assets (the raiding of pension funds and their decimation by stock and corporate collapses) by credit and stock manipulations – all of these become features of our capitalist system.[14]

3   Managing and manipulating crises through the debt trap and economic shock therapy

The springing of the debt trap is a key method of accumulation by dispossession. This was brought home to me vividly when I visited Seoul in October 2006 to lecture. South Korea fell into the debt trap in the late 1990s, when the currency was devalued by 80 per cent. This enabled foreign corporations to move in and buy up Korean assets at fire-sale prices. My literary agent in Seoul, Klaus Jang, had been taking his PhD in Germany. He had to stop his degree and come home, because overnight the savings he depended on had been destroyed.

The debt trap was reinvented during the early 1980s when Paul Volcker of the US Federal Reserve raised interest rates to 20 per cent in 1981. This started a prolonged recession that put companies out of business, made people unemployed, undermined unions in the US, drove debtor countries further into debt and initiated the age of structural adjustment programmes. The Volcker shock led to Mexico defaulting on its debt in 1982–4. Mexico was 'bailed out': the debt was rolled over, and the country had to agree to neo-liberal reforms such as privatisation, reduced welfare and relaxed labour laws. The World Bank, the IMF and the US Treasury then combined to impose such measures on Third World countries.

Nicanor Perlas analyses this process of dispossession through four interacting levels. He considers that economic globalisation has benefited the rich global corporate elite and that such globalisation is also history's greatest poverty-generating machine. At Level One, he describes the phenomena of elite economic globalisation and its disastrous economic, ecological and social impact. Think of the huge Indonesian rain forest fires, the pauperisation of ordinary people, fire sales of assets, unemployment, increasing rural poverty, the anti-IMF riots and social dislocation. These are the symptoms of dispossession.

At Level Two, he describes the neo-liberal structural adjustment polices (SAPs) that have caused these phenomena. Countries had to accept draconian SAPs to get IMF loans. These forced countries to adopt market liberalisation, allow unrestricted foreign investment, reduce wages, devalue currency and reduce government spending, except for security, the police and armed forces, needed to counter the inevitable anti-IMF riots.

Level Three is the ruling ideology of neo-liberal economics as a framework of values and policies, including the Social Darwinist principle of the survival of the fittest. Lastly at Level Four Perlas describes the powerful institutions that have been driving elite economic globalisation. These are the transnational corporations and banks, which have co-opted the international financial institutions – the World Bank, the IMF and the World Trade Organization – into a global poverty-creating machine on the one hand, and a wealth-creating machine for the global elites on the other.

The WTO, according to Perlas, is a permanent structural adjustment programme, to be imposed multilaterally. 'It embodies trade and investment liberalisation, and stops nation states stepping in to protect customers from product health hazards. For example, South Korea had to stop blocking the import of high pesticide contaminated US grain, because this was a "trade restraint".'[17] South Koreans demonstrated in 2008 against the importation of frozen US beef, which goes against their food culture, but which is being forced through by WTO rules.

Perlas describes SAPs starkly as pushing back the boundaries of the state so as to free and expand the market. Culture is seen as a barrier to trade, and cultural services such as education or health are commoditised and marketised. He summarises the essence of SAPs as '"Free" the market, while reducing the power of the state to intervene in the economy and in social services.' The market can be freed by a host of ingenious schemes to liberalise trade, investments and financial capital. The power of the state can be reduced through deregulation and privatisation.' SAPs, according to Perlas, lead to ruthless, jobless, voiceless, futureless, rootless and meaningless economic growth.

Dispossession by debt crisis redistributes assets. According to Harvey, since 1980, equivalent of over fifty Marshall Plans, or $4.6 trillion, have been sent by poor to rich countries. Joseph Stiglitz comments, 'What a peculiar world in which the poor countries are in effect subsidizing the richest.' Neo-liberals mask accumulation by dispossession by calling it 'confiscatory deflation'. As Perlas observes, this happened in the 1997–8 Asian crisis, where Japanese and Western corporations were the big winners. Huge national currency devaluations and IMF-imposed financial liberalisation enabled the biggest transfer of assets from domestic to foreign owners in fifty years.[18]

Naomi Klein's *The Shock Doctrine: The Rise of Disaster Capitalism* analyses how economic crises have been manipulated in country after country to benefit rich power elites and corporations. It is worth noting that this shock effect is happening in Britain with the credit crunch and provides the rationale for the government to mortgage our future to keep the band playing. Feeling comfortable and denying the possibility of collapses, we could be facing protracted financial meltdown from banking failure, toxic debts coming home to roost, unemployment, house dispossession, the loss of confidence, oil peaking, the credit crunch, a £1.3 trillion personal debt overhang and the resulting social dislocation. We should be prepared for the possibility of further rounds of neo-liberal 'shock therapy' in Britain, just as Iceland has gone down.[19]

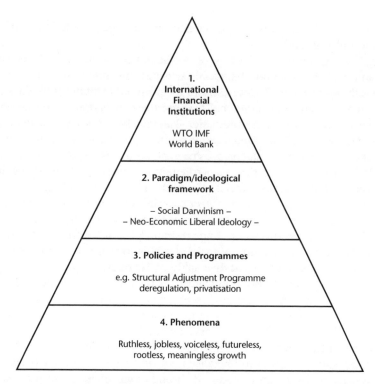

Figure 7.2   The power structure of neo-liberal dispossession
*A wealth-creating machine for corporate, financial and political elites, and for creating
the conditions for poverty*
Source: Nicanor Perlas, Shaping Globalisation, 2000, adapted from the Social Pyramid, p. 64

According to Klein, neo-liberal capitalism spread from the 1970s through the opportunistic exploitation of crises. Milton Friedman wrote that 'Only a crisis – actual or perceived – produces real change. When that crisis occurs the actions that are taken depend on the ideas that are lying around.' Klein examines key neo-liberal turning points, such as Chile in 1973, when Pinochet and Friedman's Chicago Boys imposed free-market economics, Britain in 1983, China and Poland, Russia in 1993, East Asia in 1998 and Iraq since 2003.

Crises were used opportunistically to embed neo-liberal values, so that Margaret Thatcher could eventually say 'there is no alternative'. Joseph Stiglitz, serving as the World Bank's chief economist, described the shock doctors such as Jeffery Sachs and President Yeltsin's own Chicago Boys in Russia in the early 1990s as 'market Bolsheviks'. 'Only a blitzkrieg approach during the "window of opportunity" provided by the "fog of transition" would get the changes made before the population had a chance to organise to protect its previous vested interests', wrote Stiglitz.[20]

In autumn 1991, a week after Gorbachev resigned, Yeltsin launched his economic shock programme of lifting price controls, free trade, the start of the privatisation of Russia's 225,000 state-owned companies and an overnight devaluation of the currency. Many people lost all their savings. The market Bolsheviks believed that if the right conditions for business were created, then the economy could rebuild itself without any planning. Things would get worse for six months, and then recovery would lead to Russia becoming a great world economic power, according to Yeltsin. But after a year, a third of the population fell below the poverty line, consumption fell by 40 per cent between 1991 and 1992, and millions of workers went unpaid because of cuts. People were selling their belongings and their bodies on the streets because they had no jobs or savings.

The sale of Russian assets accelerated under privatisation minister Anatoly Chubais, once described by Sachs as a 'freedom fighter'. The oligarchs and foreign corporations took the lion's share of public wealth. For example Yukos, a huge oil company, was sold for £309 million and, as of 2007, earned profits of more than £3 billion a year. Fifty-one per cent of the Sidanko Oil Company was sold for $130 million, a stake valued at $2.8 billion two years later. Russia's public assets were sold off for a pittance, funded by oligarch-controlled banks and using public money. According to James Bruges, the capitalist liberation of Russia resulted in huge inequality with 36 billionaires, 88,000 millionaires and an average annual wage of $3,300 for ordinary people.[21]

Naomi Klein concludes that 'National salvation through the harnessing of greed was the closest thing Russia's Chicago Boys and their advisors had as a plan for what they were going to do after they finished destroying Russia's institutions.'

The manipulation of crises resulted in disaster capitalism, where the hollowed-out state pays corporations to take over privatised security, reconstruction, utilities and public services, as has happened in New Orleans in the wake of Hurricane Katrina. Klein considers that a capitalist system that needs perpetual growth and which rides roughshod over the environment will anyway produce a reliable stream of profitable economic, military or ecological disasters for corporations to exploit.

However, the dream neo-liberal project for disaster capitalism was the reconstruction of Iraq after the 2003 war. Using shock and awe tactics to rapidly defeat Saddam, the US installed Paul Bremer as the head of the Coalition Provisional Authority (CPA). Stiglitz observed that Iraq was receiving 'an even more radical form of shock therapy than pursued in the former Soviet world'. Iraq became a new profit frontier for US corporations. Paul Bremer's aim was to build a client state with an extreme free-market economy. Like Russia, Iraq was a neo-liberal experiment. State assets were privatised, as 'Getting inefficient state enterprises into private hands is essential for Iraq's economic recovery.' He implemented a neo-liberal wish list of reducing corporate taxes to 15 per cent, 100 per cent ownership of Iraqi assets by foreign companies, foreign investors having the right to take all of their profits out of the country, contracts to last for forty years and the CPA, whilst not privatising the state oil company, did claim $20 billion in oil revenues. A new currency was launched with a virtual absence of any financial regulation.

The Iraqi intended 'dream economy' would have been impossible to develop in the US, given the 'blockages' of democracy, trades unions, regulation and civil society. Furthermore, Iraq was run from the Green Zone, a Halliburton-managed city state, and even though Bremer's CPA was the transitional authority, most government functions were outsourced to corporations. In analysing the CPA, Naomi Klein concluded that:

> Iraq under Bremer was the logical consequence of Chicago School theory: a public sector reduced to a minimal number of employees, mostly contract workers, living in a Halliburton city state, tasked with signing corporate friendly laws drafted by KPMG and handing out duffle bags of cash to Western contractors protected by mercenary soldiers, themselves with full legal immunity. All around them were furious people, increasingly turning to religious fundamentalism because it's the only source of power in a hollowed out state. Like Russia's gangsterism and Bush's cronyism, contemporary Iraq is a reaction of the fifty-year crusade to privatise the world. Rather than being disowned by its creators, it deserves to be seen as the purest incarnation yet of the ideology that gave it birth.[22]

So the opportunistic exploitation of crises for corporate benefit has been one of the engines of accumulation by dispossession. You could also argue that war, and the fear of war, has been one of the ways in which taxpayers have been persuaded to pay more taxes for defence, thus benefiting arms corporations. This leads to state redistributions, the last engine of wealth transfer to the elite.

4   State redistributions from poor to rich, from the public to the private

There was a redistributive flow of wealth and income in Britain from rich to poor, from the private to the public, from the 1940s to the 1970s. But, from Thatcher onwards, the neo-liberal state became an agent for reversing the flow of public wealth back to the rich elite. The state uses the following methods.

- Privatisation and cutting state spending that contributes to the social wage. For example in Britain, dentistry has been effectively privatised as a £2.2 billion service, despite the rhetoric. One-off gains for the modestly off, such as council house sales at give-away prices, result in long-term negative effects. For example, newly privatised central London council homes soon became gentrified, with the loss of affordable social rental homes for low-paid service workers, who are then faced with long, costly travel to work.
- The redistribution of wealth and income through income tax code changes, for example to favour returns on investment rather than wages, to promote regressive sales taxes, to leave higher incomes relatively untaxed so that only 'little people' pay tax, relaxing inheritance tax, less tax on large company profits financed by more tax for small companies, lowering capital gains taxes – and the provision of a range of tax breaks, tax avoidance opportunities and subsidies to corporations, such as arms companies. (The Serious Fraud Office spent £2 million showing BAE had paid £1 billion to Prince Bandar of Saudi Arabia and £1 billion to Swiss bank accounts controlled by agents of Saudi royals.)[23]

- As a result of government's tax changes, the IMF declared Britain a tax haven. Tax havens have created an offshore financial world that offers the 'secrecy jurisdictions' of low or zero taxes, secrecy and light-touch regulations. The big accountancy firms and the City of London use tax havens to avoid tax and hide assets. Corporations offshore their brands and intellectual assets to legally avoid tax, so for example there is a big tax gap between the profits companies such as Shell, GlaxoSmithKline make in Britain and what they pay in tax. The total tax gap could be between £3.7 billion and £13 billion according to the Inland Revenue. The Tax Justice Network highlights the offshore avoidance schemes.
- Gordon Brown and Alistair Darling have given private equity firms very low taxes of 18 per cent.
- Allowing price increases way above inflation for privatised industries, such as gas, water, electricity and transport. Taxpayers subsidise rail transport in Britain at much higher levels than in pre-privatisation days, and rail travellers pay much more as well.
- Allowing companies to dump their pollution costs on society and the environment. Instead of requiring every drinks container to be refillable, reusable and recyclable, these are dumped or recycled voluntarily.
- Allowing companies to avoid tax. According to the National Audit Office, nearly a third of Britain's 700 largest businesses paid no corporation tax in 2005–6, and a third paid less than £10 million each. Del Monte Fresh Produce UK, Chiquita UK and JP Fresh reported combined sales of over £400 million in their most recent accounts, yet they paid a total of only £128,000 in UK tax. Profits and capital are increasingly going untaxed.[24]
- Using off-public-balance-sheet tricks such as PFI to transfer both capital and land assets to corporations and guarantee income/profit streams for thirty years. Gordon Brown as Chancellor has committed British taxpayers to pay £170 billion by 2032 to banks, investors and corporations for more than 800 PFI schemes for new hospitals, schools and prisons. Gordon Brown wasted £450 million on just the contractual paperwork for the London Underground Metronet PFI that then soon went bust. Various PFI schemes, such as Fazakerley Prison near Liverpool, have already recouped their original investment by refinancing the deal at lower interest.[25]
- Allowing developers significant planning gains from granting planning permission, and not charging property owners benefiting from public infrastructure investment, such as the new Jubilee Line, which raised property values along the line by £3.5 billion.
- Poor regulation, which has led to a series of financial mis-selling, and takeovers which undermine pensions. For example the pension provider Friends Provident Life was allowed to demutualise, and is now being taken over by Resolution, an offshore, tax avoiding shell company that will no doubt milk FPL at pensioners' expense. The government acknowledges the lax regulation of Equitable Life but has still not paid proper compensation to pensioners. The commons of pensions are not safe. The light-touch regulation of the City and the financial sector has resulted in the taxpayer bailing out the banks and mortgaging the future at a huge cost.

- Allowing generous bonuses and pensions to both failed and casino bankers; this is mirrored on a smaller scale by some MPs and ministers themselves exploiting the common wealth of taxpayers' money through a hitherto secretive expenses system.

To summarise, there has been a massive redistribution of wealth from society as a whole over the last thirty years to the wealthy corporations, financial institutions and the political and economic elites. They have accumulated wealth in the following ways:

- the privatisation, corporatisation and commoditisation of public assets and the commons;
- financialisation through a whole range of asset-stripping, private equity takeovers, speculation, hedge funds and ever riskier lending, such as Northern Rock and sub-prime mortgages;
- the management and manipulation of crises, such as springing the debt trap and using the shock therapy for dispossessing whole populations of their national wealth as in Russia and Iraq;
- using wars to extract huge profits from the state, such as the $3 trillion debt the US government now owes for Iraq;
- state redistributions to turn the flow of redistribution from poor to rich, such as making Britain a tax haven for the wealthy, where only the 'little people' pay tax.

Conclusion and discussion: unleashing capitalism

The purpose of this chapter was to analyse the story of neo-liberal capitalism, so that we can name what is happening and who benefits.

To summarise, neo-liberal capitalism has fed on the process of accumulation by dispossession and the use of economic shock therapy that takes advantage of a series of financial crises. Neo-liberalism has been exposed as a uniquely self-serving ideology for the rich and powerful. Historically, the 'golden age' of 1945–79 saw the increase of public, common and ordinary individual wealth and incomes. There was significant redistribution in the context of a more egalitarian, social democratic society.

This golden age was reversed after 1979 by the unleashing of selfish capitalism by neo-liberals such as Thatcher. Inequality has since risen significantly. There was a striking turnaround after 1979 in the relative fortunes of labour and capital, so much so that Ben Bernanke of the Federal Reserve in 2006 called on corporations to pay their workers more from their increased profits.[26]

According to Larry Elliott and Dan Atkinson, the neo-economic liberal gods have failed, and the financial elite have gambled away our futures. 'They promised economic stability, and have delivered chaos and volatility. They promised an economic order based on enterprise, thrift and personal effort and have delivered one based on chronic instability and wild speculation.'[27] Furthermore, they suggest, Western societies are run in the interest of 'moneyed oligarchies', rather than for ordinary people.

Andrew Glyn, the Oxford economist who charted the 'neo-liberal turn' from 1979 in his book *Capitalism Unleashed*, concluded that history was being run backwards by melting down the gains of the 'golden age' and returning to an older form of laissez-faire liberalism. He asked two key, prescient questions in 2007:

1.   Will the current financial system implode in a major crisis and bring prolonged recession?
2.   Can the social democratic welfare states of Northern Europe survive the pressures of globalisation and free-market ideology and keep developing in an egalitarian direction?

Will Hutton analysed how the financial sector has profited from a one-way bargain with society, hiding behind market fundamentalism whilst offloading its losses and risks on us. Part 3 asks how we can reverse this 'one-way bargain' and argues for the reclaiming of land, labour and capital as commons. The practical understanding of land, labour and capital as commons offers entry points for developing a creative, just and sustainable society that we can engage with now.

So how can capitalism be captured?

Summary

Type of society	Neo-liberal capitalist	Tripolar
Economy	Neo-liberal economy, based on free market competition, deregulation, globalisation, free capital movement, flexible labour	Associative, green, economy organised by mutuality and collaboration between producers, distributors and consumers
Polity	Captive corporate state, where property rights are dominant in a market democracy, with privatised public services; surveillance society and wars (e.g. against terrorism, Iraq, etc.) to ensure compliance	Representative and participative democracy focused on human rights, entitlements, social justice; a planning, enabling, resourcing and human-security-enhancing polity based on equality and social inclusion
Culture	Monocultures, suppression of cultural diversity, corporate media, privatised education, health and public services; commercialisation	Autonomous, self organising cultural organisations (education, health, media), communities and civil society, based on freedom
Education	A commodity to be paid for as a private good, hence paying fees for university courses, and 'modernising'/privatising education support services for private profit. Students as customers, teachers as producers	Free education is a cultural right, a public good and investment in society's future. Not-for-private-profit delivery. Students are active learners and inquirers as clients with rights

Health	A commodity to be bought on the market, delivered by privatised, for-profit health companies. Patients as consumers with private insurance	An integrated, comprehensive, autonomous public health service, with health as a commons, a public good. People responsible for their own health and engaged in health service governance
Arts and media	The arts and media captured by corporate industries for mass markets	Free, independent media and self organising arts sector for diverse groups, funded from member gifts, grants, business and creative commons fees
Science	Captured for profit and private patents, using public funding subsidised via university research bodies	Free, independent scientific research for its own sake. Applied research addresses priorities agreed with government, civil society and business
Family and community life	Commercialised, with children as commodities; nationalisation/ bureaucratisation of children, families and communities	Respect for rights to childhood and free, creative, diverse family and community lifeways
Land, capital	Reduced to commodities on the market; private ownership; concentration of ownership and power	Commons held in social trusteeship bodies, stewarded for social benefit and leasing for individual/business initiative. Private and statutory ownership
Nature, the earth, natural resources	Corporate profit from environmental destruction, extraction, dumping, externalising costs	Living within the earth's resource limits using environmentally sound technologies, recycling, repair and re-use; carbon-capping and sharing; redesigning for resilience
Consumption	Hyper-consumerism through stimulating wants	Needs-based, sustainable consumption
Growth and development	Jobless, ruthless, futureless, rootless, meaningless, voiceless growth, measured by GNP	Sustainable, resilient, equitable growth in a steady-state economy, measured by ISEW (Index of Sustainable Economic Welfare)
Income and wealth	Widening inequality of wealth and income; common wealth seizure by corporate and political elite sense of entitlement; workfare	Citizen's income as the basis for inclusion, security and equity; self-provisioning; redistribution for common wealth and public service access

Dominant driver	Acquisitive, competitive self interest – 'no such thing as society'	Balance of individual self realisation and growth, citizen engagement for the common good, and economic association for mutual benefit
Dominant groups	Corporate and plutocratic elites, with a subservient political elite; celebrity, 'winner takes all' culture	Dispersed, widespread leadership and agency/activism through cultural excellence, public service and economic collaboration
World Governing bodies	National political elites cede power upwards to dictatorial economic bodies such as the WTO, IMF, World Bank, and to military alliances, with the UN largely sidelined	Reinvention and democratisation of the UN, WTO, IMF, World Bank through world tripolar forums. Bodies such as the International Criminal Court are strengthened; human security through meeting millennium goals, fair trade, human rights, environmental protection, social justice, peaceful dispute resolution and good governance
Civil society	A way of offloading welfare, cultural and public services to cut business and government costs. (No general or politician would dream of using jumble sales to finance missiles.)	Leading body of the community/cultural sector with other cultural organisations, creating exemplars, raising the human spirit and changing values
Business	Private business dominated by ever larger corporations and finance through world markets, relying on government paid infrastructure, bailouts and the light-touch regulation of a self-correcting market	Social business with a growing mutual, co-op sector working through associative fair trade. Governance secured through well-integrated consumer, distributor and producer agreements. Localised, viable small/medium business economy integrated with world economy
Government	Government tasks include security, outsourcing services, securing citizen compliance, maintaining a supportive judiciary and legislature, creating good conditions for big business including light regulation, cut-price sell-off of public assets, tax breaks, tax havens, bailouts and revolving doors	Works with an independent legislature and judiciary to secure human, political, economic and cultural rights and entitlements; agrees resources needed for public and cultural services with business/economic sector and develops policy participatively through widespread public discussion and inquiry
Image of human being	Rational, competitive economic man who seeks self-interest and gain	Producers and consumers who associate for mutual benefit; engaged citizens and self-realising individuals who seek a balance of private and common good

Figure 7.3   Summary: a comparison of neo-liberal capitalist and tripolar society

PART 3

Redrawing Boundaries

Part 3 outlines some entry points for redrawing boundaries and restoring the fences torn down by unleashed capitalism. Redrawing the social ecology of society with three distinct systems of politics, culture and economics will help business, government and civil society to contribute their strengths for the common good. Here are four entry points:

- transforming capitalism: stewarding capital as a commons
- land for people and affordable homes
- citizen's income: wealth for all
- freeing education.

How to get there? An emergent change strategy

But how do we get there? Rather than impose an abstract, 'not invented here' programme, the four entry points listed above are *already* emerging. The method is to observe what is emerging and how this can be helped. Try asking, 'Where are the positive seeds for the future? How can these be understood and supported?' Take the community-supported food and farming movement. Starting in the 1980s, this is now a worldwide movement, including farmers' markets, community-supported farms and producer/consumer co-operatives. Or take the appropriate technology and natural capitalism movements. Businesses the world over are trying to do more with less, with leaner technology and processes. The learning accelerates the more it is spread around, like muck. One way of recognising positive emergent movements is that they don't need much pushing; rather, the virus spreads through example, inspiration, word of mouth and learning.

The emergent change strategy contrasts with the 'revolutionary' state-driven approach, political party manifestos or a top-down change plan rolled out by a remote management or government. One British default government change method is to blame, shame and coerce with a top-down plan implemented by statute law. However, the emergent change approach does not need patronising politicians 'incentivising' or 'nudging' people to do the required things, like more recycling. Rather, by engaging with people around burning questions, analysis, identifying the key questions to tackle, describing the current situation, learning from good practice, changes to implement a desired future can be realised through participative planning and design.

But, if the growing points for change coming from people, communities and organisations are ignored by political, civil society and business leaders, the situation will get worse, and then only breakdown may possibly lead to change. It took the 1929 Wall Street Crash, the Depression and the 1939–45 war to show the door to disastrous laissez-faire liberal capitalism and push back 'the market' with the Keynesian mixed economy and the welfare state. The peace movement and eminent British soldiers such as Sir Michael Rose wanted to bring about a better future in Iraq in 2002–3 through a variety of peaceful economic, cultural and political means. But Bush and Blair pushed through their $3 trillion war with disastrous results. Many young people the world over want to care for the planet, but will government, civil society and business follow their lead and support them?

So the first step is to ask, 'What are the positive growing points?' The second step is to understand human beings and the principles of development so as to guide social change. For example, one principle is that the more a commons, such as capital, water or land, is treated as a commodity, the more market failure and inequality there will be. Or the more that schools or health care systems are bureaucratised and politicised, the less real education and health there will be, and the more it will cost because discretionary, values-led motivation will disappear. Understanding these basic principles helps emergent changes.[1]

So the next three chapters argue for treating land, labour and capital as socially created commons. I will argue for the development of community land and capital trusteeship for securing community interest on the one hand, whilst leasing land and capital for individual initiative on the other. This crucial step of pushing back 'the market' by conceptualising land, labour and capital as commons offers a lever for developing a creative, wealthy, just and sustainable society.

Chapter 8

Transforming Capitalism: Stewarding Capital for Individual Enterprise and Common Good

The process by which banks create money is so simple that the mind is repelled.

J. K. Galbraith

The government should not borrow capital at interest as a means of financing government work and public enterprise. The government should create, issue and circulate all the currency and credit needed to satisfy the spending power of the government and the buying power of consumers.

Abraham Lincoln

When land, labour and capital are turned into commodities to be bought and sold on the market, the result is market failure, social injustice and widening inequality. Capital markets concentrate wealth in fewer and fewer hands, as do unfettered land and housing markets. This results in a huge disparity of income and wealth, and what John Ruskin called 'illth' rather than wealth. The aim of this chapter is to suggest ways of transforming capitalism, so that capital can be stewarded as a commons to lease for individual enterprise, whilst securing the common good. Enterprising people and businesses need access to capital, and at the same time society has an interest in stewarding capital for community benefits, such as an income stream for funding public services, whilst also lending capital to enterprising individuals who work productively.

This chapter will cover:

- what happens when market fundamentalism dominates
- from capital as a commodity to capital as a commons: circulating capital to enterprise
- giving by individuals and businesses

- giving royalty income
- limits to wealth: copyright law for fortunes
- transferring private and state capital ownership into commons capital trusts
- mutualising capital through community benefit co-operatives, commonwealths and partnerships
- channelling new capital created by the Bank of England into public investment
- setting up a national people's investment and pension fund
- global capital and environmental commons trusts
- from free to social enterprise.

What happens when market fundamentalism dominates?

To begin with, some theory. Neo-liberals believe that markets can best serve as a guide for decision-making through prices, and that most things can be treated as commodities. This means that there are property rights over things, processes, commons and relationships, that these can be priced and traded. But different societies set the boundaries between commodities and the commons in various ways. Native Americans such as Massasoit of the Wampanoag were astonished by the white settlers arriving in Cape Cod in the 1620s when they enclosed land and established private property. The land was the Great Spirit's – it 'belonged' to everyone, with custom guiding use. Indians were angry at the drug multinationals that patented products from the Neem tree, their traditional pharmacopoeia.

The creation of land, labour and capital markets is therefore central to neo-liberal economic theory. However, these are really commons, which are either socially created like capital and labour or nature-given like land and such resources as oil or water. You can certainly buy the products of labour from workers, but not labour itself. You can buy or lease the right to use land or a bundle of land related rights, but not the land itself, as it is not a commodity. You can buy or lease the right to use capital, but it is not a commodity that wears out like a chair. It is different in kind. Karl Polanyi considered that land, labour and capital 'are obviously not commodities ... the commodity description of labour, land and money (capital) is entirely fictitious'.

Leading thinkers of the last 200 years, such as John Ruskin, John Stuart Mill, Gandhi and Rudolf Steiner, advocated similar arguments to Polanyi's. They all considered that land and capital are rights to be held in trust for the community and that the use rights can then be leased to individuals. Mill embedded his ideas on the productive association of individual enterprise and community benefit into a legal form, the Industrial and Provident Society, which he got through parliament. This unique legal form still thrives. John Ruskin, who excoriated the extremes of capitalism in his day, famously said that human capital is the most important asset of a country: 'There is no wealth but life. Life, including all its powers of love, of joy, and of admiration. That country is the richest which nourishes the greatest number of noble and happy human beings.'[2]

Polanyi was blunt about what unfettered, free markets in land, labour and capital would do. They would demolish society, the economy, culture, people and the planet.

> To allow the market mechanism to be sole director of the fate of human beings and their natural environment, indeed, even of the amount and use of purchasing power, would result in the demolition of society. For the alleged commodity, 'labour power' cannot be shoved about, used indiscriminately, or even left unused, without affecting also the human individual who happens to be the bearer of this peculiar commodity. In disposing of man's labour power the system would, incidentally, dispose of the physical, psychological and moral entity 'man' attached to that tag. Robbed of the protective covering of cultural institutions, human beings would perish from the effect of social exposure; they would die as victims of acute social dislocation through vice, perversion, crime and starvation. Nature would be reduced to its elements, neighbourhoods and landscapes defiled, rivers polluted, military safety jeopardised, the power to produce food and raw materials destroyed. Finally, the market administration of purchasing power would periodically liquidate business enterprise, for shortages and surfeits of money would prove as disastrous to business as floods and droughts in primitive society.[3]

With Polanyi, we can also see the destruction caused by the 'flood and droughts' of speculative capital on the global markets and the destruction of the planet when the earth is treated as a commodity to be exploited. Look at the human waste caused when the market Bolsheviks imposed shock therapy on Russia in the 1990s under Yeltsin, with the resulting human dislocation and the plummeting of life expectancy.

So what are the practical alternatives for transforming neo-liberal capitalism through treating capital as a commons to be stewarded?

From capital as commodity to capital as trusteeship for common good and enterprise

To summarise the last chapter, the transfer of capital upwards from the poor, from the commons and the public sphere and the global free movement of capital result in wealth being concentrated in a plutocratic elite. This concentration of capital is caused by the system of the private, absolute ownership of capital. We allow capitalists to retain their private ownership of the capital that their business activities have created, with profits and inheritance taxes taking only a small amount of the capital created for public services and investment. This system of the private ownership of capital may have been economically and socially healthy in the early days of small businesses, where there was a personal, entrepreneurial relationship between the family owners and the business. The success of early capitalism was partly due to ethical foundations that built trust, interest, fair dealing and credit. However, with the growth of large corporations and the erosion of the old ethics, this private, corporate system of capital ownership no longer serves society well.

The excesses, injustice and waste that can come from private and corporate capital ownership are there for all to see. However, many business leaders of integrity deplore such waste. They argue that they make a highly responsible use of capital, supplying much-needed goods and services, employing people, paying taxes and creating wealth. Many entrepreneurs are far more interested in creative business development, developing new products to meet human needs, than in amassing wealth for its own sake. Think of Dame Anita Roddick, who built the Body Shop on ethical business principles and gave her money away to good causes. Think of the business people who tithe their time and money to the community. Think of the Quakers whose wealth was second only to their godliness. However, those pioneering days are largely gone, except perhaps in emerging markets. With global transnational businesses, some of which are free-riding on societies around the planet, it is time to transform capital ownership.

Even capitalists are calling for the control of the private equity firms. They say these are endangering capitalism as we know it because private equity firms get such big tax breaks from the government. Nicolas Ferguson of private equity firm Permira reckons that private equity capitalists pay less than 10 per cent tax, arrogantly saying that we 'pay less tax than a cleaning lady'. New Labour doesn't mind. Peter Mandelson famously said in 1997 that 'New Labour is intensely relaxed about people becoming filthy rich as long as they pay taxes.'

Take the Blackstone Group, which owns Madame Tussauds, Centre Parks and Café Rouge. Blackstone started with $400,000 and now manages funds of $88 billion. It buys low-priced companies with cheap loans, asset strips them, restructures them and then sells these off. In Britain, because the taxes on private equity firms are so low, people argue that this fundamentally undermines capitalism.[4] In October 2004, private equity group Charterhouse invested £481.8 million in the £1.35 billion acquisition of Saga. Two years later Saga refinanced, so Charterhouse was repaid the £481.8 million in full, plus interest of £101.5 million, a return of more than 20 per cent. In the Saga and AA merger, £4.8 billion was borrowed and £3 billion was used to pay the AA/Saga borrowings, leaving £1.8 billion to be divided between investors Charterhouse, Permira and CVC and management.[5]

No wonder Polly Toynbee wrote in the *Guardian* that 'the Babylonian excesses of the rich have to be tackled if we are to stop our society being wrenched apart'. She asked 'Does this wealth matter?' 'No' say a government unwilling to tax private equity firms fairly, 'the poor are not have-nots obsessing about the have yachts: they need basic things. London is booming with jobs created by billionaires' wants. Chase away the zero taxpayers with tax demands and no one gains. What London looks like is the last days of Rome. Complete with imported slaves. The nation thrives, and there is more money collected for social projects.' But Polly Toynbee points out the downside. House prices are high, top salaries are up, there is a deepening social divide and social programmes like Sure Start are under funded. It is hard to see how the untaxed capital gains and profits of private equity firms and zero-taxed private equity capitalists benefit ordinary people and the nation.[6] When Chancellor Alistair Darling proposed in January 2008 that highly paid non-domiciled City executives should pay tax, there was such a storm of protest that he dropped his plan. This left ordinary British taxpayers angry that rich non-doms are even allowed to be members of the House of Lords.

So what are the alternatives? When businesses grew into large companies in the nineteenth and early twentieth centuries some capitalists were concerned about the wealth and power that the private ownership of capital brought. Some did not like the idea of their incompetent children inheriting the businesses they had created and wasting the capital. They wanted to see their business continue to employ people, create wealth and provide needed goods. Andrew Carnegie, the US steel tycoon, famously said, 'Those who die rich, die disgraced.' He set up philanthropic foundations to give his money away, for example to create Carnegie libraries in US towns. Others, like Joseph Rowntree and George Cadbury, set up garden towns on land-trust principles at New Earswick in York, and Bourneville in Birmingham. The Joseph Rowntree Charitable Trust was to set up fund work that addresses the causes of poverty. Some went further and put their businesses into trusteeship for securing the future of the enterprise and also for social benefit.

For example, the leading quality supermarket Waitrose and the John Lewis department stores are owned by the John Lewis Partnership. This was set up in the early twentieth century by the Methodist John Lewis, who was shocked to find that he earned more than all his staff combined. So he put the business into the ownership of the Partnership, and to this day, each staff partner gets a share of the profits, after tax and the allocation of capital needed for reinvestment in the business. The Scott Bader Commonwealth is another example of a company where there is common ownership of the means of production. The philanthropic owner also endowed it.

Such business entrepreneurs realised that capital is socially created – that enterprises require people with knowledge and skills, a secure society, a legal system, markets, a transport system and communications to manufacture goods profitably. Without society, it is not possible to create capital. Directly as a result of this key insight, many creative business people have made sure that some of their surplus profits go back into society – to the arts, to scientific research, to the community, to education. Farsighted entrepreneurs set up foundations to give away the income from their investments, so that this generosity continues long after they die.

But this still leaves the key question of the claims of society to capital after the pioneer start-up phase of a business, when there is a healthy personal connection between the entrepreneur and the growing business. In the development of a business beyond the pioneer phase, there comes a time when society needs to step in to preserve its capital base, for example, to prevent a firm moving offshore, or to stop a takeover that will negatively affect jobs, pensions and the business or result in asset stripping. One way of doing this is through a capital transfer process, whereby the capital is put into a public capital equity trust, and then leased to the business entrepreneur who makes the best ethical, social, environmental and business bid through a rigorous selection process.

The Takeover Panel of the Department of Trade and Industry offers an existing business transfer process to build on. Currently, the Takeover Panel has a limited remit, ruling on things like whether a takeover helps or hinders competition.

However, the remit could be widened with a panel composed of public interest, stakeholder and business members. They can decide on takeovers, not on the basis of which bidder has the most money, but on a wider set of criteria such as which bidder has the best business, ethical and environmental plan; whether capital, jobs and pensions are secured; which bidder has the competence to develop the business most productively; and which bid offers the most value. This process can be likened to a job interview, or the French Safer process for choosing which farmer can buy a farm that has been put up for sale, in order to keep farms affordable, locally owned and working. The Takeover Panel, after a careful selection process, can conclude a full repairing lease with the successful bidder, with transparent conditions for securing public benefit and business interest, rather than allowing a sale to the highest bidder.

Currently, the stock market and the government in the shape of the Takeover Panel can be applauded by anti-capitalists for allowing so many takeovers and mergers that result in a significant long-term destruction of company value. An extreme example was Daimler Benz, which took over Chrysler in 1998 for $36 billion and ended up selling it in 2007 in a complex deal that cost Daimler $500 million. The AOL–Time Warner merger once had a combined market capitalisation of $350 billion, whereas as of May 2009 it is $28.8 billion, a value loss of $321.2 billion. As John Lanchester says, 'for anti-capitalists, merger = fiesta'.[7] Takeovers and mergers clearly benefit stockbrokers, financial institutions and the management of the 'winning' company in terms of bonuses, but not necessarily customers, staff, investors, society or the local community. Businesses need protection from predatory financial capitalists.

The basic principle underlying the business transfer process is that capital is socially created, so society has an interest in the successful business. The careful selection of capable new people will ensure that the business continues to prosper. The business and its capital can be understood as a commons leased for productive use to a competent entrepreneur, rather than as an individually owned commodity

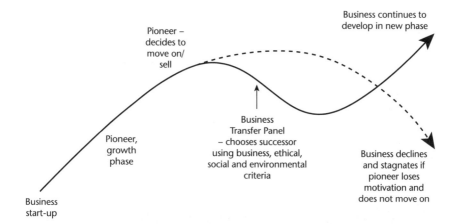

Figure 8.1   The business transfer/takeover process to secure enterprise and capital stewardship

to be disposed of only for private benefit. However, the personal, creative relationship between the business and the entrepreneur or enterprising team is crucial for continuing success.

A Marxist, of course, would say that all capital is the surplus amount withheld by the capitalist from the workers in his business, which they would have otherwise have received as wages. However, this ignores other capital-creating factors such as the better use of science and technology for innovation, better management, cost savings, reduced interest payments for capital used, quality improvements, investment in better tools, increased demand, as well as various forms of windfall profits and tax breaks. The business transfer process would ensure both that society benefits, that the business continues to be run well by capable people and that the outgoing entrepreneur gets a fair share.

The urgent need for a public interest overhaul of the business takeover process is brought home regularly on the stock exchange, where those with the most money take over good businesses, with the business, shareholders, society and customers losing out. For example in July 2009 the offshore, Guernsey-based tax avoider Resolution made a bid for the once mutually owned Friends Provident. If 'successful', i.e. in terms of stockbrokers' fees, with extra bonuses for Resolution and Friends Provident directors, the takeover will probably mean bad news for staff, shareholders and people saving for pensions. Capital needs saving from the destruction of value by a hostile financial system.

It is striking how much capital is given away. For example the American multibillionaire investor Warren Buffet has given much of his wealth to the Bill Gates Foundation, which amongst other things aims to improve health in Africa. But welcome as such philanthropy is, this disposal is still a private decision. Society as a whole needs to secure its shared capital commons for enduring social benefit. This commons will enable businesses to continue to provide needed goods and services, rather than be 'offshored' or asset-stripped and loaded with debt.

So, building on the emergent, established practices of successful capitalists giving their assets away for philanthropy and business leaders like John Lewis putting their firm into trusteeship, I propose nine ways of capturing capital. All are based on the principle of treating capital as a commons to be held in trust for society, rather than capital as a market commodity. The purpose is to create a virtuous circle of putting capital into trust, where an increasing pool of public wealth is fed by a stream of capital in the form of profits, royalties from inventions, taxes, contributions and gifts. This capital pool as our 'common wealth' can then be stewarded, invested in business or given for public and cultural benefits. These ways are:

- giving by individuals and businesses
- giving royalty income from the creative industries
- limits to inherited wealth: copyright law for fortunes
- transferring private and state capital ownership into commons capital trusts
- mutualising capital through community benefit co-operatives, commonwealths and partnerships
- channelling new capital created by the Bank of England into public capital investment

- setting up local and national people's investment and pension funds
- establishing global capital and environmental commons trusts
- culture change and regulation.

Giving by individuals and businesses

Many people and businesses give time, skills, resources and money for social benefit. Organisations working in the cultural sector such as NGOs, charitable, environmental, educational, arts, religious, voluntary and community organisations rely on such gifts for core funding, for the services they provide or investment in new projects and facilities. In 2005, British people gave £8.9 billion to charity.

Grant-making foundations and trusts rely on a stream of gifts and endowments, so that they can then make grants. The National Lottery, though run by the government and often raided by politicians for their pet projects like the £790 million Millennium Dome and for the 2012 Olympic Games, is a big source of grants. Changing the governance of the National Lottery from a government dominated to a joint government and civil society run foundation could ensure autonomy from direct government control, to prevent pet political projects such as the Millennium Dome and the Olympic Games starving other good causes of funding.

The government encourages charitable giving through Gift Aid, so that charities can claim back 28 per cent of an individual's gift from the Inland Revenue. (Gift Aid could be raised to 40 per cent on all gifts, not just for higher rate taxpayers, to increase income.)

The result of this stream of giving by individuals and businesses is the development of a huge pool of social, cultural, human and financial capital and assets for enduring community benefit. Gifts liberate initiative, enable innovation and lead to a more creative world. The more we give, the wealthier we are. The glorious diversity resulting from free giving enriches life in so many unexpected ways. And giving encourages giving.

Giving royalties: the arts pay for the arts

One way of building creative artistic, scientific, technological or cultural capital is to encourage royalty-giving to build the creative commons. Inventors, scientists, artists, writers, performers, musicians and designers working in the creative industries can gift or part-gift the royalty income from their patents, copyrights, designs and performances to cultural foundations. The royalty rights can also be given on death. These gifts can then support creative individuals, artists, theatres, research and work as part of the creative gift economy. Businesses or organisations that share the benefits from exploiting such creative inventions can also give a share of the income.

Whilst there are creators who want to give away their inventions, others are more cautious. For example, the 'creative commons' agreements allow free individual, research and educational use provided there is acknowledgement, but requires a fee if there is any financial gain from use. And huge gifts are being made

---

Box 8.1   Can the arts support the arts?

When members of the American Federation of Musicians became concerned about recorded music crowding out live performances, and thus jeopardising musicians' jobs, they set up the Music Performance Trust Fund. Equally, the record industry was concerned because they benefited from working musicians' talents, and wondered how the industry's success could support musicians in turn. An agreement between the industry and musicians created a tithe of a fraction of 1 per cent of records, tapes and CDs that went into a trust independent of recording companies and musicians. The money is then used to pay musicians who play live music in public places, schools and parks. Musicians play music at both ends of the chain, and in the middle is the royalty system that allows the art to support the art.

Lewis Hyde also suggests other ways of replenishing the creative commons whilst also rewarding individual creators. He says, 'The best idea I've seen is for a two-stage copyright system. During the first stage, copyright fees would still be collected, but the income would go to the copyright holder, as it does now. In the second stage, copyright fees would still be collected, but the income would go to endowments for the arts and humanities. After that, all works would enter the public domain.' The key to managing the creative commons is to respect it as a gift, as creating is also about giving – but creative people also need financial support so they can keep productive.

See Lewis Hyde, The Gift *and www.friendsofthecommons.org*

---

to society by creators. Take the Linux operating system. A computing student called Linus Torvalds at the University of Helsinki initiated this operating system in October 1991. He invited other programmers around the world to work together on 'his' new operating system. The Linux open source movement was partly motivated by computer programmers who were outraged by the poor quality of Microsoft's Windows MS DOS, or 'dirty operating system', the exploitative licensing fees charged by Bill Gates and Microsoft's monopolistic practices. They believed passionately in the global open communications mission of IT and the Internet as civilising cultural forces. Since Linux first appeared, thousands of people around the world have worked to improve it. Linux is far superior to any Microsoft operating system and freely downloadable.

The proposal would be for those benefiting from Linux, and similar inventions, to give royalty income, such as tithing a proportion of the profits, to creative commons trusts for supporting creative work.

Companies benefiting from creative inventions could also be required by government to give part of the income stream from patents to creative foundations for supporting the arts and science. For example, many publicly funded scientific discoveries have then been exploited by companies, without any social pay-back. Public interest royalty income could be levied, to support further original research and to support research in less profitable, but no less important areas.

Limits to inherited wealth: copyright law for fortunes

How much is enough wealth? After all, you can't take it with you when you die. This is one reason that more socially or spiritually minded people make sure they give their wealth away to good causes, donate to foundations and ensure their businesses are handed on to those who can direct them productively for social benefit. And how much in this life is enough? £10 million? Society is not served by people acquiring large fortunes and passing them on to unproductive heirs who as 'trust fundies' can be morally crippled by living on unearned income from large inherited fortunes. One idea suggested by Rudolf Steiner was to subject large fortunes to a capital copyright law, a bit like a copyright in a book. Just as the copyright on a book enters the public domain after the author has been dead for seventy years, the capital copyright for fortunes could be set at, say, ten years after death. Any business capital would then be put into trusteeship for continuing productive use, and other remaining capital given direct to cultural life.[8]

Transforming private and corporate capital ownership into capital trusteeship: growing the family silver

Ownership is different in kind from trusteeship. Most people readily understand this distinction. When setting up Fordhall Farm community land trust in 2005, I phoned the Inland Revenue to ask if community land ownership would qualify for Gift Aid, if people donated money for a community farm buy-out. They said, 'No, ownership as such is not charitable.' Remembering John Ruskin, I then asked,

---

Box 8.2   Tolkien Trust received only £32,000 royalties from the £3 billion sales of the Lord of the Rings films

The Tolkien Trust has received only £32,000 from the blockbusting Lord of the Rings films distributed by New Line Cinema. Tolkien set up the trust in 1969 with an agreement for the film rights of 7.5 per cent of the gross receipts of films of his works, once the films had made 2.6 times the production costs. The trust's lawyer said the case was 'an extraordinary example of how enormous financial success can breed unabashed and insatiable greed'.

Think of how some of the royalties could have been used to nurture creative work and education. There is a need for authors, artists and inventors to make common cause through developing stronger forms of copyright and royalty.

'Would community land trusteeship qualify for Gift Aid as an objective?' After a pregnant pause, the answer was 'yes, trusteeship for community benefit would qualify'.

So what I propose is a new capital commons sector where community capital trusts are an alternative vehicle for trusteeship, rather than corporate owner-ship of capital. Trusts that require trustees to serve beneficiaries in line with the objects cannot be taken over. They are more appropriate than statutory bodies for preserving gift capital assets for present and future generations, and for leasing such assets for a range of economic, social and cultural enterprises and benefits.

In practice, a variety of trust vehicles are already emerging such as community capital trusts, capital transfer bodies, community benefit co-operatives, founda-tions and partnerships.

The purpose of a commons capital trust (CCT) is to receive, acquire, hold and invest capital for enduring economic, cultural and social benefit. CCTs would be non-profit and would acquire capital through gifts and through investing in a range of ventures from risky to safe. Surpluses would be reinvested. The state could use CCTs as a neutral but professional, public-interest conduit for investing sover-eign funds or for the communalisation, rather than the privatisation, of previously state-owned assets and enterprises. CCTs could receive capital assets from compa-nies at the point of takeover and from companies where the founders wanted to sell up. CCTs could act as a transfer vehicle for the leasing of assets according to an agreed business, social and environmental plan.

CCTs would start to make up for the capital loss to society by the state privatisa-tion and corporatisation of often-undervalued assets and enterprises. This capital loss happened not just at the original sale, but every time the asset was sold on. This loss happened because of politicians' short-term desire for capital receipts for spending and their neo-liberal ideology that 'public enterprise is bad, private is good'. The Treasury wants capital receipts, civil servants do not have the time or expertise to really value a business, and they lack the entrepreneurial vision for spotting the potential business added-value.

Take the 2003 privatisation of QinetiQ by the Ministry of Defence, which made a £107 million profit for the ten civil servants involved in the privatisation. Edward Leigh, Tory chair of the Commons Public Accounts Committee, said, 'QinetiQ's top managers … won the jackpot. They got a mind-boggling return of almost 20,000 per cent on their investments.' The National Audit Office told how ten former civil servants running the privatised QinetiQ devised their own incentive scheme, which later gave them huge returns. It enabled non-executive chair Sir John Chisholm to see his £130,000 investment rise to £25.97 million and CEO Graham Love see his £110,000 rise to £21.35 million on the day the firm was floated on the stock market. Carlyle Group took a part-share of £42 million in the undervalued QinetiQ, which was then worth £374 million on flotation. Baroness Taylor, Minister for Defence Procurement, told the NAO lamely that the sale had, 'delivered excellent value for money, generating more than £800 million for the taxpayer'.

As Vince Cable MP said, 'This deal didn't sell the family silver; it gave it away.' Clearly, QinetiQ was grossly undervalued by the Ministry of Defence, no doubt eager for a sell-off to get capital receipts, even at a knock-down price. The ten civil servants who profited so much from the eventual flotation clearly did know the potential value of QinetiQ, which is why they invested so heavily in it. Only expert valuation and defence professionals, like the Carlyle Group, would know of the real current and potential value of the various patents, products and research services of QinetiQ. Given that this is a very expensive, scandalous way of selling off public assets, which sacrifices both capital receipts and future income, it would have been far better for the British taxpayer to secure its present and future capital, to transfer QinetiQ to an expert, public-interest CCT.[9] That is, if it had to be privatised at all.

Capital and business owners could also transfer their wealth to CCTs, confident that their assets would continue to be used fruitfully long after their old age and death, and not wasted by incompetent family members. CCTs would have professional financial, legal, business and management expertise to act as a public equity trust, rather than as a private equity firm like Carlyle.

CCTs, like venture capital firms, could also help finance entrepreneurial start-up businesses, with an agreement to transfer a share of the ownership of the business with its capital into trusteeship. At some point, the original entrepreneur wants to retire, move on, sell or dispose of the business and make sure it continues successfully. The CCT can then take full or part trusteeship of the business and act as a broker for competent bidders who have to submit a comprehensive business, environmental, ethical and social plan for how they will run and develop it. A transfer panel, made up, say, of the outgoing entrepreneur, competent business people and stakeholders can assess the bids, and conclude a full 'capital repairing and increasing' lease with the successful bidder. The outgoing entrepreneur gets a mutually agreeable package of benefits. The CCT builds the capital commons, with an income stream for further investment, and the business will continue to develop in new, competent hands within the framework of a social ownership lease, as for example with the Scott Bader Commonwealth.

Currently, entrepreneurial start-up businesses are taken over by other corporations, who may have the capital but not the expertise to run the businesses well, by asset strippers, by hostile bidders who then close them down and sell off the capital equipment, by competitors who have less ethical practices and by companies that close down the business, sack staff and move abroad.

The CCT solution, depending on the context, offers a way of circulating capital to competent entrepreneurs and management who can keep developing the business, keep staff employed and serve customers. CCTs also treat capital as a commons held in trust, soundly stewarded for public benefit. One key benefit could be a major shift from running business primarily to make a profit for personal gain, to running a business to profitably meet customers' needs. CCTs could remove the power that comes with control over accumulated wealth, after the healthy entrepreneurial, capital-creating phase of a business, when the personal connection of pioneer and business is vital. But CCTs could also ensure the continuation of this personal connection by leasing the use of capital to suitable managements who know the business. So CCTs are a bit like a tool-hire firm, where people borrow tools. Questions that entrepreneurs on the one hand and the CCT on the other might ask on start-up and or transfer could include:

- E: How can I get access to the capital needed to set up and or develop this business?
- CCT: How can the loan, lease or share issue enable effective start-up and secure the community's interest? How can this be reflected in the business plan, and does this include a triple bottom line?
- E: How can I, when I am no longer able, or no longer have the will to carry on, transfer my business to competent successors?
- CCT: How can the current business and the potential business be valued? How much capital can be given away without harming the business? What is an appropriate 'entrepreneurial share' to cover personal, retirement and family needs?
- CCT: How can the capital and business continue to deliver both community benefit – in the form of jobs, taxes, training, needed goods and services, respect for the environment, new investment – and individual benefit for the incoming entrepreneur or management?
- CCT: What are the business, environmental, social and ethical plans of the business?

So CCTs share some features with private equity firms, venture capital companies, social banks, sovereign funds and some charitable foundations now beginning to invest in worthwhile ventures. The purpose is to enable asset transfer to competent users, so that a commons capital trust is developed for enduring social, economic and cultural benefit.

Mutualising capital and businesses through community benefit co-operatives, foundations and partnerships

There is a large mutually owned financial services sector, originating in the co-operative movement in the nineteenth century, when people formed member-benefit co-ops, usually constituted as Industrial and Provident Societies. Many mutual pension funds, insurance companies, banks and building societies were constituted in this way. Many, like the Nationwide Building Society, are member-owned.

Sadly, the directors, managers and members of many mutuals failed to reinvent the businesses with renewed co-operative values in the neo-liberal heydays of the 1980s and 1990s. Directors pushed for demutualisation, with all the share options and increased salaries that brought them personal gains. Members voted for the windfall cash and share gains that represented the accumulated assets of the mutual saved up over generations. They valued windfall gains over the benefits of slightly better interest and loan terms, stability and the community contribution of their mutual.

Community benefit co-operatives with an asset lock cannot demutualise for member benefit, but have to hand on assets on winding up, for example to bodies with similar community benefit aims. This is why many emerging community land trusts have chosen this legal form for holding land and property in trust for community benefit.

However, there is a fascinating history of entrepreneurial family firms putting business ownership into trusteeship. The aim is usually to keep the business thriving, with effective management, through a combination of gifting the profits not needed for reinvestment in the business to a foundation and sharing the profits with all staff. The John Lewis Partnership is a leading British example, where all staff are partners in the business and regularly receive an annual profit share of over 10 per cent of their usual salary. When the original John Lewis realised that he earned more than all his staff put together, he was shocked at the inequity. Rather than give the business away to staff, though, he put the capital into a Partnership body that ensured effective business management leadership, guarded against takeovers and ensured all staff were benefiting partners. Today, Waitrose supermarkets and John Lewis department stores are legendary for quality, price, customer service, profitability, working conditions and business management. It is significant to realise that a business's capital can be secured in a Partnership, protected from the stock market drive for 'shareholder value', that management is free to develop the business whilst partners share in the business's success. The John Lewis Partnership has worked well for nearly a hundred years.

Box 8.3   John Lewis's success

Sir Stuart Hampson, chair of John Lewis for thirteen years, considered that the group's partnership structure was key to its success. 'When you come in to one of our stores, you are not being served by an employee, you are being served by an owner of the business and customers do really notice the difference.

'Also there is the ability to take long-term decisions – the fact that we have said we are going to double our size and know we will not be subject to a takeover or a restructuring. We can tackle the long term decisions without being driven by a need to deliver an increase in profits every few years.

'Being a partner is about being a decent citizen in a decent business. It is the thing that singles us out from the rest of business.'

In March 2007 partners received a bonus of more than nine weeks' pay totalling £155 million. The total value of the staff benefits was £300 million, with £85 million going to the group's non-contributory final salary pension scheme, £65 million for staff discounts, subsidised holiday homes, dining rooms and societies.

Overall sales for 2006 were £2.7 billion for department stores and £3.7 billion for Waitrose.

Source: Julia Finch, 'John Lewis shares £155m', Guardian, 9 March 2007

The Scott Bader Commonwealth is another example of putting capital into trust. Entrepreneur Ernest Bader assigned all the shares of his Scott Bader Company to the Commonwealth, a holding company based on democratic membership control by all staff. If liquidated, the remaining capital would pass to a charity. The Commonwealth members collectively own the capital. Bader developed a successful plastics and paint firm, guided by strong pacifist and Christian values. He disliked the wage system and working in a command and control, hierarchical enterprise. He felt this was undignified and against the spirit of Christianity. So the Commonwealth worked on three levels: economically as a well-run, profitable business; socially as a community of members with equal status and collective ownership; and culturally through the giving away of half the profits for cultural and charitable purposes. There is a ratio of 1:7 of the highest to lowest paid, with a carefully worked out pay system. The annual bonus, usually half the profits after tax and capital set aside for reinvestment, goes into an equal bonus for the 360 staff members.

The British co-operative movement is a successful example of how capital assets can be mutualised and thriving social businesses can be run for staff, community, member and customer benefit. Customers and members can clearly see the social dividend going back into the community in the form of gifts for community projects. For example Mid Counties Co-op gives £500 community dividend grants to community groups and start-up community-benefit co-ops. Recent speculative attempts to demutualise co-ops, such as in financial services, resulted in 2003 in legislation to strengthen asset locks, which protect the capital developed mutually.

Since the essence of the division of labour that underpins the economy is mutual exchange, in cooperating together for mutual benefit, it is not surprising that the co-operative movement is today a massive, worldwide movement. The rewards of cooperating together effectively are often practically greater than the rewards of competing in a cut-throat way. As Benjamin Franklin once said, 'We either hang together, or hang separately.' The modern British Co-op was started in 1844 by the Rochdale Pioneers, and then spread around the world in less than fifty years. This is their story.

> In 1844 28 working men gathered together to set up the Rochdale Equitable Pioneers Society and opened a co-op shop on Toad Lane in Rochdale. They sold basic items such as flour, butter, tea and candles, but it was how they ran the business that made them different.
>
> They had decided it was time shoppers were treated with honesty, openness and respect, that they should be able to share in the profits that their custom contributed to and that they should have a democratic right to have a say in the business. Every customer of the shop became a member and so had a true stake in the business.
>
> This way of doing business was revolutionary. These businessmen didn't adulterate products, by putting foreign leaves in tea or chalk in flour. They didn't simply see customers as the way to make a profit at the expense of others.

They believed that pooling resources and ensuring everyone benefited, was the way to do business. Unsurprisingly, and to the annoyance of other traders, the reputation of the co-op shop was soon established and customers flocked to it, certain that they would be served quality products at affordable prices.[10]

A co-op is an association of people who join together voluntarily to meet their common economic, social, or cultural needs through a jointly owned and democratically controlled enterprise. A co-op is a social business, with members on a one-person, one-vote basis, electing a board of directors who then choose and supervise the effective management of the enterprise. The guiding values are those of self-help, self-responsibility, democracy, equality, equity and solidarity. Members, following the founders' traditions, believe in the values of honesty, openness, social responsibility and caring for others. These values are put into practice through the seven co-op principles of:

- voluntary and open membership
- democratic member control
- member economic participation
- autonomy and independence
- education, training and information
- cooperation among co-operatives
- concern for the community.

The purpose, values, principles and working social business models of the British co-operative movement came from the enterprising experience of working people, addressing practically how their needs can be met. So where businesses choose to go down the co-operative route, provided that there are asset locks in place, the capital of the co-op is secure for continuing business and community benefit.[11]

It was striking that all the demutualised banks such as HBOS (once the Halifax Building Society), Bradford and Bingley, Northern Rock, Alliance and Leicester got into trouble in the credit crunch and had to be taken over. The Co-op Bank is the only bank that had surpluses to lend to the Bank of England during the crunch. Certainly, the governance of co-op and mutual banks and building societies, with one-member one-vote, is a far better model for banks and utilities than private banks aiming at maximising 'shareholder value' and big bonuses for directors. The big caveat though is the vital importance of member education and participation to make mutuals work well, otherwise members will forget co-op values. And it was the carrot of jam today from sharing out the assets built up over generations by old mutuals which was a major cause of demutualization.

Channelling £45 billion a year of new capital created by the private banks into public capital investment

New capital can be captured by a new capital stream for public capital investment that is currently worth up to £45 billion a year. Surprisingly, private banks currently capture this £45 billion a year for themselves. This fact has been an open secret, a conjuring trick that bankers prefer not to discuss. The proposal to capture all this new debt capital for public benefit would remove the current privilege the Bank of England allows private banks, that of spending new money into circulation through debt creation. This proposal is to allow only the Bank of England, say through a designated People's National Investment Bank, to create such new money and to spend it into circulation through investment in new schools, public infrastructure, social housing, health, education, culture and the environment. So how, the reader may ask, do the banks currently create such huge amounts of debt capital from nothing?

J. K. Galbraith once famously wrote, 'The process by which banks create money is so simple that the mind is repelled.'[12] According to James Bruges, it is illegal to make money by forging bank notes, but banks, which are privately owned businesses, can legally create money. How? By making us loans and mortgages, which put us into debt and which we pay back with interest. Banks need not borrow money and can create the loan needed on the computer, as information. Lord Josiah Stamp, a former Bank of England director, said in 1937, 'The modern banking system manufactures money out of nothing. The process is perhaps the most astounding piece of sleight of hand that was ever invented.'

Here is how this sleight of hand works. When you get a loan from a bank, you sign an agreement and the bank manager credits your account with the loan on his computer and the money is put into circulation. The bank may not actually have the money, but has had to lodge a fraction of the new money created with the central bank as a reserve. This is called 'fractional reserve banking'. It is only our 'confidence' that the bank will pay back our savings that keeps the whole show going. Only about 5 per cent of the money in circulation is physical paper and coins. Northern Rock shows what happens when people – and bankers – lose confidence in a bank.

If you borrow, say, £100,000 for a flat, you will pay around £100,000 in interest by the end of the loan. According to Bruges, over 95 per cent of the capital in use has been created by privately owned banks putting their customers into debt: 'These institutions own the nation's money and we pay them interest for using it, not just once, but year after year. If the government allowed the central bank, instead of commercial banks, to create the UK's currency it would be returning the country to a sane banking system – one that existed before it was hijacked by the commercial banks.'[13]

So the proposal is to channel the creation of new money via CCTs for public investment. This proposal is backed by respected advocates of monetary reform like James Robertson, who said in 2005 that 'It should be illegal for commercial banks to create money denominated in the national currency, just as it is illegal to forge coins or counterfeit banknotes.' This call for monetary reform follows Thomas Jefferson, US President from 1801 to 1809, who said: 'If the American people ever allow the banks to control the issuance of their currency, they will deprive the people of all property. I sincerely believe that the banking institutions having the power of money are more dangerous to liberty than standing armies.' Abraham Lincoln tried to go further with monetary reform, saying that: 'The government should not borrow capital at interest as a means of financing government work and public enterprise. The government should create, issue and circulate all the

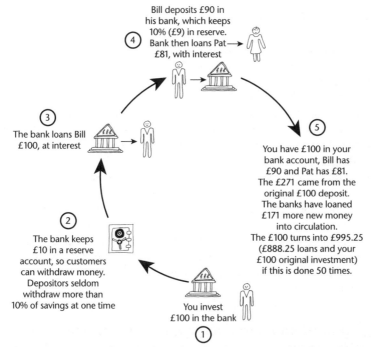

Figure 8.2   Money from nothing: how banks create capital from thin air
Source: James Robertson, 'Money from Nothing', Yes! Summer 2009, www.yesmagazine.org

currency and credit needed to satisfy the spending power of the government and the buying power of consumers.' It was shortly after this that he was assassinated – whether this was a coincidence is debatable.

James Robertson, co-founder of the New Economics Foundation and former director of the Inter Bank Research Association, describes how monetary reform could be implemented:

1.   The central bank, independent of government, should bring into being as much money as it decides is needed for the money supply. Government should spend it into circulation like it does with its other revenue, such as money from taxes.

2.   Commercial banks would then have to borrow money in order to make loans. They would become brokers charging a fee for their services. There would be no restriction on borrowing and lending except that the money must already exist. Banks would not be allowed to create money out of thin air as they do now – just as you and I are not allowed to forge banknotes and lend them to people, at interest.[14]

These two measures would increase UK national investment income by as much as £45 billion a year. Elaborate off-public-balance-sheet deceptions that mortgage our future to corporations like Gordon Brown's PFI would not be needed. Public investment could be financed without tax increases or mortgaging future genera-tions. The losers would be the banks. The government would get the public benefit of issuing money. A People's National Investment Bank could be a channel for investing and stewarding such new capital for enduring public benefit.

The government could choose to spend far more money into circulation than the current free £45 billion a year or so that they allow the banks. The Bank of England printed electronic money to the tune of up to £175 billion in 2008–9 by means of quantitative easing through the banks, when the alternative could be to spend this directly into circulation through real activities like building houses and rebuilding Britain's decaying transport infrastructure. (Japan recently got out of recession by putting cash into people's hands to spend in the real economy.) Rather than borrow huge amounts of money and increase the national debt, the government and Bank of England could issue new money, for the banks to then borrow, pay interest on and lend out. Currently, one thing that central bankers such as 'Helicopter' Ben Bernanke are doing is dumping printed money on banks as a free lunch 'to get the economy going'. However, instead of the bank-friendly helicopter approach, why not let the new money go directly to businesses via a People's National Investment Bank who can then use it productively in the real economy?

Setting up local and national people's investment and pension funds

The real pension scam is that we have invested current income, hard-earned from our work, into the assets of over-valued stock-market-quoted companies. Our money has been siphoned off to pay for the fees and bonuses of pension fund dealers, brokers and shareholders. Anyone investing in a private pension in this way will have paltry pensions and will have seen the value of their pension pot tumble. Those like teachers with index-linked public sector pensions are fortunate.

Local and national asset funds for investment and pensions could be one way for people to free themselves from the casino pension firms and banks. This would mean the renewal of the local, mutually owned and governed friendly society, credit union, building society and pensions sector. Investors would be able to see their pension investment going into local real assets. For example, Stroud Common Wealth raised £170,000 in grants for renovating The Exchange for workspace for co-op and social enterprise development and £45,000 in fair-interest-bearing loans from local people. There is growing experience from around the country of such successful direct community investment, for example in wind farms.

The purpose in setting up people's investment and pension funds would be to develop an independent capital commons for both public investment and indi-vidual benefits such as a citizen's income and pensions.

The funds would receive pension contributions from individuals and from companies wanting to protect their pension scheme assets from predatory take-overs and asset strippers. The local funds would be less risky than the casino pension and investment funds. Other sources of capital flows could include wind-fall capital and property gains, a proportion of company profits, resource taxes

Box 8.4   Quantitative easing, printing money and creating debt-free money

Mervyn King, Governor of the Bank of England, is printing or issuing new money from thin air to buy the assets of banks, in order to get these banks lending again. He is doing this because the lowering of the bank rate to 0.50 per cent has largely failed to get the banks lending through creating debt, as banks want to build up their capital reserves. The central banks are calling their creation of new money 'quantitative easing'. However, rather than the £175 billion quantitative easing money to prop up the banks, government could send money that is created in this way direct to people, say via the Citizen's Income and business loans.

Molly Scott Cato writes that, 'This is one of those moments – like when Tom Lehrer gave up satire to commemorate the award of the Nobel Peace Prize to Henry Kissinger – when you feel that all comedians should retire because the whole universe has been created by an almighty stand-up comedian. Not so much intelligent designer as cosmic joker.

'Yes, the deputy-director of the Bank of England is really called Mr Bean and he really is undertaking a national tour to convince us of the seriousness of the policy of Quantitative Easing. The BBC managed to post an online story about this with every sign of a straight face:

"Mr Bean is in Leeds on the first leg of a tour of the UK, attempting to explain what the Bank calls its 'conventional unconventional' measure to counter the recession. Armed with a box of explanatory pamphlets, optimistically entitled Quantitative Easing Explained, he is on a single-handed mission to bring the world of gilt yields, money velocity and commercial paper to the people." ...

'It is good enough that the Bank has admitted that money was always created from thin air, that the whole time they have been creating money as debt – at huge cost to citizens and the planet – it was completely unnecessary. That has given me great satisfaction. But that they leave the task of explaining this policy in the hands of Mr Bean is just a delight too far.

'Indications are that the public are unconvinced – questioning why the money is not reaching the small businesses it was apparently created for. The explanation is simple: the vast majority of the thin-air money has been used to buy up national and corporate debt and not sent to small businesses that are strapped for ready cash.'

Source: Molly Scott Cato: gaianeconomics.blogspot.com/ 14 July 2009

Reclaiming Money and Capital as a Common Resource

Whatever form money takes, whether metal, paper or an electronic bank account, it must be created. Money does not emerge fully fledged from

Continued overleaf

some secret money mine, even if it is made of gold. It is brought into being through a combination of processes, private (borrowing to invest), public (government issue of money and authorisation of money as legal) and social (people's trust in the money system). Most new money in society is now created as debt through the banking system and used primarily for the benefit of the issuer (profit for the bank) and borrower (access to goods and services). For most borrowers (including the government) the cost will be high, but for speculators the reward can far outweigh interest charges.

As a product of society, money effectively emerges out of 'fresh air'. When issued, it provides for the holder a claim on future resources and labour. As something that is produced out of fresh air, the social resource of money is akin to a natural resource. Like natural resources, money can be made subject to property rights or can be seen as a Commons, that is, something that should not be owned by any individual or group, but used for the benefit of all. Commons resources are those which 'belong' to the people as a whole, and in the case of the natural environment to the nonhuman world as well. Capitalism has been built on the privatisation of Commons resources, and the harnessing of the money system is no different. Land and other resources have been expropriated or enclosed by private ownership through the expulsion of inhabitants, or the removal of their rights to use previously common land. Historically this grab of assets was often achieved by force, but money is even more effective. Privately 'enclosed' money is used to buy productive assets in the same way that colonists bought Manhattan for strings of beads (wampum was valued money in the area at the time). Privatisation of the social resource of money is central to capitalism. If money is to be used for the benefit of all it must be reclaimed as a democratically controlled social and public resource.

Source: Mary Mellor The Future of Money:
From financial crisis to public resource. *Pluto Press April 2010.*

and revenues. By replacing the for-private-profit financial service companies, the funds would capture the unearned value and fees presently captured by brokers, financial advisers, sales people, insurance companies and the finance industry for individual and community benefit. The funds, independent from government, would invest in a range of public infrastructure and businesses on a sound business, ethical and social basis. Investors can see where their pension money is being invested, rather than losing sight of it in obscure global casino and stock market pension Ponzi schemes.

One example of such a fund is the Alaska Permanent Fund. Initial capital came from oil leases on state land. Today, a $23 billion diversified portfolio pays every Alaskan an annual dividend. In 2004 this was $1,540. The Norwegian Oil Fund was

---

Box 8.5   SCARF: Stroud Community Asset Reinvestment Fund

Stroud, like many places, has a successful tradition of raising public gift
and loan money for securing local assets, such as the public performance venue, the Subscription Rooms, and the SPACE, the performing arts
centre. Whereas credit unions are social banks that enable individuals
to save and get loans, community asset reinvestment funds enable individuals and organisations to invest, and organisations to then borrow
to build local assets such as the eco housing that was funded by the
Somerset-based Ecos Trust. Stroud is a dynamic community in transition
to a low-carbon future. This requires projects to be funded and assets to
be purchased. SCARF will be a fund to which local people can donate
regularly on a small scale and/or loan to at a fair rate of interest, enabling
the community to fund its development. The Bangor University and the
Miners' Institutes of South Wales were initially paid for in this way – by
local people on modest incomes making small but regular donations.
Action research by Wessex Reinvestment Trust found that people would
readily donate and invest when they saw a clear benefit from making
gifts and/or loans, as with wind farms, housing schemes or Fordhall Farm.
As a result, WRT has created the Wessex Community Asset model rules
for others, like SCARF, to adopt.

Source: www.wessexrt.org.uk

---

set up by the Norwegian parliament in 1990 and is now known as the Norwegian
Government Pension Fund (Global), with assets of £250 billion, though this will
have fallen with the credit crunch. Once known as the Petroleum Fund of Norway,
it invested oil licenses, oil taxes and dividends from Statoil Hydro globally, using
ethical criteria. So BAE Systems is excluded because of its arms manufacturing and
also Wal-Mart because of its poor human rights record. Norway, as the world's third
largest oil exporter, wanted to make sure that current oil wealth benefits future
generations and that it is invested ethically. The second fund, the Government
Pension Fund Norway, was set up in 1967 to invest domestically for pensions and
national insurance purposes.

The Swedish Wage Earner Funds offer another proposal for a commons capital
stream going into a national investment and pension bank. In 1976, Swedish trade
unions proposed that firms with between fifty and one hundred employees would
issue new stocks at 20 per cent of the value of the annual profits. These stocks
would be owned by funds representing wage earners. This reform would counter
the increasing concentration of wealth, and the higher the profits, the higher the
wage-earner funds. Some of the dividends would go to re-educating workers in
their new ownership role.[15]

The Quebec Federation of Labour Solidarity Fund is a successful working
example of a variation of the Swedish idea. This is a voluntary pension scheme

---

**Box 8.6   *Norwegian Oil Fund shows way forward for Scotland's future*

The Scottish National Party has obtained figures showing the extent to which Norway's Government Pension Fund has grown since it was first established. Set up in 1990 as the Petroleum Fund with an initial payment of £174 million Sterling, the value of the Government Pension Fund Global at 30 June 2007 was 1,939 billion Norwegian Kroner – the equivalent of a staggering £174 billion Sterling at current prices. By 2010, the fund value is forecast to have spiralled to a staggering 2856.4 billion NOK – or £257 billion Sterling at today's prices.

Commenting, SNP Treasury Spokesman Stewart Hosie MP said:

'These figures are simply extraordinary. From a seed corn investment equivalent to just £174 million pounds in the 1990s – made almost 20 years after the first oil started flowing ashore – Norway's careful husbandry of her oil and gas resources has seen the national fund grow in value a thousand-fold.

'Even Energy Minister Malcolm Wicks recognised recently that the Norwegian approach was the correct one. However, with oil prices currently nudging US $100 per barrel and the resulting revenues, which are flooding into Treasury coffers, now is exactly the time to start investing this extraordinary windfall for future generations.

'The last 30 years represent a sad story of missed opportunities and squandered resources. By seizing the initiative and establishing a Fund for Future Generations, instead of repeating the failures of successive UK governments over the past 30 years, Scotland can begin to mirror the successes of our neighbour across the North Sea.'

Source: SNP Westminster press release, 11 July 2007

---

of over 550,000 shareholders, assets of $4.6 billion, with capital in around 1,900 small and medium-sized businesses that created, saved or maintained 100,000 jobs. The Fund aims to make a profit, in order to promote workers' rights and training. It conducts a thorough social audit of firms before investing. It aims to stimulate the Quebec economy through strategic investment and to help workers both save for retirement and invest in the local economy.[16]

Global capital and environmental commons trusts

Taxpayers guarantee the global financial system, with governments as lenders of last resort. This is a shared financial commons that we all use and contribute to. But the windfalls and speculative firms in the financial services sector cream off the lion's share of the benefits of this global commons for the freeloading financial elite. This is the casino economy. Think of the hedge fund and currency speculator George Soros, who made over a £1 billion from betting on the exit of the pound from the ERM in 1992 on Black Wednesday. Our global currency system originated to serve the trading needs of companies, but now only a small fraction of money on the financial markets is needed for trade. Every year $912tn or £561tn is traded on the world's foreign exchanges. Currency speculation, however, has been growing at 15 per cent a year, is untaxed and unregulated and causes financial instability.

James Tobin, an American economist, proposed in 1972 a tax on foreign currency transactions, at 0.1 per cent to 0.25 per cent. Governments could use this Tobin tax to protect their economies from currency speculators. The Tobin tax has two objectives: firstly to make exchange rates reflect the real long term value of a currency, as opposed to short term speculative gain from trading and currency betting, and secondly to secure the autonomy of national economic policies. Tobin believed that this simple tax had the key benefit of calming down the international financial system, securing financial stability by penalising short term round trip trades. It would not affect commodity trading or long-term capital investment.

Opponents of the Tobin tax dislike the interference in free financial markets. It would drive exchange dealing offshore and it would not prevent currencies being at the mercy of speculators a foreign currency. However, in August 2009 Adair Turner, the FSA chair warned bankers that the Tobin tax would be one way of curbing excessive profiteering, reducing the size of the swollen financial sector and taxing some of the City's 'socially useless' activities. He identified the key Tobin tax benefit of securing financial stability as, 'a nice sensible revenue source for funding global public goods.' This income steam could be used to counter climate change and for development aid. But not everyone is waiting for regulators like the FSA to implement the Tobin tax. Ethical Currency has become the first foreign exchange broker to ring fence 0.005 per cent from its exchange transactions, which will be channelled into a Global Fund currently underfunded. Alastair Constance of Ethical Currency believes that a currency transaction levy or CTL is easy to implement, as forex transactions are electronic. Initially the City and Wall Street will oppose it, but over time the tax would be hardly noticed. The Tobin tax can be seen as a fee for the benefit of being able to use the global financial capital commons, a user fee that would deter speculators who would otherwise freely undermine the stability and wealth of the shared financial commons. The income from an international Tobin tax could also go into global capital and environmental commons trusts, to invest in environmental protection, education, health and holistic sustainable development. Larry Elliot suggested that the Tobin tax could be the 'Forgotten brainchild that could transform the banking casino'.[17]

The most advanced proposals for stewarding the environmental commons of the sky is the capping of carbon emissions, and the sharing of the benefits equally. This is in essence like the common fell grazing rights I was brought up with as a hill farmer's son. Each farm had grazing rights for a traditionally agreed number of sheep that were grazed on the fell. The farmers themselves, who held periodic round-ups of stray sheep and sorted out any problems arising, regulated this system.

Simply put, excessive and rising carbon emissions are causing global warming and unstable climate change. The solution is that emissions must be capped. The simplest way of controlling carbon emissions from oil, gas and coal lies with the large mining, oil and gas companies at source. But who owns the air and the sky? We all share the commons of the sky, which can process a limited amount of carbon emissions. One estimate of the monetary value of one sky service, carbon dioxide absorption, is $400 billion annually. Rather than give emission-trading rights to big polluting firms free of charge, which delivers an annual windfall profit of £800 million to British energy firms alone, better to use the cap and share system.[18]

How would this work? A global, independent regulator, such as a UN body, would set a safe emission level and allocate emission coupons equally amongst the world's people. Independent agencies for each country could either auction the emission coupons to extractor companies, and then give the surplus equally to every citizen, or issue emissions rights coupons to each citizen to sell through the banks.

Whilst aiming to restrict carbon emissions to safe levels and distribute shares from the sale of emissions rights equally, some of the proceeds could also go to global CCTs for investing in environmental, economic and social development in clean, low-carbon farming and transport systems, for example. Income from other resource taxes and the licensing of commons user rights could also go for investment in global CCTs and other international co-operative institutions that build common wealth for humanity's benefit.

The shift from free to social enterprise

Whilst since 1979 there has been a shift to free enterprise through the neo-economic liberal model, there is also a counter-shift from free to social enterprise. This is partly a matter of original social enterprise, such as the co-operative movement, reinventing itself around the world. There are also the ethical finance and micro-credit movements, as exemplified by Triodos Bank and the Grameen Bank respectively, and the CSR or corporate social responsibility movement. Some corporations are practically engaged in partnerships with aid organisations, from a mixture of business and public benefit motives. The French company Danone is partnering with Grameen to develop the Bangladesh yoghurt industry with a cheap, nutritional yoghurt for malnourished children. The Nobel laureate Muhammad Yunus has seen the Grameen Bank which he founded in 1982 help millions of Bangladeshis with microfinance to set up small businesses. Grameen has 8 million borrowers, 97 per cent of them women, lending around $100 million a month, with average loans of $220, repayments of nearly 100 per cent and lending a cumulative total of $6 billion. He has proved that the poor are creditworthy and that loans given without collateral but guaranteed by lending circles are repaid. He sees social enterprise, rather than charity, as the way out of poverty and the best means of tackling social problems, and welcomes the potential to channel the resources of profit-making business into social business. He also sees the current recession as an opportunity to create a more equitable world.[19]

An increasing number of businesses are being set up as social enterprises. These aim to deliver not just a profit or surplus, but also social and other benefits. The statutory sector has started to give service contracts to local social enterprises.

Businesses are keen to sponsor local social enterprises in their host communities. Jeff Skoll, an entrepreneur who pioneered eBay, has endowed the Skoll Foundation at Oxford's Said Business School to research, support and offer courses in social enterprise.

Fair trade can be another form of social enterprise, where companies – such as coffee companies – develop a short, associative supply chain that delivers a fair price to growers.

Contrary to neo-liberal stereotypes like the fictional Gordon Gecko in Oliver Stone's 'Wall Street' with his signature line 'greed, for want of a better word, is good', much of business is anyway inherently social. The division of labour means that we are all serving each other's needs. Businesses agree to send their goods all over the world, trusting that they will get paid. Moral, social terms like 'interest', 'trust' and 'credit' are at the heart of 'good' business relationships. But the emerging social enterprise sector makes the 'social' more conscious, for example with triple bottom line accounting and with profit or surplus distribution.

Social enterprise and mutuals may come to run not just a significant share of the financial sector, but also utilities such as the water system, as with Dr Cymru, Wales Water. It may be that just as the publicly owned, not-for-private-profit Network Rail successfully took over the bankrupt privatised rail company Railtrack, so many private banks, temporarily nationalised banks and utilities may well become member- and consumer-owned mutuals.

Summary: transforming capitalism and the emerging social economy

This chapter has offered an account of some ways of transforming capital and putting it into trusteeship. These ways treat capital not as a commodity, but as a socially created commons. This means a profound shift from the absolute private ownership of capital with a sense of entitlement to acquire and keep vast fortunes, to capital trusteeship for social benefit. The purpose of a CCT is to steward assets for enduring individual business enterprise and the common good. A variety of such commons capital trusts are emerging, ranging from the Alaska Permanent Fund and the Norwegian Oil Funds to charitable foundations, commonwealths and partnerships created by entrepreneurs to steward assets. Another way is to transform entrepreneurial capital into capital trusteeship through a business transfer process, so that the benefits of leasing to enterprise and preserving the public interest are secured.

Conclusion

I have argued that whereas neo-liberals see the engine of economic growth as profit-seeking, selfish entrepreneurs, the reality can often be different. A significant number of farsighted, public-spirited entrepreneurs are both interested in providing for human needs and want to see their businesses continue to thrive for community benefit. The various ways of holding capital in capital commons trusts both serve as a vehicle for transferring capital assets for productive use to competent people, as well as benefiting society. Treating capital as a socially created

---

Box 8.7   Scrooge Nouveau and the Spirit of Earth Day Past

Margaret Atwood's *Payback: Debt and the Shadow Side of Wealth* ends with a conversation between Scrooge Nouveau, a selfish hedonist believing he owes nothing to anyone, and the Spirit of Earth Day Past. The Spirit's message is that there are limits to growth, consumption and population:

> Mankind made a Faustian bargain as soon as he invented his first technologies, including the bow and arrow. It was then that human beings, instead of limiting their birth rate to keep their population in step with natural resources, decided instead to multiply unchecked. Then they increased the food supply to support this growth by manipulating those resources, inventing ever newer and more complex technologies to do so ... The end result of a totally efficient technological exploitation of Nature would be a lifeless desert: all natural capital would be exhausted, having been devoured by the mills of production, and the resulting debt to Nature would be infinite. But long before then, payback time will come for Mankind.

At the end of the book and the conversation, Scrooge Nouveau tells the Spirit:

> I don't really own anything ... Not even my body. Everything I have is only borrowed. I'm not really rich at all, I'm heavily in debt. How do I even begin to pay back what I owe? Where should I start?

Source: Margaret Atwood, Payback: Debt and the Shadow Side of Wealth,
Toronto, Anansi, 2009

---

commons, as trusteeship, is a key entry point for developing a creative, just and sustainable society. Capital is too precious a socially created resource to be left to the predatory financial capitalist system to waste for private gain.

This, however is not to ignore the need for other far-reaching reforms to 'humble proud finance' so that finance serves the economy and society, rather than dominates it. This is a serious point – remember that British taxpayers have bailed out banks with up to £1.3 trillion. Stakeholder governance is needed so that boards can steward capital and businesses responsibly. There is need for accountable, transparent and independent audit and credit-rating bodies. A new Glass-Steagall Act needs to separate retail banking, best done by mutuals, from casino investment banking. Tax havens with their destabilising, secret, tax-avoiding, money-laundering activities need closing down. Triple bottom line assessment of performance on environmental, ethical and business criteria should be implemented. Large banks should be broken up, so none is too big to fail. The government, whilst regulating finance overall, should insist on the financial sector growing up, insuring and regulating itself at its own expense – not by the taxpayer. It is all very well to blame government 'light-touch regulation' for the credit crunch, but in fact the financial sector failed to regulate itself and strongly opposed more government regulation, to all our cost. The private financial sector did not care for the shared financial commons, with the notable exception of most of the mutual building society sector. The full complexities of the backstage, self-serving, intertwined political and financial interests that played into the financial meltdown need thorough analysis.

What would help is a clear separation between the political and financial systems, and a grown-up financial sector that had the capacity to care for the financial common wealth for all, serving society, not acting with a sense of entitlement as 'the masters of the universe'. Otherwise there will be low trust, rising inequality, low confidence and market failure.

But what of labour and land?

Chapter 9

Citizen's Income: Social Inclusion and Common Wealth for All

Who gets what?
Source: The fruits of labour by Ken Sprague

This chapter examines the Citizen's Income, which offers the benefits of social inclusion, security and common wealth for all. Social inclusion and wealth redistribution can be achieved; this is also an equitable way of helping people through the recession, particularly young unemployed people who need supporting by a Citizen's Income into community service, work, education and training. When Andrew Glyn analysed the devastating effects on society of unleashed capitalism, he saw that the Citizen's Income was one way that the social democratic welfare states of Northern Europe could survive the pressures of globalisation and free market ideology by securing more equality.

The recession has triggered the current debate about the Citizen's Income, with rising unemployment on the one hand, and continuing bank bonuses on the other exposing unequal Britain. Many members of the financial and political elites running Britain seem to care mainly for their personal enrichment and power. Big finance and government have failed to serve ordinary people. People were astonished by the exposure of the staggering salaries, bonuses and pensions that City bankers pay themselves. Never have so few paid themselves so much with the expectation that the public would bail them out. Ordinary bank workers and customers were equally angry. Many financial 'masters of the universe' had a powerful sense of entitlement that meant even after failure they felt they deserved all this and more. The real connection between individual performance and rewards was tenuous. The overwhelming drive for 'shareholder value', for the increasing profit culture, meant gambling to the extent the law allows, pursuing ever more dodgy, edgy deals using abstract mathematical models untested in the real world. And as of summer 2009, the 'bonuses are back' for banks such as Goldman Sachs which have profited from the recession, to the cost of the financial commons.

At the same time, the Westminster political elite were too busy claiming their expenses for parliament to do its proper jobs such as holding government to account, pushing back the market from the provision of public goods like health and wise law-making. Whilst many MPs were ethical in their expenses claims, many were not. Michael Gove claimed £8,000 for furniture whilst also voting against an increase of the minimum wage. Phil Hope, a care minister, claimed £41,000 for furniture. Expenses were claimed for chandeliers, moat cleaning, a floating duck house and a tennis court. Hazel Blears, who as Communities Secretary was responsible for affordable housing, claimed a £13,332 capital gains tax exemption and flipped her homes to her advantage. Some MPs claimed for trivia, like 38p for a yoghurt, exploited the 'no receipt rule' for claims up to £250, flipped their homes to gain expenses, rented out second homes, overspent on renovations, spent up to the monthly limit on food and claimed for second homes they didn't need because they already lived in London. Some had an arrogant sense of entitlement, like Gerald Kaufman, who claimed £8,865 for a television set, unsuccessfully as it turned out, and £1,262 for a gas bill in credit by £1,055. The Speaker of the House, Michael Martin, who opposed revealing details of MPs' expenses under the Freedom of Information Act, benefited himself from large taxi fare claims, a £1.7 million renovated official home, a £1.4 million pension pot and the reward of a peerage, with all the perks this brings.

Though the Westminster expenses scandal is small beer by City standards, it indicates just how out of touch MPs and the government are in an unequal society. There is a big gap between citizens and privileged rulers. When you are on Jobseeker's Allowance of £64 a week or a median family living on £393 a week, MPs' expense claims are astonishing. Tax-avoiding MPs on £150,000 a year pay and expenses can hardly call for people to 'tighten their belts' in the recession, or criticise 'social security scroungers'. Inequality is now higher than under Thatcher. Over the last ten years, the wealth of the top 1 per cent went up dramatically, whilst average incomes hardly changed, with the poor getting poorer.

The neo-liberal approach favoured by government and corporations treats labour as a flexible commodity to be paid for. This causes social dislocation and human misery. Individuals are stripped of their identity, character, values, skills, feelings and relationships by being treated as a dispensable factor of production. Work is important for human dignity. Some of the motivating power behind the development of the trade union movement came from being treated just as a 'hand' or as a 'head'. Rights, decent conditions of employment, security, the minimum wage and pensions were fought for by trade unions and established by legislation so that the worst aspects of wage slavery were overcome.

But these employment rights were hard won and are preserved only through vigilance. British governments have attracted foreign companies to come to Britain by offering tax breaks, relatively low pay and comparatively weak rights for workers. In February 2009, there was a stark contrast between Prime Minister Brown's decision to allow the failing Royal Bank of Scotland (which had received a large taxpayer bailout) to pay bonuses to bankers of £775 million whilst BMW Oxford sacked 850 agency car workers with an hour's notice. Tony Woodley of Unite wrote to BMW saying: 'You have treated your workforce with utter contempt. The difficulties of the car industry globally are well known but the manner in which BMW has sought to address the reduction of its volumes at the Cowley plant is nothing short of disgraceful … You would not treat a dog this way, never mind loyal and committed employees.' BMW could sack the agency workers with impunity because successive governments had opposed signing up to all of the provisions of the European Social Chapter.

The contrast between the way City bankers and agency car workers are treated raises the old questions of social inclusion ('the social question' – who matters and who doesn't, who is included and who is not) and of how our common wealth is shared, the redistribution question. There are now such inequitable pay differences that some people are advocating a maximum as well as a minimum wage and a review not just of directors' pay but also the whole salary system in the interests of public health as well as equity and fairness. Richard Wilkinson advocates for greater equity because the afflictions of inequality are so costly. His research shows that the more wealth inequality there is, the unhealthier a society is.[1] The social and health effects of large income and wealth differences are a very powerful reason for reducing such inequality.

The neo-liberal project aims to reduce or remove the rights and protections gained by organised labour. How is this achieved? Firstly, the state and employers establish 'flexible labour markets' by curbing trade union power, by limiting labour rights, by reducing state welfare provisions and by shifting employment away from unionised sectors such as coal mining in Britain in the 1980s to less unionised service sectors. Isolated workers increasingly work on short-term contracts; job security declines and individuals become responsible for their own health, pensions, sickness insurance and training – things that were previously the responsibility of the state or employers. Then the state relaxes the conditions on company take-overs, so that people lose their pensions from the hedge fund asset strippers. Individuals have to buy health insurance and private pensions on the risky financial markets, but with the financial institutions benefiting from mandatory fees. Most people find that these private pensions stand no chance of matching the benefits from index-linked state pension schemes and end up with relatively little. In any case, government can fail to protect those saving for private pensions through poor regulation, and then using deliberate delaying tactics to avoid compensation as with Equitable Life, and by allowing predatory take-overs that endanger pension funds and saving, such as the take-over of Friends Provident by the offshore shell company Resolution.

Secondly, the global mobility of capital and business means that there is a race to the bottom for jobs. So manufacturing jobs go to China, or wherever there is a docile, exploitable workforce for the world's sweatshops. Some people do benefit from the rewards and mobility this brings in the South, but for the 2 billion people who live on $2 a day, there is little choice. As in the early days of the Industrial Revolution in Britain or even recently with the British gang-master labour system that was tragically exposed by the drowning of the twenty-five Morecombe Bay cockle pickers, the neo-liberal ideal of the disposable, flexible worker emerges. John Berger describes the disposable worker:

> The new world order works night and day according to the principle that anybody who does not produce, who does not consume and who has no money to put into a bank, is redundant. So the emigrants, the landless, the homeless are treated as the waste matter of the system: to be eliminated.

Rudolf Steiner campaigned after the First World War for a just society in Germany. Often speaking to large public meetings, he argued that there were two seismic forces driving the workers' movement in his day.

In the first place, industrial workers had lost the sustaining power of their relationships and culture and felt alienated from bourgeois modern culture, which they experienced as empty ideology. Turning instead to the dynamic forces of management, science and technology that were transforming industry and the economy, workers wanted a share of the material wealth this brought. However, material wellbeing alone was not enough, and never would be enough by itself, as it would not feed the soul and the human spirit. Compared with the dynamic power of modern technology, science and production management, bourgeois culture was weak. But working people also longed deeply for a creative cultural life to give them meaning and human dignity in the empty, soulless new world they found themselves in. Modern materialism did not meet the profound human need for dignity, meaning, personal freedom and education of the whole person and a creative culture that renews the human spirit. The liberal bourgeois 'top drawer' culture on offer was empty and deeply hypocritical given the harsh economic conditions imposed by the bourgeoisie in the mines and factories.

The other motivating force was working people's hatred of being treated as objects, as wage slaves, as commodities in the modern economy. They felt deeply alienated. Capitalism tends to treat everything such as labour as commodities if no boundaries are set: 'Instead, one must find a way of removing labour from the economic process, so that it can be determined by social forces which no longer impose a commodity character on it', said Steiner.[2]

So how can labour be treated as a right, rather than a commodity? How can the dignity of people in employed work be respected? And how can individuals and their work – not just paid work but part-time work and gift work such as caring – be integrated into society?

Firstly, how can labour be treated as a right, rather than a commodity? Social democracies respect labour as a right. Employees now have a range of economic rights that are protected by employment law, by health and safety law, by trade unions and by the courts – with an underpinning state welfare safety net. As well as a wage or salary, we all get a 'social wage' in terms of a bundle of health and social benefits provided by the state. Good employers provide good working conditions, both because they feel it is the right thing to do and also because it makes business sense. The last thing good employers want is a 'race to the bottom' in terms of working conditions. But the current market fundamentalism means that employers have to be vigilant in maintaining the competitive position of their company. The threat of takeover and competition is a constant feature of the market. Against the background of rumours of a private equity interest in taking over Cadburys, the firm shed 9,000 jobs worldwide as a defensive measure.

Secondly, how can the dignity of people in employed work be respected? Good employers want productive workplaces where human dignity and needs are respected. The old hierarchical command and control management structures are being replaced by flatter, participative, high-performance organisations where there is mutual support and respect, learning, elbow room for decision-making, variety, challenge, meaningful work and a desired future. Participative work and organisation design has resulted in increasing workplace democracy as well as more productive workplaces. Some companies also contribute to the community in a variety of ways,[3] through volunteering and funding community projects. When Northern Rock was a mutual building society, for example, its Foundation gave away a lot of money.

Thirdly, how can individuals and their work be valued and integrated into society?

This is a big question, and also begs the questions why work, what is work, how can work be justly rewarded? One solution is a basic citizen's income for every person, regardless of the nature of the work or whether it was paid work. This is as much a way of achieving social inclusion and equitable wealth distribution as a just pay system. It would redistribute wealth, reverse widening inequality and restore fairness. Moreover, it would dignify work by providing an income as a right.

The purpose of this chapter is to explore how people's labour can be valued through treating it as a commons, as a right by means of the Citizen's Income. Social inclusion and wealth redistribution can be achieved through a basic citizen's income. This is also an equitable way of helping people through the current deep recession, with job losses and growing youth unemployment.

The plan of this chapter is:

- the citizen's basic income
- how would the Citizen's Income work?
- discussion and questions
- implementing Citizen's Income.

The citizen's basic income

The Citizen's Income (CI) is being considered all over the world. It is the BIG or Basic Income Grant proposal in South Africa. The government is concerned that with unemployment at around 50 per cent means-tested welfare payments would be too expensive to manage efficiently with fairness, efficiency and without corruption. The BIG is being considered as an alternative. This would be given to all citizens equally and raised from people paying higher-rate income tax. It overcomes the need to means test for welfare, and the tax system does not have to change.

CI is known as the unconditional basic income in Germany, the Universal Income in New Zealand, the Guaranteed Annual Income in Canada and the Citizen's Dividend in the US. The CI is Green Party policy in Britain and in October 2006 was even included in the Queen's Speech outlining the New Labour government's proposed legislative programme: 'My government will take forward legislation to reform the welfare system and to reduce poverty. A Citizen's Income would make it easier for many families to earn their way out of poverty.'

One aim of CI, to quote Martin Luther King, is 'to civilise ourselves by the total, direct and immediate abolition of poverty'. Other aims include:

- to affirm a social contract between society and the individual affirming their worth as citizens and human beings, rather than as a labour commodity;
- to be a means of sharing wealth from the commons, whether from nature, such as land, or whether socially created from the economy;
- to provide the motivating conditions for working, not just for money, but to meet the needs of other people;
- to make huge savings on the cost of administering government welfare and benefits systems;
- to remove the poverty and benefits trap that penalise poor people who want to work;
- to create a dignified, flexible safety net for low paid people whose jobs, hours and contracts vary from week to week – a feature of employment that the benefits system cannot cope with
- to provide a secure foundation of a socially just society for the majority. The government currently increases social inequality by guaranteeing the long term profits of PFI companies, allowing bankers' bonuses, giving taxpayer insurance for risky casino dealing and doling out generous expenses to MPs. A citizen's income, however, would guarantee security and social inclusion for all.

Molly Scott Cato argues in *Green Economics* that the rationale for CI is that it is based on natural human rights, and that human welfare is dependent on caring for the earth. If people cannot meet their basic needs, they will plunder the earth. The efficiency argument for CI is that it is a single tax policy that makes work attractive and simplifies the baroque, costly-to-administer benefits system. Whereas social democratic welfare systems were based on protecting the weak and vulnerable and always required the individual to work (if one was able) in return, CI is different. It is a 'social dividend' based on citizenship rather than contribution. It represents a fair share of the nation's wealth, as a universal entitlement like the child or family allowance.

How would the Citizen's Income work?

CI would be paid monthly as a tax-free income to every person as a right of citizenship. It would be age-related, with more for adults than children and more for the elderly. CI would replace the state pension. There would be supplements for disability, housing and other exceptional circumstances. CI would replace all existing benefits and tax allowances. CI levels would not be affected by income, wealth, work status, gender or marital status. It is a right, not welfare, pay or charity. It is a share of the nation's wealth.

James Bruges considers that CI would free people to improve their lives and that CI offers the following benefits:

- It would provide them with a financial platform from which they could choose the life they want to lead.
- It would give them the independence to seek decent wages and conditions.
- People would be able to leave a job that is unsatisfying, making way for others who want it instead.
- People could avoid work that harms the environment.
- Small-scale farmers and marginally viable businesses and cultural organisations could better survive.
- Local shops within a community would become more viable.
- The centralisation of economic activity would be reversed, making it possible to curb the excesses of corporations.
- Small-scale employers, and larger employers during the recession, would only need to top up the Citizen's Income and could therefore employ more staff.
- There would be no need to produce unnecessary or short-lived products just in order to generate employment.
- People would no longer need to adjust their behaviour to maintain eligibility for the benefits; intrusive means testing would end; many perverse consequences of the current benefits and welfare system would end as people realised their lives were in their hands, not the dependency-creating nanny state.
- People would feel more secure, not needing to amass excessive wealth for their old age or even to pass it all on to their children.[4]

People use different but interesting rationales when arguing for the Citizen's Income. James Bruges argues strongly that it is possible to build a world without poverty because we have a greater ability than ever to create wealth. The wealth created together, whether by workers, farmers, the service sector or industrialists, is a commons from which we should all benefit, rather than wealth that is enclosed by the rich and powerful.

However, with 220 billionaires owning more wealth than the joint income of half the world's population, and their elite wealth growing, wealth and income are concentrating in fewer hands. The rest of us are concerned about our mortgages, losing our jobs, of getting ill, poor or hungry. The question is: 'Do we really want a world of conflict and cut-throat competition that impels ever-expanding businesses into destructive competition, sweatshops and environmental destruction?'

Professor Goetz Werner, founder director of the DM drugstore chain in Germany, also advocates a form of CI called the 'unconditional basic income'. He was inspired as an entrepreneur with Rudolf Steiner's idea that 'The welfare of the community is the greater, the more the individual lives not from the proceeds of his own work done, but from the proceeds of work done by others.' Werner points to the fact that with the modern division of labour, today's economy is dependent on world sufficiency, not the perceived self-sufficiency of the self-employed person who works for him or herself. In reality our needs are not met from the proceeds of one's own efforts but from those of many others. The division of labour means working for others, serving their needs. Altruism – serving others – is an in-built feature of modern economic life. You can see on your dinner table products from all over the world that many different people and companies have added value to and brought there through mutual exchange along multiple supply chains. Since the division of labour means working for others, this can have greater meaning if work can be performed independently of one's income – for the love of the work itself, working with other people, the meeting of others' needs and developing your skills to be of better service. So the unconditional basic income for every human can be a step towards this. One can be motivated, not because of the money one earns, but out of interest in meeting others' needs.[5]

Discussion and questions

Firstly, would people go on working if they got a Citizen's Income?
Currently most people of working age choose to seek paid work. But parents and other carers find that paid employment for a few hours a week brings only small extra financial gains, because they lose benefits in the so-called benefits trap. CI would remove this blockage, so carers who cannot or do not wish to seek full-time paid work would be more likely to look for part-time work. Research shows that most people are motivated to work, and that there are many people who, in spite of the current benefits trap, go on working even though they are penalised for doing so.

Secondly, is it fair to ask working people to pay for everyone to receive CI?
We currently fund benefits to those not in paid work from taxation, from the wealth created by society. Those in employment pay for the benefits received by people who are not in work. With CI, both those receiving means-tested benefits and tax credits and those *not* currently getting them, for example those in paid work,

would receive a CI. This is fairer than the current system. In addition, CI would not cost more than the various state subsidies to those in work on low wages.

Thirdly, are there better ways of preventing poverty such as a minimum wage and securing the right to work?
Well-paid work is the best way to remove poverty, and CI frees people up, encourages people to work and creates the security for a more flexible labour market. A national minimum wage can also help remove poverty.

Fourthly, wouldn't the work ethic be undermined – some people just wouldn't bother to work?
There would indeed be some people of working age who would decide to study, engage in interests such as art, music, environmental work, caring and travel, as well as undertaking part-time work. CI would certainly have a profound and interesting impact on the work ethic. A whole variety of work and life options would develop. However, the powerful incentives that paid work offers would still operate, and work fulfils such a number of important needs for security, survival, respect, status, service, companionship and self-realisation that it would continue to motivate people positively.

One way to introduce CI as a pilot is to support young people and the long term unemployed into work by providing well designed programmes whereby people do up to two years community service, with training and guidance, and receive CI. There is a lot of work, such as caring and environmental work, that will otherwise never get done, and this would be socially useful as well as providing meaningful work. The Community Programmes of the 1980s were examples of this kind of community service. The Green New Deal could be the basis for new programmes. The 1980s Enterprise Allowance scheme also showed what initiative people had for self-employment and small business when granted £50 a week for a year.

Lastly, wouldn't CI be too costly? Where would the money come from?
CI offers big savings on current administration costs, as it can be delivered via tax allowances and flat-rate benefit systems like the family allowance or the state pension. CI would largely prevent benefit fraud, which in 2006 cost the British government £2.5 billion.[6] According to the Citizen's Income Trust:

> A small Citizen's Income could be introduced on a cost neutral basis by reducing income tax allowances, means-tested benefits, National Insurance benefits and tax credits. A larger Citizen's Income would require a higher marginal rate of tax (though net incomes of earnings + CI would still be greater than before for everyone below or slightly above median earnings). It would be for a government to decide how high a Citizen's Income to pay and thus whether tax rates would need to be raised.[7]

There are other sources of sustainable revenue to draw on for paying CI without raising income taxes. There is land taxation, resource taxes such as carbon taxes and creating a Norwegian-style People's Pension Fund such as the National Petroleum Fund of Norway, now known as the Government Pension Fund. And of course, the

Bank of England can use quantitative easing, creating money to part-fund a CI, rather than help banks build their balance sheet non-productively. As CI would be spent on necessities, it would give a big stimulus to the real economy – as has happened in Japan where there have been direct payments to citizens as one way of getting out of the recession.

Ideally, all citizens would have the right to an income sufficient to cover all their basic subsistence needs – a 'full' Citizen's Income. In 2002 the Irish government published a Green Paper on a Basic Income that suggested £100 per week for adults.[8]

Implementing the Citizen's Income

The pressure for change often now comes from Ireland, Wales or Scotland and is taken up by England when tried and tested. The smoking ban was first implemented in Ireland and Scotland, then in England and Wales. So if Ireland or Germany does implement CI, then this experience can be learned from. The implementation of CI would be a major turning point for working people, following the landmark introduction of National Insurance by Lloyd George in 1910 and the creation of the welfare state after 1945. The right to CI would dignify human work, end the vestiges of wage slavery, decommoditise labour and provide basic security for all. CI is a major entry point for a more socially just society.

So CI would help bring in a socially just, inclusive and equitable society, and would help roll back the commoditisation of labour. James Robertson argues that:

> The result will be doubly progressive. The CI will be progressive because the same amount of money is worth relatively more to poor people than rich. The taxes will be progressive because they will impact rich people both in terms of their spending and in terms of their income and wealth. Their higher spending as consumers will mean that they pay more than poorer people, for example for the energy that has been used in producing the goods and services they buy. The larger proportion of the incomes and wealth (salaries, dividends, capital growth, etc.) derived directly or indirectly from land ownership and the use of other common resources like energy, will mean they pay proportionately more tax (indirectly) than their incomes.[9]

A starting point for implementing CI could be well organised, two-year community service programmes, some based on the Green New Deal, for young unemployed people. To conclude, just as the basis of a Roman's citizenship, security and wealth was owning a piece of land, so the Citizen's Income offers social inclusion, security and common wealth in our time, as a way of countering the social exclusion, insecurity and devastation caused by neo-liberal social Darwinism.

The next chapter, 'Land for People, Homes and Communities', offers a third transformative entry point.

Chapter 10

Land for People, Homes and Communities

The earth shall become a common treasury to all, as it was first made and given to the sons of men.

Gerrard Winstanley, 1649

When we see land as a community to which we belong, we may begin to use it with love and respect. There is no other way to survive the impact of mechanized man.

Aldo Leopold, *A Sand County Almanac*, 1949

In this country we have long enjoyed the blessings of Free Trade and of untaxed bread and meat, but against these inestimable benefits we have the evils of an unreformed and vicious land system.

Winston Churchill, 'The People's Land', 1910

I will not allow house prices to get out of control and put at risk the sustainability of the recovery.

Gordon Brown, first budget speech, 1997

We argue that there have been failures of vision, collective memory, strategy and regulation that have wasted many billions of taxpayers' money. The deregulation of financial markets in the 1980s sparked off a flood of house purchase lending that has underpinned massive house price rises and consumed £600 billion of investment that could have found a better use renewing our infrastructure or in research and development to make Britain more competitive in a global market rather than in bolstering house and land prices. The increasing commitment, from 23% to 72% of GDP since 1980, to house purchase loans seems unsustainable. Furthermore the increasing flow of demand-side subsidies is working to enrich landlords and land vendors, not to stimulate more housing output. The analysis shows that more money has gone into housing but fewer houses have come out. Housing benefits and allowances have imposed a huge and increasing burden on state finances.

The Zacchaeus Trust, Memorandum on Unaffordable Housing to the Prime Minister, May 2005, p. 10

We need land for people and affordable homes. The more that land is treated as a commodity to be bought and sold on the market, the more there will be market failure, widening social inequality, house price inflation, social exclusion and the lack of affordable houses to rent or to buy. And the more that land is treated as an untaxed monopoly, the more inequality there will be. Winston Churchill saw land as the mother of all other forms of monopoly. He spoke passionately of 'the evils of an unreformed and vicious land system' and wanted to reform this vicious system with inheritance taxes, a Land Value Tax and land registration in his 1910 election manifesto, 'The People's Land'.

This chapter proposes practical solutions to the land for people question, beginning with proposals for a Land Value Tax so that, in Winstanley's words, 'the earth shall become a common treasury to all', and then exploring ways of reclaiming land as a common wealth through Community Land Trusteeship and co-operative solutions for increasing the affordable access to homes, farms and workspace. Affordable access to and ownership of land are critical for human dignity, making a living and social relationships.

Since the introduction of the 'right to buy' council houses in the 1980s (the transfer into private ownership of housing developed using public funds), the idea of housing as 'property', an investment, rather than a shelter and a home, has taken hold of the national psyche, penetrating our language, dominating government policy – largely unchallenged. As a result, homeownership is a mark of social acceptability, a 'ladder' to be climbed, rented housing often a mark of exclusion.

Treatment by the government, the banks and individuals of land and homes as speculative commodities has led directly to a massive credit bubble and recession. Housing for rent has become a distinctly old-fashioned as policy; shared ownership such as Homebuy schemes[1] were offered as compromises and forced prices up even further.[2] An overall shortage of housing fuelled this speculation. The absence of decent, affordable rented housing for permanent homes forced everyone into the race, irrespective of their personal circumstances, aspirations and priorities, despite the rhetoric of 'choice'. Moreover, the idea of a 'property-owning democracy' has taken us back to the days when not to own 'property' effectively entailed exclusion from participation in democracy.

Against this background of pressure to acquire that first home, a 'foothold on the property ladder', the deregulation of lending to first-time homeowners was seen by many as a means of unleashing the creativity of the genie in the bottle of the City of London to enable people who would otherwise never have had the opportunity to gain access to property ownership. This became the driver of the economy, the engine of the consumer boom, the engenderer of sense of wellbeing: everyone was drunk on money.

Interest-only mortgages, or Northern Rock-type sub-prime mortgages, were made available with only the most cursory of financial checks to young first-time buyers, enabling them to borrow five or more times their annual income. Confidence that prices could only continue to rise, combined with fear that failure to take up these mortgage offers would put homeownership permanently out of reach, encouraged people to borrow recklessly.

And who could resist the corrosive promise that this 'investment', in future years, would generate an unearned fortune all by itself? Certainly, more was to be earned that way than from proper work. And people who reached the great age of thirty without a foot on the ladder were left in a state of panic, as well as with unstable and over-priced living arrangements. Meanwhile, those who had benefited from the boom borrowed against their 'equity' in buy-to-let investments, cashing in on the spiral, forcing up house prices even further.

The equivalent to two years' national output, £2.5 trillion, was added – temporarily as it turned out – to the notional wealth of those owning houses by means of house price inflation over a ten-year period. In many parts of the country, the average house price rose to more than nine or ten times the average income, as opposed to a more sustainable three to four times.

So house prices went up and up, more than tripling between 1997 and 2007. With them rose the risk of default and repossession, to the point that the viability of the financial system itself was brought to the point of collapse. In the USA, over-mortgaged people facing negative equity, their mortgages far greater than the value of their houses, are simply walking away from their homes, leaving banks with potential losses of at least $1 trillion.[3] In Britain, around one in nine homeowners is, as of summer 2009, in negative equity. Essential urban workers on modest incomes cannot afford to live near their jobs. Many young families spend over half their net income on rent or mortgage payments, and the English countryside is being cleared of the low-paid. Intergenerational inequity sets young families against the old. A new term, 'social cleansing', has entered our vocabulary. On top of this, speculative priorities have left a legacy of shoddy new housing. So, what is the solution?

The landscape changed with the credit crunch. A survey by the Chartered Institute of Housing conducted in 2009 suggests that only about one-third (37 per cent) of people aged between 18 and 24 believe that homeownership is right for them. Meanwhile, house prices have fallen dramatically, accompanied by a deep recession in the wider economy and escalating unemployment.

Over £24 billion was loaned by the British government to Northern Rock in autumn 2007 to stop the first run on a British bank for over a hundred years. Banks have been forced to curtail their risky lending practices and are no longer willing to lend on terms that make it possible for those on modest incomes even to contemplate homeownership.

This chapter examines the options and proposes two positive ways forward, a Land Value Tax and Community Land Trusts. The chapter covers the following plan:

- Land Value Tax: sharing our common inheritance
    - how does LVT work?
    - why is LVT opposed?
- Community Land Trusts: capturing land value for people and communities
    - what is a Community Land Trust?
    - origins of Community Land Trusteeship

- · the rationale for Community Land Trusts
- · support for CLT schemes
- · the CLT experience
- · CLTs elsewhere
- where does the land come from?
- bridging the affordability gap
  - · restricted resale price
  - · equity mortgage
  - · Declaration of Trust lease
  - · Mutual Home Ownership Society
  - · co-housing and housing co-operatives
  - · tenant co-operative homes
- the future of Community Land Trusts
- conclusion: letter to Gordon Brown
- summary

Land Value Tax: sharing our common inheritance

Landlords grow rich in their sleep without working, risking or economizing. The increase in the value of land, arising as it does from the efforts of an entire community, should belong to the community and not to the individual who might hold title.

John Stuart Mill, Principles of Political Economy, *1848*

Firstly, what is the story of LVT? Adam Smith argued that a Land Value Tax was a 'peculiarly suitable' way to raise revenue because it did not harm the incentive to save, invest or work. When Henry George asked in *Progress and Poverty* (1879) why both poverty and wealth were increasing, he argued that it was the landlords who were taking most of the benefits of progress, in the unearned increment in increased land value. His LVT ideas were soon adopted in the US and Canada, with municipalities in Australia, China, Denmark, New Zealand, South Africa and now parts of Russia using LVT.

When Lloyd George and Winston Churchill proposed a modest land tax, a land registry and death duties in the budget in 1909, the House of Lords rejected them on the grounds of the land valuation this involved. Big landlords, at a time when the upper chamber was still significantly a 'House of Land Lords', opposed a land survey that would show how few landowners owned so much of Britain. They also opposed death duties and of course LVT for long enough for them to make alternative tax avoidance plans such as family land and property trusts held offshore.

The rejection of the budget by the House of Lords caused a constitutional crisis with two general elections in 1910, and even though prominent Liberals like Winston Churchill argued cogently for 'land for people', the movement for LVT and land valuation was headed off by the war, by powerful landed vested interests

---

Box 10.1   Experiences with Land Value Tax in various countries

Country	Experience
Australia	Some form of LVT in every federal state
Russia	Following privatisation of land in 2001 land tax was set at fixed rate per hectare
Denmark	Land tax levied on all private property, at a rate that varies between municipalities
USA	Two-rate property and land tax used in Pennsylvania; two-rate system used in Pittsburgh between 1913 and 2001
Canada	Some cities and provinces tax land values at higher rates than improvements – a commitment to the principle of Land Value Tax

Source: Molly Scott Cato, Green Economics: An Introduction to Theory, Policy and Practice, *London, Earthscan, 2008, Table 12.1, p. 192*

---

and by the rise of Labour. Churchill said in 1909, 'Roads are made; electric light turns night into day; water is brought from reservoirs a hundred miles off – and all the while the landlord sits still. He contributes nothing to the process from which his own enrichment is derived.'

But today, current housing market failure and renewed interest in reclaiming the commons such as land for resource taxes have reawakened interest in LVT, as shown in Labour's Land Campaign, in Green Party policy and in the Liberal Democrats' proposed alternatives to council tax.

Resource taxes, such as LVT, are in fact already being levied. Chancellor Gordon Brown raised around £22.5 billion in 2001 from mobile phone company licences for the use of the electromagnetic spectrum for 3G phones. Ken Livingstone introduced a congestion charge for driving into central London, thus licensing access to the roads as a commons.

Whenever there is public investment in infrastructure there is a debate about how LVT can help pay for it. The £3 billion public investment in the Jubilee line resulted in a massive £10 billion increase in property prices near the new stations. This raised questions of how such public investment could be paid for in the future from LVT by Transport for London. Capturing land value is an opportunity for fairer taxation. Writing in 2005, Sam Brittan of *The Financial Times* reported that 'The government estimates that the value per hectare of "mixed agricultural land" averages £9,287 in England but rises to £749,000 if it is used for business development and to £2.46m if it is switched to residential use.'[5]

The purpose, then, of LVT is to tax the site value of the land, but not the buildings on it, so that the community benefits from the increased value of the land and owners can improve their property. LVT taxes the land, not the buildings. Owners of car parks or empty brownfield sites will pay the same LVT as nearby home or business

---

Box 10.2   Britain's feudal land ownership system

The UK comprises 60 million acres: 41 million acres are designated as agricultural land, 15 million are 'waste' as forest, mountains and rivers and 4 million acres are 'urban plot', where most of the 60 million people live. Sixty-nine per cent of Britain is owned by 0.6 per cent of the population, i.e. 158,000 families own 41 million acres, whilst the rest live on 4 million acres. The UK's top five landowners are the Dukes of Buccleuch (270,900), Northumberland (132,000), Westminster (129,000), Atholl (147,000) and Cornwall (141,000). They get large agricultural subsidies: the more land owned, the more area land payment subsidy. Ten per cent of British land is still owned by the Plantagenet descendants benefiting from William of Normandy's 1066 land grab.

'There is a myth in this country that land is scarce. It is not scarce. There is 41m. acres of it out there, about a third of it so uneconomic that it has to be subsidized, hidden behind nothing but a myth. The problem is that there is simply not enough land coming onto the market for housing, which puts fierce pressure on the little land that is available, and thus dramatically inflates its price.'

Source: Kevin Cahill, Who Owns Britain, *Edinburgh, Canongate, 2001*[4]

---

owners. LVT challenges our attitudes to land owning. In Britain, many of us accept without question that a few thousand landowners own a disproportionate amount of land. Indeed, around 10 per cent of Britain is owned by aristocratic descendants of the Normans who were originally granted land by the king in return for providing soldiers for war. But when this costly obligation fell into disuse at the end of the Middle Ages, families such as the Percys of Northumberland just kept the land without having to provide soldiers any more. Britain never had any fundamental, egalitarian redistribution of land as occurred at the French Revolution. Quite the opposite: from Tudor times there were clearances of people and land enclosures, which continued well into the nineteenth century. These eventually were countered in Ireland by the nineteenth-century land reform movement and the Scottish 2003 Land Reform Act.

So our attitude to land owning in Britain is still medieval. Having been excluded from so much of our country, we are astonished to discover in Sweden that there is 'everyman's right' to roam, provided one respects privacy, nature and farming.

LVT, in contrast, is based on the idea that the land of a country is a commons for all to share the benefits of, 'a common treasury for all', as Winstanley hoped. Land is given value by society, by the location. Whilst people need secure use of the land on which their home or business stands, the value of that land depends on things like transport links, views and local amenities. Land in city centres is worth far more than agricultural land. The value of land is often as much as half or even 75 per cent of the value of the property that stands on it. Buildings need costly maintenance to

Box 10.3   The Development Land Tax Act 1976: how we nearly got it right

The Town and Country Planning Act 1947 introduced the concept that establishing a suitable pattern of land use was in the public interest. This involved preparing plans of which land should be used for what purpose, and denying any change of land use without permission from the Local Planning Authority. This had the revolutionary effect of 'nationalising' the development potential of land and, in the process, allowing government to plan systematically for the changing needs of its citizens. However, as 'development land' became scarce, it was patently clear that the 'winning' of planning consent, especially for houses, provided a substantial 'windfall' to the landowner, not the wider community. As a result, and following an idea first developed by the Conservative administration of 1970–4, Labour introduced the Development Land Tax Act 1976, as a means of taxing away the excess profits arising from gaining planning permission. In theory, this measure – with cross-party support – would ensure that the value arising from allocating land for development in the public interest would remain with the public. In practice, however, the level of taxation was probably set too high, thus proving a disincentive for developers to take the risks that they had previously taken, while the provisions governing the calculation of the gain were both complex and open to interpretation, making the valuation procedure expensive and cumbersome. The result, according to critics of the Act, was that the supply of development land fell, making housing (and commercial property) more expensive than would otherwise have been the case. The Act was repealed following the Conservative election victory of 1979.

In recognising that the failure of the Act lay in its technical detail, not its principle, the Labour administration elected in 1997 brought the idea of a land tax back onto the political agenda. Unfortunately, it stands little chance of progressing to the statute books since our memories (jogged by the developers who stand to lose out) are of punitive taxes that made development land scarce and raised the cost of housing. But it need not have been so.

Source: Dr Neil Ravenscroft, University of Brighton, 2009

keep their value. However, the value of the land on which the house stands may go up or down depending on the location. For example, property prices are booming in London's King's Cross, fuelled by the opening of St Pancras station as the Eurostar terminal, and will climb in areas improved by the 2012 Olympic Games investment.

Currently, we have a perverse council tax and business rating system that punishes the improvement of buildings by higher taxes. Adding a garage, a conservatory or another bedroom results in council tax rising. But you can leave your office or home empty, or derelict, and not pay any tax at all.

To summarise, there are three arguments for taxing land – fairness, efficiency and to reduce the concentration of British land ownership. Molly Scott Cato argues for LVT because it is fair: 'Land is the most valuable resource available to the human community and thus the value derived from it should be shared between all members of that community.' Secondly, the economic efficiency argument holds that there should be no reward for keeping land and property unused, hoping for a rise in price, or to keep land empty to stop others using it, or to live off rent as an alternative to making the most productive use of the land. The third argument is that LVT would help break up the concentration of land ownership by the 157,000 owners that hold 69 per cent of Britain.[6] As has been convincingly demonstrated in Scotland by the community land buyouts, this results in better access, jobs, democracy and social development.

These are some of the benefits of LVT.

- Property owners can make improvements without tax increases – only the underlying land rental value gets taxed.
- The community benefits from any rise in value of the land.
- Owners of empty sites are encouraged to develop or sell their land because they have to pay LVT.
- Britain's 750,000 or so empty houses, currently untaxed, would be brought into use.
- Currently, taxing empty buildings has resulted in some owners demolishing them to avoid tax, but LVT would still be levied on the land on which such buildings stand, obviating the need for demolition.
- Brownfield sites would be redeveloped, to address most of the problem of shortage of land for homes. Consider the 13-hectare Battersea power station site, derelict since 1982. It was bought by a developer in 1993 for £10 million and sold in 2006 for £400 million. It is still vacant. Or consider the Cashes Green Hospital Site in Stroud, which the NHS and government has allowed to sit vacant since 1994. LVT would have taxed all these sites into productive use much earlier.
- The price of land would fall as more land came on to the market and the supply increased.
- LVT is excellent for local taxes because it gives local government big incentives to improve the environment and community facilities, to attract people, investment and businesses. The more attractive the area, the higher the LVT.
- LVT is easy to implement, as land is much simpler to value than the buildings on it. The valuation of buildings can be challenged because each building has to be separately assessed.
- When public investment is made, as for example with the jubilee line, LVT could help pay for it.
- LVT is cheap to collect and cannot be easily evaded.
- LVT encourages enterprise, as landowners have to make the most productive use of empty land such as city-centre car-parks on derelict land.
- It is one way of capturing the increased value of land which has had planning permission granted by the local authority (e.g. when agricultural land worth

£5,000 per acre gets planning permission for housing, this may raise the land price to £1 million an acre). It would make land ownership more accessible to more people.

- It is a progressive and redistributive tax, based on the fact that even though landowners have bought the right to use the land, they have not created the land itself. Society has created the value of the land.

How does LVT work?

LVT is based on the annual rental value of any plot or area of land in its unimproved state, excluding the value of structures or improvements on the land. The annual value can be assessed the same way as the old British rating system, as a rental, but as if the site were bare and unimproved. The land use and planning zone would be valuing factors. Values are easily assessed, and any surveyor with local knowledge can assess the land value separately from the buildings' value. Once there is an accurate, updated survey of land ownership, as well as data on the values of typical sites, it is straightforward to track changes of ownership. Denmark, which has used LVT for urban land for over a hundred years, holds sites on computer databases, with values being updated every four years based on local property sales.[8]

Why is LVT opposed?

Firstly, vested interests oppose LVT because it is a progressive, redistributive tax that undermines landed power, wealth and the privileges of unearned income. Turkeys do not vote for Christmas.

Box 10.4   Harrisburg cuts crime and unemployment with LVT

Harrisburg, Pennsylvania, was the second most run-down city in the USA in 1982. LVT at three times the value of tax on buildings was implemented. The results? The city has issued over 32,000 building permits, or $4 billion in new investment, over 5,000 new homes have been built and older properties renovated, businesses have risen from 1,908 to 8,864, crime has been cut by 58 per cent, unemployment has been cut by 20 per cent, vacant sites by 85 per cent and the buildings tax halved. Public revenues have increased dramatically, as has the value of land and buildings. The fact that 47 per cent of land in Harrisburg is owned by state, federal, educational and charitable bodies exempts them from property taxes, though the lost revenue has been clawed back by the increased price of water, gas and electricity supplied by publicly owned utilities companies. But in contrast, nearby Pittsburgh cut LVT. As predicted by land tax theory, this resulted in the buildings tax being raised, new construction falling by 20 per cent and businesses moving out.[7]

Secondly, landed power through the House of (Land) Lords and the political system has historically exercised huge influence over land, successfully holding up land tax and death duty legislation, for example in 1909–11, for long enough to set up family trust arrangements for inheritance tax avoidance. One indication of the power of large landowners is the historic suppression of information about landowning. For example Lord Derby was so shocked in the 1870s by the results of the land ownership survey that he commissioned that it was cancelled and most copies of the survey destroyed. The 1876 'Return on the Owners of Land' exposed the embarrassing fact that most of British land was owned by a few thousand families. Over 25 per cent of England and Wales was owned by 710 people, according to Kevin Cahill.[9]

Thirdly, people are not well informed about who benefits, and how, from the current land ownership and taxation situation. There is a lack of information; for example, agricultural subsidies to large landowners are secret.

Fourthly, many people see their homes as their main asset, incorporating their savings, representing a pension perhaps, and until recently they expected house prices to keep going up. This can give a feeling of security. They may misperceive LVT as raising taxes, rather than replacing council tax, and being a threat to the value of their houses. The sale of council houses by Thatcher, Major and Blair was a key way of embedding neo-liberal values, so anything that people perceive to threaten house prices will be opposed.

Fifthly, some LVT advocates have oversold it, for example claiming it would replace all taxes.

Figure 10.1 Land for People

Box 10.5   Freedom to roam: access ... what access?

There has been mounting pressure, over the last 150 years, for enclosed lands to be returned to the people of England. Rather than a return to mass grazing or the exercise of other production rights, people have increasingly demanded a right of recreational access, to enjoy the countryside of their heritage. Following a number of false starts, in which limited rights came with conditions so onerous that access was not improved, the Countryside and Rights of Way Act 2000, enacted as part of the 1997 Labour election manifesto, heralded a new dawn, in which the public at last had a right of access on foot to most uplands, downs and commons in England and Wales.

Following a prolonged mapping process, the public does, indeed, have a right of access on foot to much open country. However, following many exclusions for 'land management' reasons, it is unclear how much of this is genuinely new access, or merely the codification of what previously existed. There is also a concern that some exclusions now deny people like climbers access to rock faces that they have traditionally been able to reach by foot. What is also clear is that, as the new right on foot has come into being, access previously enjoyed on horseback, bicycle and motor vehicle (including disability vehicles) is increasingly been outlawed.

This is largely through the reclassification of byways as footpaths (thus restricting access to those on foot) and the use of Traffic Regulation Orders (mainly to ban motor vehicles). The argument used to defend these actions is that the Countryside and Rights of Way Act 2000 was expressly about facilitating quiet enjoyment of the countryside – individual people walking across private land with negligible impact on that land. However, it is notable that this argument has not been extended to rivers and lakes, meaning that canoeists and swimmers, who also have a negligible impact on the environment, are still excluded from most inland waters. While the Countryside and Rights of Way Act 2000 has therefore codified (and probably extended) the rights associated with one activity – walking – it has done so at a considerable cost to the public, certainly in terms of all the other opportunities that have been lost.

Dr Neil Ravenscroft, University of Brighton, 2009

Lastly, land speculators will oppose LVT because it taxes empty land and will be an extra cost. They are used to government and taxpayers maintaining the social and economic infrastructure they benefit from as a free lunch. Big landowners themselves could benefit from LVT, as if they sold their land the proceeds could be invested in more productive activities than in keeping the ancestral pile going.

To summarise, LVT is a progressive, redistributive tax on the common resource of our land. It would help fund the Citizen's Income, stimulate enterprise, fund investment infrastructure and empower people and local communities.[10]

Whilst LVT is already working successfully around the world, a complementary approach is offered by considering land as a commons to be owned and stewarded by Community Land Trusts (CLTs) for local benefit, including affordable homes. CLTs offer huge potential for engaging people in place-making, permanently affordable homes, community building and developing assets for the public good. CLTs can help realise in practice what the 2009 Reith lecturer Michael Sandell sees as the 'new citizenship'.

Community Land Trusts: capturing land value for people and communities

What is a Community Land Trust?

A CLT definition was passed into law in the July 2008 Housing and Regeneration Act. It is a 'corporate body which:

1.   is established for the express purpose of furthering the social, economic and environmental interests of a local community by acquiring and managing land and other assets in order –
   ·   to provide a benefit to the local community
   ·   to ensure that the assets are not sold or developed except in a manner which the trust's members think benefits the community
2.   is established under arrangements which are expressly designed to ensure that:
   ·   any profits from its activities will be used to benefit the local community (otherwise than by being paid directly to members)
   ·   individuals who live or work in the specified areas have the opportunity to become members of the trust (whether or not others can also become members)
   ·   the members of the trust control it.'

More broadly, a Community Land Trust is a body for creating the community trusteeship of land, for the benefit of a defined locality or community. It offers communities the means to:

1.   acquire land and hold it in trust for the provision of affordable housing for lower-income residents and key workers in the community – either through social rental homes or shared equity homeowners;
2.   provide the means for residents on modest incomes to acquire an economic interest in the success of their community;
3.   develop land to meet local needs for affordable workspace, farming, community orchards, land for food growing, retail units for enterprise and to provide community facilities for social and public services or community energy schemes;
4.   locally manage green spaces, community gardens and conservation areas;
5.   capture the value of the land for the community in perpetuity whilst allowing productive use of the land separate from its ownership;
6.   promote resident involvement, local democracy and active citizenship.

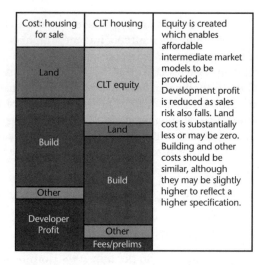

Figure 10. 2   Equity creation through a CLT

A CLT provides a unique way of capturing the value of public investment in the form of philanthropic gifts, charitable endowments, legacies and private development gain for the community interest. It keeps land and property assets under the control of local people for public benefit.

CLTs are not-for-private-profit, community-based organisations, constituted either as Industrial and Provident Societies for community benefit or as a company limited by guarantee, which can be a charity. A small professional staff, directed by a board elected by members, runs them. There are directors from partner organisations and public interest representatives as well as members and user directors.

Origins of Community Land Trusteeship

The rationale for Community Land Trusteeship goes back a long way into British social history. CLTs are a way of reclaiming land as a commons and for the community democratically to control the bundle of rights available in it. So, to the amazement of our French and American visitors, Stroud's Minchinhampton Common, managed by a commons association, has golfers playing, cows grazing, children flying kites, people out for walks and recreation, with a diversity of wildflowers on this site of scientific interest. Common land trusteeship is not new, but is a rich part of our traditions, with a deep resonance that goes back to pre-Norman times. Scotland has its own rich tradition of 'Common Good Land.'[11]

The origins of the modern forms of Community Land Trusteeship go back to nineteenth-century social reformers. John Ruskin gave his friend Octavia Hill some financial help for one of the first housing associations, the Marylebone Housing Society, in the 1860s. John Stuart Mill, John Ruskin and William Morris helped found the Commons Preservation Association, which later became the Open Spaces Society. This successfully preserved common land, including Epping Forest, Hampstead Heath, the Malvern Hills and Wandsworth and Wimbledon Commons, against private enclosures. John Ruskin founded the Guild of St George in the 1860s. This received gifts of land for rural renewal in the form of crafts, smallholdings, the preservation of heritage and farming.

The ideas came to fruition in the National Trust, an open membership land trust founded in 1895 by Octavia Hill, Canon Rawnsley and Robert Hunter, to preserve landed heritage. The 1907 National Trust Act made the Trust land inalienable, so the government cannot compulsorily purchase its land. It has 3.4 million members and owns more than 600,000 acres of land in England, Wales and Northern Ireland, including large parts of the Lake District, such as the former Beatrix Potter farms. It holds 700 miles of coastline, 1,500 tenant farms, 25 castles, 300 great houses and gardens and much else. It realised Octavia Hill's vision of the Trust as a way for people to access the countryside and the beauty of Britain. However, the National Trust is not a Community Land Trust. (Recently, though, the NT has woken up to its original values, and is piloting the leasing out of land for allotments.)

A number of garden cities, colonies and villages were established using land trusteeship principles before the First World War. George Cadbury set aside 6,000 acres for the mixed residential Bournville Village Trust in Birmingham. Joseph Rowntree founded New Earswick, with the Joseph Rowntree Charitable and Housing Trusts, and these developments still pioneer innovative, socially just forms of housing tenure to this day. Like Mill and George, Rowntree was concerned about the 'unearned increment of rising land values', and how it could be captured to help relieve poverty. Ebenezer Howard used land trusteeship principles in purchasing the 30,000 acres of land for Letchworth for his Garden City. Ground rent from the co-operative land societies he established at Letchworth funds social, cultural and community services.

The land trusteeship ideas of Ruskin were adopted by Count Leo Tolstoy, and later by Gandhi in South Africa. They were implemented in India by his follower Vinova Bhave in the 1950s with the Land Gift or Boodhan movement, and subsequently the Gramdan village land gift movement. Bob Swann picked up these ideas in the 1960s when he was working in the US civil rights movement. Swann, as a builder, observed that no matter how good the quality of his work on new houses, the price was mainly determined by the land cost. He joined with others, such as Scott King, the cousin of Martin Luther King, to set up a rural, farmland-based Community Land Trust in the South, to combat sharecropper poverty. Today there are over 200 CLTs all over the USA providing affordable homes to people on modest incomes.[12]

The rationale for Community Land Trusts

Like land value taxation, Community Land Trusts are based on an understanding of the importance of land in the social, economic and ecological life of communities. The starting point is the preservation of land for the benefit of the community in which it is situated. However, the overwhelming weight of the impetus behind the contemporary movement lies in the housing crisis and the lack of affordable housing for working people and those on low incomes. The context is government inaction in the face of massive housing market failure and inequity. So forward thinking neighbourhoods, villages and towns decide to provide housing themselves.

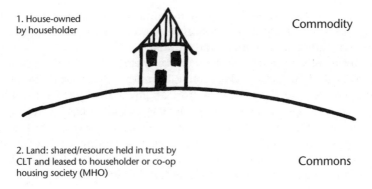

1. House-owned
by householder

Commodity

2. Land: shared/resource held in trust by
CLT and leased to householder or co-op
housing society (MHO)

Commons

Figure 10.3   House and land

One key reason for considering Community Land Trusteeship is that the building cost of a house can be one-third to a half of its market price. Get low cost land, preserve affordability through holding the land in trust off the market, and build homes for renting and part ownership.

The land-cost of a house is often as much or even more than the build-cost of the structure. This was one original rationale for CLTs. The land is understood as a commons, to be held by the CLT. The house structure is a commodity, which needs maintenance and can be bought and sold. So, put the land into trusteeship, thus preserving the community interest, and lease the land to home owners or social housing associations with restrictions to preserve permanently affordable access to housing for local people and/or those on the housing waiting list.

Community leaders from a cross-section of proactive villages, towns and city neighbourhoods see Community Land Trusteeship as one way to provide permanently affordable homes, as well as workspace, amenities and community facilities, and to conserve the local environment. Community Land Trusts are capable of playing a major role in local economic development including, as the Scottish Gigha experience described below has shown, community energy schemes.

Interest in Land Trusts was revived by work done by the New Economics Foundation. This led to the report *Common Ground for Mutual Home Ownership*, which explored mechanisms for development of a CLT within the current English and Welsh legislative framework, based on a co-operative model in the form of a Mutual Home Ownership Society (MHOS).

In autumn 2003 Bob Paterson of Community Finance Solutions at the University of Salford, Pat Conaty of the New Economics Foundation and the author went on a fact-finding visit to the US on a Winston Churchill Travelling Fellowship, in order to find out more about CLT practice there.[13] Work then developed on piloting CLTs in the UK, through the Capturing Value for Rural Communities project (2003–5). This led to the CLT National Demonstration project (2007–9), getting Community Land Trusts established with the aim of securing permanently affordable housing. Over fourteen pilot CLTs and 150 homes are now underway, with technical assistance and seed funding available.

Support for CLT schemes

Implementation of a CLT programme was in the Labour Party's 2005 election manifesto. Various reports, such as the investigation by Matthew Taylor MP into rural housing, have identified CLTs as a useful option for rural housing provision.

However, the government's focus on expanding freehold homeownership is a major blockage, a focus shared by the other mainstream political parties. There is also a reluctance to transfer public land to CLTs because the government and hard-pressed local authorities, like any landowner, want to sell land at the highest price.

Social housing does not get priority. Government in practice does little to help sustainable community development. There is no integrated approach to place-making and housing tenure, and a plethora of competing and conflicting tiers of local and national statutory agencies.

Finally, community self-help approaches on the whole are not well understood, welcomed or trusted by government. Ministers and civil servants appear to have little confidence in what communities are capable of doing. Governments' basic distrust of people and communities results in expensive government control. And the more need there is for inappropriate government control, the more communities will be put off self-help. Contrast this, say, with Holland, Germany and Denmark where local authorities are keen to practically support community led housing schemes. The city of Amersfoort in Holland has ten older people's co-housing communities and employs a community housing worker to work with local living groups, find sites and act as broker with a housing association.[14]

One example of the cost of government distrust of community led housing was the Holy Island loan of £212,000 that cost over £30,000 to access. Social Housing Grant, formerly available only to registered social landlords, was extended to community organisations in the form of the Direct Grant Agreement. But this involves completion of a detailed, highly technical questionnaire which is over a hundred pages long (the original document was over 300 pages long). It cost the Holy Island CLT over £30,000 in legal, consultancy and other technical fees to obtain a grant of £212,000 to develop four rental units of housing.

Rising inequality and the scandal of MPs' expenses have created the belief that housing ministers live in a very different world from people on modest incomes. For example, some MPs' and the former communities' minister Hazel Blears 'flipped' the designation of their second homes in order to maximise allowances and minimise tax.

The CLT experience

Stonesfield Community Trust was one of the earliest CLT ventures in post-war England, and was established in the early 1980s. Cornwall CLT is now making strides in England with several schemes, and this has fired up Conservative shadow housing spokesman Grant Shapps MP to develop a far-reaching policy to implement CLTs. Other schemes are under development, including in Devon, Gloucestershire, the northwest, on Holy Island and in Shropshire. In Wales, Land for People is providing assistance to a number of schemes in their early stages of development right across the Principality.

> ### Box 10.6   Stonesfield Community Trust, Oxfordshire
>
> In the early 1980s, as land prices began to rise rapidly in west Oxfordshire, local activist Tony Crofts donated a quarter-acre site in the village of Stonesfield to provide affordable housing in perpetuity for local people. He had seen other villages in the Cotswolds die as a result of house-price inflation, and he and other local people founded the Stonesfield Community Trust (SCT) in 1983 to save the village.
>
> Initially, with only a seed-corn grant of £3,000 from a local company, the trust was registered and planning permission negotiated. This consent alone increased the value of the donated land from £3,500 to £150,000 and enabled SCT to raise a mortgage to build their first four properties. Since then they have borrowed £80,000 from West Oxfordshire District Council to buy another quarter-acre site and developed a further twelve affordable homes, as well as converting a redundant glove factory into workspace units for the village. More recently a second commercial property development has been completed to house the village post office at a low fixed rent. All properties have been developed to high energy efficiency standards to ensure low running costs. Low-cost, below-market loans of £120,000 have been raised from private ethical investors. Additional zero-interest loans have been raised and small donations from villagers made in cash and in kind to SCT.
>
> In 2004 most of the loans were fully repaid, and the net property income from the CLT now contributes an annual surplus of £40,000 a year, which helps funds a local youth service. Stonesfield is now helping Oxfordshire Community Land Trust get started, with a new scheme in Oxford and the innovative Windsor Terrace Housing Co-op in Bristol.

CLTs elsewhere

In sharp contrast to the sluggish English government, Scotland has acted decisively to implement community land trusteeship. The 2003 Scottish Land Reform Act gave communities the right to buy land and property, as well as the right to roam, and set up a comprehensive enabling, funding and legal framework. This was implemented by the Community Land Unit at the Inverness-based Highlands and Islands Enterprise Board. There are now hundreds of community land buyouts across Scotland, which are reversing the historic concentration of landed wealth by putting land into trust for a variety of community uses. The result is more confident, vibrant and wealthier communities, and a growing social land trusteeship sector.

The land reform framework was put in place after the legendary £3 million Isle of Eigg community buyout in 1997 from the outgoing laird. Brian Wilson MP, after officiating at the foundation ceremony of the Isle of Eigg Heritage Trust in 1997, famously said 'It shouldn't have to be so difficult for communities.' He and Donald Dewar MP, then Secretary of State for Scotland, went on to put in place the Land Reform Act.

Where does the land come from?

As Mark Twain once said, 'The trouble with land is that they are not making it anymore.' Acquiring low-cost or 'free' land is a prerequisite for a CLT. Just as the National Trust started slowly with land gifts, so CLTs are taking time to acquire land from the following sources:

- gifts of land, as at Stonesfield Community Trust;
- getting land from exceptional site planning consents round towns and villages. This is when planning permission for affordable homes is given on land which is outside the usual boundary;

Box 10.7   Isle of Gigha Heritage Trust, Scottish Hebrides

When the absentee landlord put the Isle of Gigha up for sale in August 2001, residents formed a steering group to consider a 'community buyout' of the 3,400-acre island. The Scottish Land Fund provided support for a feasibility study, and a ballot of islanders secured overwhelming support in late 2001 for the plan developed. The community borrowed £1 million from the Scottish Land Fund and raised a further £3 million in grants to complete the purchase. The Isle of Gigha Heritage Trust, operating as the CLT, has taken into ownership forty-one of the sixty-seven houses on the island. It has developed six owner-occupied properties for sale and is developing eighteen houses for rent in partnership with Fyne Homes Housing Association. The CLT has formed a construction consortium with Fyne Homes and three local builders to carry out home improvements on the old properties and to build the new homes. Building apprenticeships have been created to enhance local skills and a small quarry on the island will provide local materials. The CLT has also created Scotland's first community-owned wind farm, which began generating power from three 40-metre turbines in October 2004. Funding of £400,000 has been raised for the wind farm, which will generate income of £150,000 a year. Profits from the three 'Dancing Ladies', Faith, Hope and Charity, will contribute to funding other CLT developments once the loans and investment for the project are repaid in 2009. The Isle of Gigha Trust also operates a hotel on the island and three dairy farms. In 2004 the £1 million loan from the SLF was fully repaid. The population of the island is on the increase for the first time in decades, the school is expanding and there is now a waiting list for people who want to move to Gigha.[15]

- getting a proportion of land that 'planning gain' agreements between developers and local authorities require for affordable homes. In large housing schemes, this could be up to 30–40 per cent of the land;
- land sold at a discount by developers as part of a wider scheme;
- low-cost land provided by companies, statutory organisations or individuals to provide employment-related housing;
- the transfer of publicly owned land and assets to the community at nil cost for social benefit, as the Homes and Communities Agency plans to do with some of the Cashes Green Hospital site in Stroud to dispose to Gloucestershire Land for People.

So far, pioneer CLTs have developed in villages and market towns in England and Wales where there is strong local support, land gifts from the community or individuals and low-cost land. A central challenge is to ensure that the land will remain in community ownership, so that the value of the gift remains with the community and thus stays a community resource. There are fears that housing associations will find it difficult to meet this challenge in the long term and worries that government may in the future introduce legislation extending the right to buy to housing associations (this has already been advanced as Conservative Party policy).

Box 10.8   The future is Fordhall

This community buyout of an organic farm could point the way for others.

British farming is often said to be in crisis. News emerges regularly from the countryside of farms closed down and sold off, farmers driven out of business by superstores, villages declining and the traditions being lost.

But there are exceptions. Fordhall Farm, near Market Drayton in Shropshire, was saved for organic farming and for the community on 1 July 2006. Faced with a possible hostile buyout, the third generation tenant farmers Charlotte Hollins, 24, and her brother Ben, 21, together with many volunteers and supporters, set up the Fordhall Community Land Initiative (FCLI). A public appeal enabled FCLI to raise £800,000 through selling shares in the farm to over 8,500 people. The success means that this pioneering 123-acre farm has now been placed into a community trusteeship – safe for future generations.

The Fordhall story is one of both social and environmental progress. FCLI has been set up as an Industrial and Provident Society for community benefit, to hold Fordhall Farm in trust and lease it affordably to the young farmers. The mission of FCLI is to run Fordhall Farm as an educational, environmental and social resource, helping to reconnect people to food, farming and the countryside. It seeks to demonstrate that small-scale farming, connected to the local community, offers a viable way of life for generations to come.

Right from the start, Fordhall farmer Charlotte Hollins wanted practical ways of engaging people with the farm, and making it a community resource. She came to us in early 2005 at Stroud Common Wealth and asked for ideas and assistance. We suggested that the farm could be safeguarded in the form of an Industrial and Provident Society for Community Benefit. This means that the farmland is mutualised – a democratic, one-member one-vote structure is set up, and shares are sold to the public at £50 each. Shares cannot be traded, but are returnable to FCLI if another buyer can be found. Members vote for a board which runs FCLI on their behalf, developing a variety of programmes and leasing the land to the farmers.

The basic principle is a simple one, now known as 'crowd finance'. People got together and paid to take Fordhall's land off the open market, thus safeguarding it for the future. Through supporting Fordhall, people knew they were helping conservation, preserving wildlife, saving a historical organic farm and reaffirming their relationship with the land. Small gifts really mattered. Local primary school pupils contributed £7 by each giving 20p. Everything counted. People from all over the world, as well as local people and people from across Britain, became members.

The full story can be accessed from the Fordhall Farm website, and there is a Fordhall case study on the Stroud Common Wealth website. One key learning point is that a community buyout can only work if there is considerable public support, if the land purchase price is agreed with the landlord and they give a reasonable time, say up to nine months or a year for the community buyout to raise the money. It was then up to many people signing up to the values of taking land off the market by putting it into democratically accountable forms, such as an Industrial and Provident Society for Community Benefit.

The Fordhall community buyout could be as significant for England as the 1996 Isle of Eigg community buyout was for Scotland. Eigg sparked the 2003 Scottish Land Reform Act, which gave communities the right to buy their own land. At a time when the government is busy privatising our public land on a massive scale, Fordhall shows an alternative future – saving the family silver for community benefit. We could be seeing a sea change in values from treating land as a commodity to be sold to those with the most money, to seeing land as a commons, as a right, to which the community can control access in open, democratically accountable and equitable ways.

Sources: Martin Large and Greg Pilley, www.stroudcommonwealth.org.uk for
CFLT Action Pack and www.fordhallfarm.com

Bridging the affordability gap

In order to make housing affordable, the value of the land is separated from the value of the housing or other structures built on it. The land is held by a public body such as a CLT on behalf of the community. The value of the structures is generally based on their replacement value, which in turn relates to the cost of materials and labour. Any public investment in the form of land or other investment is preserved and recycled for succeeding generations. The example of Stonesfield Community Trust, described earlier in this chapter, shows how one village does this in practice.

There are a number of models of CLTs, and the model used will largely depend on local conditions and the community's priorities. Communities must ask themselves what they want to achieve, now, soon and later, for future generations.

However, the legislative framework in the UK presents a tough challenge because of right to buy legislation, which, as we have seen, restricts the role of local authorities and, potentially, housing associations, in the provision of permanently affordable housing for their communities.

A further legislative obstacle lies in leasehold enfranchisement legislation. This was designed to protect the rights of tenants of housing under a long lease and allows them to compel the owner of the freehold to sell it to them.

A further complication lies in the terms for provision of government housing grants, which, in a nutshell, require occupants under a shared ownership scheme to be allowed to 'staircase' up to 75–80 per cent ownership, thus reducing the CLT's stake in the freehold and its ability to keep it for the benefit of future occupants.

Yet another complication is the right of borrowers under a mortgage to repay that mortgage in total. Models based on a mortgage arrangement cannot ultimately prevent the occupier from repaying the mortgage and taking full ownership of the property (this is significant in relation to the 'equity mortgage models' described below).

These legal complications make it potentially hard for CLTs to retain their land, though CLTs owning land and homes for rental, as at Stonesfield, is not a problem. As far as housing models are concerned, the examples below represent the four main types of 'part equity' ways of preserving affordability that CLTs currently use or are developing in the UK.

Restricted resale price

This is the simplest model. It simply involves a binding covenant by the buyer to resell on departure at a specified discount against open market value. This approach has problems, however, where runaway house price escalation makes even a discount of 50 per cent or more unaffordable to future generations. It also means that the community retains no ongoing benefit from the land, other than the fact that there is housing on it. It can achieve discounted housing, but leaves little scope for other aspirations.

Equity mortgage

The individual buys the freehold. He or she obtains a mortgage in the usual way for part of the purchase price. The CLT grants a loan for the remainder and retains the right of first refusal on resale, as well as a right to nominate future purchasers. In principle, however, the occupant is entitled to redeem the mortgage and obtain full ownership in due course. The CLT would then recover only the equity for future investment in other land, assuming it was available and affordable. This is the HCA's preferred method for Cashes Green, even though it neither offers permanent afford-ability nor keeps the connection of Cashes Green people to place. Basically, the CLT becomes a kind of community equity trust, rather than a community land trust.[16]

Declaration of Trust lease

The CLT grants a lease to itself and the prospective occupant on the basis of a trust specifying the shares held by the occupant and the CLT respectively. Again, the CLT retains the right of first refusal to recover the property when the occupant leaves and to nominate future residents. The occupant obtains a mortgage to pay for the price of the lease, which is set at a percentage of the open market value of the property.

In both of the above cases, the lender would have a right to take possession and sell the property on the open market if payments are not made.

Mutual Home Ownership Society (MHOS)

This model offers stronger protection for the CLT's stake in the land. The CLT holds the land in trust, and leases it to a Mutual Home Ownership Society. The MHOS is based on a co-operative structure and co-operative management of the neigh-bourhood. Essentially, the occupant pays rent, but over time builds up a capital stake based on the capital amount (not the interest) the CLT has paid in respect of its own borrowings to fund the development. This arrangement also involves a declaration of trust and a lease.

In both Declaration of Trust and MHOS, the leasehold enfranchisement problems referred to above do not apply, because the CLT is a joint lessor and cannot enfran-chise itself. MHOS schemes are best suited to larger developments of, say, fifty dwellings, so that real economies of scale can be achieved.

However, as yet, housing ministers have not chosen to give CLTs any prac-tical support in the form of land, to finance MHO pilots or to guarantee MHO schemes so they can get private finance. Margaret Beckett, the former housing minister, did however, launch the Co-operative Party's MHO Policy, developed by David Rodgers of CDS Co-operatives, on 27 January 2009.[17]Ian Wright MP, junior housing minister, said in March 2009 he wanted to support five MHO schemes in a pilot scheme of 200 homes. Welcome as this sounds, to date achieving this depends on getting finance. (In sharp contrast, government does have the money to prop up the banks and insure them.) In the present climate and without direct government support, banks are reluctant to lend on anything other than conven-tional mortgages. But, if taken up, mutual home ownership offers a practical way of building a just society using mutual solutions.

Box 10.9   The benefits of mutual home ownership

Residents can be active members of a sustainable neighbourhood community of fifty or so homes, which they can democratically control. They can get access to a decent, affordable home, build up equity and in cases of unemployment the monthly interest-only payments are eligible for housing benefit.

Living costs will be cheaper from shared facilities and environmental design for low-energy homes.

Flexible tenure-residents can join on an interest-/rent-paying-only basis and then as income rises build up equity in the scheme.

Government will value the preservation of public subsidies and land disposal by CLTs in permanently affordable co-operative homes.

The MHOS promotes social cohesion and encourages active citizenship and democratic participation in neighbourhood affairs.

The mechanism of the CLT holding the land in trust, and then leasing the land to the MHOS, guarantees a continuing connection between land and people, people and place.

This is a new form of tenure, akin to the highly successful Swedish co-op sector, which owns 18 per cent of Swedish homes.

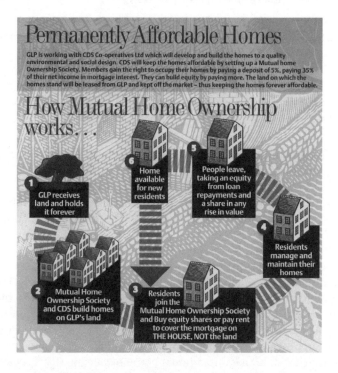

Permanently Affordable Homes

GLP is working with CDS Co-operatives Ltd which will develop and build the homes to a quality environmental and social design. CDS will keep the homes affordable by setting up a Mutual home Ownership Society. Members gain the right to occupy their homes by paying a deposit of 5%, paying 35% of their net income in mortgage interest. They can build equity by paying more. The land on which the homes stand will be leased from GLP and kept off the market – thus keeping the homes forever affordable.

How Mutual Home Ownership works. . .

1. GLP receives land and holds it forever
2. Mutual Home Ownership Society and CDS build homes on GLP's land
3. Residents join the Mutual Home Ownership Society and Buy equity shares or pay rent to cover the mortgage on THE HOUSE, NOT the land
4. Residents manage and maintain their homes
5. People leave, taking an equity from loan repayments and a share in any rise in value
6. Home available for new residents

Box 10.10   The Cashes Green Hospital story: from a Community Land Trust to a Community Equity Trust

Figure 10.4   Cashes Green Hospital, Stroud

The hospital was closed in 1994, and the allotment holders cleared off the land by the NHS. The site has been empty ever since, a common resource that has been wasted for years. This represents, in government language, 'poor value for money'. Land Value Tax would have induced the NHS and government to bring the land into use, rather than keeping it empty and unproductive for so long.

Whilst getting pilot CLTs started in villages with local resources has been successful, it can be a different matter when communities try to engage with government and the Homes and Communities Agency (HCA) on larger projects such as Cashes Green in Stroud. Housing ministers seem to come and go every six months or so, and civil servants – who themselves keep moving on in Whitehall – profess to want innovation but in practise focus on 'risk', which usually means their fear of a potentially hostile press.

Trevor Beattie, the Director of Policy and Research at the HCA, is reported to have said at a Shrewsbury conference in May 2009 that CLTs are 'not normal'. He gave the impression that CLTs are inherently risky, as well as being different enough to require 'special treatment and additional rigour in assessing their public policy worth and value for money'.[18]

Continued overleaf

Firstly, the risk. It seems to have escaped HCA's attention that there has been a negligible rate of home repossession amongst US CLT homeowners during the sub-prime crisis. Letchworth Garden City is based on CLT principles, and is successful. He also ignores the countless local charities that have owned assets for community benefit successfully for centuries. Secondly, Trevor Beattie seems to want to impose the prohibitive expense on CLTs of dealing with HCA's need for 'special treatment and additional rigour'. This cost is beyond the modest resources of community-based CLTs. Thirdly, one could be forgiven for contrasting the HCA's negative view of CLTs with the successful Scottish government's support for community land ownership.

And even though Hazel Blears, the former Communities Secretary, said she believed in community empowerment through CLTs, the rhetoric never matched reality. Peter Hetherington wrote in the *Guardian* in October 2007 that at Cashes Green, in a national pilot for land trusts, the CLT, Gloucestershire Land for People discovered that reality on the ground did not match ministerial rhetoric. He wrote that:

> The Gloucestershire town of Stroud might appear an unlikely starting point. But outward signs of prosperity obscure a deepening housing crisis for locals priced out of the market by second homeowners. At stake is a 4.5-hectare (11-acre) former hospital site, known as Cashes Green, on which a local Community Land Trust wants to build 77 houses; 50 affordable units cross-subsidized by the 27 for sale. In June, the government's regeneration agency, English Partnerships [EP, now HCA], under the wing of Blears' department – which acquired a string of former NHS sites for housing – announced it had agreed to hand over Cashes Green to the Community Land Trust, subject to ministerial approval. In a statement, the agency stressed its support for innovative methods of delivering homes for renting and buying.
>
> But when the deal reached Whitehall, matters stalled. Some believe EP was asked to think again. Now, it seems, a revised plan will propose that between a third and half of the site goes for mainly social housing. Most of the rest will go for private development. This will effectively end the mutual ideal, scuppering the plan. It seems that, in the culture of short-term Treasury accounting, Cashes Green is less 'valuable' as a community resource; i.e., more private houses will yield a better return. The matter has gone back to EP for further consideration. The Community Land Trust, Gloucestershire Land for People, is perplexed. Stroud's Labour MP, David Drew, is 'worse than annoyed ... we're [now] struggling to get it off the ground'.

No matter that those ministers are committed to increasing England's level of social house building – almost doubling levels to 50,000 annually after three years. 'If the government wants to increase supply to these levels, it's crucial to use public land,' says one official close to negotiations. 'It needs to weigh the long-term gains in providing decent housing against the short-term gains of increasing capital receipts.'[19]

So in November 2007, housing minister Yvette Cooper, advised by her senior civil servants, turned down a community-designed scheme that included the reinstatement of all the allotments, community facilities such as play space, a much-needed GP surgery, work space and green space. Local people wanted 'a garden neighbourhood at the heart of Cashes Green' that had twelve homes for social rental, fifty homes piloting the new co-op housing tenure option of MHO, with GLP stewarding the land. The sale of fifteen freehold homes would have helped cross-subsidise the building of the scheme.

Various reasons were given for turning down the scheme, for example 'poor value for money', though the minister refused an independent evaluation of her decision, which could have been a way ahead. There were rumours that the Treasury wanted more money for the site; that if the CLT and Mutual Home Ownership scheme went ahead, the NHS would claw back overage money, the extra money from the freehold sale value of the land. This was supposedly valued at around £3.5mn, even though a year later a local surveyor valued the site at £1mn. Government agents English Partnerships raised none of these reasons in a timely way during the 2005–7 Options Appraisal process conducted by Gloucestershire Land for People and CDS Co-operatives. The government's approach on Cashes Green was described as 'mushroom partnership' – keep communities in the dark and manure them without warning.

At the time of writing, HCA wants seventy-eight dwellings at Cashes Green, thirty-nine of them affordable, i.e. twenty social rented and nineteen shared equity houses for the CLT, Gloucestershire Land for People. There would be an ecological protection zone of 0.1 hectares, open space including a play area of 0.17 hectares and an allotment area of 0.69 hectares with a community building.

However, HCA's equity mortgage plan does not ensure permanent affordability of the nineteen shared equity 'CLT' homes at Cashes Green in perpetuity. As explained earlier in this chapter, the home buyers have a right to redeem the mortgage as and when they are able to do so, and the CLT is only assured of recovering its own equity investment. The equity can then be applied in the purchase of further loans for development,

Continued overleaf

but this fails to resolve the problem of the shortage of such land and the problems associated with planning permission and the like, which necessitates the intervention of the CLT in the first place. The 'equity' can be used to help part-equity home purchase elsewhere, but this severs the connection of people and place. Gloucestershire Land for People is going along with HCA's proposals for pragmatic reasons – at least some houses will be built at last, and the allotments reinstated. Mutual home ownership, the original preferred option, has not been possible because of the lack of funding

So HCA's proposal will sever the link between land and people in time, undermining the development of a cohesive neighbourhood. It would appear that HCA officials, bogged down in technical details and the need to make money from selling freehold homes at Cashes Green, have missed the whole point of Community Land Trusteeship. This is about sustainable community building, placemaking, the stewardship of land, re-connecting, participative democracy, social inclusion and permanent affordability. Basically, the HCA wants a community equity trust, not a community land trust. The HCA wants to financialise the Cashes Green land value and turned it into 'equity' to be then used around Stroud District to make other homes elsewhere affordable. This is in fact the opposite of what CLTs aim to do, which is to take land off the market in a particular place and community for enduring public benefit. The 'Homes and Communities Agency' will never achieve its aims with this abstract concept of land as money. The Cashes Green story shows that HCA does not understand the central importance of land for placemaking and community building, the connection between land and people as the foundation for people's homes and vibrant communities. Rather than re-connecting land, place and people at Cashes Green, the HCA is continuing the English landlord tradition of the dispossession of people and land, of enclosure. When GLP carried out the original participative conferences on what people wanted for the Cashes Green hospital site, they supported more housing than the forty homes designated in the local plan provided these were permanently affordable to local people in a garden neighbourhood that would strengthen the heart of the community. HCA's scheme will not do this.

It is deeply puzzling why the government, senior civil servants and HCA find it so hard to help CLTs develop family-friendly, permanently affordable, sustainable garden neighbourhoods. Why does the English government, unlike the Scottish government, make it so difficult for communities?

Sources: see www.gloucestershirelandforpeople.coop, 'Briefing Paper on Mutual Home Ownership'; www.cdscooperatives.coop; see www. communitylandtrust.org.uk for more information on CLTs

Other options: co-housing and housing co-operatives

MHOs and co-housing share common features, though unlike co-housing, MHO aims to bring the cost of affordable homes way down to modest income levels.[20] Both aim to reinvent co-operative approaches to housing, with all the benefits of social cohesion, affordability, common spaces for play, community gardens, low carbon homes and garden neighbourhoods.

Co-housing, short for co-operative housing, was invented in Denmark in the 1960s by an architect and a parent who wrote an article called 'Children Should Have One Hundred Parents'. One driving force was single-parent families wanting to share common facilities with others yet keep a private living space as well. Danish co-housing schemes stress low-rise, clustered housing, with residents involved in designing homes and common facilities like laundry, district heating, gardens, play space and a common house with communal kitchens. Co-housing is a popular housing tenure, supported by the government with generous loans for equitable access, and accounts for 5 per cent of Danish homes. Many co-housing design features, such as keeping cars on the edge of the neighbourhood, common facilities, eco design and a range of homes of different sizes and tenures, have spread to the private and state housing sectors.

In Britain to date, only pioneering co-housing projects of middle-income people who can afford a mortgage have been successful. One successful example

Figure 10.5   Springhill co-housing, Stroud

is Springhill co-housing in Stroud with thirty-four homes. Like all forms of co-operative housing, co-housing helps build sustainable, more inclusive communities and is a popular choice in the US, Holland and Denmark.

Tenant co-operative homes

Tenant co-operative homes are another tried and tested option for low-income households. Coin Street Builders, for example, near the OXO Tower on the South Bank in London, are a leading example of a tenant-housing co-operative with over 220 homes and community facilities. These give control to tenants in human-scale neighbourhoods, which are managed by residents.

Redditch Co-operative Homes is the largest provider of new-build co-operative housing in Britain with 266 homes built to date for five neighbourhood tenant co-operatives. Since 2001 RCH has pioneered the design of socially cohesive and environmentally friendly homes with co-op residents. Co-op members help plan their neighbourhoods and then manage them, resulting in dynamic, active communities. The low-carbon homes, whether flats, bungalows, terraces or semis, are manufactured offsite using the Norwegian Hedalm eco-home system. These are timber framed, with wood cladding, and their low energy costs result from insulation, photovoltaic solar panels and heat recovery. Build costs are around £1,300 per square metre. Space inside the homes is very generous, of Scandinavian standard, and the quality shows. RCH houses people registered with the council who are

Figure 10.6   Redditch Co-operative Homes

prepared to take an active part in their neighbourhood and who do a co-op housing training course. The homes are social rental, with no right to buy. A board made up of five directors from Redditch District Council, five directors from the parent housing association, Accord, and five tenant representatives of the tenant co-ops governs RCH. Carl Taylor, the general manager of RCH, considers that 'Mutuality is the forgotten solution for meeting Britain's housing needs as an effective way of increasing community ownership and resident control, of building trust, community and garden neighbourhoods.' He quotes a resident of RCH's Breedon co-operative:

'Here is a company that has reinvented the old ways and brought them back to the twenty-first century. Since we moved in, my social life has taken on a whole new meaning. No longer do we sit in front of the TV every night. Now we have friends we can visit, go out for meals, laugh at jokes long forgotten and, most importantly, look forward to a brighter future. And I don't have to go far because all my best friends are my neighbours.'[21]

The future of Community Land Trusts

The practicality of Community Land Trusteeship and the benefits are clear. For Grant Shapps, the Conservative shadow housing spokesperson, 'seeing was believing', thanks to a visit to the Cornish CLT of St Miniver, of fourteen self-build homes. We may have to wait for a Conservative government for real practical support for CLTs, as Labour have been so slow.

CLTs offer a variety of different tenure choices, for example social rental homes, a range of tenant co-op, permanently affordable mutual homes or co-housing as alternative options to freehold housing. There are early successes, like Stonesfield Community Trust, and village-grown CLTs are now arising across the country.

And people are not just supporting Community Land Trusteeship for houses, as the case of Fordhall Community Land Initiative described above shows. However, the successes of putting farms into CLTs, the growth of conservation land trusts like the RSPB and county wildlife trusts contrast with the tougher challenges of developing CLTs for homes and community facilities. It took the dogged determination and community spirit of Tony Crofts to get Stonesfield Community Trust going, or years of work by David Brown at High Bickington, in Devon, to implement CLTs.

The pressure on the government for Community Land Trusteeship solutions for permanently affordable homes, work space and community facilities will continue to build as the demand for social rental and part-equity homes increases. So far, the HCA has been like Henry Higgins in *My Fair Lady* complaining to Eliza Doolittle, 'Why can't a CLT not be more like the HCA?' So far, government has been making things very hard for communities to help themselves on housing.

However, CLTs could go from heresy, from 'not being normal', to being mainstream. Stephen Hill, a land economist and spatial planner writes that rather than being 'way out', 'CLTs are the new paradigm. They are focussed placeshaping investors and community builders, agents for delivering the well being outcomes required by spatial plans, sustainable community strategies and local area agreements. It's the traditional developers who are now inefficient, obsolete and not fit for purpose.'[22]

Just as the National Trust took time to get going, there are now enough pioneer CLTs to spread the concept. There is a value shift from seeing land not as a commodity, but as a shared commons. There is an emerging recognition of the right to decent, affordable, low-carbon, well-designed homes in sustainable, self-provisioning, social, supportive neighbourhoods that have a mix of social rental and co-operative tenures. And an emerging view that a partnership of housing associations as social businesses, government and civil society bodies such as community land trusts can implement this right.

Summary: a common treasury for us all

Treating land as a commodity has resulted in housing market failure in Britain. Classical economists, such as Adam Smith and John Stuart Mill, saw land as a commons. This is in sharp contrast to the neo-liberal treatment of land as a market commodity, as only equity or money. Land Value Tax is one way to reduce inequity and make the best use of our land as commons. Another way is Winston Churchill's idea of 'Land for People'. Community Land Trusts are one way of securing land and affordable homes for people. CLTs were first developed by pioneers like Ebenezer Howard for Letchworth and are now being reinvented by the land trust movement for reclaiming the commons and securing affordable homes.[23]

So what about people as the fourth transformative entry point? How can education be freed so that people can reach their full potential and can contribute?

Afterword: letter to Gordon Brown

To conclude, Stonesfield pioneer Tony Crofts points out the opportunities offered by the CLT solution. He wrote this letter (unanswered) to the incoming Prime Minister Gordon Brown in June 2007:

> Be faithful to your words about devolution, and people having control over their own lives. Community Land Trusts are an answer, building small, locally wanted, locally designed developments in villages, towns and urban areas all over. Not huge estates flown in by big developers at the behest of central government.
>
> The current housing crisis is the result of a complete market failure, and the Government's refusing the take any responsibility for managing it.
>
> Encouraged by property supplements in every newspaper, and silly TV programmes about doing up old houses and selling them for a profit, English people have convinced themselves that if they keep selling their homes to each other at ever-higher prices, they are getting richer.
>
> This is the ultimate pathetic fallacy: the only people getting richer are the moneylenders who drive the process. Ever since banks were de-regulated and allowed to lend money they don't have, they have all been falling over each other to gather in mortgage business because it is safe and profitable. The result has been to push house prices up and up.
>
> For the British economy to continue to grow, therefore, it is necessary for house prices to continue ever upwards. This means that, if you haven't got a

house yet, you are officially sunk: and that's government policy. 17.4 million adults in this country are now unable to afford a home, either to buy or to rent; and the average home-owner is now spending 51 per cent of income on keeping a roof over his/her head.

Spin-driven pronouncements about 'helping more people onto the housing ladder' are foolish and completely irrelevant. They ignore the fact that everyone on the housing ladder has a great millstone of debt around their neck, and is standing on the fingers of someone else who hasn't got on yet. Increasing the supply of houses at market price only aggravates the situation, even if they are subsidised. As soon as you sell a low-cost house, it becomes a high-cost house.

This also means that, when you have paid off the mortgage you took out to buy your home, you can take another mortgage to provide your children with deposits for theirs; and when you have paid that off, you are encouraged to 'release equity' in your home by taking a third mortgage to pay for your care in old age – because your children are too busy looking after their homes to do anything for you.

The continual price rise is produced, not by the actual cost of constructing houses, but by competition for land. If you buy a house today, the rebuilding cost for insurance purposes is less than half of the market price of the house. The only way of stopping this escalation is to take land out of the equation, and hold it in public ownership for the benefit of the community.

Ebenezer Howard realised this when he set up Letchworth Garden City, where the freeholds are held by community land cooperatives, and everyone's ground rent helps fund proper social services.

The truth that needs to be recognised and accepted is that it is only by pulling together to secure and protect land for common benefit, that the housing problem can begin to be solved. Through Community Land Trusts, any public investment in such schemes is preserved permanently, and constantly recycled for the benefit of succeeding generations.

So far, no public policy has given any recognition to the need to provide for future generations or the continuing life of communities. Permitted development in small rural communities is often only allowed for proven agricultural/forestry workers – whose numbers are not increasing – with no provision for their children to stay in the community where they grew up. There is no provision, either, for young couples to have close family support when building relationships and bringing up children.

And so the process continues: cowardly government, greedy moneylenders, suffering citizens without homes, unstable markets and a total failure of proper society-building. More fear and isolation, less communal solidarity. When will we get together and say 'Stop'? We can organise things better for ourselves.

Chapter 11

Freeing Education

The Stalinist overtones of a 'state theory of learning' enforced by the 'machinery of surveillance and accountability' - league tables, testing targets - are as unattractive as they are serious ... The general air of pessimism and powerlessness [among teachers] could be an accurate reflection of how people feel, anywhere, when their freedom of action and thought in the area which lies at the heart of their work is reduced.
Professor Robin Alexander, *Cambridge Primary Review*, as quoted by Richard
Garner in the *Independent*, 16 October 2009

Freeing education will create the most common wealth. This is the common wealth of whole people who fulfil their creative, physical, spiritual, moral, emotional and intellectual potential; who contribute, as creative individuals, citizens and productive makers. Parents want their children to realise their potential to lead fulfilling lives of love, wellbeing, work and meaning. Employers welcome young people who can take responsibility, are motivated, keen to learn, can work in teams, take initiative, have good communication, ICT and numeracy skills – and who have a sparkle in their eyes. The community needs people who can take part in civic, political, social and cultural life. Our environment, the earth, needs caring for. Consequently, there needs to be free cultural space in schools, communities and families to nurture, support and invite children and young people to be who they really are and for them to realise their talents. Our children are our future.

But all is not well with English education. There are some challenging contradictions and paradoxes:

• Firstly, government has instituted a highly regulated, costly system of increasingly centralised control, inspection and audit, rewarding what they define as 'good' school performance with resources, and punishing, blaming, naming and shaming so-called 'failing schools'. Yet at the same time, governments have trusted the City and the commercial sector with light-touch regulation. A strange conundrum: just why did government trust the bankers so much, and our teachers so little?

- Secondly, there is the contradiction of governments introducing (allegedly) 'parental choice' into the schooling system through league tables and 'marketising' education. Yet when parents then take up the government's invitation and try to choose popular schools, they find them full, and there is selection (overt or covert), even lotteries, for places. A systemic contradiction.

- Thirdly, there is the paradox that more money than ever is being spent on education with the aim of making English schools 'world class', yet international comparisons are often getting worse, with schools on average not much better than 'bog standard'. So how and why has so much extra money produced so little educational improvement?

- Fourthly, there is the paradox of English school children falling behind those in other countries, as measured by PISA tests, yet their UK exam results seem to be constantly improving. This paradox prompts awkward questions: Have grades in GCSEs and A levels been inflated by easier marking? Why, in spite of much effort and more funding to bring about educational change, has there been so little improvement? Might it be that the pervasive 'teaching to the test', recently exposed by the UK Children, Families and Schools Select Committee, has meant that inflated examination results are reflecting little more than school pupils who are well programmed for test-passing, rather than having their more general learning horizons appropriately nurtured and expanded? Have 'standards' become politicised, since allegedly rising standards please the politicians, who can then claim success? Academics such as Peter Timms of the University of Durham came up with awkward research showing that literacy standards have barely improved in the last fifty years.[1]

- Fifthly, there is the contradiction that more (rhetorical?) attention is apparently given to supporting children's individual wellbeing through 'Every Child Matters', which advocates 'be healthy, stay safe, enjoy and achieve, make a positive contribution and achieve economic wellbeing', yet it is raising measurable school performance standards that *really* seems to matter, and which gets the money. This is what schools are rewarded for.

- Finally, on the one hand Ed Balls, Secretary of State for Children, Schools and Families, says he wants teachers to exercise more responsibility, professional judgement and leadership. On the other, he trusts teachers so little that – to give just two examples – he signed the Early Years Foundation Stage (EYFS) into law in September 2008, and he has recently announced the regulatory 'licensing' of all teachers every five years. Ed Balls has not yet signed into law how surgeons should conduct operations, but does coerce teachers through the law. This is in sharp contrast to the EYFS adoption by the Welsh Assembly as voluntary guidelines for educators. Furthermore, Ed Balls said that teachers who refuse to carry out SATs tests in 2010 would be breaking the law.[2]

Discussion of the aims of education engages our values, our image of the human being, our view of society and our education paradigms. For example, how is education different from training? And why is ICT one of the core themes of the new primary curriculum, and not the arts? Gordon Brown's education paradigm, for example, sees the primary goal of education as economic, because there is a 'global skills race' and Britain has to have a 'globally competitive national economy'.[3]

There seems to be a basic conflict between, on the one hand, the government's desire to train children for a productive working life so that Britain can compete economically, and on the other, teachers and parents who want to educate children to realise their full creative, emotional, physical, spiritual and intellectual potential.

These are important educational content questions. However, the main focus of this chapter on freeing education is to analyse the nature of the relationship, of the boundary, between the two quite different systems of education and government. Crucially, this is a system boundary question. Whilst it is appropriate for government to ensure that every child has an equal right and entitlement to education, children (and the teachers teaching them) also need to be free to learn (and free to teach), with teachers who are in a position to create the best possible conditions for child development, learning and personal and social growth. The two system principles are, respectively, *equality* in the political system, and *freedom* in the educational, cultural system.

So, to what extent is the current relationship between government and education a real partnership, where each sector plays to its strengths? Is it a partnership of equals? To what extent does one sector dominate the other? Is there too much or too little equality or freedom? Some say, for example, that teachers had too much professional discretion up to 1979, and now there is too little. So how can the optimal balance be struck?

There is more real partnership and respect between government and schools in the Welsh and Scottish education systems. This is partly cultural, with traditionally liberal ('free') views of education and respect for teachers underpinning the relative autonomy of Scottish and Welsh schools. The northern European and Scandinavian countries, which regularly come top of the international educational comparisons, all respect partnership working between education and government. These countries have liberal, child-centred educational and community cultures, rather than the industrialised, 'schoolified', quasi-authoritarian English model. Educators are held in high regard, with a 'Greek' respect for learning, rather than the English approach of regarding teachers as the Romans did, as slaves who 'delivered' the curriculum, who 'stretched' children like Procrustes, so as to ensure their child got a place in the middle-class meritocracy and not to let poetry get in the way of a working-class boy getting a good plumbing job.

So, in what follows I will argue for transforming the domination by government of English education into a real partnership for mutual benefit. The purpose of this partnership is to unleash the learning capacities of educators, students and parents by freeing education. The benefits of this will be many and diverse; for example:

- more learning;
- rising levels of motivation, in particular freeing more discretionary effort;
- real ownership of education;
- more distinctive individual schools;
- better results;
- lower costs from the scrapping of expensive (and often counter-productive) auditing systems such as SATs, saving teacher and student time for real learning as opposed to 'teaching to the test';
- schools making optimal use of education and community resources for student learning;
- a variety of educational approaches growing from students' needs and the local context;
- attracting and keeping more creative, professional teachers;
- more schools as creative community centres for cultural and social renewal (i.e. open rather than closed systems, learning organisations rather than transmission belts); and
- transforming social and personal development through cohesive, human-scale education and respect for children's rights.

So freeing education, by moving from a low-trust to a high-trust system, will transform learning in a whole host of beneficial ways.

If you think such benefits are a fairy tale, then look for inspiration to the US small-school educational movement, and English state schools working with human-scale education such as Countesthorpe in Leicestershire, Stantonbury Campus in Milton Keynes, Brislington Enterprise College, Bristol, and Stanley Park High School, Surrey, which are 'lead schools' for the Human Scale Schools project. The purpose of this chapter, then, is to argue the case for freeing education, to illustrate the many benefits, how it can work in practice, and some first steps. It will cover:

- the nationalisation and commercialisation of children
- how England's free education system was taken over by the state
- emerging human-scale schools: from over-regulation to partnership
- freeing education: from the audit culture to partnership.

The nationalisation and commercialisation of children

An increasing number of commentators maintain that free cultural space for children, families and schools has been crowded out by both commercial and bureaucratic forces taking over childhood and education. Childhood has effectively been nationalised by government diktat and commercialised by business through pervasive marketing. For example, the government now heavily audits schools. Early years educators have been prescribed a so-called 'nappy curriculum' with its sixty-nine learning goals. The Early Years Foundation Stage (EYFS) was made compulsory in September 2008 by executive order, replacing the previous Curriculum Guidance framework, which 'suggested ...' rather than 'prescribed' to practitioners. The curriculum was therefore made a statutory requirement, with a whole range of legally sanctioned learning targets for pre-school age children, including literacy and numeracy activities on screen.

The nappy curriculum was imposed in the face of widespread, well-argued opposition from parents, childminders, early years educators and academic researchers, including a national campaign specifically formed to challenge aspects of the EYFS — the Open EYE Campaign (www.savechildhood.org). Campaigners were concerned about EYFS's arbitrary and developmentally inappropriate age-related learning goals, the legalisation of a controversial one-size-fits-all, state-defined model of child development, toddlers being exposed to the anxieties of practitioners' anxiety-driven surveillance and assessment, compulsory IT, 'structured, directed play' as opposed to free play, and 'too much too soon' in terms of formal, cognitively based learning. They pointed to nations like Finland with enviably successful educational outcomes, where formal literacy is introduced at six-plus, when children are developmentally ready, rather than too early. Yet ministers Ed Balls and Beverley Hughes refused to amend the status of EYFS to voluntary 'professional guidelines' that would allow professional discretion in what is anyway a *pre-compulsory* school age domain.

Their only limited concession was to offer childminders, nurseries and kindergartens wanting to opt out of the EFYS learning 'requirements' a labyrinthine thirty-four-page application for exemption. The process was clearly deliberately designed to make it both procedurally difficult and costly to seek, let alone gain, exemption. Each request for exemption requires an interview with the local authority and a ballot of the parents that should result in at least a 75 per cent majority in favour of exemption, before the QCA will even consider an application. Applications then require detailed thought before answering the questions on the form, backing them up with in depth background information about the philosophy and methodologies used at the setting together with any documentary evidence such as policies, flyers or prospectuses. This is difficult enough for a school or nursery, but well nigh impossible for a childminder who wouldn't normally have such documentation. Then, if successful, each exemption will only last for a maximum of two years because the EYFS is to be reviewed in 2010.

One respected childminder, who has cared for children over the last 22 years, whilst happy to use the EYFS as voluntary guidance, was refused exemption by the QCA. This means that, on inspection, OFSTED (the Office for Standards in *Education*, notice) will fail this experienced childminder even though the parents of the children she looks after are fully supportive of her approach, which is informed by a coherent educational philosophy. The Department of Schools and Families says: 'It is nothing to do with us, we just make the laws. We don't apply them!' Local authorities won't fund early years settings with no QCA and OFSTED approval.

Apparently, OFSTED also has to have evidence for the early years profiles of four- and five-year-old children, so educators are making videos, keeping copious notes so they can tick the requisite EYFS boxes.[4] Early years settings not adopting the compulsory guidelines may eventually have their funding cut by local authorities,

Box 11.1   The 'Open Eye' Campaign – for Open Early Years Learning

The 'Open EYE' Campaign was founded in late 2007, with an Open Letter and a front-page lead report published in *The Times,* and an Open Letter published in the *Times Educational Supplement.* Since its launch, the campaign has helped to spawn a major national debate and protest against certain aspects of the EYFS, with a Downing Street petition signed by 10,000 British citizens, and an Early-Day Motion in the British House of Commons, sponsored by Shadow Minister Annette Brooke MP, and signed by approaching 100 MPs.

Open EYE stands for the following broad principles:

The right of every child to spend their pre-school years in a developmentally appropriate, play-rich holistic learning environment, free of unnecessary and overly intrusive assessment and pressure, with suitably trained practitioners trusted to exercise their own professional discernment in their work.

The right of every parent, as laid down in the European Convention on Human Rights, to have access to pre-school care and/or education which accords with their own religious, philosophical and pedagogical convictions.

The campaign has seven principal areas of concern:

(1) Too Early Literacy

The EYFS literacy goals are both compulsory and developmentally inappropriate, including the compulsion to use a particular reading and writing scheme. The way in which the government's well intentioned goal of supporting disadvantaged children is being pursued is misguided – for these are the very children who need a solid foundation in socialisation, listening and speaking skills, and fine motor skills, before proceeding to the demands of reading and writing.

(2) A Play-Based Experience?

Much has been made of the allegedly 'play-based' nature of the EYFS framework. However, the notion of play used in EYFS is one that has lost its true meaning, being narrowly 'adult-centric', and seriously neglecting the subtleties of truly authentic imaginative play with its attendant rewards. For many holistic educators, to speak of 'directed' or 'structured and purposeful' play is to negate the whole concept of play.

(3) An 'Audit Culture' in the Early Years?

Early-childhood experience is the very last place where 'audit culture' values and practices should hold sway, with their distracting bureaucratisation and anxiety-generating practices.

(4) Assessment-Mindedness Affecting the Under 5s

A mindset of observation and assessment saturates the new framework.

> The very existence of an assessment apparatus at a given age has direct consequences for children significantly below that age, as settings 'drill' or prepare their children for the assessment procedure. This 'filtering down' of assessment pressures *always* occurs, and there is no reason to believe that it will not happen with the EYFS profiling process.
>
> (5) The Effects of the Eyfs on Early-Years Practitioners
>
> A utilitarian approach dominates the EYFS guidance throughout, which verges on a kind of 'developmental-obsessiveness', and which is anti-time, and quite contrary to any reverential or *spiritual* dimension to early-childhood experience.
>
> (6) State-Defined 'Normality' in Child Development
>
> In EYFS the State has defined its own paradigm for what is 'normal' child development, and then compulsorily enshrined its model in law – a quite unprecedented development in modern political life, and one which raises very grave concerns, not least about just where the boundary between the public and private spheres in education should be appropriately drawn.
>
> (7) Human/Parental Rights
>
> The EYFS legislation is directly compromising of parents' rights to choose the pre-school, pre-compulsory school-age environments that they wish for their children, which, under European law, constitutes a major infringement of parental and, therefore, of human rights.
>
> *Source: www.savechildhood.org*

which effectively means forced closure in all but name. What a brilliant way to impose and enforce a centrally defined state definition of child development and learning on an entire sector of mostly compliant, uncritical practitioners!

Parents who keep their children out of the non-compulsory early years settings where EYFS now applies are also afraid of losing a place for their child in the local school – so in effect, there is no 'choice', and families are effectively being coerced into placing their pre-school age children into learning environments that many are claiming will damage a significant number of children. Little wonder that legal action in the courts may be on the horizon in this sorry saga of overweening and inadequately thought-through government intrusion.

A key boundary issue is that the government has imposed a compulsory early-years curriculum and guidelines on to *non*-compulsory early years, pre-school and childminding settings. So what next? A government-imposed baby and toddler curriculum and inspection regime for all parents and families?

The take-over of education and the creeping nationalisation of childhood by government, together with the commercialisation of childhood, has contributed to what Sue Palmer and the Alliance for Childhood call 'toxic childhood'.[5] This seems a peculiarly, though not exclusively, British phenomenon. Surveys confirm that our children's mental health is suffering, not to mention rising levels of obesity and learning difficulties. A 2006 UNICEF study found that British children had relatively poor wellbeing, ranked at 23 in the survey, as compared with other developed countries, with Scandinavian children enjoying relatively good levels of wellbeing. In spite of all the government's best efforts, 2007 PISA research shows that the performance of British school children is middling in maths (24), reading (15) and science (14).[6]

According to Andrew Cooper, there is now a yawning chasm over approaches to children's education between government on the one hand, and, on the other, teachers, parents and researchers. The government does not want partnership. It distrusts teachers so wants to control them through the audit culture – hence SATs at seven and eleven, school league tables and endless tick boxes. Just like a Victorian schoolmaster, the government points its finger at 'failing' schools and 'failing' teachers, prescribing what is to be taught, how and when.[7]

Professor Robin Alexander of the University of Cambridge, leading the independent Cambridge Primary Review, reported the first research findings in October 2007, thus:

> In spite of our careful attempts to elicit and record differences, what is striking about the Community Soundings is the extent of consensus which they reveal, especially in the key areas of educational purpose, curriculum and assessment, the condition of childhood and society, and the world in which today's children are growing up. What is no less striking is the pessimistic and critical tenor of much of what we heard on such matters. *Thus we were frequently told that children are under intense and perhaps excessive pressure from the policy driven demands of their schools and the commercially driven values of the wider society.*[8] [author's italics]

To illustrate the gulf and lack of dialogue, an unnamed government spokesperson replied defensively that 'The vast majority of children go to better schools, enjoy better health, live in better housing and in more affluent households than they did 10 years ago … The government does not share the view that children are over tested. Tests help parents and teachers monitor the progress of children and ensure they get the help they need.'

The chasm between government and educators was also well described by Peter Hyman. He resigned in 2003 from his job as a Labour speech writer and No 10 spin doctor to teach at an Islington comprehensive school. He pointed to the big power imbalance between politicians and teachers, and the basic lack of respect of politicians for teachers:

> Now, looking through the other end of the telescope I see how unequal is the relationship between politicians and the people … Those at the centre relish ideas and, in the main, are bored by practicalities. Those who suggest better ways of making policy work are too often dismissed as whingers … Why can politicians not acknowledge that those in the front line might know more?[9]

It was not always so. Until 1979 education as a maintained sector was organised as an equal partnership between schools on the one hand and mainly local government on the other.

How Britain's free education system was taken over

But how did the state take over English schools? According to Lord (Michael) Young of Dartington, Britain once was proud of having one of the freest education systems in the world. This was in marked contrast to countries where governments decided what, when and how children should be taught, as in France. Schooling was often seen as the means for making children compliant, as Rudolf Steiner observed of state schooling in Germany in 1919:

> The State will tell us how to teach and what results to aim for, and what the State prescribes will be bad. Its targets are the worst ones imaginable, yet it expects to get the best possible results. Today's politics work in the direction of regimentation, and it will go even further than this in its attempts to make people conform. Human beings will be treated like puppets on strings, and this will be treated as progress in the extreme.[10]

The Allies and German leaders in postwar Germany shared Steiner's analysis of the fascist dangers of a state-dominated education system. So a thoroughly pluralist, inclusive school system was established which included a variety of state and church schools, along with different pedagogical approaches such as Steiner, Montessori, Freinet and Jena plan schools. This pluralist system was a democratic way of offering real diversity, choice and competition in education.

Lord Young described how education in Britain was once a semi-autonomous public service organised by democratically accountable local education authorities, with schools largely free to educate at teachers' professional discretion. The boundaries between state and education were clearly set by the liberal Conservative Rab Butler's 1944 Education Act. This enshrined the minimum role of the state as a partner, whose job it was to maintain the legal and financial framework and fund specialist support services. The only compulsory curriculum requirement was religious education. The content was left free, though there had to be school assemblies.

So, from 1944 to 1979, the government supported schools and left them free to do the best job they could. British people used to say proudly that our schools had educational freedom, unlike France, where the Minister of Education knows what is being taught at any time of day. How ironic.

Paradoxically, from the 1980s, during the same period that governments deregulated the financial sector, the state rolled back the boundaries of educational freedom by instituting centralised control through finance, the National Curriculum and Ofsted. As a result, education was politicised through prescribed state curriculum content, bureaucratised through audit, control and targets and privatised, as the government increasingly contracted with private companies for various support services and the running of 'failing education authorities'.

The British education system shifted from a high-trust to a low-trust control model, where teachers were told what to teach and how to teach it, except that teaching came to be described as 'delivering the curriculum'. Educational officials and politicised educators like Chris Woodhead, Chief Inspector of Schools under the Conservatives and then New Labour, distrusted teachers. According to Professor Ted Wragg, writing tongue in cheek but seriously, 'No less a figure than Chris Woodhead (and there is no less a figure) once wrote that it was dangerous for teachers to think up their own ideas. But thinking up fresh ideas is what teachers are paid to do.'[11] So what happened?

The 1944 Education Act provided education for all young people in England and Wales, according to age, ability and aptitude. There was a mutually respectful, working partnership between central government, teachers, local education authorities (LEAs) and the churches. Central government supported the legal and financial framework for schools. LEAs were the employers of teachers and owned most school buildings. There were no 'state schools', only maintained schools within a state-supported system. For practical purposes, teachers and schools decided what was taught and how, with LEA overall control. The churches owned around a third of the schools, as until the second half of the nineteenth century they provided education, not the state. Church schools were either voluntary aided or controlled, and had more independent governance although they remained within the state system. Parents and the local community hardly featured in this partnership, which was a major shortcoming.

The striking feature from today's perspective was that LEAs and teachers had real influence over the curriculum and the learning environment in schools, with the government in support. The relatively small Ministry of Education played a respectful, strategic role, initiating conversations, investigations and research to improve education. Just as government ministers today still have enough respect for boundaries and professional expertise not to dare tell surgeons how to operate, so, once politicians respected teachers' discretion. It was believed that teachers and schools were the experts, normally possessing far more 'coal-face' experience to know what was best for children's education than either bureaucrats or career politicians with other (not necessarily child-centred) agendas. They were the guardians of education, and politicians should support, not interfere. This tradition was maintained, and protected from government interference, by Her Majesty's Inspectorate, who inspected schools, defended and helped develop education as an independent service that was accountable but free of political constraints.

In this way, then, education was conducted outside of the party-political sphere; whereas now, career politicians stake their success on better SATs test scores, exam results and narrowly defined, measurable literacy improvements. Professor Richard Pring of the University of Oxford described how a friend, on being appointed to the Central Advisory Council in 1947, was told by the Permanent Secretary of the Department of Education that the responsibility of members was to 'be prepared to die at the first ditch as soon as government gets its hands on education'.[12] Educational policy was developed through central advisory councils, which included teachers, academics, LEAs and the community. Teacher-led bodies such as the Schools Council worked on curriculum development.

From 1945 to 1988, when the Conservative Education Act was passed, England and Wales had a relatively free education system, where the dominant partners were teachers and LEAs with government in a support role. So what led to the shifting of the boundaries from a free, liberal education system to a government-controlled system?

Firstly, the 1960s saw an upsurge of educational innovation partly encouraged by the Plowden Report. In the 1970s schools were challenged by criticism of their failures. There were real problems that needed addressing. There was criticism of educational standards and teaching methods in schools. A significant proportion of children leaving school had not acquired reasonable literacy and numeracy skills. Many teachers were not well trained in reading techniques and literacy methods. A disproportionate number of children leaving school with poor skills and no qualifications came from disadvantaged backgrounds or were from ethnic minorities. The Black Papers argued that low standards were the result of poor teaching of literacy and numeracy, and that this was influenced by the pursuit of equality through comprehensive schools, for example. Authors perceived that the brightest suffered and that Britain's economic rivals had better schools.

However, the actual research evidence to back up the anecdotal assertions made by the Black Papers about the supposedly dire state of education was patchy. Educators visited Britain from all over the world to learn from inspiring, innovative comprehensive schools like Leicestershire's Countesthorpe College or the creative approaches to education in British primary schools exemplified by Sybil Marshall's *Experiment in Education* and advocated by the Plowden Report. (In contrast, British educators now visit Scandinavia for inspiration.) But negative education stories became a continuing theme in the press, feeding parents' fears, causing moral panics and creating the openings for authoritarian politicians like Kenneth Baker to make changes.

Secondly, Prime Minister Callaghan gave a speech at Ruskin College, Oxford in 1976 and initiated a debate on education reform, where he wanted more economic and vocational relevance in secondary education. A successful British economy depended on schools with positive attitudes to business, so work experience was introduced. Even though a direct, causal link between education and national economic performance is highly debatable, schools were criticised as being out of touch and as not economically relevant. Politicians, of course, were looking to apportion blame for Britain's relative economic decline. (It is, however, widely accepted that a well-resourced further education and vocational training system *is* important for Britain's economic performance, otherwise there wouldn't be so many Polish plumbers.) Moreover, a significant proportion of young people left school in the 1970s with few or no qualifications and were alienated from education. Clearly secondary schools needed to make big changes to engage them productively.

Thirdly, these serious criticisms prepared the ground for Kenneth Baker, then Secretary of State for Education, to use them opportunistically to take more and more power from LEAs and teachers. However, the Thatcher government drew heavily on neo-liberal thinking, which saw professions such as (progressive-thinking) teachers, doctors and lawyers as blockages to a healthy free market and to the propagation of an individualistic right-wing ideology. Another political aim was to reduce the power of the teaching unions and Labour-controlled metropolitan authorities like ILEA, the Inner London Education Authority. And yet another aim was to introduce 'market reforms' into education so as to shake it up with informed 'competition'. More central government control via a 'strong state' was the answer, rather than really analysing the serious problems facing education and coming up with effective, lasting solutions. Such intractable challenges include improving literacy and tackling the growing number of young people 'not in education, employment or training' or NEETs. And there were ideological agendas and hobby-horses that came through 'political educators' such as Chris Woodhead, who, it now turns out, really believed all along that better middle-class school performance is down to better genes, and that, even though young children may not be developmentally ready for reading, 'high expectations of children' is what really matters. One 'political' educational hobby-horse, for example, was instituting the teaching of history by means of kings, dates, battles and the concept of 'progress', as opposed to using history to develop students' ability to argue from evidence.

The resulting 1988 Education Reform Act gave the Secretary of State for Education the powers to determine in detail the National Curriculum for five- to sixteen-year-olds, with targets and study programmes. Central curriculum control, maintained by Ofsted, was matched by a decentralised 'delivery system' offering consumer/parent power by means of apparent 'choice and diversity' of schools. High-stakes testing (SATs) of children at seven, eleven and fourteen created school league tables so that parents could in theory see which schools were 'best'. Competition was supposed to 'drive up' standards – a tell-tale quasi-authoritarian discourse that has come increasingly to dominate all government pronouncements on the schooling system. The role of LEAs was reduced by local management arrangements whereby schools had their own budgets, schools were encouraged to opt out of LEA control and become grant maintained, and City Technology Colleges were established. All this, plus the privatisation of support services and LEAs, the Academies programme, Sure Start and excellent attempts to widen participation and social inclusion, has continued under Labour.

The education system we have now is controlled by the state, not by LEAs, teachers or parents. The young mother who takes her six-year-old out of school occasionally to garden is frowned on by an 'incentivised' head teacher worried by being penalised for a poor school attendance record. 'Failing' or underperforming schools are now the fault of government, as the architect of the current education system. However, despite the market rhetoric, unless parents have the money to move into the catchment area of a 'good school', there is little real choice of school. Most parents would in fact prefer their local school to be a good one. Teachers, whilst welcoming the improved partnership with parents and the community, have now to 'deliver' the government's micro-managed and audited curriculum. For example, infant teachers are legally required by the Early Years Foundation

Guidelines to stop several times whilst telling a story, to ask pupils questions about comprehension. Young children cannot just enjoy the story.

The philosophy of successive governments is clear. Parents have to accept the government's education offering. There is room for some specialisation, but no space for alternative educational approaches, like in Northern European countries such as Sweden, Finland, Denmark, Holland and Germany, where there is a variety of schools with different pedagogical approaches in the maintained state system. Academies with more discretion over varying the National Curriculum have been introduced, but unlike, say, Finland, these academies are not designed as state-supported, integrated school exemplars of a variety of pedagogical approaches that can be learned from to improve practice overall.

On the one hand there is central government educational control, and on the other there is the rhetorical ideology of parent/consumer choice. Parents can shop around for the best education for their child. They clearly do not have a choice over a nationally delivered curriculum; they can only choose the school they want their child to attend – if there are places. Consumer-parents need to be well informed, hence the need for school league tables based on national tests. Professor Richard Pring commented that 'Thus, it might be argued, there have been created the ideal conditions for a consumer-led choice of educational provision – a diversity of producers aiming at the same standardised product with an open and objective labelling of that product. The state's job is twofold: to ensure the appropriate labelling of the product and to regulate the market competition for the support of the consumer.'[13]

The government has also commodified and commercialised education as a product to be sold to consumers rather than to students or learners. Teachers do not teach, they 'deliver' the government curriculum. Education has become filling buckets rather than lighting fires. Instead of education being a creative process of learning, it becomes a conveyor belt. Standards become 'performance indicators', language adopted from production management. Knowledge, judgement, skills become a list of competences. Advisers, once there to support teacher development, become 'auditors' in a school 'audit culture'. Ofsted inspectors sometimes tell deputy heads that their real job is to audit the school.

Richard Pring describes how schoolchildren became customers in the Nuffield 14–19 Review, the biggest review of education and training in fifty years. The report notes that the dominant aim of education is to help improve the economy, quoting Tony Blair: 'education now is the centre of economic policy making'. The central control of education has resulted in corporate values ruling schools, using 'performance management' language. Hence:

> The customer or client replaces the learner. The curriculum is delivered. Aims are spelt out in terms of targets. Audits (based on performance indicators) measure success in terms of hitting the targets ... As the language of performance and management has advanced, so we have proportionately lost a language of education, which recognises the intrinsic value of pursuing certain sorts of questions ... of seeking understanding [and] of exploring through literature and the arts what it means to be human.[14]

A major challenge facing the current education system is that the monolithic curricular, audit and surveillance system hasn't addressed the real needs of the 20 per cent or so deeply damaged, disadvantaged children who feel deep down that they are not remotely realising their potential. One such disadvantage is the incidence of low birth weight in Britain, which at 8 per cent is on par with Romania and Mongolia, and in some inner city areas reaches 11–15 per cent. Low birth weight is a strong predictor of poor learning and behaviour from brain disadvantage.[15] So quick behavioural fixes and tick boxes won't help at all. Furthermore, the system is inflexible, at a time when schools need to be constantly changing, learning and adapting to thrive, not just survive, in a changing world and changing communities. A further point of concern is that many schools, particularly secondary schools, are too large to deal with the social and personal needs of learners. Teachers see too many students to be able to establish the good relationships so essential for learning and growth. Lastly, there is a huge amount of innovation and good educational practice that teachers are quietly getting on with – like the proliferating forest schools movement in the early years. Much of this (thankfully) is well below both Ofsted's and the government's radar.

Freeing education: from the audit culture to partnership

So it is time to free education from the audit culture through developing an equal partnership between government and education – including communities, parents, learners – where each sector plays to its strengths. The 'yawning chasm' that Professor Andrew Cooper sees as separating government and education needs addressing. The cause of this chasm is the fundamentally different dynamics of the political system on the one hand and educational dynamics on the other. Crudely put, education is not at all like running an office or a production line. The leading principle of the education system is freedom, which leads to a diversity of educational provision because the needs of children, the family, the community and cultural contexts are so diverse and impossible to predict, let alone control. Prescriptive, top-down, 'equal', one-size-fits-all approaches are just not appropriate. Teachers need the professional freedom and discretion to educate, in partnership with parents and the local community.

In contrast, the state bases its whole approach on a grossly simplistic notion of 'equality' – on treating everyone the same. Government is rightly concerned with minimum standards, a respect for children's human rights and equitable resourcing. But when the state becomes school master, it will naturally want to bureaucratise, control and deliver, with a prescribed National Curriculum, compulsory ways of teaching such as literacy and numeracy hours, inspection, testing, ticking boxes, naming and shaming, payment by results. This is how the state does things if it can, its default position. But this approach steps way over the system boundaries between culture and politics, education and the state. Schools are not post offices or machines for education delivery, they are creative, learning organisations.

To summarise, one common critique of the current system attacks box ticking, too much bureaucracy, inspection anxiety, teaching to SATs tests, the external imposition of the curriculum, mandatory professional guidelines, the erosion of the professional autonomy of teachers, a one-size-fits-all approach to child development and the educational methods prescribed by the National Curriculum. Teachers with this perspective say: 'Reduce the load to manageable proportions, tell us what to teach, cut the red tape and control-freakery, and education will improve.' According to Andrew Cooper, this approach addresses only the 'how'. It does not address the more fundamental 'why' or the 'what' of the national educational system.

His critique of the current education system is that:

> The values and practices of education in a liberal, democratic society have been hijacked and subordinated to a single overarching aim – from the start to the end of the educational process it is to secure the right knowledge and skill set for our economy to survive and prosper in the world market. As one core aim of a nation's education system ... this ... has become absolutely the overriding, universal, 'one size fits all' driver of the system we now have.

The Kindergarten teacher, psychotherapist and Roehampton academic Richard House goes further. He is concerned about the effect of intrusive teaching methods on the personal wellbeing of children:

> In Britain, the problem with overbearing State educational policy-making from the National Curriculum onwards, is that it has necessarily stifled creativity and innovation, encouraged normalisation and uniformity, and disempowered, deprofessionalised, and infantilised teachers. It can be potentially catastrophic when (albeit well-meaning) Governments dictate their own narrow view of healthy child development and learning, especially when the model upon which they are drawing with its 'earlier is better', prematurely cognitive-intellectual, and education-as-commodity world view is, from the standpoint of many developmental theories, highly damaging to children.[16]

This analysis is a serious challenge to a hyperactive, anxiety-driven government and its education officials. Academics such as Richard House argue that some government educational policies are actually damaging children. For example, the 'one-size-fits-all, early formal learning is better' approach of the Foundation Stage 'curriculum' can be seen as one of the causes of poor learning and wellbeing later on, for example amongst boys who are not so 'school ready'.

However, the nature of cultural activity is that the gifts, talents, initiative and creativity of people keep welling up. Education, by its nature, is full of creative responses to challenges. One way of rebalancing the education and state systems is to let go of the tight audit culture, and then recognise, encourage, research and spread the good practice arising in schools. One good story is the emergence of small schools within schools and the introduction of the concept of 'human scale' in education as a way ahead. The 2004 Woods Report suggests how mainstream education can learn from the Waldorf approach.[17]

Human Scale Education (HSE) is an organisation that offers both a critique and working solutions from the heart of education, based on research and good practice in state schools. These solutions, whilst achieving the educational outcomes the government wants and more, also reframe the relationship between government and education. Teachers and schools take Ed Balls at his word, taking on professional responsibility for leading major school innovations from the bottom-up, on the basis of meeting students' needs.

HSE considers that big secondary schools suffer many problems due to their sheer size, and draws on the research of Ted Sizer of Brown University in the USA. He founded the Coalition of Essential Schools to develop high schools that were small (i.e. up to 300 students), equitable, personalised and intellectually challenging. One principle was that 'less is more', or 'depth over coverage', with teachers having a personal relationship with the students – up to a maximum of eighty – that they taught in a week. There are now hundreds of CES schools in the USA. Research studies in the US suggest that students in small schools do better academically and in terms of wellbeing than students in large high schools.

So in Britain, HSE worked with innovative schools like Bishops Park College in Essex, to introduce a 'schools within a school' model with its principal, Mike Davies. There were three, 300-pupil schools, with their own team of teachers and facilities on the same campus. The vision was to nurture the wellbeing of each individual student within a context of equity and social justice, which was reflected in the school design, policy, practices and educational approach. Teachers saw no more than ninety students a week, teaching a cross-disciplinary, thematic curriculum. This school flourished between 2002 and 2007. Its innovative curriculum, 'A Curriculum like Tartan', was featured on the QCA website as an example of a successful thematic curriculum. During this period, there were no teenage pregnancies and the NEET figure was 2 per cent. This was a school in a particularly deprived area with the largest intake of 'looked after children' in Essex. But the school fell between the conflicting demands of the 'Every Child Matters' agenda, which is geared to student wellbeing, and the standards agenda geared to SATs and GCSE results. Happy, purposeful and engaged young people did not reach the required 30 per cent grades A*–C benchmark and the school was put into special measures by Ofsted in October 2007. The reasons underlying this included the fact that a visionary, gifted head moved on before the culture was embedded, the difficulty of attracting and retaining teachers and a disadvantaged catchment area.

A key challenge to twenty-first-century education in Britain is the persistence of the values and practices of a nineteenth-century mass education model. The 1988 National Curriculum, according to Mary Tasker of Human Scale Education, is a nineteenth-century relic devoid of any fundamental philosophical aims and values. It is a 'schoolified' rather than an educational, child-centred paradigm. As an example of what she means by aims and values, she describes how the Norwegian Department of Education is guided by six main educational goals. These encourage students to become a person who is: searching for meaning, creative, working, enlightened, cooperative and environmentally friendly.

Mary Tasker sees human-scale education as grounded in three overarching values:

- the importance of community

Box 11.2   A practical manifesto for education on a human scale

Human Scale Education suggests the following eight key practices that schools might follow:

1.   Small size: schools or learning communities of 250 to 300 students.
2.   Small teams of between four to six teachers, learning mentors and learning support assistants who will see no more than eighty to ninety learners each week.
3.   A curriculum that is thematic, cross-disciplinary and holistic.
4.   A timetable that is flexible, with blocks of time that make provision for whole-class teaching, small-group teaching and individual learning. Time for teachers' planning and evaluation is timetabled.
5.   Pedagogy that is inquiry-based, experiential and supported by ICT.
6.   Assessment that involves the assessment of learning approaches of dialogue, negotiation and peer review and develops forms of authentic assessment such as portfolio, exhibition and performance.
7.   Student voice: involving students in the learning arrangements and organisation of the school.
8.   Genuine partnership with parents and the community.[19]

Each of the schools has its own suite of generic rooms and resources, cohort of students and staff. Within each 5–14 mini-school there is extensive wireless networking and mobile provision to allow practical and experimental work, for example, in science, although there is also the abailability of more specialist resources in the 14–19 school. Overall admission arrangements, pedagogy, curriculum and ethos are set across all schools. Staff are an integral part of the stable learning group and stay with the young people and their families throughout the school. There is some sharing of facilities such as library/resources, leisure centre. There is a strong emphasis on locating facilities e.g. a galley kitchen, in the home bases. This mode builds on the traditions of the Danish Folk Schools. Hellerup in Copenhagen is a contemporary example of the use of home bases.	**School 1 nursery** **School 2 5–14** **School 3 5–14** **School 4 5–14** **School 5 14–19+**

LEADERSHIP:	single campus	school specific	collegiate
TEACHER ORGANISATION:	subject departments	cross-disciplinary teams	learning tutors
SITES OF LEARNING:	teacher rooms	home bases/grounds	community/virtual
USE OF TIME:	long blocks (days)	organised by teaching team	negotiated by task

Human Scale by Design (2009), Mike Davies, Human Scale Education

- respect for the individual
- the primacy of human relationships.[18]

Mike Davies, the founding principal of Bishops Park College, successfully implemented the schools-within-schools design. He echoes Winston Churchill: 'We shape our buildings and afterwards they shape us.' So he believes that students and teachers in human-scale schools should be able to design and shape their learning conditions, as this increases dignity, ownership and empowerment. He thinks it vital that the curriculum should fit the child's needs, rather than the child being fitted to the curriculum, and that trusting relationships are a basis for support and challenging students, with authentic expectations. He writes that 'The creation of smaller learning communities is not an end in itself but rather an enabler. They make possible fewer bureaucratic organisational structures and processes, less reliance on externally set targets as a means of monitoring progress, fewer mechanistic control measures and tariffs for those who offend, less hierarchical dependency on "one size fits all" national strategies for change.'[20, 21]

Davies then describes a range of schools-within-schools design options, based on well-researched exemplar working schools. There are design differences according to the autonomy each school has and the degree to which the curriculum is fixed for all, negotiated, student-centred or offered as a range of alternatives for students and parents to choose. Eight human-scale schools are offered as design choices including:

- Mission Hill School, Boston: five autonomous kindergarten to grade 8 schools share a building;
- Stantonbury Campus, Milton Keynes: five mini-schools, each with a specialism (performing arts, media, technology, sport, science);
- SPF/Youth Town, Copenhagen: generic home bases with access to a range of authentic, multi-provider, experiential centres;
- Hellerup Danish Folk High School, Copenhagen: series of five to fourteen all-through schools with applied post-fourteen provision (see Box 11.2)
- Bishops Park College, Essex: series of self-contained mini-schools within an 11–16 college;
- Brislington Enterprise College, Bristol: schools within schools with specialist facilities and a resource and community hub; (see Box 11.2)
- Morialta High School, Adelaide, Australia: five mini-schools with different pedagogic styles, including teacher-directed formal mode, enquiry-based, performing arts and community/applied.

But above all it's up to the teachers, students, parents, local community, local business and the local authority to enable their school to thrive as a good school, not the government. There is no magic bullet, no quick fix. The human-scale school examples offer beacons of inspiring practice and learning, but it's up to each school to make the most of its potential for meeting students' holistic educational needs. This also means redrawing boundaries between government and education. The more schools take a constructive educational lead, the more government can be a supportive but equal partner. The more government stands back, the better education will be.

Practical first steps for freeing education could include:

1.   Start to free teachers and schools from the audit culture by abolishing SATs and school league tables. This would end the marketising of education with all its perverse unintended side-effects. It would also save a huge amount of time, paper, energy and money. Teachers would no longer have to waste time on 'teaching to the SATs test'. Schools could then focus on *real*, authentic education.

2.   Make the National Curriculum and EYFS into voluntary guidance, and instead ask every school to regularly renew its own purpose, mission, values, structure and curriculum, involving students, parents and the community.

3.   Strengthen the advisory services for teacher coaching, mentoring, supervision, for school improvement, management, leadership, organisational development and administration.

4.   Strengthen LEAs' ability to provide support services for and with schools so that schools can federate for common services and/or buy in centrally provided services as appropriate.

5.   Support ongoing teacher education, training, professional development and learning as the foundation of thriving schools, and use sabbaticals to help teachers remain resilient, creative, open to change and effective.

6.   Pilot small schools within big secondary schools as a way of introducing diversity of provision, social cohesion, increased wellbeing and learning.

7.   Like Holland and Finland, selectively promote innovative schools of a different pedagogic type to the mainstream that can then spread the learning and good practice – rather than the Swedish free for all model. One suggestion is to invite every LEA to fund such an innovative school.

8.   Research and evaluate a range of education paradigms, particularly the entrenched English 'schoolified' paradigm and the child-development-centred Nordic, Middle European and Reggio Emilia whole-child approaches.

Lastly, enabling cultural change in the education sector is tough, as we are up against embedded strong cultures and deeply held assumptions about children, about our image of the human being, our values and society. Education is a political football and needs to be taken out of party politics. There are conflicting educational paradigms that need surfacing. For example, a teacher described her shock when visiting a Norwegian kindergarten, as most play and activity was outside in the open air. Six-year-olds were teaching 5-year-olds very competently how to abseil down a small cliff, with not an adult in sight! I once accompanied an eighteen-year-old Norwegian student with her father for a day-study hike up precipitous mountain paths. She was leading a mountain pony carrying cement for restoring part of an old 'summer farm' for a camp of school students. They were milking the goats and cows for cheese-making and learning about the old farm ways. Working with horses was part of her project for her high-school graduation certificate.[22] It is eye opening to compare the open Nordic/Middle European early years education paradigm with the 'schoolified' English EYFS paradigm.

The Nordic early years education paradigm sees the child as having the human right to autonomy, wellbeing and self-directed development. According to John Bennett of the OECD: 'The child is an agent of their own learning, a child rich with natural learning and research strategies … The child as a member of a caring community of peers and adults, in which the agency of the child is promoted … An outdoors child of pleasure and freedom. Awareness that there is a time for childhood that can never be repeated.' He remarks that the British 'readiness for school' tradition sees 'The child as a young person to be formed, as an investment in the future of society; the productive knowledge worker, the compliant well-behaved citizen … A benevolent, utilitarian approach to childhood in which state and adult purposes are foregrounded. Pedagogy focussed on "useful" learning, readiness for school.'[23]

The 'readiness for school' tradition harks back to the nineteenth century and still dominates English educational policy. Part of the yawning chasm in understanding between the government and the education sector can be explained by

---

Box 11.3   Pluralist, free education systems

Social democratic countries in Northern Europe have pluralist education systems where there is state support for a range of religious schools and schools such as Montessori and Steiner Waldorf Schools which offer alternative educational approaches. One rationale for establishing a pluralist education system in West Germany after the Second World War was that diversity of education and decentralisation created free education for democracy. In Holland, around 60 per cent of schools are independent, but maintained within the state system

Denmark offers the most pluralist example, with a tradition of free schools that are government supported. The free school and folk high school ideas of Grundtvig and Kold were written into the Danish Constitution of 1849, which legislated general compulsory education, not compulsory school attendance. About 10 per cent of children attend free schools. These are recognised and receive state support regardless of the ideological, religious, political or ethnic motivation of the schools. One key benefit is that state schools can learn from the experience and competition with the free schools and vice versa. Schools have to meet minimum educational standards and it is up to the parents to make sure the schools perform well.

The thinking behind Sweden's Freedom of Choice and Independent Schools Act 1992 was that politicians should not dominate education by picking ideal school types, curricula and methods, but should trust schools and parents to make the appropriate choices for children's growth and learning. The Act requires local authorities to allow parental choices between government-run schools and to give funding to licensed independent schools. This has resulted in a quite remarkable diversity of provision, with over 585 independent schools, 12 per cent of the total, educating 74,000 pupils. Before 1991, Swedish schools were centralised and prescriptive, with parents having to send their children to the local school. The profit-making thirty Kunskapsskolan are small, with no class-rooms but different learning spaces. Parents are involved but don't have the time to set up and run them. There is now some concern that the Swedish schools are socially divisive and are driving up overall costs.

Michael Gove, Conservative shadow education minister, wants to introduce this Swedish-style reform into England, with parent-run non-profit schools. This would, he says, allow parents real choice. That is, if busy parents have the time to set them up. The Kunskapsskolan have already been an inspiration for some English Academies and political party thinking. One concern is that education businesses such as Global Education Management Systems (GEMS) based in the United Arab Emirates, COGNITA linked with Chris Woodhead in the UK and Edison in the USA are interested. The Conservative policy could lead to further opening education to the market.[24]

It might be better to engage in a far-reaching, thoroughgoing dialogue and action research process, learning from current good practice and renewing education as an ongoing process.

Sources: F. Carnie, M. Tasker and M. Large, Freeing Education, *Stroud, Hawthorn Press, 1996; Colin Taylor, Institute of Directors, 'Big Picture', 2007*

such paradigm differences. Norwegian parents, hearing of desk-bound English five-year-olds having to learn to read are shocked. Unlike some British educators, Scandinavian, Reggio Emilia and Middle European educators have a good knowledge of child development and gear learning activities to developmental readiness. These approaches are based on sound research, theory and practice. However, many English educational officials and ministers just may not understand such approaches.

Finally, it could be high time to free education from both government and from business by implementing the tripolar society concept, rather than the endless search by politicians for piecemeal, magic bullet solutions that get votes, such as academies. An autonomous body such as the Education Council would take overall lead responsibility for our education system, though in partnership with government and business interests. Education could then take a creative lead in deepening and renewing our culture. Education would be taken out of politics, though the government would ensure the provision of the human right to education through funding entitlements. Business would welcome the fresh energy, maturity and talent of young people had been fired up for learning by an education sector free at last to educate. The education sector would reinvent itself as the cultural dynamo of society-free to light fires, rather than fill buckets.

Conclusion

To summarise, Britain once had a semi-autonomous education system, where government and the education sector each respected the other's respective contributions and boundaries, though education took the lead. In the 1980s government stepped in and radically shifted the boundaries in England. There have been improvements, but at the cost of the audit and surveillance culture which crowds out real learning. The costs of this alien culture far outweigh any resulting benefits. 'Marketising' education has been a costly diversion from tackling complex problems such as real literacy, NEETs and the needs of disadvantaged children. There is a conflict between children's wellbeing, as enshrined in 'Every Child Matters', and standards, with standards winning over wellbeing. In spite of all the extra effort and money spent in Britain, countries like Finland do much better. Rising GCSE grades themselves may be inflated to give the impression of progress, say some academics. International comparisons of children's relative wellbeing and school performance are either middling or poor, which is astonishing. More of the same and the search for magic bullets will make things worse. There needs to be transformative change, in a social learning process for improving education that includes students, educators, government, parents and business.

At the heart of the education question is the yawning gap between the government on the one hand, and the education sector on the other. This reflects two different systems, the political and the educational/cultural systems, each with its own unique contributions to make. But optimise one at the expense of the other and things get chronically one-sided, as we have seen. Free up schools and teachers, end the audit culture, encourage emergent, well-researched good practice such as the human-scale schools, respect an equal partnership of education and government and education will flourish. The more schools and teachers are freed up, the more discretionary, creative effort there will be.

Lastly, a story of national educational success. Finland now consistently comes top or near the top of most international surveys of children's wellbeing and academic achievements. But Finland, like England now, was once well down the surveys. The government and educators recognised that there was a problem. They decided to listen and learn about what worked and what didn't, and why. They visited other countries and also evaluated what worked and didn't work in Finland. They decided what to keep, what to drop and what new features needed creating. This took some time, but they learned much more as a result. They learned from a variety of pedagogic modes, such as Froebel, Montessori and Steiner, and from good practice. They welcomed a diversity of pedagogical provision as providing learning and live action research. They engaged students and parents in this process in a range of participative conversations and as part of a democratic culture. This led to the changes that make Finnish education today so successful.

Chapter 12

Common Wealth: Leading from the Social Future as it Emerges

How can we put an end to unrestrained market fundamentalism and financial capitalism, that are void of morals or moderation, in order to protect the finances and livelihoods of our citizens? That is the issue we are now facing ... In these times, we must return to the idea of fraternity – as in the French slogan 'liberté, égalité, fraternité' – as a force for moderating the danger inherent within freedom.

Yukio Hatoyama, Prime Minister of Japan[1]

Ever since the ideals of *liberté, égalité, fraternité* were thrown up by the French Revolution, people have longed for a society where they can be respected equally as citizens before the law, where they can experience cultural, religious, educational, artistic, scientific and personal freedom, and where they can work for mutual benefit with dignity in a fraternal economy.

But people puzzle about the fact that these principles can be contradictory when applied. However, *Common Wealth* suggests that the free, equal and mutual (or brotherly/sisterly) society dreamed about during the French Revolution *can* be realised when applied in the 'home spaces' of the cultural, political and economic systems respectively. Equality, whilst being the basis of the polity, doesn't apply in science. Voting on which theory is correct is nonsensical. Brotherliness doesn't work well in the political system if this means passing inequitable laws, but works well when guiding the economy, which depends on cooperation. Freedom is the informing principle of cultural life. However, freedom doesn't work well in the economy when a free-for-all destroys the banking system.

So a tripolar, or threefold, society can enable the principles of freedom, equality and mutuality to be realised in their respective home spaces. These useful guiding principles are stars to steer by. *Common Wealth* argues that the more that freedom informs our culture and civil society, the more equality informs the state sector with its human rights, entitlements and responsibilities, and the more that mutuality guides business and economic life – the healthier, juster, wealthier and the more resilient society will be.

When these principles kept coming up while I was facilitating strategic planning with businesses, government and civil society, I felt challenged to write this book as a response. People wanted a strategic 'big picture' to guide their community, business, and organisational and individual direction. Their burning questions were:

- How can we build a more efficient, collaborative, sustainable economy that meets people's real needs?
- How are we building a more peaceful, democratic, just and equitable society?
- How are we enabling every human being to reach and maintain their full human spiritual, creative, social and physical potential?
- How are we caring for the earth with all its living beings and building human capacity for this task?

These seed questions well up from people's inquiring minds, open hearts and good will when there is the space. Others have noticed them too. Otto Scharmer, working in organisational development at MIT, also considers that we are faced by three similar 'root questions':

1. How can we create a more equitable global economy that would serve the needs of all, including today's have nots and the future generations?
2. How can we deepen democracy and evolve our political institutions so that all people can increasingly directly participate in the decision-making processes that shape their context and future?
3. How can we renew our culture so that every human being is considered a carrier of a sacred project – the journey of becoming one's sacred self?[2]

To conclude this book, the following themes will be explored as a help to analysis and action:

- how did we get here? The evolution of society: from theocracy, democracy, capitalist market economy to ...?
- the gods that failed: the crisis we are now in and the way forward
- three-way strategic conversations for vision and action: seeing and acting from the heart of society
- openings for transforming capitalism and democracy
- community-building and placemaking: creating common economic, cultural and social wealth together.

How did we get here? The evolution of society: from theocracy, democracy, capitalist market economy to ...?

So, how did the economy, polity and cultural life separate out as distinct systems in history?

Firstly, cultural life was dominant back in the early dreamtime of humanity. Theocracy is the rule by priests and was prevalent in ancient civilisations. For example, the pharaohs, the priest-god-kings, ruled Egypt and guided religious, legal and political life. Religion dominated. People experienced themselves as living in the 'great house of Pharaoh.' Everyone instinctively 'knew' their place in a hierarchical, pyramidal system. Economic and legal life was sacred, governed by religion. Egyptian theocracy was a onefold, religion-controlled society with a dominant cultural system.

Some after-echoes of theocracy still live on today in the Roman Catholic Church. In business, some CEOs still insist on a command and control, pyramid style *hierarchy* or 'sacred order'. The industrialist Henry Ford and the banker J. P. Morgan even went as far as to liken themselves as 'captains of industry' to the old pharaohs! When people say 'they' should do something, or give up their power to a charismatic leader, you can see theocratic after-echoes at work. Osama bin Laden invokes the return to a theocratic caliphate, and Iran came under the rule of the ayatollahs, with Sharia law, in 1979.

Ancient Greece and then Rome saw the birth and separation of a distinct politico-legal system out of ancient theocracy. Society became twofold or bipolar with distinct religious-cultural and politico-legal systems, with the economy still subservient. Rome saw the establishment of the first real laws, with one legal system for Roman citizens and another for relationships between Roman citizens and others, such as women and slaves, who did most of the economic work. Increasing individualism amongst citizens led to the concept of a last will and testament being established, which for the first time in history determined who got what after a man's death. Citizenship was based on land ownership.

So law and the rights of citizens stem from Roman times, and with this the legal status of the labour of workers. Slaves and women had no rights. However, ideas about workers' rights started to develop, and these evolve today as the last vestiges of wage slavery are removed through the full implementation of economic and social rights. The British government only recently signed the minimum wage into law. It has been dragging its feet on the full introduction of the European Social Chapter, thus making it easier, say, to fire workers in Britain than in Germany.

But as labour and capital became emancipated in the late Middle Ages, the challenge of growing individualism arose. Guilds had once made sure that people were productively placed in work, and put limits on egoism through craftwork controls. Rudolf Steiner observed that the struggle of people coming to grips with individualism, egoism and selfishness was one driving force for democracy or 'the rule of the people'. He described humanity as striving, more or less unconsciously, 'to come to grips with Egoism ... and in the last resort, this striving culminates in nothing else than modern Democracy – the sense for the equality of man – the feeling that each must have his influence in determining legal rights and in determining the labour that he contributes.'[3] Another democratic cultural underpinning was the recognition that every human is equal before God and therefore also equal before the law.

The modern politico-legal system of rights and democracy developed from Magna Carta in 1215, the first elected English parliament in 1265, the victory of parliament over the king in the English Civil Wars and Revolution, the 1689 Bill of

Rights, the American Revolution of 1775–81 and the subsequent Constitution, the French Revolution, the extension of adult suffrage to all, the Universal Declaration of Human Rights in 1948, and the 1998 adoption of the European charter of human rights into British law with the passing of the Human Rights Act – just to mention a few key milestones. These democratic advances had to be fought for, and each generation has to reclaim them or lose them.

However, the after-echoes of outdated imperial and monarchical forms still live on strongly in Britain on Planet Westminster. The government does not see itself as the 'servant of the people' but as the crown-in-parliament. 'We the people' are not sovereign in our own land as power sits 'at the top'. Some ministers and MPs claimed excessive expenses because they had a sense of entitlement and little sense of the common good. What the historian David Marquand calls our 'parliamentary monarchy' is in basic conflict with the 'democratic imperative' that originated with the American and French Revolutions.

Britain lacks a written constitution, so the unwritten checks and balances can be readily abused by political and business power elites. Big business and government run Britain as a captive state, hence the government's inability to put proud finance in its place.

The parliamentary monarchy lets the Prime Minister be the 'king in parliament' with huge executive powers allowed by a largely compliant parliament. The judiciary, the House of Lords and the people occasionally check these powers, as with the successful anti-poll tax campaign. The parliamentary monarchy allowed Prime Minister Eden to go to war in Suez without the approval of cabinet or parliament. Tony Blair could run his sofa government, asking eager-to-please Attorney General Goldsmith to give the required form of legal 'weasel words' required for invading Iraq, and deceiving parliament through the information control of weapons of mass deception. Many MPs, of course, failed to get informed about the case for war, despite expert information readily available on the Internet, or from sources ranging from the Oxford Research Group to the Royal United Services Institute. Parliamentary monarchy allows the Prime Minister and Home Secretary to create a surveillance state and erode civil liberties, *because they can* – there are no real checks and balances.

So the full developmental potential of British democracy that successive movements such as the Levellers, the Chartists, Charter 88, the Power Inquiry and the 2009 Convention on Modern Liberty stand for is still being realised. The collapse of legitimacy of parliament and government, brought about by such things as the Iraq War, the credit bubble, rising inequality, helping the corporate seizure of vast amounts of common wealth for example through the £251 billion PFI scams, failing to defend civil liberties, failing to reform banking and finally the expenses scandal, offer a historic opportunity to transform the Westminster shamocracy into real democracy.

The economy separated out as a distinct system from the sixteenth and seventeenth centuries. It freed itself slowly from the constraints of religion – such as the prohibition of interest on loans – and state, which controlled companies through legal charters. The scientific and technological revolutions led to systematic innovation being applied to industry and agriculture. This resulted in the market system described by Adam Smith in *The Wealth of Nations* in the eighteenth century. The Industrial Revolution led to the independent development of the economic system, in the helpful capitalist context of free-market, laissez-faire economic liberalism.

Adam Smith identified the division of labour as one of the important secrets of increased productivity in the emerging market economy. His ideas were misused much later by social Darwinists and neo-liberals to justify excessive market competition, private capital accumulation and profit. Smith, however, always emphasised how important the moral sentiments – such as trust – were for successful market economies.

But the specialised division of labour in the modern economy can be understood in a quite differently way to the neo-liberal institutionalised greed interpretation. The more there is specialisation in the division of labour, the more we rely on each other. Self-sufficiency of meeting one's needs was to an extent possible with land-based, agrarian livelihoods, but not with modern industrial life. The more interdependent we are in the modern economy, the more we rely on each others' efforts, the more we need mutuality or brotherliness/sisterliness as a guiding principle that is both practical and also moral and social. What goes around comes around. Steiner once observed that 'Whoever works in a society which is based on the division of labour never really earns their income by themselves; he or she earns it through the work of all the others.'

So the economy was the third societal system to separate out in history from the religious-cultural sector and the state and it became especially dominant in the West, in the English-speaking nations.

The unleashing of the neo-liberal capitalist economy in the 1980s now dominates the cultural and political systems, having largely captured both culture and the state. The result is the systemic breakdown we see now with the credit, inequality and environment crunches, as the captive cultural and political systems are unable to check, balance and transform a runaway capitalist economy. Prime Minister Brown, for example, bailed out the failing RBS with taxpayers' money in autumn 2008, and Lord Myners, minister with responsibility for the banks and the City, allowed the failed RBS boss Sir Fred Goodwin a £703,000 annual pension and then permitted bankers' bonuses of £750 million. Goodwin's pension was later cut down to £500,000 a year. Stephen Hester, the new RBS chief executive, will get a package of salary, incentives and shares worth between £9.6 and £15 million, and in spite of RBS making a £35 billion loss; the bank spent £300,000 on Wimbledon 2009 entertainment. Such pay deals are made by UKFI, which supervises the bailed-out banks for the Treasury and is composed of a majority of bankers, mostly drawn from failed banks.[4] This is an example of how the captive state works for the banks.

In spite of proclaiming the end of the Washington neo-liberal consensus at the London G20 Summit in April 2009, Brown helped increase funding by $750 billion to the arch-neo-liberal IMF. He continued his policy of toxic market fundamentalism at home by proposing a hugely expensive £5 billion 'PFI plus' contract for widening the M25, which need only have cost less than £500 million, as another handout to the banks. He also opposed real banking reform, like separating casino investment banking from High Street retail banking, reducing bank size, raising taxes on bank profits to cover banking insurance, and opposed tighter EU regulation of the hedge funds and bankers' bonuses.

Leading Westminster politicians failed to make a clean break with the disastrous neo-liberal model of society which benefits the financial and corporate elites, a model that is now bust. John Lanchester summarises: 'There needs to be a general acceptance that the current model has failed. The brakes off, deregulate or die, privatise or stagnate, lunch is for wimps, greed is good, what's good for the financial sector is good for the economy model; the sack the bottom 10 per cent, bonus driven, if you can't measure it, it isn't real model; the model that spread from the City to government and from there to the whole culture, in which the idea of value has gradually faded to be the idea of price. Thatcher began, and Labour continued, the switch towards an economy that was reliant on financial services at the expense of other areas of society.'[5]

At the same time, market thinking was applied to all aspects of life, to areas where it did not belong, like health, education, housing, the environment, education, employees' rights, democracy and culture. The market-dominated government knows the price of everything and the value of nothing. For example, in 2007, housing minister Yvette Cooper turned down the community's proposals for a garden neighbourhood of social and co-operative housing with health and other social facilities for Stroud's Cashes Green Hospital site. She thought the plan was poor value for money, compared with the government's aspirational land valuation of £3.5 million, even though the land market had crashed and a realistic valuation was £1 million. For her, the issue seemed to be technical, securing cheap social housing, getting as much money as possible money for the site, and ignoring community value for money. She and her senior civil servants did not understand the Cashes Green community plan which was based on the values of sustainability, permanent affordability, equitable access to homes, participative democracy and community cohesion and placemaking.

John Lanchester argues that in areas such as education, culture, housing and health 'the first conversation to happen should be about values; then you have the conversation about costs. In Britain in the last 20 to 30 years that has all been the wrong way round. There was a reverse takeover, in which City values came to dominate the whole of British Life.'[6]

Michael Sandell's 2009 Reith Lectures invited values back into the heart of politics, now market fundamentalism has collapsed. There needs to be moral and political imagination in rolling back the market, otherwise the momentum for civil renewal that carried Obama to victory will be lost in a politics of technical fixes. He considers that things have gone so far that perhaps the only way of securing public good from the banks, which enjoy such huge private advantages, is to nationalise them. He further considers that democratic societies will fall apart if they get too unequal. The challenge is to put markets back in their proper place. He asks where the public debate on the hollowing out of the state is, for example, pointing out that from 2007 there were more private contractors or mercenaries in Iraq than US soldiers. And lastly he asks 'How do you get changed politics without changed politicians?'

Paradoxically, the unleashing of capitalism in the economy and the corporate capture of the state has created the conditions for a resurgent civil society, cultural and community sector. Civil society is now growing locally, nationally and globally to create a transformative cultural counterforce. Just as in the 1980s civil society movements for peace, environment and human rights across Europe fatally exposed the moral hollowness of communist regimes, now civil society is exploring a new politics that has the potential to transform the market state.

At the same time, business, government and civil society are paying more attention to putting their own respective houses in order. The private financial sector, currently dominated by profit, shareholder value and bonuses, faces what Adair Turner, chair of the FSA, calls the 'biggest crisis in the history of market capitalism'.[7] Banks were carrying out many 'socially useless' activities. The financial meltdown forced the government to step in to save the whole financial system, to regulate more and to invest public money. But this raises a systemic conflict of interest, as the government is both a large owner, funder, borrower and a regulator of the financial sector. So in the medium term, the finance and economic sector should develop the capacity to govern itself for common good, just as the mutual financial sector has for long regulated itself through good governance, prudence, shared co-operative values and member/customer democratic control. Member-owned mutuals could better govern the utilities and High Street banks.

Government and parliament need fundamental democratic transformation, as recommended by Helena Kennedy QC's Power Inquiry, with real subsidiarity applied to levels of government down to parish and ward sovereignty. Thirdly, civil society organisations face their own development challenges, as they move from protest and advocacy to prototyping exemplars, trisectoral partnerships and engaging with business and government to create social enterprises for service delivery. Cultural and community organisations in the health and education sectors need help to become effective semi-autonomous public services, as the reassertion of healthy boundaries pushes back commercial market and state/bureaucratic forces.

The gods that failed: the crisis we are now in and the way forward

With the meltdown of the capitalist financial system, some people look to government for solutions. In the face of perceived terrorist threats, some think that 'security is better than freedom'. But others are cynical about the current self-serving political elites who have let society be fleeced over the last thirty years, and gained from this personally.

But what happens if both the god of neo-liberal financial capitalism and the god of the state have failed? By April 2009, the British government had bailed out the financial sector with vast sums, including insuring huge toxic bank debts, which will rise as the property market falls. We have already mortgaged our grandchildren's future and big cuts are coming after the next election. At best, more government bailouts of the banks will delay financial collapse rather than offer breakthrough solutions to a resilient, mutual economic system. Bankers have been likened to zombies, thirsting for more bonuses and public money, the more bailouts they get. Gillian Tett of *The Financial Times* wrote in March 2009 that the financial system could be 'lost in creative destruction', because the value of toxic bank assets is at least four times more than global annual GDP. She suggested that the financial system is too big to save.

So, we seem stuck between bankrupt market fundamentalism on the one hand, and dreams of the social democratic welfare state on the other. But it is easy to look nostalgically to Scandinavian and Northern European social market democracies and back to our own 'golden era' of 1945–79. We can forget that this came unstuck in a destructive conflict between capital and labour, which, after the miners were brutally defeated in 1985, unleashed the full power of finance capitalism with the 1986 City of London 'Big Bang'. Poisonous nationalistic, racist and religious fundamentalisms are also lurking, waiting to be mobilised given the opportunity.

Blatcherite market fundamentalism was implemented opportunistically step-by-step in Britain from 1979 to 2007. The rationale was that the postwar welfare state was costly, intrusive, bureaucratic, inefficient and dependency creating. So there needed to be a smaller state, through the hollowing out of statutory functions and a shift from a service-providing state to a leaner and meaner enabling state that outsourced public services to corporations, with a shift from welfare to workfare.

Paradoxically, 'modernisation', as Blair called it, led to the most centralised government in Europe and an even bigger statutory sector than before. Rather than getting more public services with less money, there was less public service with more money, as with PFI. Britain became a surveillance society at home, and, since 1997, an aggressive state permanently at war somewhere on the planet. There was a massive transfer of common wealth – such as the capital and assets of the nationalised industries or public housing – into private hands. This transfer of public wealth is now accelerating as Brown pours public capital down the bankers' throats, further allowing the enclosure of the financial commons. Brown's light-touch regulation of the City, with his government being seriously relaxed about the filthy rich getting richer, led directly to the credit crunch. The New Labour government, which helped cause the financial meltdown, continues to allow bonuses to bankers, despite Angela Merkell and Nicholai Sarkozy wanting tight controls. The government has ownership but no real control of the banks, refusing to put directors on to banks' boards even when there is a majority state shareholding. The nationalised Northern Rock bank was the toughest prosecutor of home repossession for mortgage-payment default, despite ministerial pleading. Big finance rather than the government seems to be the boss.

The government, the Westminster political elites, Whitehall and the central British state are in a moral, political and financial crisis. The system is out of control. Prime Minister Brown does not accept responsibility for helping allow the most grotesque credit bubble in history, but blames it on the global economy. The greater the number of hyperactive government initiatives, the more we suspect there is denial, underlying panic, poor analysis and lack of strategic vision. The

Westminster shamocracy faces a crisis of legitimacy. This means collapse as confidence and trust dive. The New Labour 'minority' government was elected with a comfortable majority of sixty in 2005 by around a paltry 25 per cent of registered voters because the British political elite favours the antique first-past-the-post, winner-takes-all system. The government kowtows to powerful corporate lobbyists, so we are likely to get privately run Titan gaols because these give the politicians' corporate sponsors more profits. We have Jack Straw, the current 'Minister for Justice', who some think should be brought to trial in the International Criminal Court for the illegal war against Iraq, keeping the relevant cabinet Iraq minutes secret, perhaps to save his skin. Foreign Secretary Milliband and his predecessors failed to protect British residents like Binyamin Mohammed from torture at Guantanamo, and only reluctantly acted after years of abuse because of his lawyers' courage, British judges and President Obama. Even then, Milliband tried to cover up the truth. Former Home Secretary Jacqui Smith, whilst extracting the maximum amount of expenses for her second home and £10 for hiring adult movies for her £40,000 p.a. husband-assistant, kept building the surveillance state and undermining the civil rights she was supposed to defend. Industry Minister Lord Mandelson, with support from Conservative and fellow Bilderberger Kenneth Clarke MP, meanwhile prosecuted the part-privatisation of Royal Mail. This was despite constructive alternatives advocated by John Cruddas MP for reinventing RM as a public service and as a People's Bank.

Whilst stuffing the bankers with bonuses and pensions, the government implemented the banker David Freud's workfare proposals. In return for a Jobseeker's Allowance of £64.30 a week, anyone unemployed, such as single parents, will be required to prepare for work – or else. Workfare is presented in the New Labour language of 'personalisation', 'individually tailored advice', to enable 'people to take control of their journey back to work'. In practice, benefits are dependent on the jobseeker actively seeking work for sometimes inappropriate or even non-existent jobs. So, just when unemployment is rising rapidly, former minister James Purnell now sets up a punitive, complex, arbitrary workfare system, which has perverse, humanly destructive results, in sharp contrast to the potential of the Citizen's Income to free people to contribute.

Workfare is an example of the big, inequitable gap between Westminster and ordinary people, with one law for MPs and another for the rest. Unlike the MPs who have been claiming expenses for a floating duck house, bags of horse manure, hanging baskets, wisteria pruning and second homes, ordinary self-employed people who claim wrongly on allowable expenses incurred in the course of work, are fined by the Inland Revenue. Similarly with those on benefits. That the government can allow Freud's fellow bankers such bonuses on the one hand, and introduce workfare at the same time is staggering.

Astonished people all over the world see the fall of the Houses of Westminster and the City. They ask, 'How much of this can British people take before they protest? What is stopping them?' The political elites well know how angry people are, and with what utter contempt they are held. They are dreading principled leadership and popular opposition arising, but continue as usual because they can.

They know that information control reduces protest. The corporate media restrict the reporting of critical opposition and alternatives. Some people are afraid of protesting because of brutal, illegal policing. For example, Val Swain, 43, and Emily Apple, 33, are both mothers of young children. When they challenged police at Kingsnorth for not displaying their numbers, the officers nearly throttled Emily for taking photographs, bundled them to the ground and arrested them for assault and obstruction, releasing them after four days in prison without charge.[8] Many say, 'This is not affecting us; it is nothing to do with us.' As Gillian Tett remarked, most politicians, journalists and people are too financially illiterate to really know what is happening to the financial system in our name.

A Conservative government may mean more of the same or worse. The same political and corporate elites will be in control through the Westminster shamocracy where New Labour and Conservatives jump for the corporate jellybeans in turn. There is a crisis of government legitimacy as well as potential national financial bankruptcy. We could be seeing the strange death of party politics, with what Peter Jenkins calls 'the worst parliament of modern times, a tawdry somnolence of sleaze and squander mania, authoritarian in its law making, reckless in its war mongering and immoral in its self regulation.'[9] But at the same time, there is a rump of freethinking, principle-led individual politicians from all parties who could join with civil society to reinvent British democracy, civil liberties and governance. For example the 28 February 2009 Modern Liberty Conference brought a range of people together on the common platform of preserving civil liberties, and there is democratic change in the air in the wake of parliament's expenses scandal.

This raises the question of how more freethinking Conservatives, Greens, Labour and Liberal Democrats can remake society. The four parties can each be seen as drawing on civil-society-based social movements. Each is trying to realise values in society through implementing laws, policies and resourcing. One problem is that the values that originally motivated political parties have been lost in the pursuit of power. Politicians' prime aim is to get elected and stay in power. The less politicians are informed by guiding values, the more cynical citizens become about politics. This is why so many people like Obama – he is clear about his values as a moral compass for action. However, the four parties can still reinvent themselves by strengthening their commitment to their original values – and find common ground.

Conservatives have traditionally been the cautious party of law and order, believing that everyone is equal before the law. Laws shouldn't be changed without good reason, otherwise the law itself falls into disrepute. So real 'conservatives' regret the government passing thirty-five criminal justice acts with over 3,500 new offences since 1997, as this devalues the law. Community and social cohesion is important for traditional rural land-owning Tories and social justice is important for one-nation Tories. Think of Harold Macmillan, a Prime Minister who really valued human life as a result of having fought in the trenches in the First World War. As MP for depression-ravaged Stockton, he believed passionately in social justice – for example through house-building and keeping Britain's 'family silver' of common wealth rather than privatising it for pet political projects. The one-nation

Conservative tradition can be well expressed through the guiding principle of equality of rights in the political system.

Thatcher was not a real Conservative, but rather a reborn nineteenth-century free-market liberal who let rip corporate free enterprise in the economy. Her Conservatives almost destroyed British society and industry, giving power to finance capital. Phillip Blond, the 'red Tory', argues that:

> Most crucially, Mrs Thatcher dispensed with the idea that nation's private capital surplus should commit itself to the realm in which it was generated. She severed completely the notion of a 'national capital', loyal to locality, community and country. There was a systematic erosion of all subsistent mutual relationships in the national economy.[10]

However, it is vitally important to distinguish between free-market economic liberals like Thatcher on the one hand, and cultural liberals and libertarians on the other. Cultural liberals and libertarians value the central guiding principle of cultural and personal freedom – hence civil liberties, a free press, no taxes on knowledge such as books, a free, independent BBC and a semi-autonomous education system. Think of the Conservative R. A. Butler, who nevertheless implemented the deeply liberal 1944 Education Act, which established educational autonomy. There is a big overlap with civil society organisations and the cultural system, where liberals feel most at home. So freedom is what traditionally the Liberal Party stood for, and can bring this into politics through supporting the growth of cultural and personal freedom.

Labour is a hard one, as many of the original inspiring principles have now long since gone, and leaders like Brown, Blair and Mandelson are economic neo-liberals like Thatcher. One principle, the common ownership of the means of production, was distorted by Labour into nationalisation rather than into the mutualisation of assets and common ownership. Socialism has long gone, and any understanding of 'social' or 'community' was destroyed by the competitive individualism of opportunistic neo-liberals like Blair, who hijacked Old Labour. The succession of neo-liberal housing ministers with which the Community Land Trust movement has tried to engage do not appear to understand the values of altruism, co-operation, private action for public good or mutuality.

However, the pearl in the Labour oyster is the Co-operative Party, which has twenty-nine Westminster MPs. The Co-op Party supports Labour, which is astonishing as New Labour ignores Co-op values, cooperators and mutual business practices. Co-op shared values are honesty, openness, social responsibility and caring for others. These values are put into practice through the seven co-op principles of voluntary and open membership; democratic member control; member economic participation; autonomy and independence; education, training and information; cooperation among Co-operatives; concern for the community. Clearly, these are values that Liberal Democrats, Conservatives, Labour and Greens can also sign up to.

The Co-operative values can be summarised as mutuality, as associating for mutual benefit, as practical fraternity. So mutuality is the guiding governing principle, and the Co-operative movement, whilst originating as a cultural, civil society movement, is clearly 'at home' in the economy when working as a Co-op social business. Think of Robert Owen, the Co-op pioneer who was also a successful entrepreneur and educator. Think of the current strength of the Co-op Bank, which

---

Box 12.1   The Exchange, Stroud

The Exchange is a civil-society-led project providing a unique support service for small social enterprises and, in so doing, reinvests its surpluses locally. Income from affordable rents (just £5 per day) enables the public use of excellent facilities. Further surpluses will form a fund to enable local projects. The benefits of the £240,000 raised for refurbishing a 1830s stone building are thus used over and over to support the local economy – economic permaculture! And it's sustainable, with ground-source heat, photovoltaics and solar thermal.

Source: Max Comfort, www.stroudcommonwealth.org.uk

Source: Stroud News and Journal. 'Princess Ann opening The Exchange on 25 September 2008, with Max Comfort and Lola, Stroud Common Wealth'

Source: Copyright www.stroudpound.org.uk: increasing local trade and retaining local wealth. Designed by Ronan Schoemaker

was so awash with deposits that it was the only bank to be lending to the Treasury during the credit crunch! And think of the 169,000 co-operators who own 2009 European Cup winners Barcelona FC and how Barcelona gives $1 million a year for the privilege of wearing the UNICEF logo. This is in contrast to the losers, the debt-ridden Manchester United plc, which is owned by US millionaires, rather than by the people of Manchester. Today, the Co-operative party supports the establishment of 100 co-operative trust schools as an effective way of involving parents, staff, students and local communities in running schools; supporting co-operative housing, mutualising energy supply, former building societies and Network Rail.

The Green Party originally focused on the core value of environmental sustainability, of care for the earth and how we can reinvent a green economy, participative politics and social justice.

So the four main parties each has a particular, though not exclusive, connection to the guiding values of mutuality, equality, freedom and sustainability. These values are also the governing principles of the economic, political, cultural and natural systems respectively.

As there is potentially strong support for a society shaped by these four guiding principles, the four political movements could agree common ground. They can recognise the significance of each other's core values for transforming democracy, our economy, culture and environment. It is possible to be a conservative, green, liberal co-operator, thus going beyond the stalemated, divide and rule, conflictual system of party politics.

But what openings are there for building a free, equal, mutual and sustainable society?

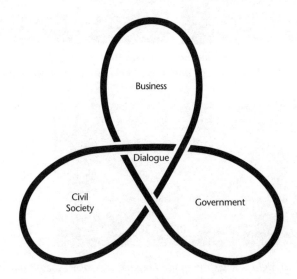

Figure 12.1   Dialogue between government, business and civil society

Three-way strategic conversations for vision and action: seeing, analysing and acting from the heart of society

One high impact intervention is to create regular, open dialogue space between the leaders of the three sectors. The purpose is to then stand back and make sense of what the community, city, district, region or society as a whole needs. As the old saying goes, 'Don't just do something, stand there and reflect!' There needs to be considered dialogue, rather than the PR-driven, hyperactive 'initiativitis' of government, characterised often by poor analysis, lack of participation by affected people followed by more initiatives if the original ones don't work.

Well-facilitated, dialogue can lead to sensing, analysis, common agreements, plans and taking action. This is already happening in Britain in an intuitive practical way on the district or city level with local strategic partnerships. However, effective trisectoral dialogue comes from participants having a clear practical grasp of the strengths of the three sectors and what each sector brings to the table. If trisectoral dialogue is effectively planned, convened and facilitated, this 'heart space' can surface new sources of leadership, vision building and direction, especially if there is participation by wider circles of people in issues that affect them (see Appendix 1).

Take health as a complex issue. There are limits to government and private spending on health. More money spent does not necessarily mean more health. Dialogue on how to improve health can offer ways of reframing the issue that go beyond quick fixes and, by addressing systemic and cultural issues, start a health culture shift. For example, Finland was a very unhealthy country, with high heart disease rates, until government, civil society and business worked hard to create a culture for health. 'Simple' actions, like regular exercise, had far more impact than expensive hospital programmes. In Britain, doctors are catching on with prescribing walking, which English Nature has been promoting for well-being. Dialogue on health can result in widening circles of action inquiry and reflection on how we can improve health in our lives, families, workplaces and community.

The key to such dialogue is to build relationships and communication. Conversation deepens through attention to listening and speaking. At first, there is downloading and offloading. People speak their usual scripts, rant, say what they think others want to hear, use clichés and do not say what they really think. A second mode is debate and discussion, for and against. People say what they think and there are diverging viewpoints and point scoring. Dialogue proper starts when people start to risk themselves, admit ignorance, ask questions, test their understanding of what others are saying, open up to new thinking and even admit that they are part of the problem: 'Well, my carbon footprint from car driving is …' or 'As health professionals, we accept that a significant proportion of illnesses are caused by the medical system itself, for example infections acquired in hospitals.' People start to reflect that 'It's not only them. It is us, too. We are part of the problem.' A fourth stage of profound dialogue surfaces when people converse with open minds, hearts and will, shifting through golden moments into a sense

Box 12.2   Dialogue: Mayor on a bench

Town councillor Andy Read is Stroud's new mayor. He took over John Marjoram's 'mayor on a bench' surgeries in Kendrick Street, outside Tony the butcher's, every Monday morning. 'It's about going to where people are, and not expecting people to come to you', he said. 'People complain about politicians that you never see them except at election times.'

Source: David Wiles, Stroud News and Journal, *17 June 2009*
(photo SSS 1007V09)

of presence, connection and fresh insights. Otto Scharmer calls this 'presencing', where people can see the whole system they are in, and can analyse, co-create and act generatively from a sense for the whole.[11]

What can help trisectoral dialogue on issues like improving sustainability, health or housing in a locality is to firstly convene a half-day conference of between twenty and sixty invited active people and 'leaders'. These are a cross-section of active, bright sparks from the top, middle and working levels of the relevant business, statutory and civil society sectors. From the inviting process, you know they are already potentially keen on tackling a burning question, have some relevant knowledge, resources and connections – and are prepared to give some time as long as the process is well facilitated and followed up. It helps if a respected leader champions the event and introduces the purpose and possible desired outcomes, such as setting up a partnership to agree and implement a plan for the desired future of x – which could be local food culture, affordable housing, health, a sustainable transport system, whatever the burning strategic issue chosen.

However, the medium-term aim is to create a cross-sectoral space for dialogue between leaders and activists from the three sectors who can firstly recognise the strengths and unique contribution of each sector, and secondly develop the capacity to see and act from the needs of the whole community, place or system. One warm-up process that can help create these conditions is to invite participants to separate out into three sectoral groups and ask them to note down on a flip chart:

1.   What do you see as the unique knowledge, skills, resources and strengths that (a) the business sector; (b) the statutory sector; and (c) civil society and the community sector can bring?
2.   How do you think that the other two sectors see your sector, e.g. your sector's strengths and weaknesses?

The three groups then present their conclusions to the plenary, followed by a lively discussion as more understanding of the qualities, leading values, competences and working fields of the three sectors emerges. What can help shift to deeper dialogue and listening is to invite real stories that show the sectors at their best – things they are proud of and want to build on, as well as things they are sorry about. Further questions can include 'How can the three sectors best work together on *x*?' and 'What can we realise through these partnership conversations?' This can then continue if there is the will, leadership, facilitation and resources to create open partnership conversations, and also practical partnership work on specific issues where cross-sectoral input is needed. Ros Tennyson of the Prince of Wales Business Leaders Forum has developed a range of tried and tested useful tools for engaging the public sector, business and civil society for development[12] (see Appendix 1).

So a key action point is to facilitate meaningful, relevant, practical conversations that help people to see and act from the whole. This lays the foundations for partnerships and then leads to focused work on specific burning questions. There is now a range powerful tools and processes to help small and large groups engage in participative business, community and statutory planning. When well designed and facilitated, these processes can make the most of people's energy, knowledge and experience in coming up with plans and implementing them. The tools for participative democratic working are there – they just need using more.

Consider how the leading open source software, Linux, was co-created by thousands of designers, or how participative design enables online input into difficult technical, social and political challenges like a desired waste management system for London. Over a thousand people created a Community Plan for Stroud in 1994–5, creating a vibrant economic, social and cultural magnetic field for all kinds of UP2US people and projects to develop. The civil-society-led Transitions Towns movement draws on a range of community planning processes to chart a transition to a low-carbon economy and more resilient way of life.

Openings for transforming capitalism and democracy

So, what are the openings for transforming capitalism and Westminster democracy, which are both now in a systemic crisis? It is important to first recognise current reality – where we are now. Currently, Britain has an authoritarian, disconnected government running the most centralised state in Europe, a government without a legitimate mandate that operates as a parliamentary monarchy supported by a compliant elected body that has forgotten its purpose of serving the public good. Political and corporate elites have used governments to unleash neo-liberal capitalism over the last thirty years with disastrous results. The government is disgraced by using the 'war on terror' to systematically attack our civil liberties to the point of condemnation by the UN. Our common wealth has been sold from under our feet, as the plutocratic elites accumulate vast wealth through various forms of dispossession while up to a third of Britons live in post-industrial poverty. The Treasury has estimated that there is an £110 billion annual tax loss to Britain through allowing the individually wealthy to hold their capital in offshore tax havens – enough to fund the National Health Service.[13] The government, with no real public, democratic debate let alone parliamentary debates and proper scrutiny, is forcing taxpayers to bail out a broken banking system with massive toxic debts. Except that until after the next election, the Westminster elite is keeping quiet about how much extra taxpayers will have to pay, and what will be cut.

This is a legitimacy crisis for both capitalism and Westminster democracy. Where, for example, was the public debate about the merits of 'queezing' – 'quantitative easing' or creating £175 billion electronic money to further bail out the banks? Twenty billion pounds of this 'new money' could have been directly spent into circulation to create green jobs for retrofitting homes to reduce energy use and to build the 3 million homes we need – or used for piloting the Citizen's Income with the young and the long-term unemployed. How is it that Yvette Cooper and the Treasury can block the Stroud community plan for Cashes Green Hospital for investing in permanently affordable homes for public benefit as 'poor value for money', yet when she then becomes first secretary for the treasury, helps bail out the bankers?

What is needed is the capacity in business, government and civil society to see the whole picture – to see and act from the whole, to clarify guiding values and to enable conversations in workplaces, communities and government about what desired future we want and how to get there. Business will then shift from a narrow profit focus to embracing the social, environmental and sustainable bottom line. The public sector can embrace real participative democracy through a whole range of processes such as participative budgeting, community planning and a variety of deliberative public dialogues, which can build a more democratic culture. Civil society can lead on cultural and community development from the bottom up, sponsoring social enterprise for service delivery, and leading on cross-sectoral partnership working for sustainable solutions rather than just advocating, or reactively opposing, business and government. So what openings are there for renewing the political, economic and cultural sectors?

Firstly, Britain needs democratic renewal so as to shift from a state-focused to a citizen-focused public sector and to create a participative, inclusive democratic culture. The Power Inquiry has already mapped out the changes needed, such as a written constitution, Bill of Rights, the right of recall, fixed-term parliaments, strengthening parliament to scrutinise the government, a voting system based on proportional representation, an elected House of Lords and real subsidiarity of taxation and decision-making from national through regional city, county, district and parish levels. Various groups have taken up this process. The *how* is as important as the *what*, so the democratic process needs to engage citizens in debate and discussion, as with the 1647 Putney Debates, so that people can see real tangible results from their participation. One key element is good information and developing open democratic forums at all levels for considering burning questions and

---

Box 12.3   *Stroud Community Farm*

Stroud Community Agriculture is a community-supported farm, leasing two farms totalling forty-five acres. Constituted as a member-owned and run co-op, there are 180 family members that get vegetables weekly on a share system. Members pay a monthly membership fee and pay for food shares. Members guarantee the two farmers' salaries from year to year and agree a yearly budget and cropping plan. A core group of elected members manage the farms, which are mixed, with vegetables, animals, hay and grass – all farmed organically. Seasonality is important, as is the reduction of 'food miles'. There are social activities, celebrating festivals and voluntary work days. The Soil Association uses Stroud CSA as a practical exemplar for Community Supported Agriculture training workshops.

Source: www.stroudcommunityagriculture.coop
Photo by Nick Weir

for sensing strategic direction. The renewal of democracy can result in the statutory sector working from the heart of society – sensing what is needed, deciding how cultural, political, social and economic rights can be translated into entitlements, making plans and policies, resourcing and enabling delivery in partnership with civil society and business.

Secondly, the economy and the market need renewal so as to shift from a capitalist-dominated to a more associative, mutual and sustainable focus that nevertheless retains the best aspects of free enterprise, personal initiative and the personal connection with capital – the pearl in the neo-liberal oyster. The mutual sector is expanding, and so the healthy banking sector can be mutualised rather than nationalised, along with the utilities, so that managers, workers, stakeholders and consumers own and control these social businesses, sharing the risks and rewards and investing in sustainability. When Macquarie, the bank famous for making millionaires of its senior staff, announces a 17 per cent above inflation price increase for its subsidiary Thames Water, whilst making a record £605 million profit, it is time to mutualise such businesses as a way of taking back such utilities into common trusteeship.[14] Associative working is the essence of the economy, to be encouraged as a key economic governance principle. You can see associative production, distribution and consumption in the local food movement. For example, the members of Stroud Community Farm agree each year on a budget, what food should be produced and monthly shares and then negotiate an agreement with the two farmers. We guarantee their income.

Associations also work on a global scale, for example the International Energy Agency, which researches, monitors and advises on overall global energy resources, production and needs. Fair trade looks at the whole coffee supply chain, for example, and agrees a leaner supply chain and fair levels of profit so as to guarantee farmer income. However, what is needed to build a sustainable economy are associations that oversee whole systems, like food, energy, finance and transport, associations that sense and act from the whole picture. For example, Britain has an antiquated, costly, wasteful transport system that does not work well for all, the product of a captive, corporate state. A national transport association would research the whole system, engage transport users, providers and planners and come up with an integrated, sustainable transport system that worked effectively, efficiently and sustainably for all. The introduction of the basic citizen's income would shift many people from welfare state dependency to a culture of initiative and self-reliance. The introduction of local currencies, local community investment mutuals and community asset holding vehicles like Community Land Trusts would further build a local, mutual, living economy.

Thirdly, the community and civil society sector can develop through a shift from state-dominated services such as education and health to publicly resourced but autonomous, community/civil society provided services and, where appropriate, social-business-provided services. This was part of the liberal Beveridge's vision for the post-1945 welfare state. He saw that the welfare state was not only about welfare and health service reform. He suggested that the role of the state was to resource 'private action for social advance' as the key weapon in the fight

---

Box 12.4   Stroud Communiversity: Spreading the Learning

Stroud Communiversity
Building Vibrant Communities

www.stroudcommonwealth.og.uk

---

against 'the five giants on the road to reconstruction ... Want, Disease, Ignorance, Squalor, and Idleness'. According to Steven Hill, Beveridge 'believed that the spirit and experience of voluntary action was at the heart of what it means to be free'. The involvement of people was needed to humanise the provision of public services, which needed to be independent of government control.[15] Little did Beveridge foresee how public services would become so colonised by the statutory sector.

So, an independent judiciary, for example, can work with the probation service, police, social services and civil society in developing finely tuned sentencing that makes the punishment and restorative justice sentence fit the criminal and, above all, prevent reoffending. Prisons could be transformed into non-profit 'social businesses' for education and a life-changing transition to a productive life. Education can become a semi-autonomous public service, in partnership with the state, and reinvented so as to encourage lifelong learning. Freeing, rather than nationalising or privatising, schools will enable teachers, students and parents to make the most of local resources for learning, as the Forest School movement has already demonstrated for the early years. The media also need freeing up from commercial and political agendas, so as to enable more dialogue, more awareness and information. Democracy is unviable without a free, independent media, which has been made more possible with the Internet, for example with the Open Democracy website. The outstanding *Guardian* website has made it major source of global news and information access, even the world's liberal voice, and this has been made possible by the charitable, independent C. P. Scott Trust, which owns the *Guardian*. The more the BBC is freed from government influence over content, the more the BBC can become an independent public service, for the world, not just for Britain. One argument for the citizen's income is that it would free up time for people to get engaged in more community work, honouring the old tradition of tithing time.

The danger of the above openings for transforming democracy and capitalism is that they are yet more lists of initiatives that are 'not invented here'. The place to start or keep going is where you are, in your place, neighbourhood, community or workplace to focus on what you can do, whilst trusting others will be similarly engaged on their questions.

Community-building and placemaking: creating economic, cultural and social wealth together

So how can we build a free, equal, mutual and sustainable society locally as well as globally? People are working on this question in many places. Some of the Stroud responses to this question have been covered in boxes throughout the book, offered as a tapestry of growing points that are renewing the local culture, community and economy. Firstly, cultural renewal has raised the creative human spirit to the point of releasing energy for more cultural initiative, political work and business development. Cultural projects include a community play celebrating Stroud's story; a widespread 'UP 2 US' community planning process; The SPACE, Stroud's performing arts centre; the Stroud Valley Artspace for affordable studios; a range of creative projects; the Stroud Valleys Project for environmental improvement; Stroud Preservation Trust for heritage; the Painswick Inn for training and housing young unemployed people; a range of festivals; educational initiatives; a thriving Stroud district council run museum; and a significant arts, crafts and cultural industry sector. Raising the creative spirit has attracted businesses and new start-ups – everything from publishing, baking, local breweries, new small and co-op businesses, now supported by The Exchange to provide social enterprise backing. The local food movement is strong, with a national award winning farmers' market, community orchards, food growing on shared allotments and community-supported agriculture. There are housing and neighbourhood-building initiatives such as Stroud CoHousing and the land trust, Gloucestershire Land for People. Plans are afoot for a local currency and a community mutual asset investment fund. The transition town movement connects Stroud with developments elsewhere.

These projects all help build a variety of dynamic social, economic and cultural spaces. They build community and a sense of place in Stroud's five valleys. They are examples of building economic, social and cultural wealth together, of common wealth. This is a conversation between place, work and people, bringing the stories out, enjoying the cultural landscape and creating good work. At a time of change, it is important to reconnect, to be grounded in place and community. In a way everything is local in the end.

One last story. As people heard of various innovative Stroud projects, they wanted to visit, to see, to learn and develop their own plans. So Stroud Communiversity was founded as a learning exchange with those locally and nationally who were similarly engaged. Participants walk round the various projects, hearing the stories, getting acquainted with the underlying values, concepts and methods and work on their own questions. Links are being built with other communities around Britain and Europe, for example with a Norwegian civic delegation from Aurland near Bergen making a study visit in March 2009. 'Walking the land' of Stroud's five valleys and experiencing the power of place through connecting with the cultural, social and economic landscape was a high point of their visit.

Inspiring, practical change principles are emerging with the Stroud story, and from other active communities around the world.

- These include developing a variety of 'thought leaders'. These are practical examples of environmental, cultural, social and economic innovation that can offer useful exemplars to learn from.
- The underpinning theory, values, methods, evaluation and learning of the exemplars needs research and communicating.
- Good facilitation and brokering for capacity-building through taking reflective action are crucial.
- Drama, storytelling and community arts are key transformative agents. (One of my recent golden moments was being surprised by an energetic group of teenagers rehearsing a play called *After Juliet* and numerous songs outside my office in preparation for their performing tour in Uganda.)
- Finally, there needs to be a network of facilitators, cultural, political and business leaders from a web of creative, active communities across the planet for collaboration, perspective, learning, inspiring change, sense-making and prototyping. These principles can support what Otto Scharmer calls 'leading from the future as it emerges'.

Leading from the social future as it emerges is in sharp contrast to the backward-looking leadership of the majority of the Anglo-American corporate, banking and political elites. They seem trapped in top-down, centralised bureaucracies and elitist agendas, blinded by institutional ignorance: they are stuck. Disinformation is spread that 'there is no alternative'. There is a lack of public debate, analysis and properly evidenced solutions. This is at a time when even elite media like *The Financial Times* consider that our economic system may be lost in creative destruction, and when Nobel economics laureate Joseph Stiglitz thinks there is little evidence that the public money thrown at the banks has had any positive effect on the real economy.

It could be so different. Principle-centred corporate, financial and political leaders could recognise and support the green shoots of the emerging future social, economic and cultural order as it emerges. For example, when Brian Wilson MP said in 1997 on the ferry home after the Isle of Eigg Heritage Trust foundation that 'It doesn't have to be so difficult for communities', this led to the Scottish Land Reform Act to help communities across Scotland. Why don't English political leaders take up Wilson's idea? Or take visionary leadership action, such as Michelle Obama making an organic vegetable garden at the White House to show support for local food growing? After all, top-down support *and* bottom-up vision, values, principles and energy are needed to best remake society.

There also needs to be a shift away from the toxic grip of neo-liberalism and for a challenge to the intellectual ghosts of the past that cling on to power. For example, just when Kate Pickett and Richard Wilkinson's new book, *The Spirit Level*, demonstrates unequivocally that inequality – especially in neo-liberal-dominated Anglo-American societies – is the main driver of poor health, I met a Swedish doctor fighting health privatisation in Sweden. The warning sign, she said, was when the new 'moderate' neo-liberal government wanted doctors to call patients 'consumers'.

But above all, *Common Wealth* argues that to develop beyond the current broken neo-liberal capitalist system there needs to be clarity about the boundaries between the cultural, community and civil society sector, the political sector and the economic sector. One key boundary-shift is to treat land, labour and capital as commons to be stewarded, rather than as marketable commodities.

The other key shift is to remake society as a Common Wealth, just as once the declining British Empire was reframed as the Commonwealth. The development of the Common Wealth is guided by the principles of freedom, equality, mutuality and sustainability. The more that the principle of freedom informs our culture and civil society, the more that equality informs the state sector with its human rights, entitlements and responsibilities and the more that mutuality guides business and economic life, the healthier, wealthier, juster and the more resilient will be our society. And the more we care for nature and the earth, the more resilient and sustainable our planet.

And finally, there is John Ruskin's vision of the common wealth of Britain's rich cultural traditions to draw on when building a sustainable social future. Ruskin offers a compass in *Unto This Last*, celebrating the fact that:

> There is no wealth but life. Life, including all its powers of love, of joy, and of admiration. That country is richest which nourishes the greatest number of noble and happy human beings; that man is richest who, having perfected the functions of his own life to the utmost, has also the widest helpful influence, both personal, and by means of his possessions, over the lives of others.

Appendix 1: Tools for Cross-Sectoral and Trisectoral Partnership Building

Building partnerships for a variety of tasks has become a key strategic and practical activity for civil society, companies and governmental organisations. These partnerships can be used to build joint ventures with other organisations similarly engaged for sectoral or cross-sectoral purposes. Cross-sectoral partnerships (also sometimes called trisectoral partnerships where appropriate) are collabourative alliances between organisations drawn from the three societal sectors of business, government and civil society. These partnerships work together to clarify common interests and ways of tacking sustainable development, or other tasks.

Since a key theme of *Common Wealth* is the importance of practical ways of helping business, government and civil society work to their strengths, cross-sectoral partnerships can build dialogue, get practical work done and develop mutually beneficial ways of cooperating for public good.

Kofi Annan highlighted the importance of cross-sector partnerships at the 2002 Johannesburg World Summit on Sustainable Development in 2002 for, 'increasing the pool of resources to tackle global problems on a global scale.'

Partnerships are now used by organisations – from community-based organisations, NGOs, businesses and local government to civil society organisations, transnational corporations and governments. There are now a variety of partnership building approaches, such as The Partnering Initiative, led by Ros Tennyson, which was initiated in 2004 in association with the University of Cambridge Programme for Industry.

The Partnering Initiative, which works with civil society, business and government defines partnership as follows:

'A partnership is a cross-sector collaboration in which organisations work together in a transparent, equitable and mutually beneficial way towards a sustainable development goal and where those defined as partners agree to commit resources and share the risks as well as the benefits associated with the partnership.'

The Partnering Initiative enables learning about partnerships, sharing practical experience, contributing knowledge, offering support, training, and advice and setting standards for good partnering practice. It is a global programme of the International Business Leaders Forum. The Initiative offers training, advice, reviews and a wide range of practice-based publications including:

Tennyson, R. *The Partnering Toolbook: An Essential Guide to Cross-sector Partnership* (2003). This is a concise overview of the essential elements for effective partnering: a short book and stand alone tools.

Khaliq Hussain, S., Hurrell, S. and Tennyson, R. *The Case Study Toolbook: Partnership case studies as a tool for change* (2005). This provides tools and methodologies to improve the way partnerships are written up and to enable partnership case studies to be used more effectively.

McManus, S., Tennyson, R, *Talking the Walk: A Communication Manual for Partnership Building* (2007). A detailed and use-friendly guide to a vital topic in effective partnering

Halper, E., *Moving On Toolbook: Effective Management for Partnership Exits and Transitions* (2009). Focuses on the final phases of a partnership cycle – too often unplanned or mishandled.

Information about The Partnering Initiative and resources is taken from their website: www.thepartneringinitiative.org

Evaluation of Cross Sectoral Partnerships

Partnerships, of course, need evaluating carefully. Nicanor Perlas, for example, critically evaluates some of the success conditions, problems and pitfalls (such as the dangers of co-option) of trisectoral partnerships in his book, *Shaping Globalisation* (2000). *The Case Study Toolbook* (see above) includes evaluation methods, and evaluation is a key theme in the work of the Partnering Initiative.

Appendix 2: Feedback and Next Steps

The unfolding events of 2007–9 made *Common Wealth* hard to write. There was the danger that too much focus on the spectacular collapse of neo-liberal market fundamentalism would take away from four of the key themes which are:

1. Outlining a new, trisectoral analysis of society, of a threefold commonwealth of the economy, politics and culture, with business, government and civil society respectively as the leading institutions of each sector, as an emerging alternative to neo-liberal capitalism.
2. Showing how neo-liberal capitalism, which is dominated by the financial capital sector, has captured the state, culture and the economy with a massive ongoing transfer of wealth to the corporations and the elite.
3. Suggesting practically how the commons of land, capital and labour can be reclaimed through transforming capitalism, the citizen's income, land taxation and trusteeship, and freeing education for the public good, for a society that works for all.
4. Identifying openings for leading from the social future as it emerges, whether:

- by each sector working in its own right – for example with business transforming its relationship with the planet through natural capitalism, or mutualising the financial sector and public utilities; or the democratic transformation of the statutory sector and government; or cultural activities such as education the media or health becoming more self directing and autonomous;
- by trisectoral partnership working for sustainable development and other over-arching tasks for the common good;
- by communities across the world acting locally and globally, linking up for learning and exchange, whilst encouraging a thriving local civil society, mutual economy and democracy.

Feedback

Your feedback on *Common Wealth* would be welcome, as this book is both 'work and thinking in progress.' Firstly, in a second edition: What should be kept? What should be dropped? What should be added that's new? Should there be more case studies or examples? How can *Common Wealth* be improved?

Secondly, what would be timely follow-ups in the way of more focused books on specific themes?

Action for a more sustainable, equal, free and mutual society

What actions can be taken to bring about a more sustainable, equal, free and mutual society? As Goethe once said, in the end, all things have to be done.

Firstly, to follow up the book, there is a *Common Wealth* blog and website (www.common-wealth.co.uk) for comments, articles, case studies of emerging good practice and resources to share.

Secondly, another way of following up *Common Wealth* is to develop an MA in leadership and change for a more sustainable society. This would be for government, civil society and business leaders, managers, professionals and activists who want to learn through doing, through action research and cross-sectoral partnership working. This Masters degree, an alternative to an MBA, would help participants develop the skills, knowledge, capability, networks and vision needed by organisations wanting to make the most of their resources for better achieving their goals, and for contributing to the common good.

Thirdly, to develop a 1–2 year orientation programme for school leavers who want leadership skills, personal growth, an understanding of how society works – to be gained by making a difference in the community through projects and voluntary service.

Appendix 3: Governing and Reclaiming the Commons

The dominance of the private market sector and of the state sector can make it hard to recognise that the commons, our shared resources, creates special forms of wealth in civil society, outside the market and the state. The commonwealth is another term for society as a whole that both preserves individual rights, but also ensures the public good and general welfare for all.

Often, commons governance is taken for granted. When I took twenty-five Norwegian visitors from Telemark around Stroud's Rodborough Common, they were astonished at how it was owned by one body, the National Trust, and run by an association as a governance body, with a range of largely self-regulating users including golfers, dog walkers, kite fliers, walkers and farmers (for grazing).

People sometimes wake up to the common wealth when burning public issues come up. For example, when Stroud District Council wanted to compulsorily purchase Tricorn House, a derelict office block at a gateway to Stroud. This eyesore has been kept vacant for fourteen years by the offshore owner as an 'investment'. But government minister John Denham MP ruled that the CPO was against the owner's 'human rights', despite the community, environmental, job and economic benefits of the CPO proposal. Denham did not respect the rights of the common wealth, only the property rights of the free-riding owner.

The governance of the commons is flexible and adaptable to circumstances, whether for common pool resources such as the Internet, Linux software, grazing or fishing regimes. Elinor Ostrom, the 2009 Nobel laureate for economics, researched how common pool resources are governed. She found eight design principles for the successful governing of the commons, such as clearly defined boundaries, usage rules customised to the resource in question, participative rule making by all users, monitoring and controlling usage, a series of sanctions for violations; and economical ways for resolving disputes.[1]

According to David Bollier, for successful commons governance there needs to be:

1. *Openness and feedback,* such as the academic peer review system, or farmers getting together to monitor sheep grazing.
2. *Collective decision making:* participative approaches to decision making and making rules – if the people make the rules, they are more likely to implement them.
3. *Diversity within the commons:* diversity, with openness, results in inventiveness and creativity, for example with the software movement that says, 'With enough eyes, all bugs are shallow.'
4. *Social equity within the commons:* the aim of commons governance is to democratise the benefits from a shared pool resource, such as equitable access to water, land, housing, air, freedom from pollution, health and education. If delivered by the market, access would become more and more inequitable.

5.   *Environmental sustainability:* Ostrom found that many well-governed commons were highly sustainable over centuries, such as the communal Swiss high mountain meadows in Torbel since 1483 and Valencia huerta irrigation regimes in operation since 1435. Marine parks are enabling fish stocks to rebuild.

6.   *Sociability in the Commons – the Gift Economy:* rather than behaving as rational, self-seeking, profit-maximising individuals, commoners are motivated by local differences, cultural uniqueness, co-operation, sharing, generosity, equity, gift exchange, shared interests and values such as sustainability. The more we share, the richer we are – it takes a whole village to raise a child.

To conclude, commons governance offers a different form of governance to that of the state on the one hand, and the market on the other. Commons governance underpins the development of civil society and of cultural organisations. Building the commons needs a changed culture, a vision for the common good and of human potential.

Some enabling conditions include:

1.   Enabling democratic participation – the greater the participation in decision making, the better the governance.

2.   Setting limits on the market and on commercialisation – for example, building a social land ownership sector alongside statutory and private ownership, or making childhood a commercial-free zone.

3.   Setting limits on the state and on inappropriate bureaucratisation, so freeing health and education as semi-autonomous public services

4.   Creating protected spaces where civil society can thrive – for example, community gardens, festivals, cultural events, online groups, free media, café life, community land trusts and parks.

5.   Nurturing gift economies, such as donating blood, building the knowledge commons in academic life, the creative commons and software movements, and creating community land trusts, which then grow through gifts. Government can play a key role in enabling the gift economy to flourish. For example, by disposing land for permanently affordable housing, or allowing local exchange systems such as LETS to go untaxed.

As David Bollier writes:

'It is time to revive this tradition of innovation in the stewardship of public resources and give it imaginative new incarnations in the twenty-first century. The silent theft of our shared assets and gift economies need not continue. But it is first important to recognise the commons as the commons and understand the rich possibilities for reclaiming our common wealth.'[2]

Notes

Chapter 1
What Social Future Do We Want?

1. See John Lanchester, 'It Is Finished', *London Review of Books*, 28 May 2009. He estimates that taxpayers have spent £45.5 billion directly bailing out RBS, plus another £50 billion for the toxic assets in the protection scheme, which could go as high as £302 billion if the assets are worthless. This makes £95.5 billion, as well as Fred Goodwin's pension pot of £16 million.
2. Quotation from Molly Scott Cato, *Green Economics*, London, Earthscan, 2009, p. 162.
3. The distinction between commodities, such as a chair, and a commons we all share the use of, such as the whole financial system, leads to the question of what is true wealth. Much wealth, such as relationships, family, nature, health, community is unquantifiable.
4. Jill Treanor, 'Hedge Fund Made Millions Betting on Barclays Crash', *Guardian*, 23 January 2009, p. 1.
5. Judith Large, *The War Next Door*, Stroud, Hawthorn Press, 1997.
6. From C. Schaefer, 'Nine Propositions in Search of a Social Order', unpublished paper, 2003. Aphorism originally taken from Christoph Strawe, but adapted by the author.
7. See www.stroudcommonwealth.org.uk.

Chapter 2
Remaking Society

1. 'There is vitality, a life force, a quickening that is translated through you into action, and because there is only one of you in all time, this expression is unique ... You have to keep open and aware directly to the urges that motivate you. Keep the channel open. No artist is pleased. There is only a queer, divine dissatisfaction, a blessed unrest that keeps us marching and makes us more alive than the others.' Martha Graham to Agnes de Mille, quoted in Agnes de Mille, *Dance to the Piper and Promenade Home: A Two-Part Autobiography*, New York, Da Capo Press, 1979.
2. Paul Hawken, *To Remake the World*, New York, Orion, 2007, also see Paul Hawken, *Blessed Unrest*, New York, Viking, 2007.
3. See www.fordhallfarm.com.
4. Sami Sillanpaa, 'Enemy of the State', *Guardian*, 22 May 2007.
5. Heather Brooke, 'Unsung Hero', *Guardian*, 15 May 2009, pp. 4–6, and see also her website at yrtk.org.
6. Paul H. Ray and Sherry Ruth Anderson, *The Cultural Creatives: How 50 Million People Are Changing the World*, New York, Harmony Books, 2000.
7. See C. Schaefer, 'Nine Propositions in Search of the Threefold Social Order', unpublished article, 2006.
8. G. Soros, *The New Paradigm for Financial Markets: The Credit Crisis of 2008 and What It Means*, New York, Public Affairs, 2008.
9. See the *Guardian*, 24 October 2008, p. 1.
10. A. Roddick, *Take It Personally*, London, Thorsons, 2001.
11. Louise Carpenter, 'The Bag Lady', *Observer Food Monthly*, 27 January 2008.
12. However, I was pleased when the Community Land Trust legal definition amendment proposed by backbench MPs in summer 2008 was nevertheless passed into law by the Lords in July 2008.
13. Quoted in Roddick, *Take it Personally*.
14. See Geraldine Bedell, 'Why Six Britons Went to Ecowar, *Observer*, 31 May 2009. To read more about Nick Broomfield's Greenpeace documentary, *A Time Comes*, see the *Guardian* website at guardian.co.uk/environment.

15. See R. Rehm, N. Cebula, F. Ryan and M. Large, *Futures that Work*, Vancouver, New Society, 2002.
16. B. C. J. Lievegoed, *The Eye of the Needle*, Stroud, Hawthorn Press, 1995.

Chapter 3
Tripolar Society: Government, Business and Civil Society

1. Pa.press.net, 20 October 2008.
2. George Monbiot, *Guardian*, 14 April 2008.
3. John Carvel, 'NHS Reform like a Supermarket War', *Guardian*, 8 July 2008.
4. Margaret Thatcher, *Woman's Own*, 31 October 1981.
5. NIMBY: Not In My Back Yard, used to refer to people who object, often from a very narrow perceived self-interest, to change such as new houses on their doorsteps; hence, nimbies, nimbyism.
6. See The Land Is Ours website at www.tlio.org.uk.
7. For learning from Krakow, see Rafel Serafin and Ros Tennyson, 'Leading Edge Practice: Brokering the Partnership Idea', *Partnership Matters*, no. 4, online at www.ThePartnershipInitiative.org.
8. From Ros Tennyson and Luke Wilde, *The Guiding Hand: Brokering Partnerships for Sustainable Development*, Prince of Wales Business Leaders Forum and the United Nations Staff College, 2000, p. 13.
9. A. C. Guyton, *Physiology of the Human Body*, New York, Saunders, 1984, Ch. 20.
10. See Daniel Jones and James Womack, *The Machine That Changed the World*, New York, Simon & Schuster, 1992 and the same authors' *Lean Thinking: Banish Waste and Create Wealth in Your Organisation*, New York, Simon & Schuster, 1996.
11. Tristram Hunt, 'Stockholm Syndrome', *Guardian* 5 July 2008, p. 24.

Chapter 4
The Emergence of Civil Society: Restoring Fences

1. Naomi Klein, *Fences and Windows: Dispatches from the Front Lines of the Globalization Debate*, London, Flamingo, 2002, p. xix.
2. Nicanor Perlas, *Shaping Globalisation: Civil Society, Cultural Power, and Threefolding*, Quezon City, Philippines, Center for Alternative Development Initiatives, 2000, p. 41.
3. James Carroll, 'A Blind Eye on Soldiers' Suicides', *International Herald Tribune*, 5–6 July 2008, p. 5.
4. See David C. Korten, *Creating a Post-Corporate World*, twentieth annual E. F. Schumacher Lectures, October 2001, Great Barrington, MA, USA.
5. David Korten, quoted in Perlas, *Shaping Globalisation*, p. 22.
6. Barack Obama, *The Audacity of Hope*, Edinburgh, Canongate, 2007.

Chapter 5
Capturing the State

1. Abraham Lincoln, 21 November 1864, letter to Col. Williams F. Ekins: 'I see in the near future a crisis approaching that unnerves me and causes me to tremble for the safety of my country … corporations have been enthroned and an era of corruption in high places will follow.'
2. Mark Curtis, 'It's Thriving but Lethal', *Guardian*, 22 May 2007; see www.markcurtis.info. Also see www.caat.org.uk for UK arms subsidies.
3. *The Economist*, 29 January 2000.
4. George Monbiot, *The Captive State: The Corporate Takeover of Britain*, London, Macmillan, 2000.

5. Monbiot, *Captive State*, pp. 7, 14, quotations from Peter Mandelson, speech to CBI, 2 November 1997 and Tony Blair, speech to CBI, 11 November 1997.
6. L. Elliott and D. Atkinson, *The Gods That Failed*, London, Vintage, 2009, pp. 21–22.
7. *The Times.* See *Railrider*, June 2007.
8. See *Cadillac Desert* and the film *Chinatown*, starring Jack Nicholson.
9. See Dan Milmo, 'Tube Contractor Pins Hopes on Review as Overshoot Hits £1b', *Guardian*, 23 May 2007, for an example of the complications caused by a mixture of privatisation and PFI. The Treasury (i.e. Gordon Brown) forced TfL into a £17 billion PFI contract with Metronet, owned by W.S. Atkins, Bombardier, EDF Energy and Thames Water, and now it will take up to a year to arbitrate on the £1 billion overspend.
10. Tom Brown, letter to the *Guardian*, 12 February 2008.
11. Dan Milmo, 'Brown's Tube Policy', *Guardian*, 7 February 2008.
12. Duncan Campbell, 'UK Accused of Using Aid to Promote Privatisation', *Guardian*, 27 September 2007.
13. George Monbiot, 'A Scandal of Secrecy and Profligacy', *Guardian*, 28 December 2007.
14. Monbiot, *Captive State*, p. 56.
15. Martin Wainwright and Polly Curtis, 'Future Schools, Present Problems', *Guardian*, 23 January 2007.
16. George Monbiot, 'A Roaring Failure', *Guardian*, 30 November 2004.
17. Monbiot, ibid., p. 81.
18. Monbiot, ibid., p. 91.
19. Monbiot, ibid., p. 92.
20. Simon Jenkins, 'The Tesco Clauses Betray Big Business's Grip over Labour', *Guardian*, 23 May 2007.
21. Joel Bakan, *The Corporation*, London, Constable, 2004, p. 25.
22. David C. Korten, *Creating a Post-Corporate World*, twentieth Annual Schumacher Lectures, Salisbury, Connecticut, October 2000.
23. Monbiot, *Captive State*, pp. 208–24, 'The Fat Cats Directory'.
24. See David Leigh and Rob Evans, 'Scale of Pressure', *Guardian*, 23 January 2007, p. 1; letters to the *Guardian*, 23 January 2007; David Leigh and Rob Evans, 'Secret £1b Deal to Insure Saudi Arms Contract', *Guardian*, 14 December 2004; and *CAAT News*, February–March 2007.
25. Peter Wilby, 'Big Health Flexes its Lobbying Muscles' *Guardian*, 14 August 2009
26. Greg Palast, *The Best Democracy Money Can Buy*, London, Robinson, 2003.
27. David Craig and Richard Brooks, *Plundering the Public Sector*, London, Constable, 2006, pp. 252–54.
28. Palast, *Best Democracy*, pp. 296–309.
29. David Hencke and Robert Booth, 'Tycoons and Big Firms Fund Tory Push for Power', *Guardian*, 5 July 2008, p. 17.

Chapter 6
Capturing Culture

1. Gore Vidal, *The Decline and Fall of the American Empire*, Tucson, AZ, Odonian Press, 1992.
2. Letter, 4 August 1822, to W. T. Barry, in *The Writings of James Madison*, 9 vols, ed. Gaillard Hunt, New York, G. P. Putnam's Sons, 1900–10, vol. I, ch. 18, document 35.
3. See also Yehuda Tagar, *Humanising the Workplace*, Persephone Institute, South Africa, 2003.
4. Rory Carroll, *Guardian*, 4 September 2007, p. 16.
5. See www.blackthorn.org.uk.
6. See also Tagar, *Humanising the Workplace*.
7. Letter, 4 August 1822, to W. T. Barry, in *The Writings of James Madison*.

8. Lance Price, 'Rupert Murdoch is Effectively a Member of Blair's Cabinet', *Guardian*, 1 July 2006, p. 32.
9. Nick Davies, 'Flat Earth News', *Guardian*, 4 February 2008.
10. From a News International advertisement on its acquisition of the *Wall Street Journal*, published in the *Guardian*, 14 December 2007.
11. Edward S. Herman and Noam Chomsky, *Manufacturing Consent: The Political Economy of the Mass Media*, New York, Pantheon Books, 1988, p. 298, quoted by D. Kellner, *Television and the Crisis of Democracy*, San Francisco, Westview Press, 1990.
12. See Greg Palast, *The Best Democracy Money Can Buy*, London, Robinson, 2003, pp. 333–69.
13. See Sheldon Rampton and John Stauber, *Weapons of Mass Deception*, London, Constable, 2003, pp. 72–5.
14. See Peter A. Hall, 'Media Accuracy is Vital', *Guardian*, 17 January 2004.
15. Owen Bowcott, Matt Wells, Maggie Brown and John Plunkett, 'BBC in Crisis', *Guardian*, 30 January 2004, p. 4.
16. Richard Lambert, 'The Path Back to Trust', *Guardian Media*, 10 January 2005, p. 4.
17. Allyson M. Pollock, *NHS plc*, London, Verso, 2005, p. 18.
18. *Guardian*, 17 April 2002.
19. Pollock, *NHS plc*, p. 200.
20. Ibid., p. 204.
21. Ibid., pp. 214–15.
22. Ibid., p. 220.
23. See the National Children's Bureau, Institute for Education and the Family and Parenting Institute report, *Reducing Inequalities: Realising the Talents of All*, 3 September 2007.
24. The commercialisation of childhood is dealt with in my book *Set Free Childhood*, Stroud, Hawthorn Press, 2003, and Sue Palmer's *Toxic Childhood: How the Modern World Is Damaging Our Children and What We Can Do About It*, London, Orion, 2006.
25. See also Zoë Williams, *The Commercialisation of Childhood*, London, Compass, 2006.
26. *Guardian*, 6 September 2007, p. 7.
27. From news release, 6 September 2007, University of Southampton.
28. Julian Borger, 'Industry That Stalks the US Corridors of Power', *Guardian*, 13 February 2001, p. 3.
29. N. Klein, *The Shock Doctrine*, London, Penguin Books, 2007, pp. 250–1.
30. S. W. B. Ewen and A. Pusztai, *Lancet*, 354 (1999), pp. 1353–4. Excerpted from 'A Submission from Dr Árpád Pusztai', online at www.freenetpages.co.uk/hp/a.pusztai/NewZealand/nz-arpad.htm - 14k.
31. Rob Evans, 'Whitehall Admits Puzhtai Was "Martyred"', *Guardian*, 22 June 2002.
32. See 'The State of the Commons, 2003/2004', online at www.friendsofthecommons.org.
33. Ibid., p. 18.
34. Ibid., p. 19.
35. Sholto Macpherson, *New Internationalist*, July 2005, p. 7.
36. Vidal, *Decline and Fall of the American Empire*, ibid

Chapter 7
Capitalism Unleashed: The Seizure of Common Wealth

1. The title is taken from Andrew Glyn, *Capitalism Unleashed*, Oxford, Oxford University Press, 2007.
2. Will Hutton, 'This Reckless Greed of the Few', *Observer*, 27 January 2008, p. 35.
3. George Monbiot, 'Governments Aren't Perfect, But It's the Libertarians Who Bleed Us Dry', *Guardian*, 23 October 2007.
4. Ibid.
5. A. Sampson, *Who Runs This Place?*, London, John Murray, 2004, pp. 279–83.

6. Quoted in David Harvey, *A Brief History of Neoliberalism*, Oxford, Oxford University Press, 2007, p. 20.
7. Ibid., p. 37.
8. See J. Bruges, *The Big Earth Book*, Bristol, Alastair Sawday Publishing, 2007, p. 95.
9. George Monbiot, 'How the Neoliberals Stitched Up the Wealth of Nations for Themselves', *Guardian*, 28 August 2007.
10. When Beuys says 'Kapital ist Geist' the literal translation, 'Capital is Spirit', doesn't help, but 'Capital is creative intelligence' is another, perhaps better rendering.
11. Harvey, *Brief History of Neoliberalism*, p. 156.
12. Bruges, *Big Earth Book*, p. 81.
13. Andrew Clark, 'Merrill Lynch', *Guardian*, 30 October 2007.
14. Harvey, *Brief History of Neoliberalism*, p. 161.
15. BBC News website, 29 January 2009.
16. Andrew Clark, *Guardian*, 27 January 2009.
17. Nicanor Perlas, *Shaping Globalisation: Civil Society, Cultural Power, and Threefolding*, Quezon City, Philippines, Center for Alternative Development Initiatives, 2000, pp. 64–5.
18. Harvey, *Brief History of Neoliberalism*, pp. 162–3.
19. N. Klein, *The Shock Doctrine: The Rise of Disaster Capitalism*, London, Allen Lane, 2007; L. Elliott, 'Is This the Big One?', *Guardian*, 3 January 2008.
20. Klein, *Shock Doctrine*, p. 224.
21. Bruges, *Big Earth Book*, p. 93.
22. Klein, *Shock Doctrine*, p. 359.
23. R. Norton Taylor, 'Britain and the Saudis Finally Sign £4.43bn Eurofighter Deal', *Guardian*, 18 September 2007, p. 10.
24. Felicity Lawrence and Ian Griffiths, 'Revealed: How Multinational Companies Avoid the Taxman', *Guardian*, 6 November 2007.
25. D. Hencke, 'Taxpayer May Have to Pay £170bn for PFI Schemes, Says Treasury', *Guardian*, 27 November 2007, p. 2.
26. See Glyn, *Capitalism Unleashed*, p. 192.
27. L. Elliott and D. Atkinson, *The Gods That Failed*, London, Vintage, 2009, p. 4.

Part 3
1. See Robert Karp, 'Toward an Associative Economy in the Sustainable Food and Farming Movement', *Biodynamics*, Spring 2008, pp. 24–30.

Chapter 8
Transforming Capitalism: Stewarding Capital for Individual Enterprise and Common Good

1. See Robert Karp, 'Toward an Associative Economy in the Sustainable Food and Farming Movement', *Biodynamics*, Spring 2008, pp. 24–30.
2. John Ruskin, *Unto This Last*, 1862.
3. K. Polanyi, *The Great Transformation*, Boston, Beacon Press, 1954, p. 73.
4. Andrew Clark, 'There Are the Rich and the Very Rich', *Guardian*, 12 June 2007.
5. 'How to Make a Quick £740m', *Guardian*, 26 June 2007.
6. Polly Toynbee, 'This Wild West Capitalism is Born of Servility to the City', *Guardian*, 5 June 2007.
7. John Lanchester, 'It's Finished', *London Review of Books*, 28 May 2009, p. 15.
8. See Steven Usher's article on 'Rudolf Steiner's Threefold Social Order', online at www.rudolfsteinerweb.com.
9. David Hencke, 'QinetiQ Sale Made £107m for Top Civil Servants', *Guardian*, 23 November 2007, p. 6.

10. 'About the Co-op', online at www.cooponline.coop.
11. See David Rodgers, *New Mutualism: The Third Estate*, London, The Co-operative Party, 1999.
12. J. K. Galbraith, *Money: Whence It Came, Where It Went*, Boston, Houghton Miflin, 1967.
13. J. Bruges, *The Big Earth Book*, Bristol, Alastair Sawday Publishing, 2007, pp. 78–9.
14. J. Robertson, The Need for Monetary Reform, 2006, quoted by Bruges, *The Big Earth Book*, p. 83.
15. See Andrew Glyn, *Capitalism Unleashed*, Oxford, Oxford University Press, 2007, pp. 19–20, who quotes Pontusson 1992: 192; 1987: 13.
16. See 'Solidarity Fund', *World of Work*, no. 50, March 2004, available online at www.Caledonia.org.uk, and www.fondsftq.com/internetfonds.nsf/Anglais.
17. Larry Elliott, 'Forgotten Brainchild that could Transform the Banking Casino', *Guardian*, 27 August 2009; Philip Inman, 'City Watchdog Backs Tax on 'Socially Useless Banks' ', *Guardian*, 27 August 2009.
18. See Bruges, *The Big Earth Book*, pp. 38–41, for a more thorough treatment of cap and share.
19. Alison Benjamin, 'Money Well Lent', *Guardian*, 3 June 2009.

Chapter 9
Citizen's Income: Social Inclusion and Common Wealth for All

1. R. Wilkinson, *Unhealthy Societies*, London, Routledge, 1996.
2. R. Steiner, *Towards Social Renewal*, trans. Matthew Barton, London, Rudolf Steiner Press, 1999, p. 36.
3. See M. Weissbord, *Productive Workplaces*, San Francisco, Berret Kohler, and R. Rehm, *People in Charge*, Stroud, Hawthorn Press, 2000.
4. See J. Bruges, *The Big Earth Book*, Bristol, Alastair Sawday Publishing, 2007, pp. 110–11.
5. See Goetz Werner, online at www. unternimm-die-zukunft.de.
6. David Hencke, 'Benefit Fraud Costs the Government £2.5bn', *Guardian*, 25 July 2007.
7. Citizen's Income leaflet, online at www.citizensincome.org.
8. See www.cori.ie.
9. J. Robertson, 'Resource Taxes and Green Dividends: A Combined Package?', 1998, online at www.jamesrobertson.com/book/sharingourcommonheritage.pdf, quoted in M. Scott Cato, *Green Economics: An Introduction to Theory, Policy and Practice*, London, Earthscan, 2008.

Chapter 10
Land for People, Homes and Communities

1. These are operated by housing associations and broadly involve part ownership and part rent or, in the case of Homebuy, part ownership and a pro rata division of the proceeds of sale. They are available for those unable to access full ownership on the open market, but with sufficient income to support a mortgage in respect of a percentage of the purchase price.
2. The government's stated aim was to raise homeownership from 72 per cent of the population to 80 per cent. The building of new social housing for rent was restricted to 17,300 homes a year over the last ten years. At the same time, about half a million council houses have been sold off under right to buy legislation during this time, at an average of 48,300 sales a year. In July 2007, Yvette Cooper, then Minister for Housing, announced the intention to build 3 million homes by 2020. But even if built at a rate of 270,000 houses a year, this will only slow down the rate at which the affordability gap is growing.

3. BBC World Service, 'World Today News', 29 July 2008.
4. J. Cowley, 'Property Scandal', *New Statesman*, 20 September 2004.
5. Sam Brittan, *The Financial Times*, 9 December 2005.
6. Molly Scott Cato, *Green Economics: An Introduction to Theory, Policy and Practice*, London, Earthscan, 2008, pp. 191–3.
7. J. Jones, 'Land Value', Labour Land Campaign, 2008, online at www.labourland.org.
8. For more information on LVT, see James Bruges, *The Big Earth Book*, Bristol, Alastair Sawday Publishing, 2007, pp. 90 –1; M. Scott Cato and M. Kennett (eds), *Green Economics: Beyond Supply and Demand to Meeting People's Needs*, Aberystwyth, Green Audit, 1999, in particular the article by Richard Bramhall, 'Land Value Taxation', pp. 87–96.
9. K. Cahill, *Who Owns Britain*, Edinburgh, Canongate, 2001.
10. However, LVT also needs to move with the times. The current challenge of making the transition to a low carbon economy has prompted land use planner Steven Hill to link carbon reduction with land use and propose a variation of land tax based on carbon. So he suggests two linked ways of doing this: 'Firstly set up Carbon Trading Accounts for every citizen, every business, every public body, civil society organisation, and level of government. Secondly implement cascading Land Use Management Plan [LUMP], from National, to Personal, for every owner and occupier of land ... which defines the carbon carrying capacity of every piece of land and the annual rate at which the production of carbon on that land had to be reduced.'
    He considers that 'the link between Carbon Trading and Land is essential because: it puts all types of land on a similar footing with a carbon value; it stops Carbon Credits becoming just another commodity for speculators, and most importantly ... it will reduce the tendency to speculate in land, one of the principal causes and effects of the Great Banking and Housing Collapse of 2007–2008.' Steven Hill, RIBA Future Fair: 'Third Time Lucky', talk on 2 June 2009.
11. See Andy Wightman and James Perman, *Common Good Land in Scotland*, Caledonia Centre for Social Development, Commonweal Working Paper No.5, November 2005.
12. See www.iceclt.org – a national community development organisation promoting economic justice through Community Land Trusts. See www.smallisbeautiful.org for Bob Swann's story.
13. I took the 'land for people' motto from one of Churchill's 1910 election speeches where he condemned land monopolies.
14. See Maria Brenton, 'The Cohousing approach to 'Lifetime Neighbourhoods'', Factsheet no. 29, Housing Improvement and Learning Network CSIP Networks, www.networks. csip.org.uk/housing
15. See 'Capturing Value for Rural Communities', CLT leaflet, CFS, University of Salford, 2005.
16. 'There are still debates to be had as to which is the most effective way of delivering permanently affordable housing, but whichever method is used, CLTs must surely aspire to deliver permanently affordable units. Shared equity/equity mortgage does not do that in the long term. Consider the following two diferent methods of delivering affordable units by sale – equity mortgage and declaration of trust. Equity mortgage is intended for those sites where retaining the specific units in perpetuity is not a major driver, but re-cycling the equity released into other affordable units is considered an acceptable alternative. I do have concerns that, in a time of rising house prices (which will surely return eventually), there may not be enough equity released from sold units to buy others, or that there will not be suitable other houses to buy or build in the same locality. However, it seems that, in a time where credit is in such short supply, shared equity/equity mortgage is a compromise solution to get schemes up and running. The declaration of trust lease is intended to provide units which are retained as affordable in perpetuity and does not allow the leaseholder or his/her lender to acquire the outright interest in the property. The dilemma we have is that lenders seem more likely to lend more freely on shared equity rather than declaration of trust'. Ian Moran, Cobbetts LLP

17. See David Rodgers, *New Foundations: Unlocking the Potential for Affordable Homes*, London, the Co-operative Party, January 2009, and also see www.gloucestershirelandforpeople. coop.
18. See Stephen Hill, ibid.
19. Peter Hetherington, 'Does Whitehall Really Trust Us on Housing?', *Guardian*, 24 October 2007.
20. See www.gloucestershirelandforpeople.coop, 'Briefing Paper on Mutual Home Ownership'.
21. Matrix Housing Partnership, *Forging Futures: A Modernisation Agenda for 21st Century Housing, Consumers and Communities*, 2006, p. 60. See www.rch.coop for more information on Redditch Co-operative Homes.
22. See Stephen Hill, Housing Forum submission to the All-Party Urban Development Group, May 2009, 'New Approaches to Investment in Housing and Placeshaping'; Stephen Hill, 'CLTs: Commentary on Emerging HCA Policy Position', draft paper, 27 May 2009.
23. See www.communitylandtrust.org.uk for more information.

Chapter 11
Freeing Education

1. See Jack Grimston, 'The Three Rs', *Sunday Times*, 9 December 2007.
2. See Polly Curtis, 'Great Teachers Don't Write Any Child Off', *Guardian*, 21 October 2008.
3. Gordon Brown, 'We'll Use Our Schools to Break Down Class Barriers', *Observer*, 10 February 2008.
4. There is also the contradiction of the new Hereford 3–16 years Steiner Academy not being bound by EYFS law. Educators can draw on EYFS, as they think appropriate.
5. See www.allianceforchildhood.org.uk.
6. 'The Race Is Not Always to the Richest', *The Economist*, 8 December 2007.
7. A. Cooper, 'Anxiety, Learning and Audit Culture', seminar paper given at Roehampton University in their Policy Forum Series 'Childhood: Therapeutic and Educational Perspectives', Research Centre for Therapeutic Education, 18 October 2007.
8. Ibid.
9. P. Hyman, *1 Out of 10: From Downing Street Vision to Classroom Reality*, London, Vintage, 2005, quoted by Andrew Cooper.
10. Richard House, 'Steiner Early Years Practice and the New Foundation Stage Legislation', unpublished paper, Roehampton University, p. 1.
11. Ted Wragg, 'The Greatest Foe of Ton Zoffis', *Guardian*, 15 November 2005.
12. Richard Pring, 'Role of the State in Education', in F. Carnie, M. Large and M. Tasker, *Freeing Education*, Stroud, Hawthorn Press, 1996.
13. Ibid., p. 7.
14. See Warwick Mansell, 'How Children Became Customers', *Guardian*, 9 June 2009, reviewing the Nuffield report, *Education for All: The Future of Education and Training for 14–19-Year-Olds*, published by Routledge, 2009. For details see www.routledge.com.
15. Dr Michael Crawford, 'Women Will Eliminate Poverty in the UK', online at www.north. londonmet.ac.uk/ibchn.
16. R. House, 'Schooling, the State, and Children's Psychological Well-Being: A Psychosocial Critique', *Journal of Psychosocial Research*, 2, 2 (2007), pp. 49–62.
17. Woods P, Ashley M, Woods G: *Steiner Schools in England*. www.dfes.gov.uk/research/ data/uploadfiles/RR645.pdf. Department for Education and Skills and University of the West of England, Research Report RR645, June 2005.
18. See Mary Tasker, *Human Scale Education: History, Values and Practice*, Bath, HSE, 2008.
19. Ibid.

20. Mike Davies, ibid., p. 8.
21. 'School-within-schools is an attempt at rescuing young people from the complex and frequently alienating experiences that many urban schools and academies have become in their relentless adherence to nineteenth century forms of organisation and control. These are places where obsolete knowledge is poured into pupils, where the lives they lead are never the focus of the curriculum, where the style of learning is too frequently pre-prepared and preset, ready to be delivered. Schools within schools … radically recast the nature of learning and being in the new century.' Mike Davies, founding principal, Bishops Park College.
22. Some Norwegian educators look forward to schools without walls, realising how much schools have become divorced from community life and that the walls now need to come down.
23. See J. Bennett, *Starting Strong*, Paris, OECD, 2006, and his paper, 'Improving Early Childhood Education and Care Systems in Europe', Brussels, Alliance for Childhood, 20 September 2007.
24. See Hilary Hodgson, 'Transformation: Notes on the Educational Landscape', unpublished paper.

Chapter 12
Common Wealth: Leading from the Social Future As It Emerges

1. Yukio Hatoyama, 'A New Path for Japan', *The New York Times*, August 27, 2009.
2. O. Scharmer, *Theory U: Leading from the Future as It Emerges*, Boston, Society for Organizational Learning, 2007, p. 95.
3. S. E. Usher, 'Rudolf Steiner's Threefold Social Order', online at www.rudolfsteinerweb, p. 3.
4. See Polly Toynbee, 'Anger? What anger?', *Guardian*, 23 June 2009, p. 29, and Jill Treanor and Graeme Weardon, 'Meet Britain's Best Paid Public Servant', *Guardian*, 23 June 2009, p. 3.
5. John Lanchester, 'It's Finished', *London Review of Books*, 28 May 2009, p. 22.
6. Ibid.
7. See Jill Treanor, 'City Watchdog', *Guardian*, 24 June 2009, p. 1.
8. Paul Lewis, 'Caught on Film', *Guardian*, 22 June 2009, p. 1; see www.guardian.co.uk.
9. Peter Jenkins, 'This Gaping Hole', *Guardian*, 24 June 2009, p. 27.
10. Phillip Blond, 'Red Tory', in *Is the Future Conservative*, edited by Jon Cruddas MP and Jonathan Rutherford, published by *Soundings* in association with Compass and *Renewal*, available online as an e-book at www.compassonline.org.uk, accessed March 2009.
11. P. Senge, Otto Scharmer, J. Jaworski and B. S. Flowers, *Presence*, London, Nicholas Brearley, 2005.
12. See R. Tennyson, *Managing Partnerships: Tools for Mobilizing the Public Sector, Business and Civil Society as Partners in Development*, London, Prince of Wales Business Leaders' Forum, 1998.
13. Blond, 'Red Tory', in *Is the Future Conservative*, p. 7.
14. Paul Gallagher, 'Record Profit Water Firm Raises Prices', *Observer*, 21 June 2009.
15. See Stephen Hill, unpublished paper, RIBA Futures Fair, 2 June 2009.

Appendix 3

1. Ostrom, E. (1990) *Governing the Commons: the Evolution of Institutions for Collective Action*, New York: Cambridge University Press.
2. Bollier, D. (2002) *Silent Theft: the Private Plunder of our Common Wealth*, New York: Routledge.

Resources

Books

Barry, J. (1999) *Rethinking Green Politics: Nature, Virtue and Progress*, London: Sage

Bollier, D. (2002) *Silent Theft: The Private Plunder of our Common Wealth*, New York: Routledge

Bruges, J. (2008) *The Big Earth Book*, Bristol: Alastair Sawday

Cato, M.S. (2006) *Market, Schmarket*: Building the Post-Capitalist Economy, Gretton: New Clarion Press

Cato, M.S. (2009) *Green Economics*: *An Introduction to Theory, Policy and Practice*, London: Earthscan

Elliott, L., Atkinson, D. (2009) *The Gods that Failed*, London: Vintage

Galbraith, J. (1967) *Money: Whence it came, Where it Went*, Boston: Houghton Mifflin

Glyn, A. (2007) *Capitalism Unleashed*, Oxford: Oxford University Press

Harvey, D. (2007) *A Brief History of Neoliberalism*, Oxford: Oxford University Press

Hawken, P. (2007) *Blessed Unrest*, New York: Viking

Hawken, P. Lovins, L.H. (199) *Natural Capitalism: Creating the Next Industrial Revolution*, Snowmass, CO: Rocky Mountain Institute

Hines, C. (2000) *Localization: A Global Manifesto*, London: Earthscan

Korten, D. (2001) *Creating a Post Corporate World*, EF Schumacher Lecture: Great Barrington MA

Korten, D. (1995) *When Corporations Ruled the World*, San Francisco: Berrett Kohler

Korten, D. (1999) *The Post-Corporate World: Life after Capitalism*, San Francisco: Berrett-Kohler

Korten, D. (2009) *Agenda for a New Economy: from Phantom Wealth to Real Wealth*, San Francisco: Berret Kohler

Klein, N. (2007) *The Shock Doctrine*, London: Penguin

Large, J. (1997) *The War Next Door : Second Track Interventions in the War in Former Yugoslavia*, Stroud: Hawthorn

Large, M. (2003) *Set Free Childhood*, Stroud: Hawthorn

McIntosh, A. (2001) *Soil and Soul*: People versus Corporate Power, London: Aurum

Monbiot, G. (2000), *Captive State: The Corporate takeover of Britain*, London: Macmillan

Obama, B. (2007) *The Audacity of Hope*, Canongate: Edinburgh

Ostrom, E. (1990) *Governing the Commons: The Evolution of Institutions for Collective Action*, New York: Cambridge University Press

Palast, G. (2003) *The Best Democracy Money Can Buy*, London: Robinson

Perlas, N. (2000) *Shaping Globalisation: Civil Society, Cultural Power and Threefolding*, Philippines: CADI, Quezon City, Philippines

Polanyi, K. (1954) *The Great Transformation*, Boston: Beacon

Pollock, A.M. (2005) *NHS plc*, London: Verso

Pretty, J. *Agri-culture: Reconnecting People, Land and Nature*, London: Earthscan

Ransom, D., Baird, V., eds. (2009) *People First Economics*, Oxford: New Internationalist

Ray, P., Anderson, S.R. (2000) *The Cultural Creatives: How 50 Million People are Changing the World*, New York: Harmony

Rehm, R., Cebula, Ryan. F., Large, M. (2002) *Futures that Work*, Vancouver: New Society

Robertson, J. (1989) *Future Wealth: New Economics for the 21st century*, London: Cassell

Scharmer, O. (2007) *Theory U: Leading from the Future as it Emerges*, Boston: Society for Organisational Learning

Steiner, R. (1972) *The Social Future*, Spring Valley, New York: Anthroposophic Press

Steiner, R. (1980) *Threefolding: a Social Alternative*, translated and edited by Rudi Lissau, London: Rudolph Steiner Press

Steiner, R. (1999) *Towards Social Renewal*, trans. Matthew Barton, London: Rudolf Steiner Press

Tennyson, R., Wilde, L. (2000) *The Guiding Hand: Brokering Partnerships for Sustainable Development*, London: Prince of Wales Business Leaders Forum and the United Nations Staff College

Vidal, G. (1992) *The Decline and Fall of the American Empire*, Adonian: Tucson AZ

Wilkinson, R. *Unhealthy Societies*, London: Routledge

Wilkinson, R., Pickett, K. (2009) *The Spirit Level: Why More Equal Societies Almost Always do Better*, London: Penguin

Wodin, M., and Lucas, C. (2004) *Green Alternatives to Globalisation: A Manifesto*, London: Pluto

Websites

Alliance for Childhood: www. allianceforchildhood.org

Centre for Alternative Development Initiatives (CADI), Philippines, founded by Nicanor Perlas: www.cadi.ph

www.nicanor-perlas.com: Nicanor Perlas' website has many articles, speeches and details of his 2010 Philippines presidential candidacy

E. F. Schumacher Society: www.schumachersociety.org: useful for community land trusts, CSA, local currencies and much more

New Economics Foundation: www.neweconomics.org/gen, see *The Green New Deal*

New Internationalist Magazine, see www.newint.org

Molly Scott Cato blog on green economics: http://gaianeconomics.blogspot.com

Community Land Trusts: www.communitylandtrust.org.uk and www.caledonia.org.uk

Community Farm Land Trusts: www.stroudcommonwealth.org.uk and www.ford-hallfarm.org.uk

Co-housing: UK www.co-housin.org.uk; US www.cohousing.org

Global Commons Institute: www.gci.org.uk

Henry George Institute and land value tax: www.henrygeorge.org

Human Scale Education: www.hse.org.uk

James Robertson, author of *Transforming Economic Life* writes an informative, useful website: www.jamesrobertson.com

www.opendemocracy.com: UK based website with in depth analysis, articles and discussion of current events

Partnership building and cross-sectoral partnerships: www.thepartneringinitiative.org

Rudolf Steiner: www.rudolfsteinerweb.com

www.secrecyjurisdictions.com: How the offshore financial system undermines our democracy

www.taxjustice.net: How banks and the wealthy avoid tax and what to do about it

The Land is Ours: www.tlio.org.uk

Transition Towns: www.transitiontowns.org

Yes! for Building a Just and Sustainable World. Magazine and website on building sustainable economy and communities: www.YesMagazine.org

Threefolding: www.globenet3.org

Glossary of terms

Business-as-usual: the scenario that the economy can continue to grow in its current form, with technological innovation successfully tackling the environmental crisis.

Cap and share: the allocation of the right to produce CO_2 amongst the citizens of a state.

Carbon trading: system for exchanging the right to produce CO_2. Those reducing emissions more efficiently will be paid compensation.

CI or citizen's income: regular payments made to citizens of a state as a right.

Civil society: there are many contrasting definitions and no neat one: an overall term for cultural organisations, values and research-based advocacy organisations, voluntary and community organisations whose main activity is outside both business and the state. Civil society is both pluralist and self-organising, independent of the state and business. When civil society organisations/groups engage with business and/or the state to carve out cultural and personal autonomy, to build partnerships, to advocate for values or push back, 'the market' civil society can be seen as a zone of public associational life and activity for the common good. (The 'third sector' is a mix of both civil society organisations and social enterprise.)

CLT or Community Land Trust: a non-profit, open membership, democratically accountable body for holding land and property in trust for community benefit and individual initiative; or mutual land ownership by the community.

CSA (Community Supported Agriculture): ways of supporting farming through direct marketing, box schemes, consumer investment, consumer co-operatives and/or consumers guaranteeing farmers' incomes.

Commons: a shared resource like the air, water, land, culture or the financial system. 'Common resources are resources whose value is due to Nature and to the activities and demands of society as a whole and not to the efforts of individual people or organisations.' James Robertson.

Emergent theory of change: observe where positive change is happening so as to evaluate this, spread the learning and support the change, as opposed to top down imposed change that does not respect the context. 'Emergent' also means that the whole is more than the sum of its parts; new properties emerge – so an ice cube melts to produce water. 'Society' is a higher-level concept that emerges from the interaction of politics, economics and culture.

Globalisation: elite globalisation is where a few hundred billionaires own a large proportion of global wealth and income. Corporate globalisation is similar except that transnational corporations increasingly control global wealth, power and income.

Governance: The Governance Working Group of the International Institute of Administrative Sciences (IIAS), defines governance: 'Governance refers to the process whereby [different] elements in society wield power and authority, and influence and enact policies and decisions concerning public life, and economic and social development ... Governance is a broader notion than government, whose principal elements include the constitution, legislature, executive and judiciary.' (Source: Nicanor Perlas' website.) So governance is concerned with the interaction between politics, civil society and business.

ISEW (Index of Sustainable Economic Welfare): an alternative to GDP as a way of measuring economic activity and human well-being and the environment.

LVT: land value taxation.

Neo-liberal capitalism: an economic theory that relies on the central organising principle of the free market, or the 'invisible hand'. Or as John Maynard Keynes said, 'Capitalism is the extraordinary belief that the nastiest of men for the nastiest of motives will somehow work for the benefit of all.'

Peak oil: the concept that oil production will peak. The resulting decline of oil supply and the increasing demand for oil will have serious effects on economic activity and our way of life.

Social economy: the part of the economy that is socially or mutually owned, as with co-ops or building societies, and run as not-for-private-profit social enterprises, or run along associative fair trade principles outside 'the market'. Real markets, based on people trading needed goods and services, as with farmers' markets, are, of course, part of the social economy.

Structural Adjustment Programme (SAP): SAPs are imposed by the World Bank and IMF on developing countries as one of the conditions for obtaining loans. SAPs free the market, cut social services and education, reduce the power of the state to support the economy, and liberalise trade, investment and finance. Taxes are raised, and assets and state-run companies are privatised.

Threefold, tripolar, trisectoral: these are different ways of describing society as formed from the interaction of the economic, political and cultural systems. 'Trisectoral' partnerships, for example, are made up of business, civil society and government bodies from the three sectors, though 'trisectoral' is too superficial a term to get at the essence of economics, politics and culture. 'Tripolar' or 'three-fold' society, which *Common Wealth* uses interchangeably, describes society as emerging from the dynamic interaction of the economic, political and cultural systems.

Threefolding: the process whereby culture, politics and economics separate out as distinct systems, each with their own respective system principle of freedom, equality and mutuality or fraternity, and each with its particular task and optimal development conditions. The philosopher Rudolf Steiner first wrote about threefolding in 1918–24, and advocated this as an alternative to both the over-centralised German state, to the toxic nationalism of 'national self determination', to the domination of society by economics, and to communism.

Triple bottom line: accounts that measure the environmental and social as well as the financial results of a company or organisation.

Washington Consensus: this is used as shorthand for neo-liberal economic principles and policies, such as freeing or extending the market through deregulation and privatisation.

WTO (The World Trade Organisation): The WTO is a global structural adjustment programme or SAP, dominated by corporations and governments. Agreements are inflexible, with little respect paid to the environment and to culture conditions. So the WTO considers transparent, informative food labelling for consumers as a block to free trade for example. The *Codex Alimentarius* is a current plan for the WTO and other world bodies to control the global food supply in the interests of the large food corporations. (See: www.thenhf.com)

Index

'affluenza' 92, 126
agriculture *see* farming
Alexander, Professor Robin 221
Anderson, Sherry 22
arms industry 83–4
arts funding 151–3
asset locks 156, 159
Atkinson, Dan 138

Balls, Ed 215, 218
banking crisis: bailouts 170, 174, 240, 243; bonuses 131, 173, 174, 240, 243; reform 241
Baphumelele Educare Centre 19–20
Battle of Seattle (1999) 31, 96
BBC (British Broadcasting Corporation) 44, 101, 103–4, 106, 256
Bernanke, Ben (Head, US Federal Reserve) 130, 138
Beuys, Joseph 29, 93, 126
Beveridge, William 254–5
'Big Bang', City of London, 1986 129, 243
Blair, Tony: education policy 226; and free market 69; Iraq war 28, 62, 91, 143, 239; and PFI 72, 109; and Saudi arms contract 83
Blears, Hazel 27
boundaries, sectoral: 49–64; arms industry 83–4; business and arts 89; business and state 68, 69, 108; education and state 231; scientific research 111–14
Bremer, Paul 135
British Broadcasting Corporation *see* BBC
British Rail 71–2
Brooke, Heather 19, 90
Brown, Gordon: and Trident 26, 102; financial deregulation 120; increase of funding to IMF 240; lease of commons 71; and local planning 76; and PFI 72, 74, 137; and privatisation 73, 86; sale of public assets 70
Bruges, James 178
Buchanan, Professor James 84, 85
Building Schools for the Future 74
BUNGOs (business dominated non-governmental organisations) 51
business sector: competition 78; economic system 51; key elements 47; in tripolar society 37

Cadbury, George 195
Callaghan, James 224
capital: as commons 76, 150, 154, 167; mutualisation of 156–9
capitalism: crisis of 56, 123; disadvantages of 57, 146–7; potential for change 251–2
Capturing Value for Rural Communities Project 2003–5 196
carbon emissions 167–8
carbon trading 266n
Carnegie, Andrew 148
Carroll, James 53
'cash for peerages' 84
Cashes Green Hospital 205–8, 241
CCT (Commons Capital Trust) 154–6, 169
CES (Coalition of Essential Schools) (US) 229
charitable donations 148, 150–1, 195
Chartered Institute of Housing Survey 2009 184
Chicago School (of economic theory) 135, 136
children: commodisation of 109; effect of advertising on 110–11; obesity 110
Chomsky, Noam 101, 102
citizen engagement 27

Citizen's Income (CI) 172–81, 254; aims 177, 178; implementation 180; New Labour policy 177; worldwide 177
civil disobedience 27–8
civil rights movement 97
civil society: definition 53–4; expert power 51; as global movement 16–17; government opposition to 33; growth of 242; key elements 47; as power in society 11, 31, 58, 252; in tripolar society 37, 38, 55; types of 53
Civil Society Organisations (CSOs) 11, 31, 35, 51, 53
climate change see global warming
Clinton, Bill 85, 86
CLTs (Community Land Trusts) 193–200, 266n
Coalition of Essential Schools (CES) (US) 229
Coalition Provisional Authority (CPA) (US) 135, 136
Common Ground for Mutual Home Ownership 196
commons: disposal of 5; enclosure of 114–15, 119, 128–9; leasing of 71
Commons Capital Trust (CCT) 154–6, 169
commons resources 163–4
communication 249–51
community engagement 27
Community Land Trusts (CLTs) 193–200, 266n
'confiscatory deflation' 133
Conservative Party 7, 32, 87, 203, 245, 246
consumer choice 78
consumer debt 121, 160
Cooper, Professor Andrew 221, 228
co-operative movement 156, 158, 159, 247
Co-operative Party 246, 248
corporate power: domination of 10, 82–7; origins 80–1; use of cultural power, 90–3
corporate social responsibility (CSR) 168
Countryside and Rights of Way Act 2000 192
Convention on Modern Liberty 2009 245
CPA (Coalition Provisional Authority) (US) 135, 136
Craig, David 86
creative commons 115, 151, 152
creative culture 42
credit crunch 67, 120, 184, 243
crowd finance 200–1
CSOs see Civil Society Organisations
   CSR see corporate social responsibility movement)

CTL (Currency Transaction Levy) 167
cultural commons: defence of 114–15; freedom 95, 124, 126; power 90, 92, 93, 94, 96
cultural creatives 21, 22, 42
cultural freedom 51, 95, 98, 124
currency speculation 167
Currency Transaction Levy (CTL) 167

Darling, Alistair 34, 70, 75, 147
'debt trap' 132
Declaration of Trust lease 203
democracy 2, 3, 41
democracy movement, global 97
demonstrations, political 28, 31, 96, 119
Department for International Development 73
deregulation 80, 85, 120, 123, 129, 132
Development Land Tax Act 1976 188
Direct Grant Agreement 197
drug companies 112

Early Years Foundation Stage (EYES) 215, 217–18, 219
economic crisis, US 33, 119
economic system: collapse 2, 96, 242; deregulation 85
education 214–35; central control 225, 228; curriculum 218, 225; marketisation 6, 11, 215; politicisation 222, 223, 225; relaxation of centralised control, advantages of 217, 232, 234; standards 215
Education Act 1944 222, 223, 246
Education Reform Act 1988 225
electoral reform 253
Elliott, Larry 138
employment 2, 174, 176, 180, 244
enclosure, of land 128, 187, 192, 243
English Partnerships (EP) (now Homes and Communities Agency) 206
Enron 87, 129
environmental movement 97
environmental organisations 11, 29, 32, 53, 97, 168
EP see English Partnerships
equity mortgage 203, 207
ethical consumerism 26
ethical currency 167
Europe: education 216, 218, 226, 229, 233–4; healthcare 110; housing 209; standard of living 127
European Convention on Human Rights 97

'Every Child Matters' 215, 229
Export Credit Guarantee Department 83
EYFS *see* Early Years Foundation Stage

fair trade 41, 254
farming: 200–1; community ownership
    142; land ownership 13; subsidies 121
Federal Reserve Bank (US) 122
Financial Services Authority (FSA) 7, 86
food retailing 78–9
Fordhall Community Land Initiative 200
fractional reserve banking 160
Friedman, Milton 35, 134

Galbraith, John Kenneth 119, 160
GATS (General Agreement on Trade in
    Services) 107
GDP *see* gross domestic product
genetically modified (GM) food 29, 92, 112,
    113
gift aid 151, 153, 154
Glass–Stegall Act 1933 (US) 60, 80, 129
global warming 32, 38, 61, 92, 167
Glyn, Andrew 139
GM *see* genetically modified food
GONGOs (governmental NGOs) 51
Grameen Bank 168
Green New Deal 3, 32, 180, 181
Green Party 248
Greenspan, Alan 25, 85
gross domestic product (GDP) 125
Guardian (newspaper) 105

Harvey, Professor David 127, 129, 132
Hawken, Paul 16, 17, 95
HCA *see* Homes and Communities Agency
    205–8
healthcare: as commodity 34, 107; as
    commons 11; dentistry 136; internal
    market 106; PFI 75; US system 108
hedge funds 130
High Bickington Community Property Trust
    78
Hilary, John 73–4
Hill, Stephen 211, 266n
Homes and Communities Agency (HCA)
    (formerly English Partnerships)
housing 183–4; affordable 5, 10, 35, 202;
    associations 265n; brownfield sites
    189; co-operatives 209–11; grants 202;
    ownership 184, 265n
Housing and Regeneration Act 2008 193
Human Rights Act 62
Human Scale Education 217, 228–31

Hutton Inquiry (2003–4) 103, 104
Hutton, Will 118, 139
Hyde, Lewis 115, 152

IMF *see* International Monetary Fund
Index of Sustainable Economic Welfare
    (ISEW) 125
inherited wealth 153
Insel, Dr Thomas 53, 58
International Business Leaders' Forum 37
International Monetary Fund (IMF) 35, 240
Iraq War: demonstrations against 96;
    financial cost 143; Hutton Inquiry 91,
    103; post-war reconstruction 135
ISEW *see* Index of Sustainable Economic
    Welfare
Isle of Eigg community buy-out 201
Isle of Gigha Heritage Trust 199

James, Oliver 92, 125–6
jobseeker's allowance 244
John Lewis Partnership 148, 157
Jones, Digby 84
Joseph Rowntree Charitable Trust 148

Keynes, John Maynard 130
Klein, Naomi 125, 133, 134, 135, 136
Korten, Dr David 54, 56, 81

Lanchester, John 149, 241
Land Is Ours, The 36
land value tax (LVT) 183–92; benefits of
    189; opposition to 190–2; origins 185,
    187; worldwide 186
LEAs *see* local education authorities
leasehold enfranchisement legislation 202
Lievegoed, Dr Bernard 29
Linux 116, 152, 251
Livingstone, Ken 72, 73
Local Agenda 21 29
local education authorities (LEAs) 223
Lovins, Amory 17
Lovins, Hunter 17
LVT *see* Land Value Tax

Maathai, Professor Wangari 17
Major, John 71, 86
Mandela, Nelson 18
Mandelson, Peter 87, 107, 147, 244
Maquarie Bank 122
market democracy 84
marketisation, 241
media: concentration of ownership 93, 95,
    99, 103, 105; corporate control of 89, 98,

101, 102–4, 125, 245; freedom 102, 104, 256; regulation of 99
Metronet 72–3
MHOS *see* Mutual Home Ownership Society
Microsoft 116
military budget 102
Ministry of Education 223
Mission Musica 94
Monbiot, George 68, 74, 75, 82, 121, 126
monetary reform proposals 161
Monsanto 114, 128
Mont Pelerin Society 123, 124
MPs' expenses 19–20, 29, 173, 239, 244
Multilateral Agreement on Investment 92
Murdoch, Rupert 33, 68, 99, 100, 103
Mutual Home Ownership Society (MHOS) 196, 203, 204, 209

Nash, John 85
national curriculum 225, 229
national debt 3, 119
National Health Service (NHS): BMA view 34; internal market 86; marketisation 6, 86, 106, 107; performance targets 86; and PFI, 75, 106–9S
National Lottery 151
National Trust 195
nationalisation 119, 246
NEETs (Not in Education, Employment or Training) 225
neo-liberal capitalism: for benefit of corporations 125; commoditisation 145; ethos 139–41; instability 120; worldwide 122, 134
Network Rail 72
New Deal (US) 1932 80, 85, 88
New Economics Foundation 196
New Health Network 108
New Labour: modernization 243–4; party of business 69; privatisation of health 107–9; radicalism 86
News Corporation 68
News International 87, 99, 101, 105
NGOs (non–governmental organisations) 51, 54
NHS *see* National Health Service
Niskanen, William 81
Northern Rock 120, 121, 129, 243
NPI Institute for Organisational Development 29
Nuffield 14–19 Review 226

Obama, Barack 31, 58, 83
Ofsted 218, 222, 225

O'Neill, Onora 104
Open EYE Campaign 218, 219–20
Open Spaces Society 194

Palast, Greg 87, 102
Partnering Initiative, The 269
Paulson, Hank 33
peace movement 97
people's investment funds 164–6
Perlas, Nicanor 52, 58, 132, 133
PFI *see* private Finance Initiatives
Pickett, Professor Kate 258
planning system 76–8, 137
Plowden Report (1967) 224
plutocracy 64, 69
Polanyi, Karl 124, 145, 146
political system 31, 41, 51 , 62, 66, 69
Pollock, Professor Allyson 106, 108, 109
Post Office 34
PowerGen 87
Power Inquiry (2006) 252
Prince of Wales Business Leaders Forum 251
Pring, Professor Richard 226
prison system 34, 42, 75, 255
private equity firms 147
private finance initiative (PFI) 69, 72 , 74–6, 137, 240
privatisation of public services 35, 70–4 , 122
public capital equity trust 148
public capital investment 159–61
public utilities 5, 10, 35, 71, 73, 121–2
Pusztai, Dr Árpád 113, 114

QinetiQ 154
Qualifications and Curriculum Authority 218
quantitative easing 162, 163–4, 252

Railtrack 72
Ray, Paul 22
RBS *see* Royal Bank of Scotland
recession 35, 118, 173
Redditch Co-operative Homes 210–11
'reflexivity' 24, 98, 99
restricted resale price 202
'revolving doors' 67, 82–3, 107, 111
Ridley, Dr Matthew 120, 121, 125
Robertson, James 5, 160, 161, 181
Roddick, Dame Anita 26
Roosevelt, Theodore 67
Rowntree, Joseph 195
Royal Bank of Scotland 2, 119

Royal Mail 34, 244
Russia 134–5, 146

Sampson, Anthony 68
Sandell, Professor Michael 2, 6, 241
SAPS *see* structural adjustment policies
SATs *see* Standard Assessment Tests
Scharmer, Dr Otto 237, 250
school league tables 86, 226
schools-within-schools *see* Human Scale
    Education
scientific research 111–6
Scott Bader Commonwealth, The 148, 158
Scott Cato, Molly 178
Scottish Office Agriculture, Environment
    and Fisheries Department (SOAEFD) 113
securitisation of risk 130
Sen, Professor Amartya 3
separation of powers 12, 49, 62, 67; in US
    43–4, 64
Serious Fraud Office 83
'shadow economy' 130
Skoll, Jeff 169
Smith, Adam 35, 185, 240
Social Housing Grant 197
social inequality 125, 131–2, 144, 147,
    173–4
social mobility 86
social movements 96–7
social responsibility 24
Soros, George 24, 166
stakeholder governance 170
Standard Assessment Tests (SATs) 225, 229
state sector 47
Steiner, Rudolf 22, 238, 240; idea of
    community, 179; motivating forces,
    175–6
Stiglitz, Professor Joseph 133, 134, 135, 257
Stonesfield Community Trust 197, 198
strategic planning frameworks 38
Stroud: Common Wealth 162; Community
    Asset Reinvestment Fund (SCARF) 165;
    Community Farm 253; co-op allotments
    4; Maternity Hospital 77; Performing Arts
    Centre (SPACE) 43; UP2US 5
structural adjustment policies (SAPS) 132,
    133
sub-prime debt 25, 129, 130, 183
supermarkets 78–9
Sure Start 110, 147

surveillance society 3, 243
sustainable development 11, 29, 37, 38,
    58

takeovers 148, 149–50
tax 136–7
tax avoidance 70, 137, 147, 174, 191
Tennyson, Ros 36
Tesco 79, 84, 87
Thatcher, Margaret 70, 122
The Land Is Ours 36
theocracy 64, 237–8
third sector *see* civil society
Tobin, Dr James 167
transition movement 3, 33, 251, 256
transport 71, 72, 74, 254
tripolar society: 31–47; comparison with
    capitalism 239–41; importance of
    boundaries 60–2; dialogue 249–51;
    system interface 52, 59
Turner, Adair 167, 242

UK Economic and Social Research Council
    116
UNESCO Survey Global Education Digest
    2006 92
US constitution 44, 64

Volcker, Paul 122, 132
voluntary sector *see* civil society
von Hayek, Friedrich 33, 123

Waldorf Approach 228
War on Want 73
wealth redistribution 126–7, 133, 134,
    136–8
Wilkinson, Professor Richard 174, 258
Williamson, Marianne 18
women's movement 96–7
Wood Report 2004, 228
Woodhead, Chris 223, 225
Work Foundation 118
Workfare 244
workplace democracy 176
World Social Forums 28
WTO (World Trade Organisation) 31, 81,
    88, 92, 96, 133
Wriston, Walter CEO Citibank/Citicorp 85

Zinn, Howard 27–8

OTHER BOOKS FROM HAWTHORN PRESS
Social Ecology, Organisations and Change

••

Confronting Conflict
A toolkit for handling conflict
Friedrich Glasl

Conflict costs! When tensions and differences are ignored they grow into conflicts, injuring relationships and organisations. So, how can we confront conflict successfully?

Dr Friedrich Glasl has worked with conflict resolution in companies, schools and communities for over 30 years, earning him and his techniques enormous respect. *Confronting Conflict* is authoritative and up to date, containing new examples, exercises, theory and techniques.

You can start by assessing the symptoms and causes of conflict, and ask, 'Am I fanning the flames?' And then consider, 'How can I behave constructively rather than attack or avoid others?'

Here are tools to:

• Analyse the conflict symptoms
• Identify the types, causes of conflict, and if it is hot or cold
• See how personal chemistry, structures or environment influence the conflict
• Understand how temperaments affect conflicts and what you can do
• Acknowledge when you have a conflict, understand conflict escalation, how to lessen conflict through changing behaviour, attitudes and perceptions
• Practice developing considerate confrontation, seizing golden moments, strengthening empathy and much, much more

Confronting Conflict will be useful to managers, facilitators, management lecturers and professionals such as teachers and community workers, mediators, and workers in dispute resolution.

978-1-869890-71-1; 192pp; 216 × 138mm; pb; £14.99

••

Enterprise of the Future
Friedrich Glasl

This handy book describes how companies develop through the pioneer, differentiated, integrated and associative phases. This map of the enterprise of the future helps leaders work with stakeholders in the whole value-creating stream. This leads to an associative economy formed from 'shared destiny' relationships with staff, customers, suppliers, the community, shareholders and the planet.

The 'U' procedure is used to develop associative enterprises. Moral intuition is essential for building associative enterprises on the basis of shared values. Professor Friedrich Glasl, an international acclaimed conflict analyst and OD practitioner, argues that there are no text book solutions any more. Organisational solutions have to be lived into and not prescribed. This profoundly challenging book will help business leaders in making the enormous transition to working together in the kind of associative economy that helps build common wealth.

The Foreword is by Professor Dan Jones, a pioneer of lean production and lean service organisations.

978-1-869890-79-7; 128pp; 216 × 138mm; pb; £10.99

....

Futures that Work
Using Search Conferences to revitalize companies, communities and organizations
Robert Rehm, Nancy Cebula, Fran Ryan and Martin Large

'This time-tested approach capitalises on the tremendous power of the human spirit to create innovative plans. It is a treasure trove of practical experiences and easy to understand principles for planning success. I highly recommend this relevant book.'

Tom Devane

Futures That Work is all about the search conference – a practical way to build communities of people who want to make positive change happen for their company, organisation or community. The result is engagement, learning and energy for realising sustainable solutions.

This practical guide for using search conferences represents the latest development of this successful method, including the process, the principles underlying the method, how to plan for a search conference, design tips and compelling stories from searches done around the world.

Robert Rehm and Nancy Cebula enable organisations and communities to become more effective through the participation of their people. They live in Boulder, Colorado. Robert is the author of *People in Charge: Creating Self Managing Workplaces*. Fran Ryan and Martin Large use search conferences for enabling change in the non-profit, government and private sectors.

'Futures that Work restores one's faith in the collective capacity of people – regardless of position, status, age, race, or gender – to come together and create positive futures for themselves and their systems. The many cases reflect true democracy at work, and my fondest wish is that leaders of troubled organisations and nations will read and heed the lessons of this book.'

Barry Oshry, author, *Seeing Systems*

978-1903458-24-2; 224pp; 229 × 184mm; pb; £15

....

Money for a Better World
Rudolf Mees

Money re-works our approach to handling money and finance on a human scale. Topics covered include:
• Purchase, loan and gift money
• Consumer – producer associations
• Borrowing and saving communities
• Giving, interest and trust

Rudolf Mees was a Dutch Banker and a pioneer of the ethical finance movement that led to the founding of Triodos.

978-1-869890-26-1; 64pp; 216 × 138mm; pb; £5.99

....

People in Charge
Creating self managing workplaces using participative design
Robert Rehm
A step-by-step guide to designing self managing workplaces

'Frankly, I find most books on this subject useless. This one is different. It is filled with practical theories, and business related examples, that I can use on a daily basis.'
Kevin Purcell, Director of Organisation Consulting, Microsoft Corporation

Powerful and practical, *People in Charge* enables companies and organisations to create more productive workplaces and better results. Here are the tools for creating self-managing workplaces using Participative Design. The concepts, do-it-yourself guide and helpful examples show how people can re-design their work. The result is a more productive workplace full of energy, learning, quality and pride. And people in charge of their work.

People in Charge is a powerful but simple way of creating the conditions for good work. You can analyse your workplace, asking; 'Is there elbow room for decisions? Learning? Mutual support and respect? Meaningfulness? A desirable future?' Then you can take stock of the current structure and workflow, re-designing these to be self-managing. Finally, each team agrees goals, resources, ground rules, training needs, co-ordination and career paths – checking if their plan improves working conditions.

'Far and away the most readable and informative book on democracy and participation in the workplace. Rehm describes how to design processes based on actionable principles that can, in fact, transform a system. People in Charge *offers hope and possibility to anyone who seeks to fully utilise the creative potential of the people in an organisation. It's a gift.'*
Sandra Janoff, PhD, co-author, *Future Search*

Robert Rehm has a background in organisation development, socio-technical systems and fast cycle re-design. He specialises in participative planning, design and learning.

978-1-869890-87-2; 288pp; 243 × 189mm; pb; £14.99

....

Peace Journalism
Jake Lynch and Annabel McGoldrick

Peace Journalism explains how most coverage of conflict unwittingly fuels further violence, and proposes workable options to give peace a chance. Here are:

• Topical case studies including Iraq and 'the war on terrorism' supported by theory, analysis, archive material and photographs
• A comparison of War Journalism and Peace Journalism
• How the reporting of war, violence and terror can be made more accurate and more useful
• Practical tools and exercises for analysing and reporting the most important war stories of our time

Professional journalists Jake Lynch and Annabel McGoldrick draw on 30 years' experience reporting for the BBC, ITV, Sky News, the *London Independent* and ABC Australia. They have taught Peace Journalism in departments of Journalism and Peace Studies at several universities. Jake is Director of the Centre for Peace and Conflict Studies at The University of Sydney.

'Wholly refreshing – It is one of the strengths of this book that a range of problems are raised, from the choice of value-laden words and phrases to broader issues about the underlying ideology of the news agenda, the mind-set of journalists working to that agenda and the insidious nature of propaganda. Most importantly, it offers journalists a coherent, practical set of guidelines for facing up to these problems … the undeniable merit of the authors' approach is that it makes journalists think more deeply about their overall responsibilities to society.'
From the Introduction by Roy Greenslade,
Guardian media commentator and Professor of Journalism at City University, London

'Elegantly written, often humorous, always encyclopaedic – the most refreshing and constructive analysis of media practice for years.'
Stuart Rees, Professor Emeritus and Director,
Centre for Peace & Conflict Studies, University of Sydney

'An indispensable training tool for journalists living and working in the midst of violent conflict.'
Carolyn Arguillas, editor, *Mindanews*, the Philippines

978-1-903458-50-1; 288pp; 246 × 189mm; pb; £25.00

••

Vision in Action
Working with soul and spirit in small organisations
Christopher Schaefer, Tÿno Voors

'Explores and facilitates the vital process of social innovation.'

Hazel Henderson

Vision in Action is a user-friendly, hands-on guide for developing healthy organisations. Start- up businesses, schools, cultural initiatives and social enterprises will find this a useful resource. Chapters include: Starting initiatives; Getting projects going; Organising; Ways of working together; Funding; Vision, mission and strategic planning

'Socially oriented initiatives and small organisations play a vital role in a healthy, evolving society. Vision in Action *offers important and practical perspectives that capture this essence.'*
Will Brinton, Woods End Laboratory

'This book is excellent – a well-written exposition of organisational development and the problems that groups tend to encounter as they progress. I highly recommend it.'
Caroline Estes, Alpha Farm and facilitator

978-1-869890-88-4; 256pp; 235 × 152mm; pb; £12.99

• •

ORDERING INFORMATION/CATALOGUE

For further information or a book catalogue, please contact:
Hawthorn Press,
1 Lansdown Lane,
Stroud,
Gloucestershire GL5 1BJ
Tel: (01453) 757040
Fax: (01453) 751138
Email: info@hawthornpress.com
You can order online at **www.hawthornpress.com**

If you have difficulties ordering Hawthorn Press books from a bookshop,
you can order from:
Booksource,
50 Cambuslang Road,
Glasgow G32 8NB
Tel: (0845) 370 0063
Fax: (0845) 370 0064
Email: orders@booksource.net